I0763130

CONTEMPORARY BASKETRY

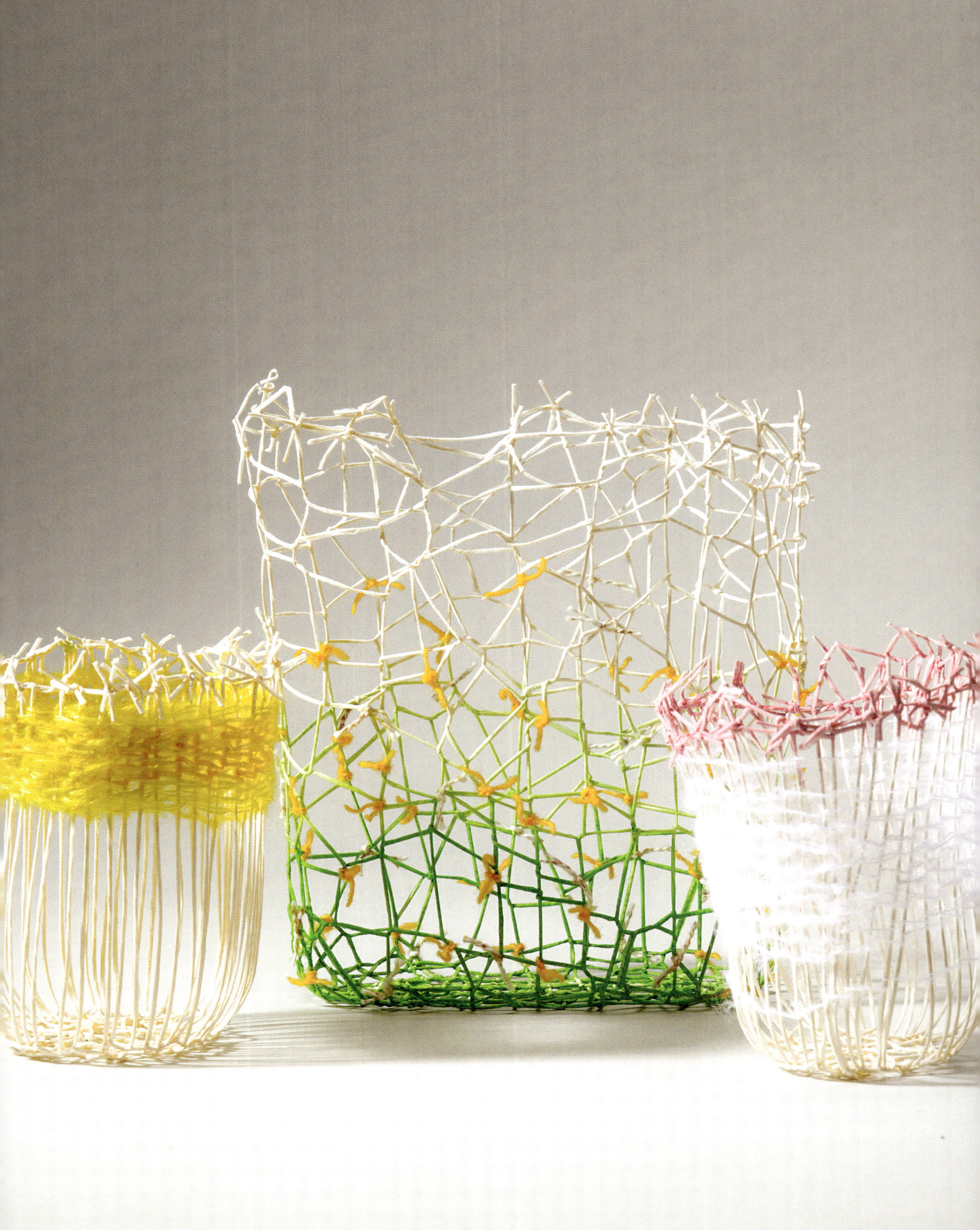

CONTEMPORARY BASKETRY

New Directions from Innovative Artists Worldwide

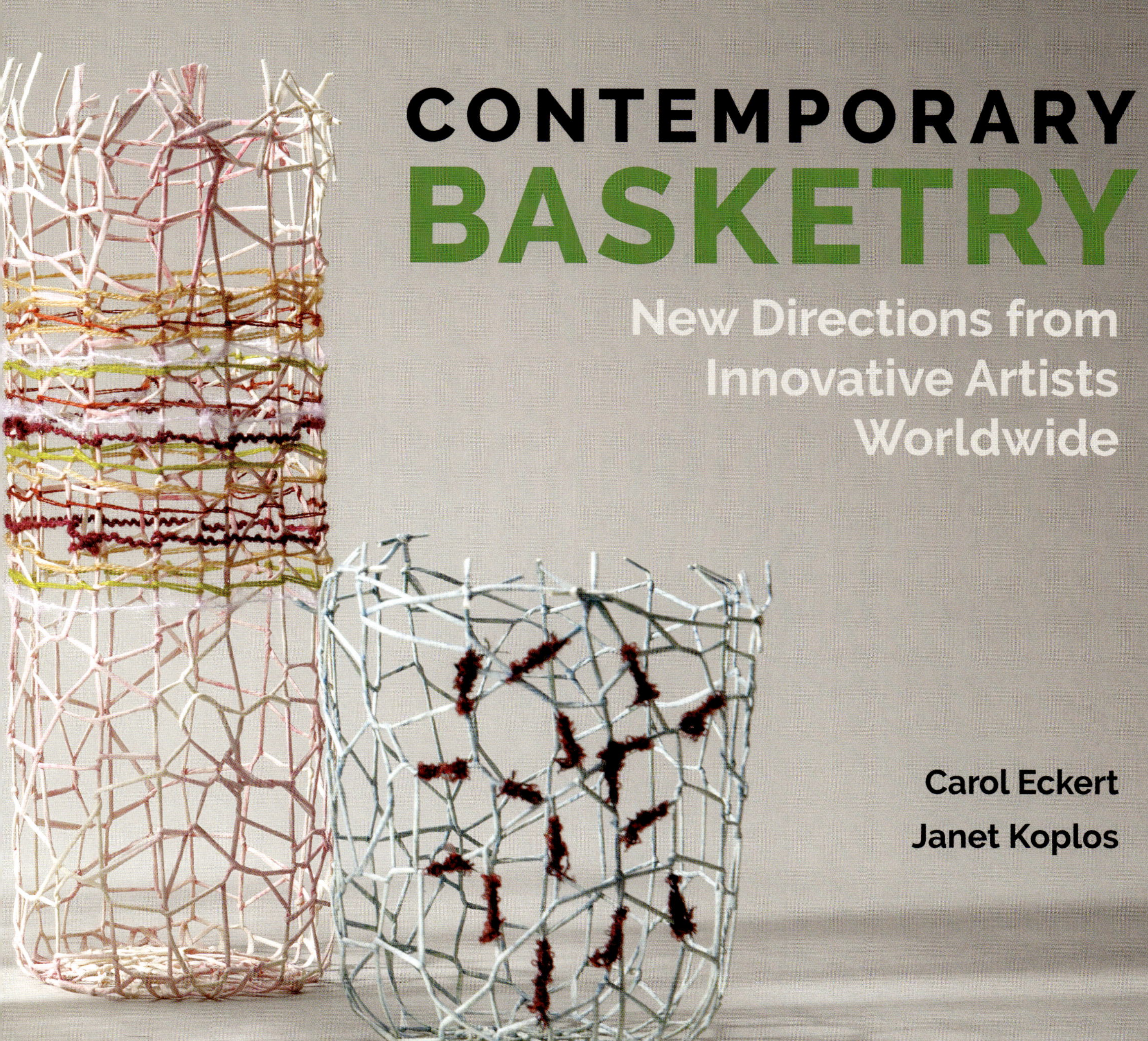

Carol Eckert
Janet Koplos

SCHIFFER CRAFT

Other Schiffer Craft Books on Related Subjects:

Rooted, Revived, Reinvented: Basketry in America, Kristin Schwain and Josephine Stealey, ISBN 978-0-7643-5373-4

The Art of Contemporary Woven Paper Basketry: Explorations in Diagonal Twill, Dorothy McGuinness, ISBN 978-0-7643-6213-2

Basketry Basics: Create 18 Beautiful Baskets as You Learn the Craft, BJ Crawford, ISBN 978-0-7643-5745-9

Library of Congress Control Number: 2025930178

Designed by Lori Malkin Ehrlich
Front cover design by Lindsay Hess
Back cover design by Lori Malkin Ehrlich
Front cover image: Dee CLEMENTS, *Things to Lean On*, 2023–24.
Photo courtesy of the artist and Nina Johnson Gallery, Miami.
Back cover images, from top: Laura LIO, *Untitled*, 2001. Photo courtesy of the artist. | Anina MAJOR, *Crawfish Armor*, 2023. Photo courtesy of the artist. | Josep MERCADER, *Arrels*, Port de la Selva, 2019. Photo courtesy of the artist. | Giuse MAGGI, *Haute Couture Series, Vessel*, 2019. Photo courtesy of the artist.
Pages 2-3: Joanne LAMB, *Imbolc* group (detail), 2023. Photo by Jan Naraine, courtesy of the artist. Page 5: Keiji NIO, *Cat Eye* (detail), 2022. Photo courtesy of the artist.

Type set in Raleway

ISBN: 978-0-7643-6999-5
ePub: 978-1-5073-0627-7
Printed in India

10 9 8 7 6 5 4 3 2 1

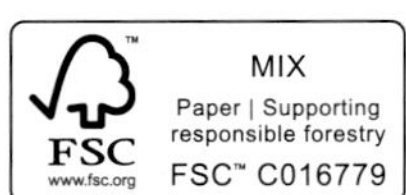

Published by Schiffer Craft
An imprint of Schiffer Publishing, Ltd.
4880 Lower Valley Road
Atglen, PA 19310
Phone: (610) 593-1777; Fax: (610) 593-2002
Email: Info@schifferbooks.com
Web: www.schifferbooks.com

For our complete selection of fine books on this and related subjects, please visit our website at www.schifferbooks.com. You may also write for a free catalog.

Schiffer Publishing's titles are available at special discounts for bulk purchases for sales promotions or premiums. Special editions, including personalized covers, corporate imprints, and excerpts, can be created in large quantities for special needs. For more information, contact the publisher.

We are always looking for people to write books on new and related subjects. If you have an idea for a book, please contact us at proposals@schifferbooks.com.

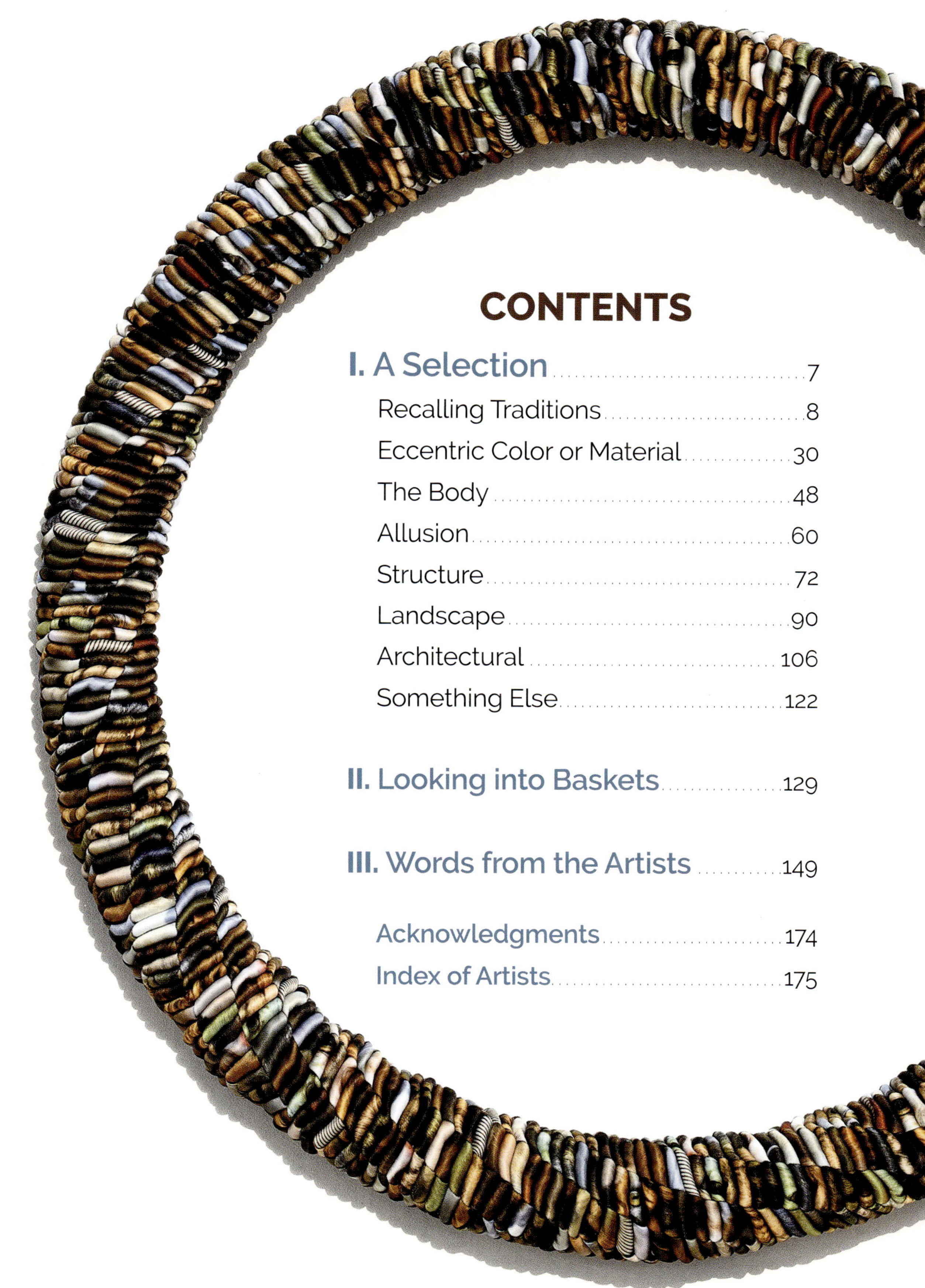

CONTENTS

A SELECTION

THE BEST ARTWORKS can never be reduced to a single characteristic or description.

In arranging these works in the present order, we suggest one quality to consider. Each work is distinctive, but each may also share some quality with the works preceding or following it. One category shades into the next just as the names of those qualities fade in and out on the pages.

For every work other qualities could be named. Most works could even be placed in another category. Identifying other qualities and considering other categories in which a work might appear can be a game for the attentive reader.

Annemarie **O'SULLIVAN**

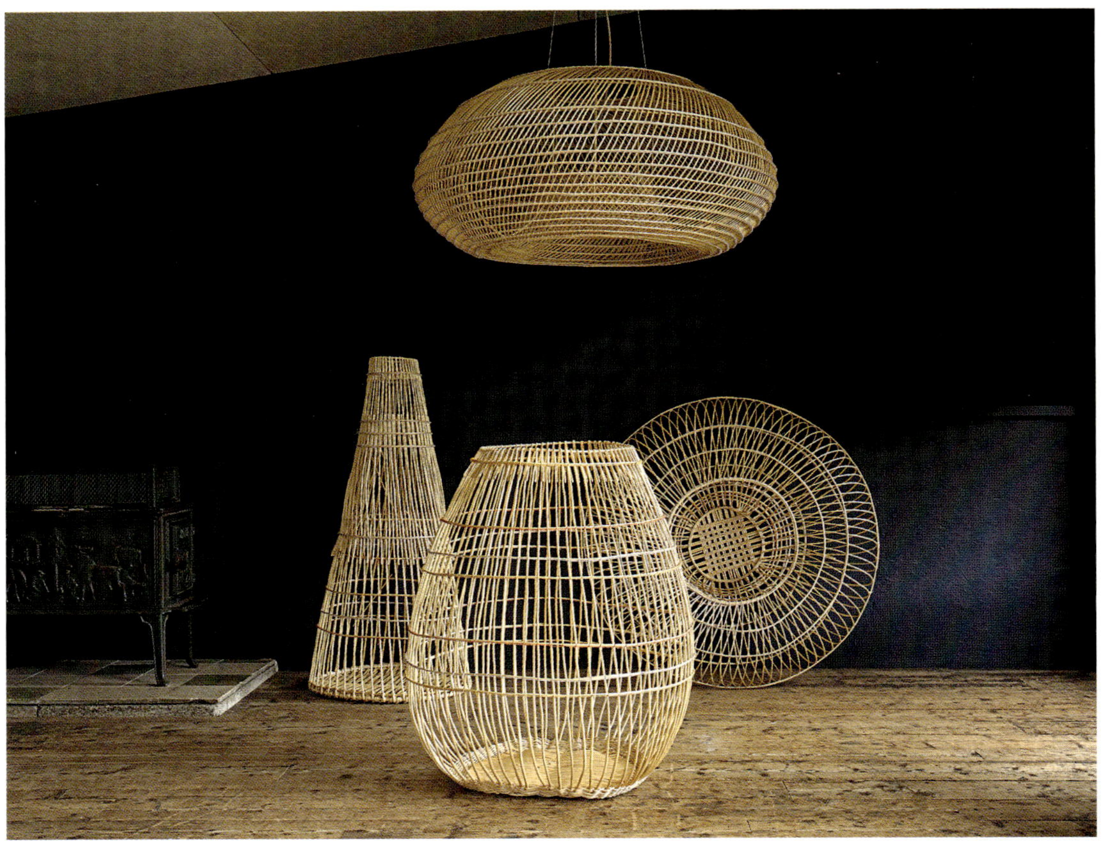

Open Work, 2022.
Stripped white willow:
various dimensions.
Photo courtesy of Jonathan Bassett

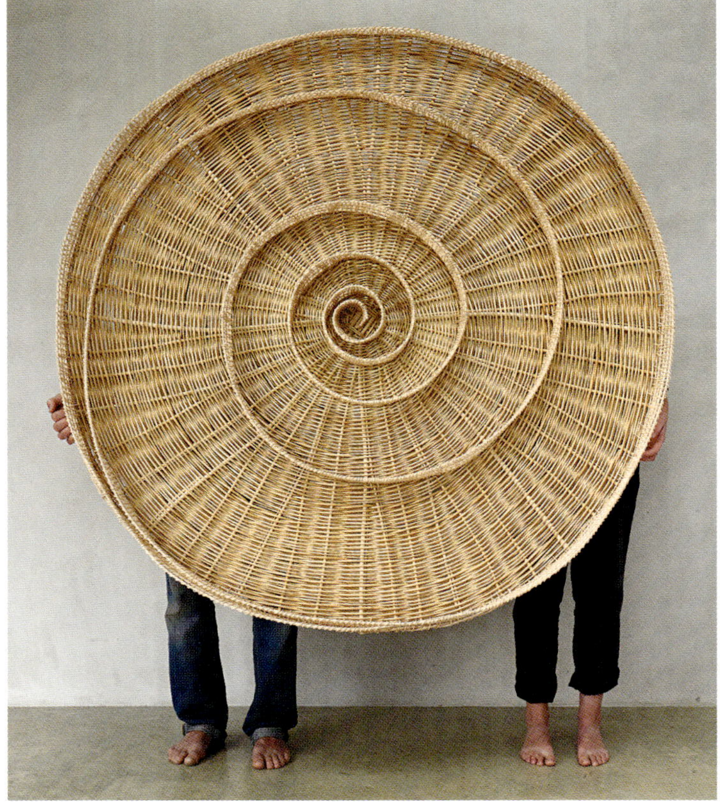

Silkworm Basket, 2022.
Stripped white willow:
120 cm (47") diameter.
Photo courtesy of Jonathan Bassett

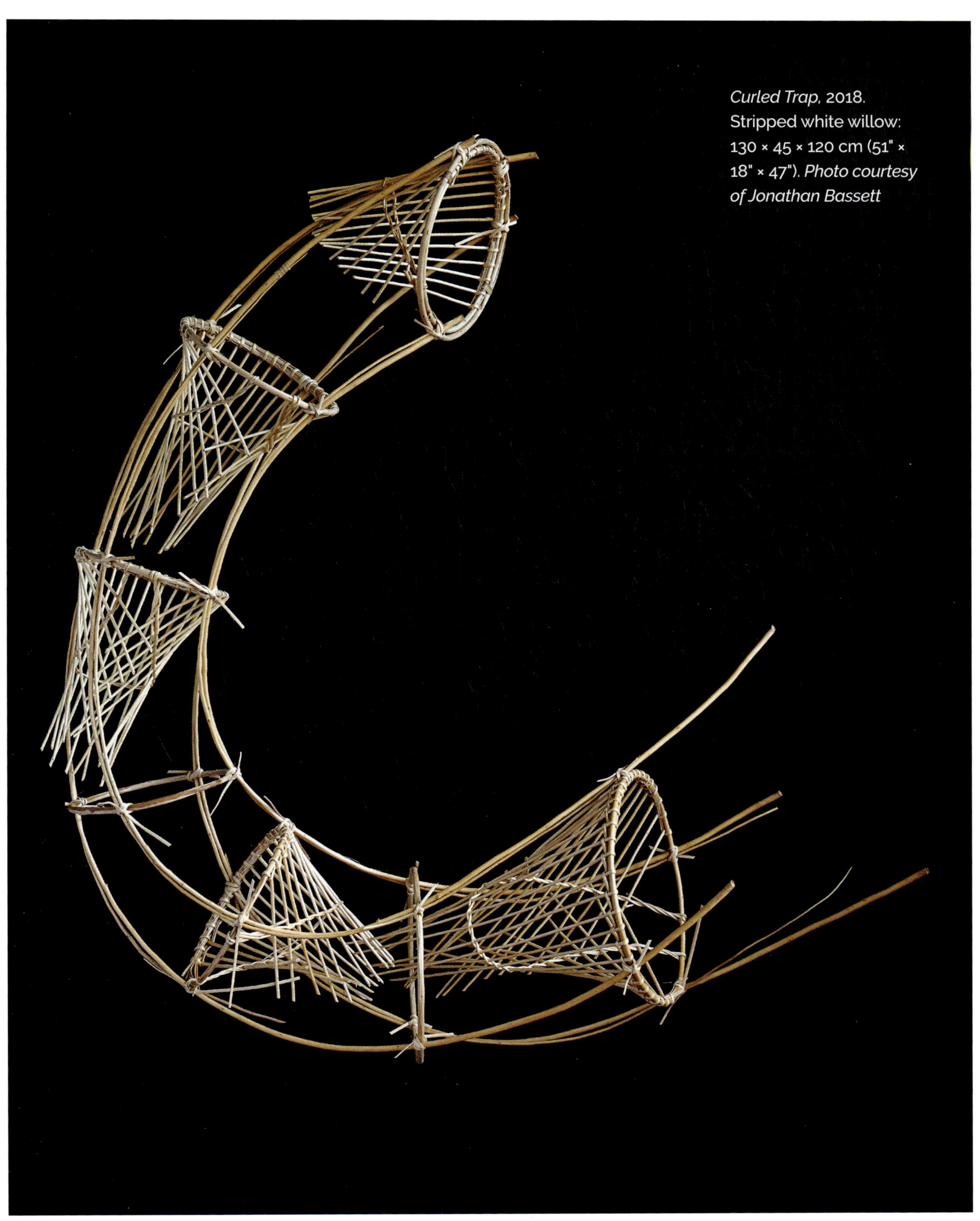

Curled Trap, 2018. Stripped white willow: 130 × 45 × 120 cm (51" × 18" × 47"). *Photo courtesy of Jonathan Bassett*

Alexandra FERDINANDE

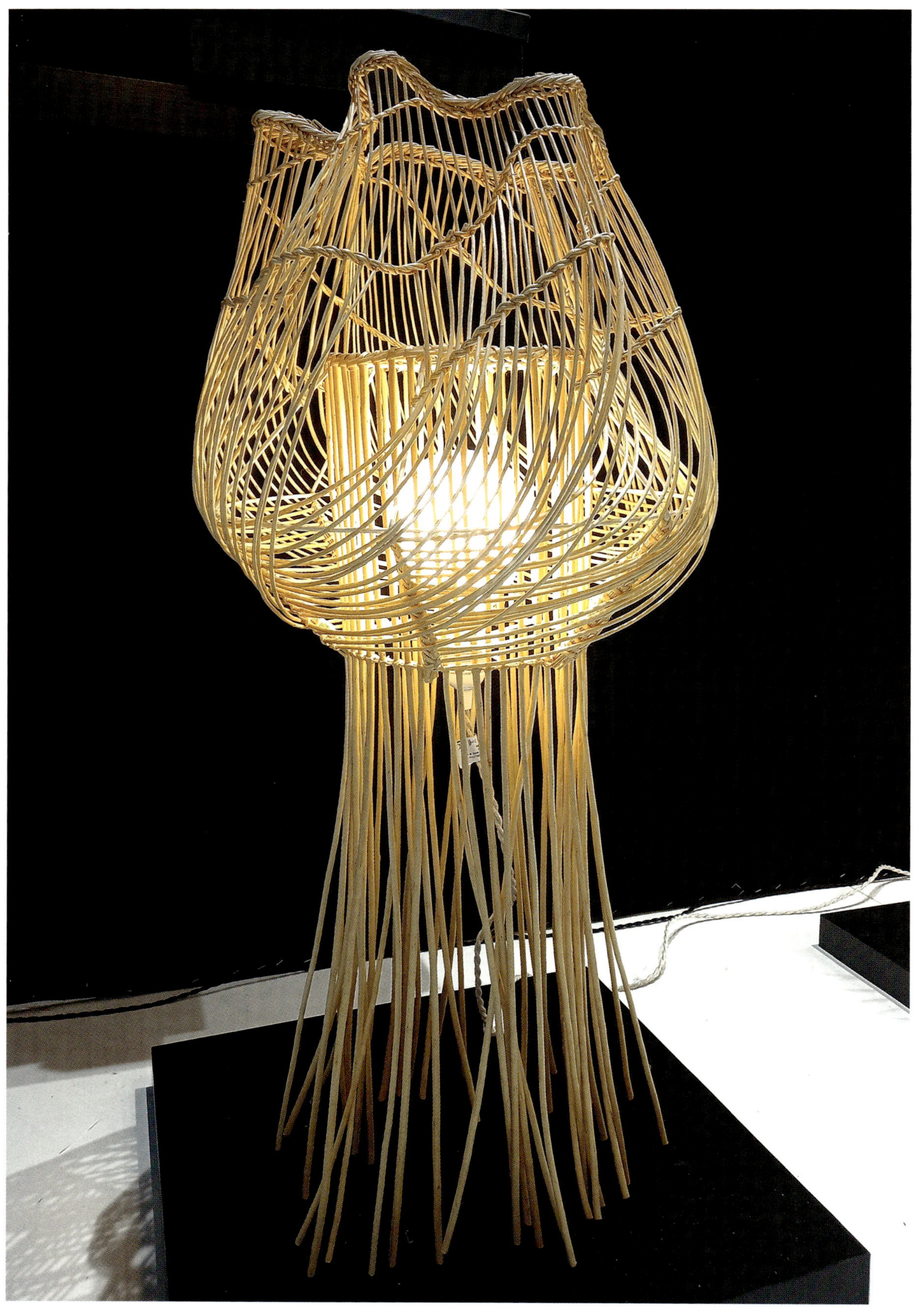

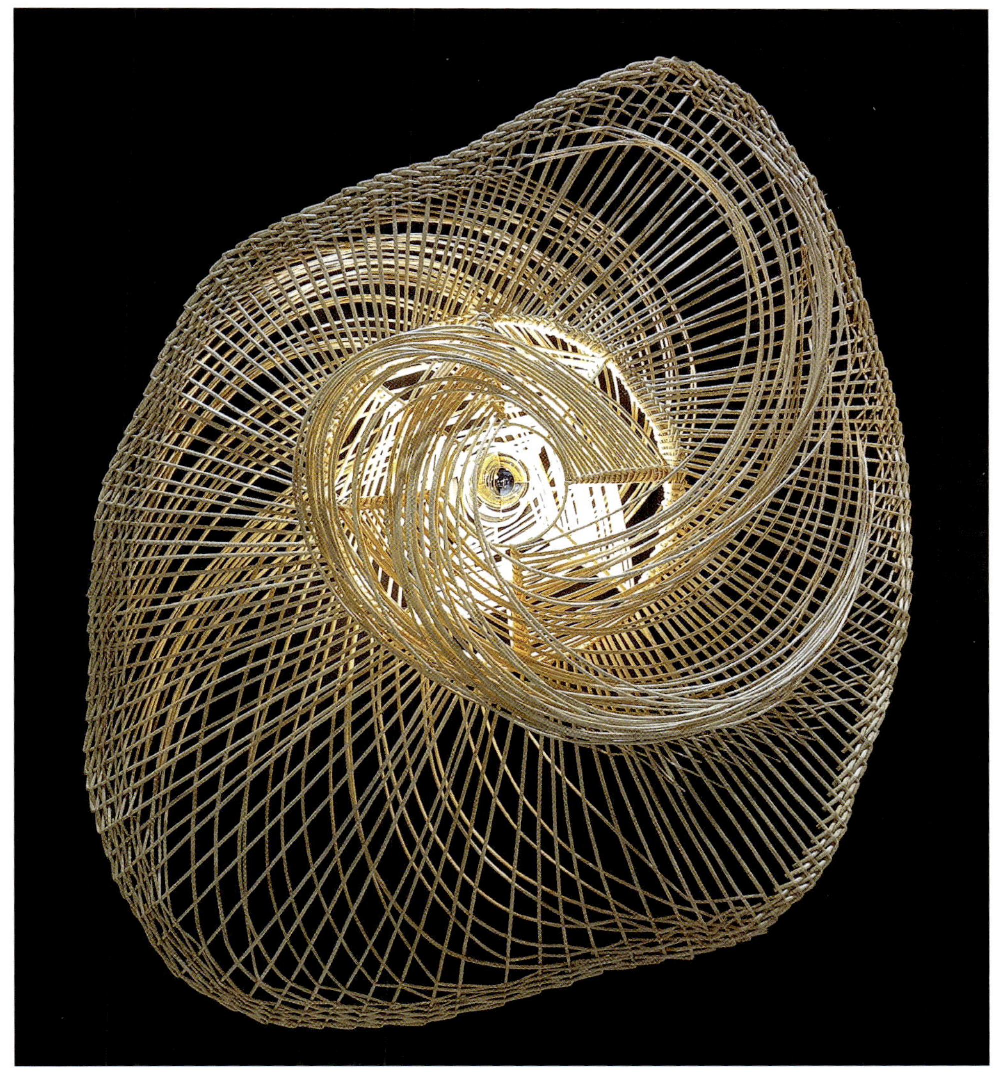

Nebulae, 2023. Debarked willow, steel structure, LED mirror bulb: 20 × 90 cm (7" × 3"). *Photo courtesy of the artist*

Nebulae (detail).

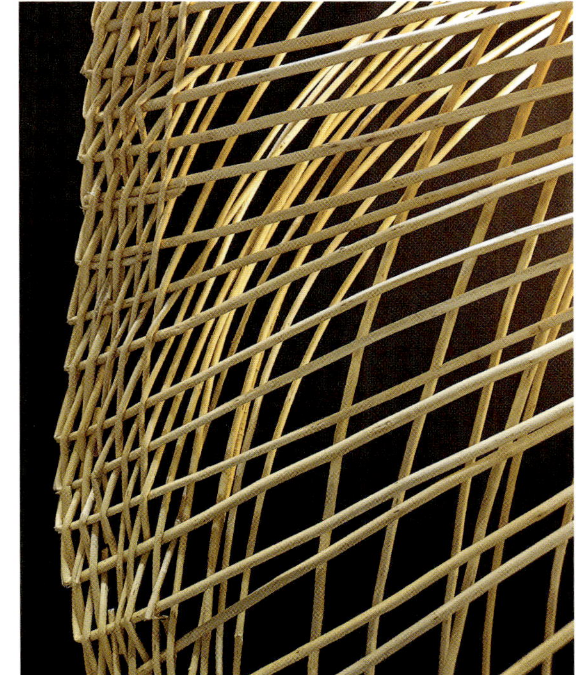

OPPOSITE: *Vibrations,* 2023. Debarked willow, steel structure, LED bulb, textile cable: 95 × 50 cm (37" × 19"). *Photo courtesy of the artist*

Joe **HOGAN**

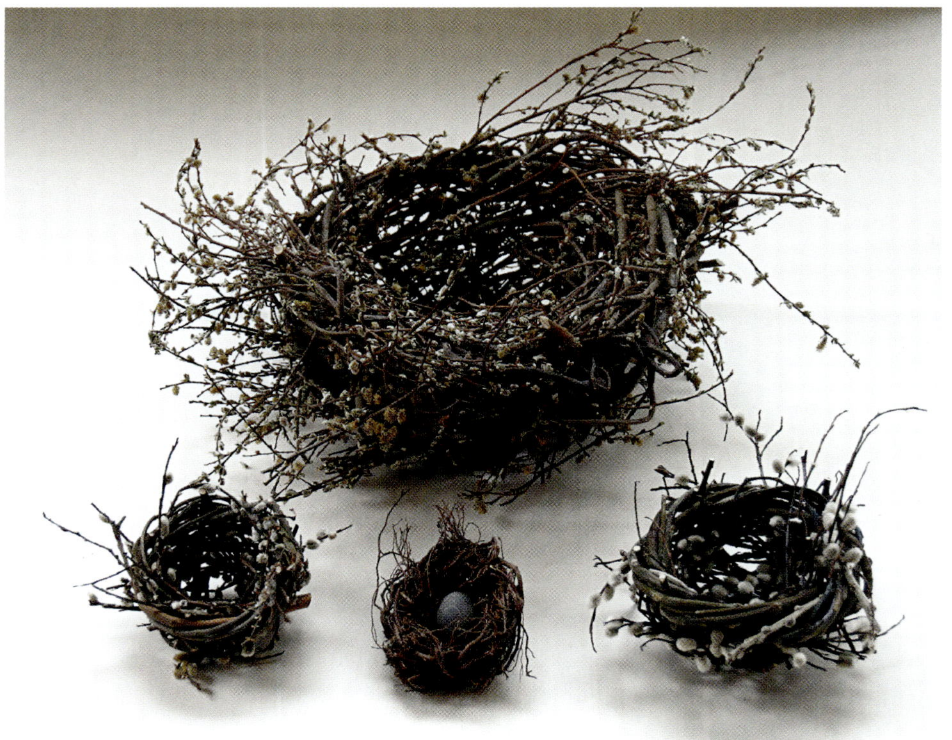

Nest Group, 2017. Catkinned willow, heather, with stone: 35, 16, 12, 18 cm diameter (13", 6", 4", 7" diameter). *Photo courtesy of the artist*

Cluster of Reclining Pods, 2018. Chestnut wood, stone, willow: 53 × 63 × 80, 80 × 68 × 100, 43 × 49 × 57 cm (20" × 24" × 31", 31" × 26" × 39", 17" × 19" × 22"). *Photo courtesy of Michael Mac Laughlin*

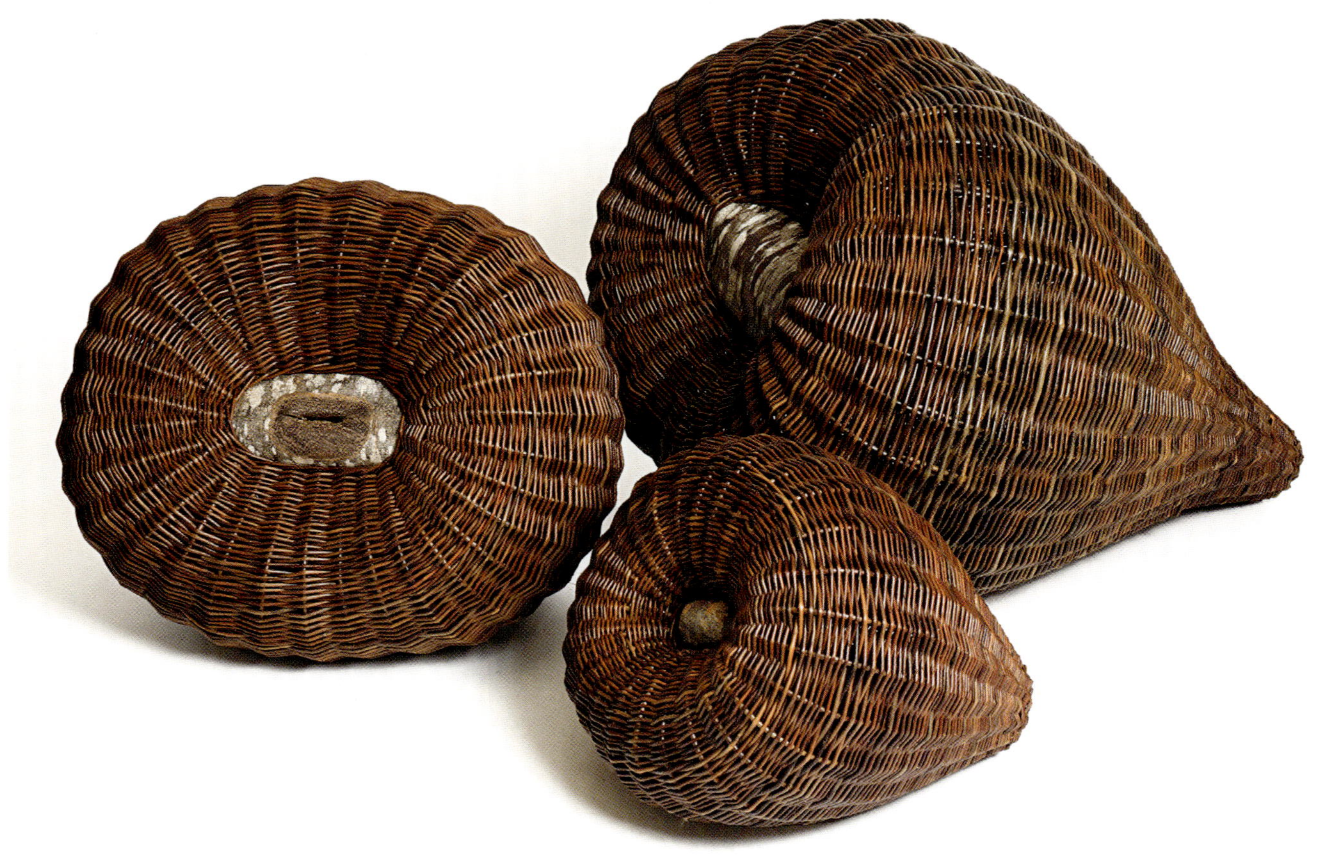

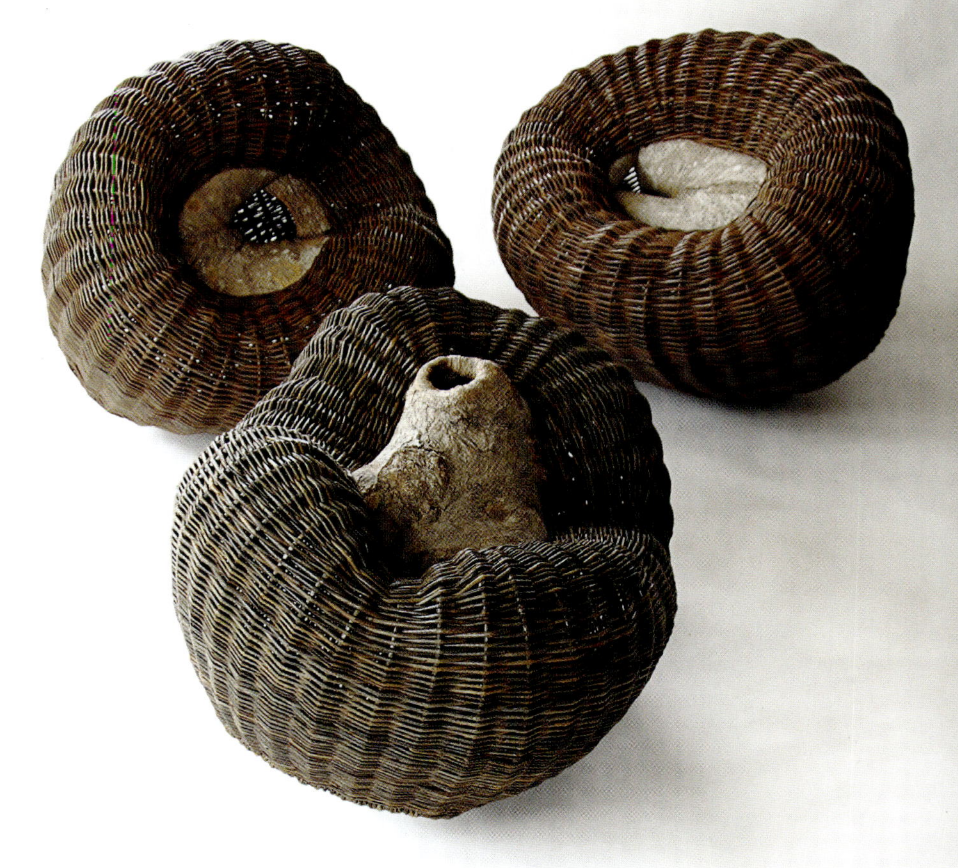

Primal Energy Series, Numbers 2, 3, 4, 2016. Ash wood, willow: *Number 2* (front), 70 × 62 × 48 cm (27" × 24" × 18"), *Number 3* (left), 77 × 60 × 50 cm (30" × 23" × 20"), *Number 4* (right), 74 × 58 × 52 cm (74" × 22" × 20"). *Photo courtesy of the artist*

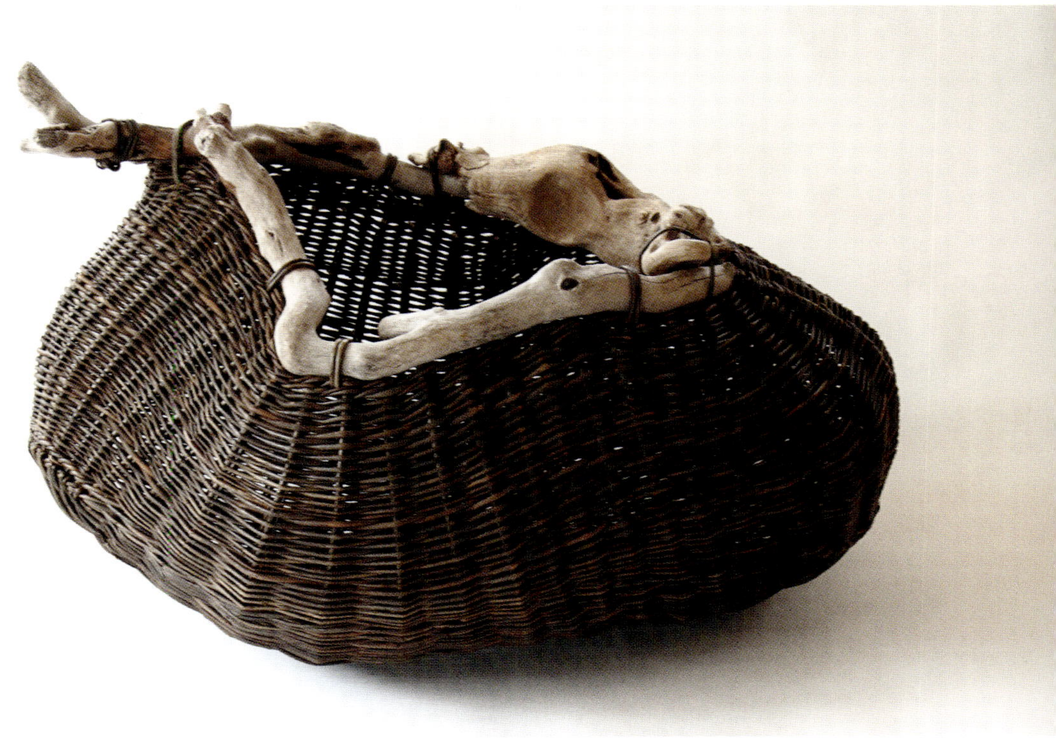

Driftwood Pouch with Embedded Stones, 2017. Willow, found driftwood: 94 × 62 × 58 cm (37" × 24" × 22"). *Photo courtesy of the artist*

Anne CODDINGTON

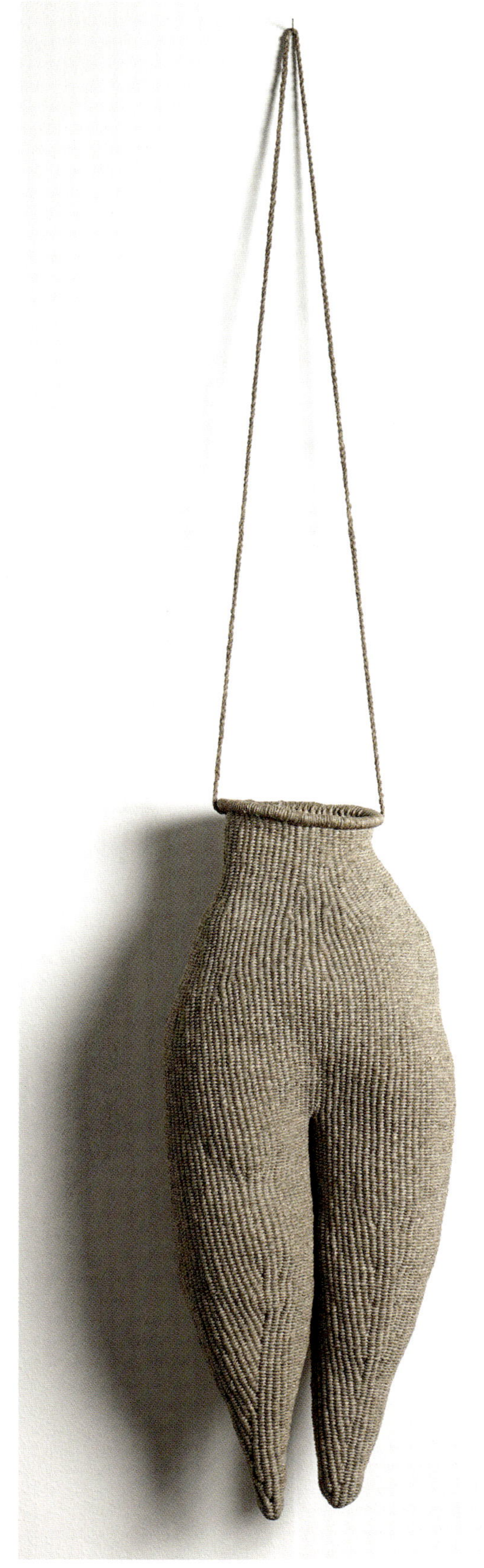

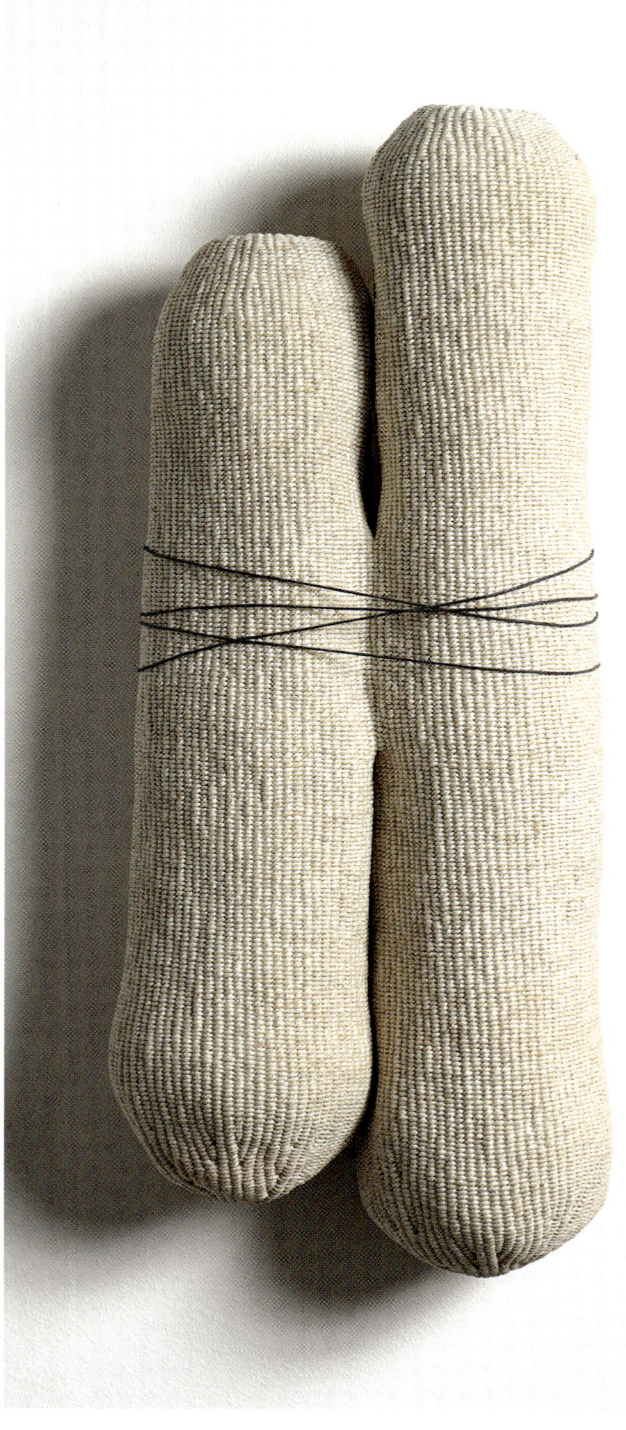

Maiden, 2024. Linen: 38 × 101 × 18 cm (15" × 40" × 7").
Photo by Brian Heaton courtesy of the artist

Bond, 2024. Linen: 50 × 81 × 18 cm (20" × 32" × 7").
Photo by Brian Heaton courtesy of the artist

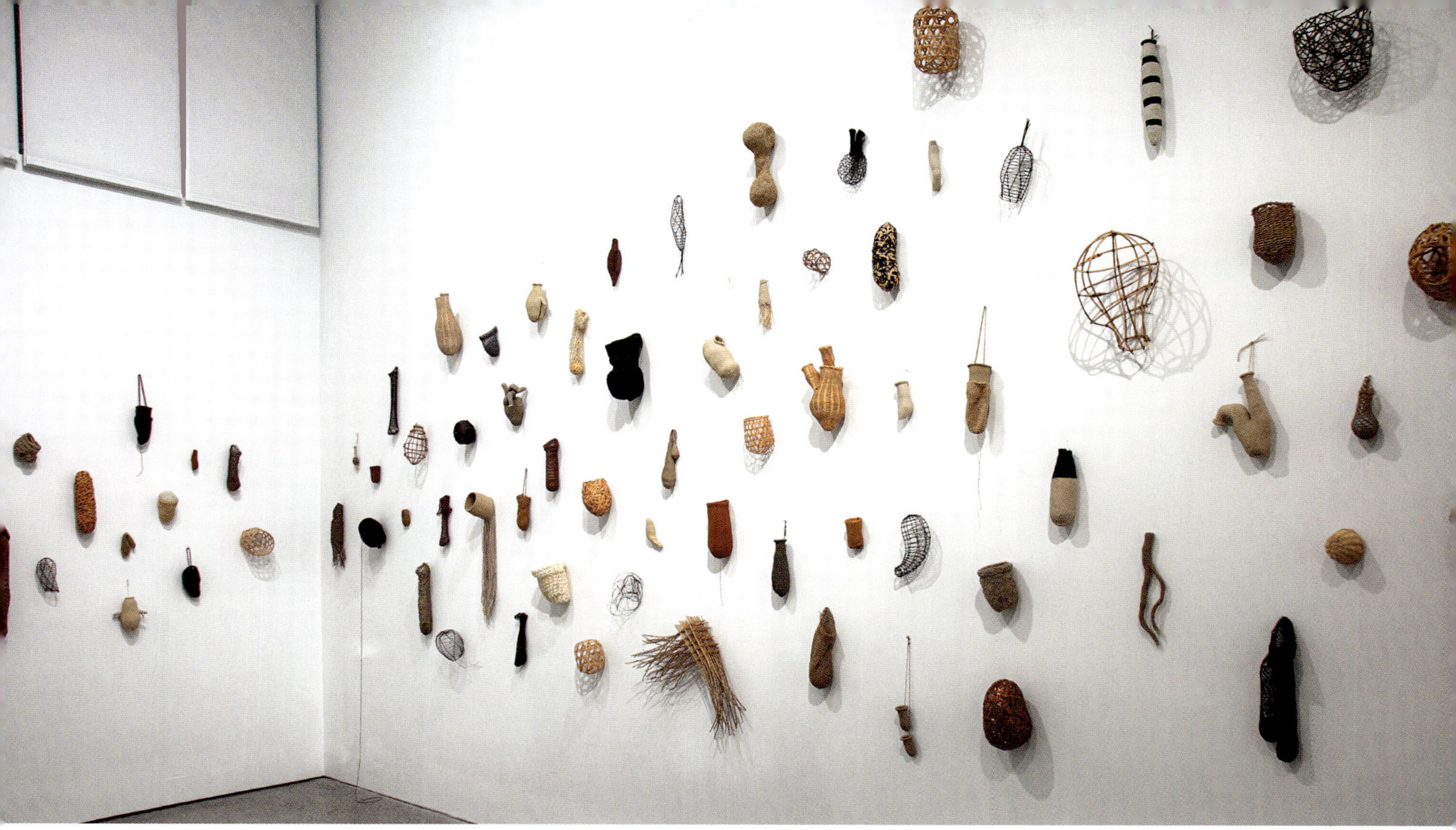

95 Forms, 2021. Mixed-media fibers: dimensions variable. *Photos by Pippi Miller courtesy of the artist*

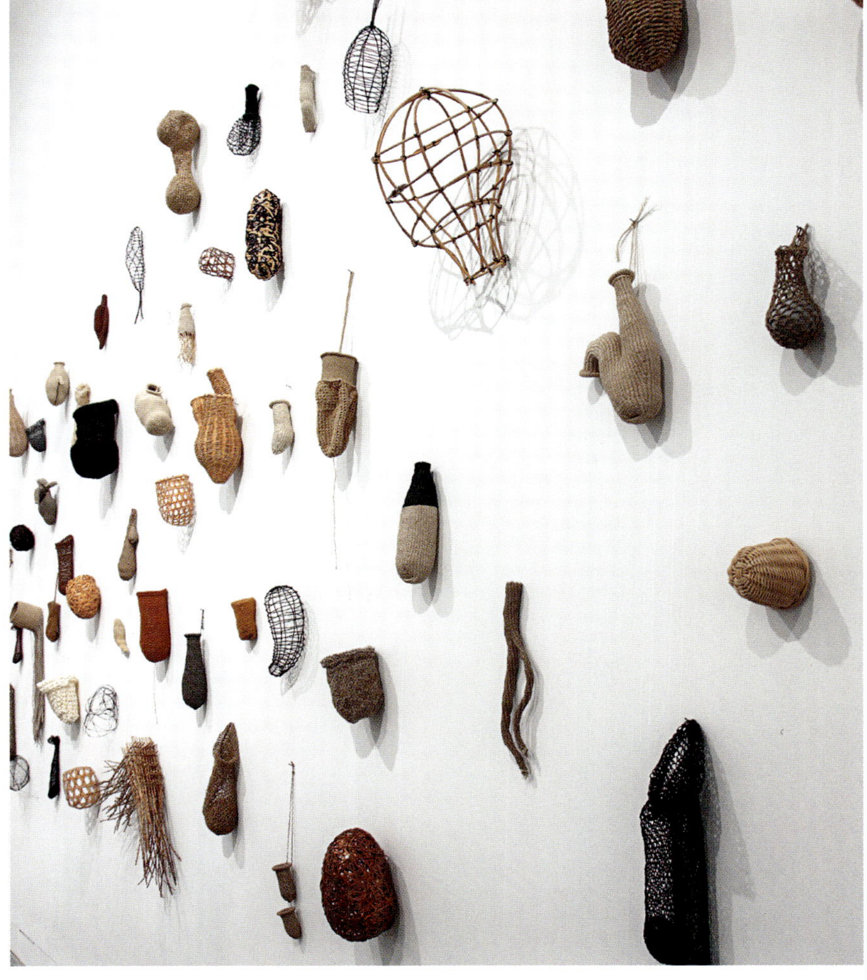

95 Forms (detail), 2021.

Tim JOHNSON

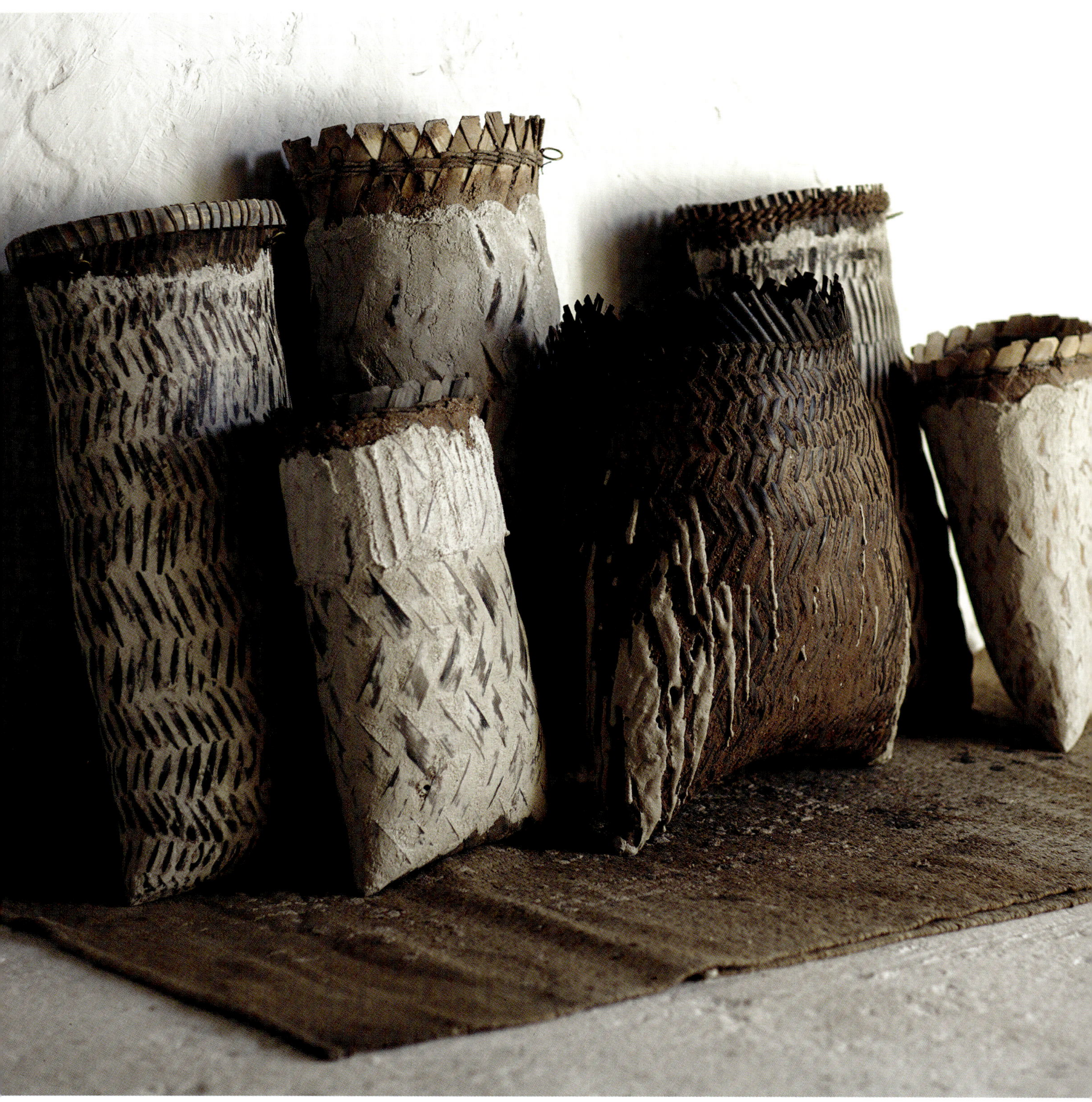

Wall Pockets, 2021. Willow skein, earth pigments, split chestnut, tarred hemp twine, sisal, crushed chalk, esparto grass; dimensions variable. *Photo courtesy of the artist*

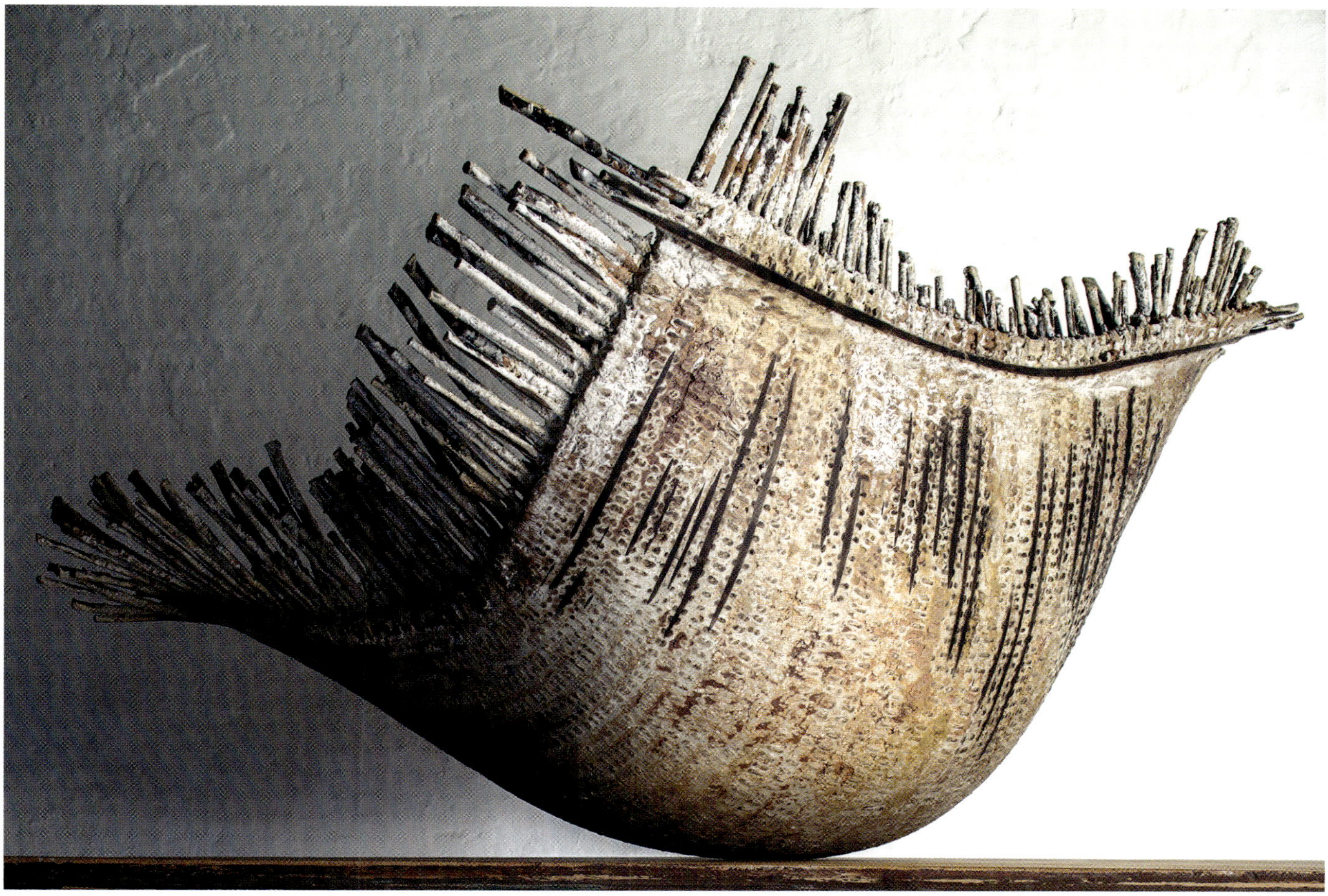

Taunt Curve, 2021. Willow, sisal, earth pigments: 95 × 82 × 43 cm (37.5" × 32" × 17"). *Photo courtesy of the artist*

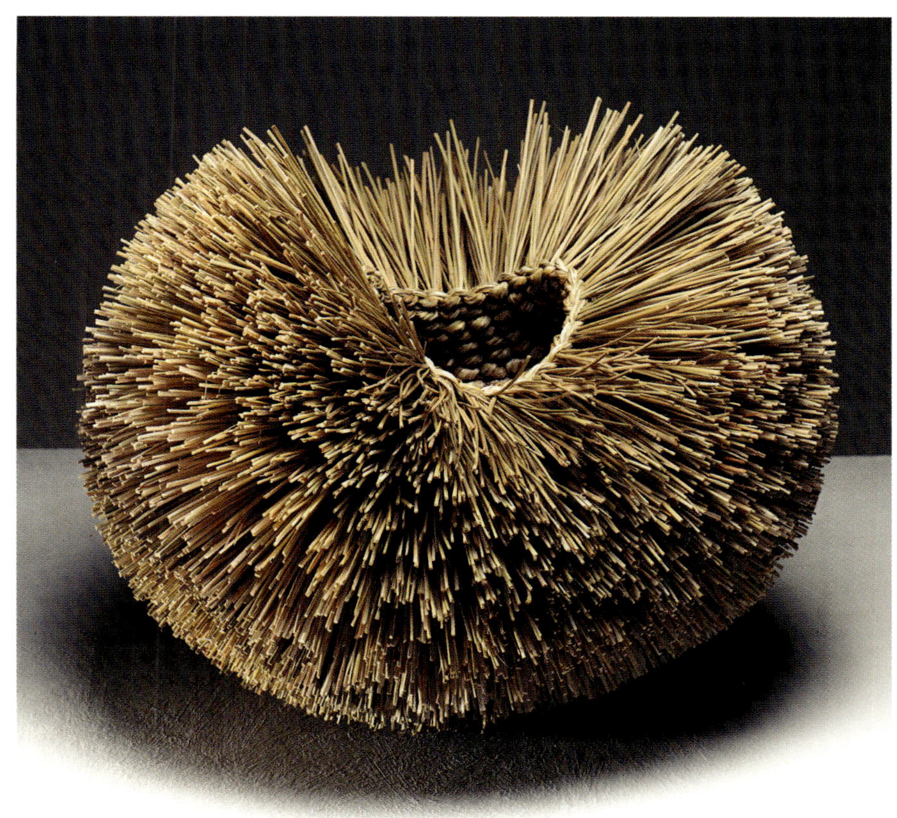

Keeping Time Basket—Split Cyperus, 2021. Split *Cyperus* stems, hemp string: 35 × 46 × 38 cm (14" × 18" × 15"). *Photo courtesy of the artist*

Beauty NGXONGO

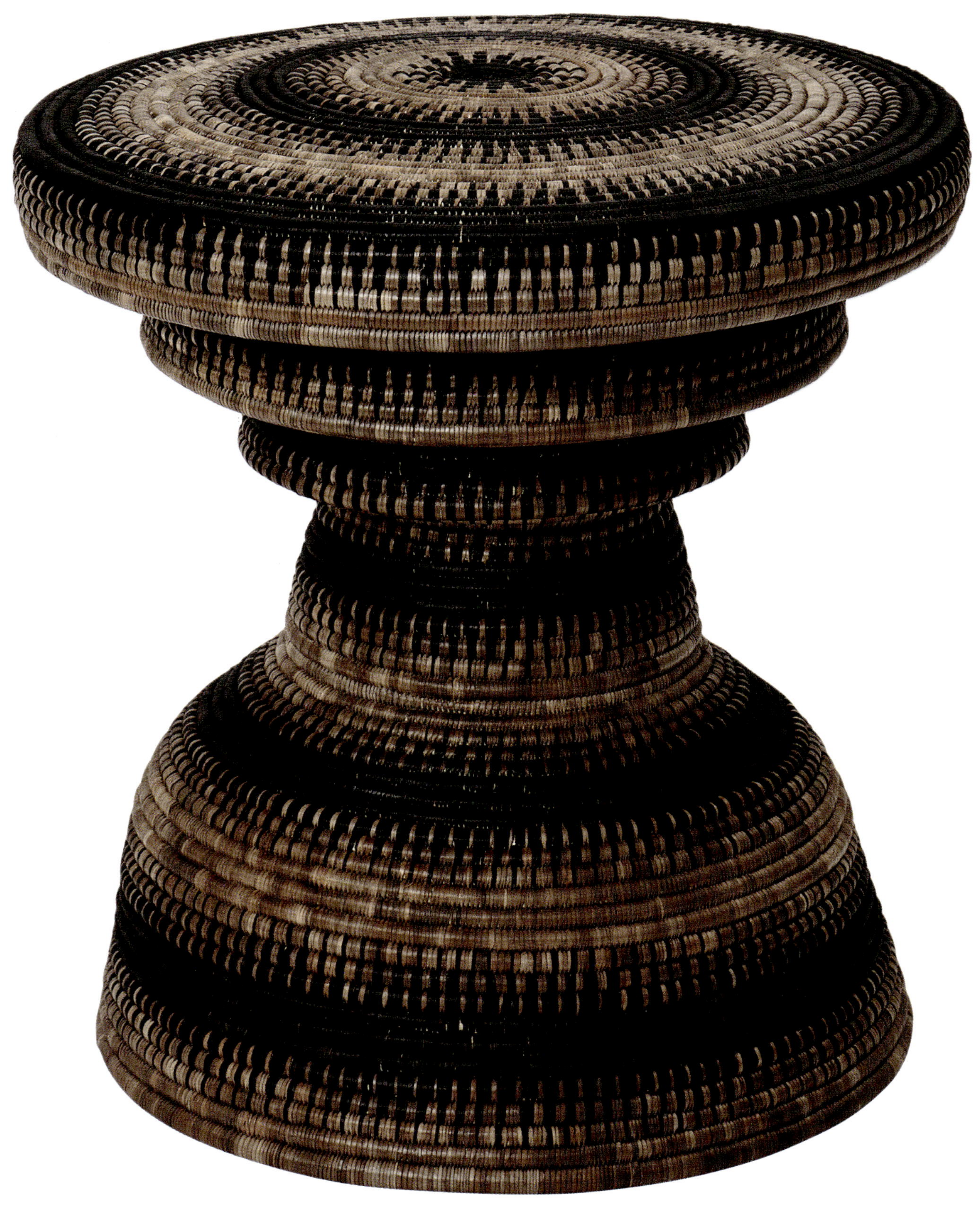

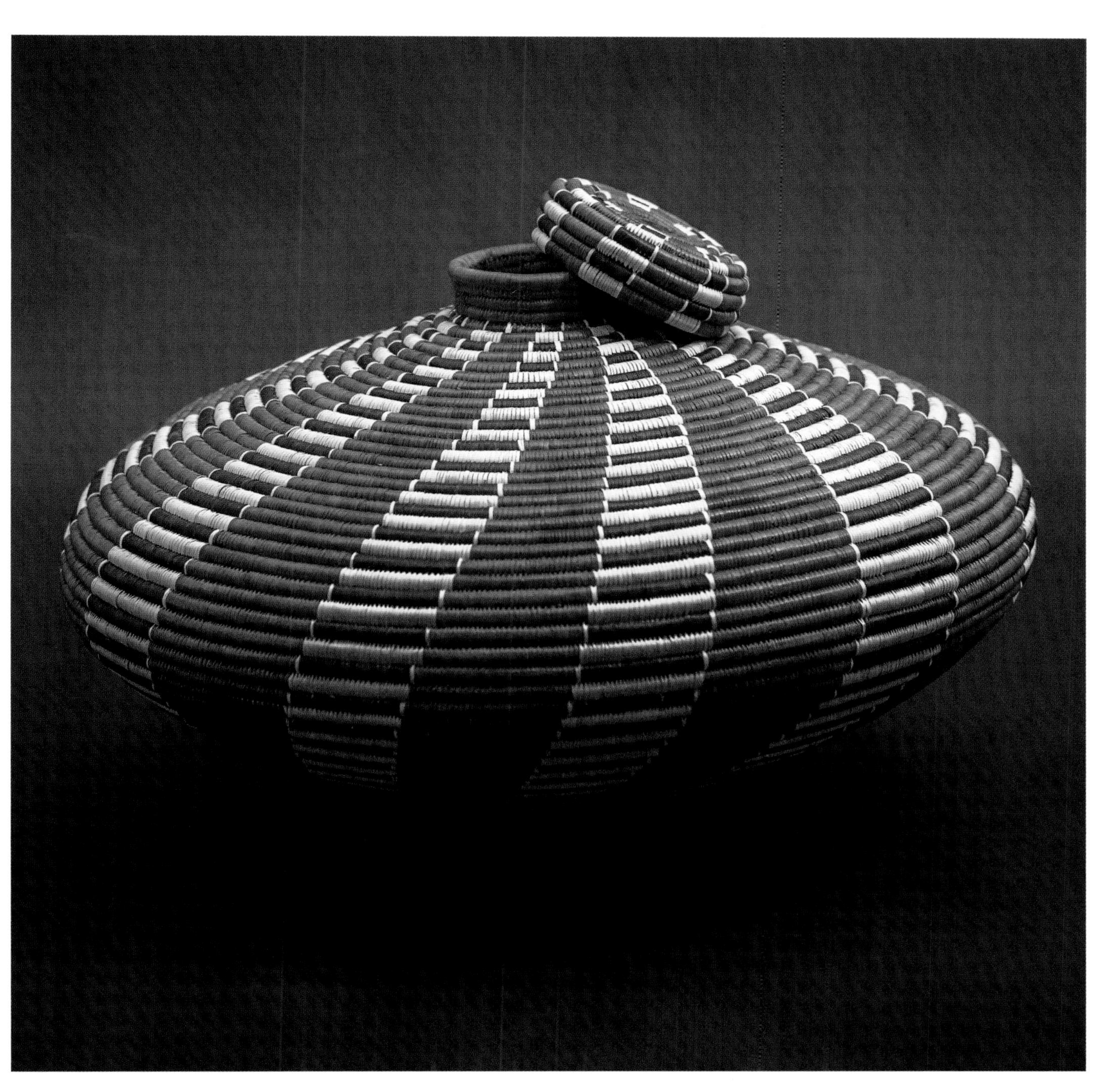

OPPOSITE: *Black/gray Table*, 2022. Plant fiber: 45 × 45 cm (18" × 18"). *Photo courtesy of Sinegugu Ngxongo*

Avocado Zebra Basket, 2020. Plant fiber: 55 × 57 cm (21" × 22"). *Photo courtesy of Sinegugu Ngxongo*

Jenna LEE

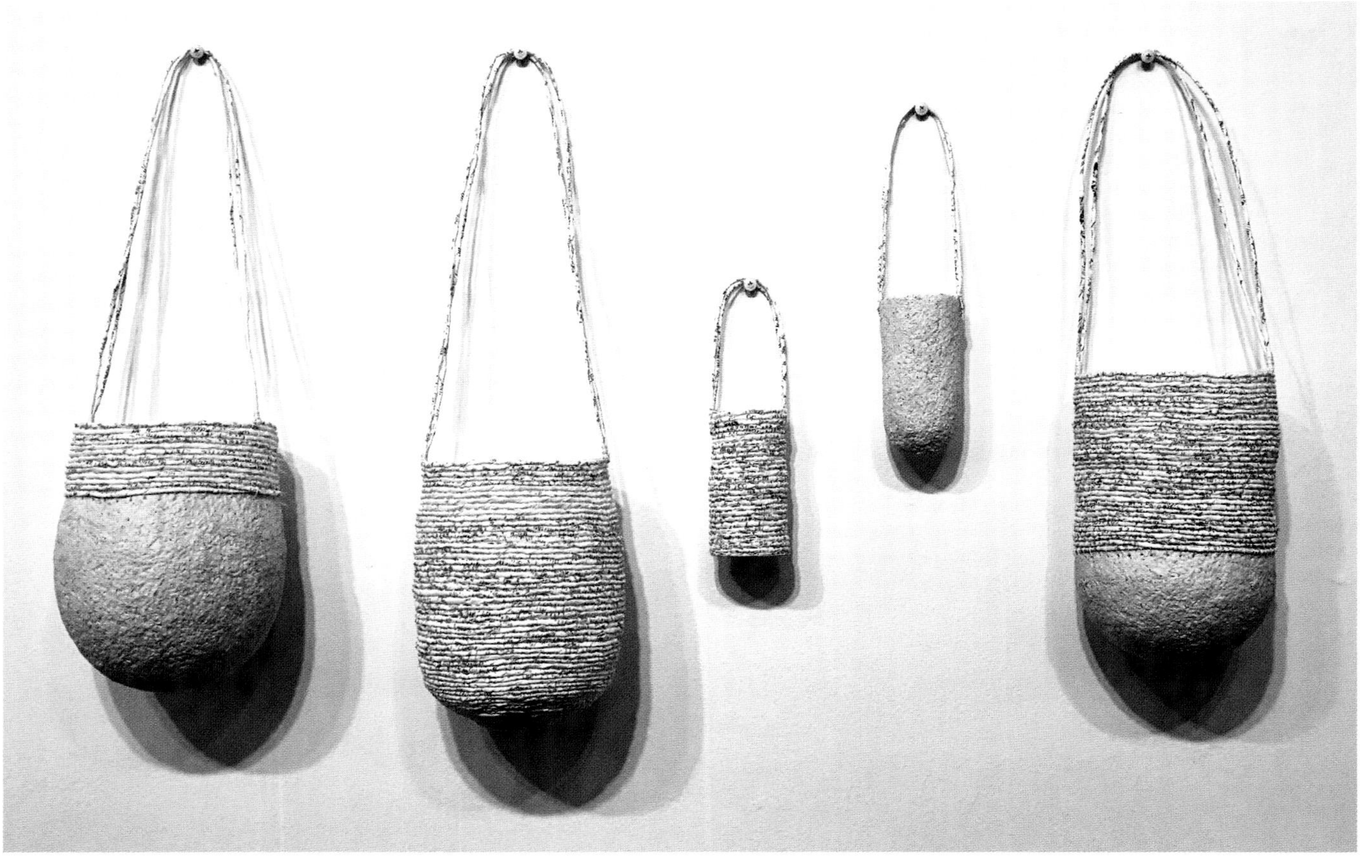

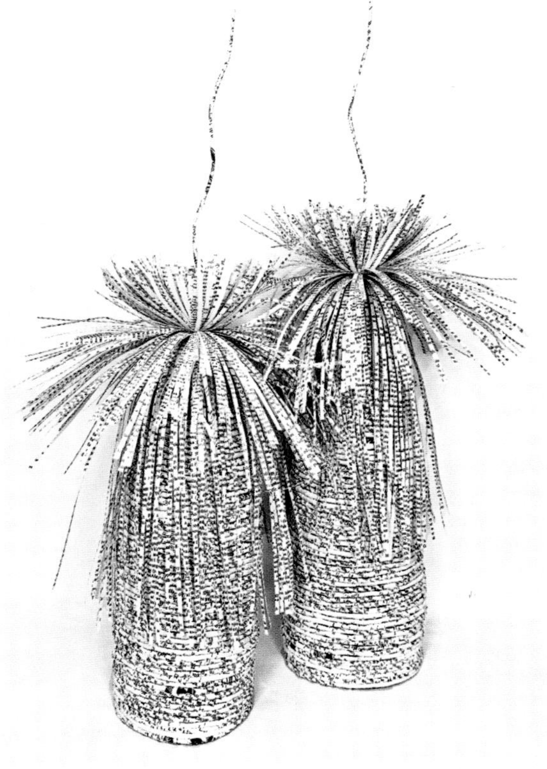

Grasstree—Growing Together, 2022. Pages of "Aboriginal words and place names" by AJ Reed (1977), bookbinding thread, book cover board, florist wire: 55 × 30 × 25 cm (21" × 11" × 10"). *Photo courtesy of MARS Gallery and the artist*

Dis/bound and Re/bound, 2021. Pages of "Aboriginal words and place names," bookbinding thread, varnish: 53 × 90 × 15 cm (20" × 35" × 6") installed. *Photo courtesy of MARS Gallery and the artist*

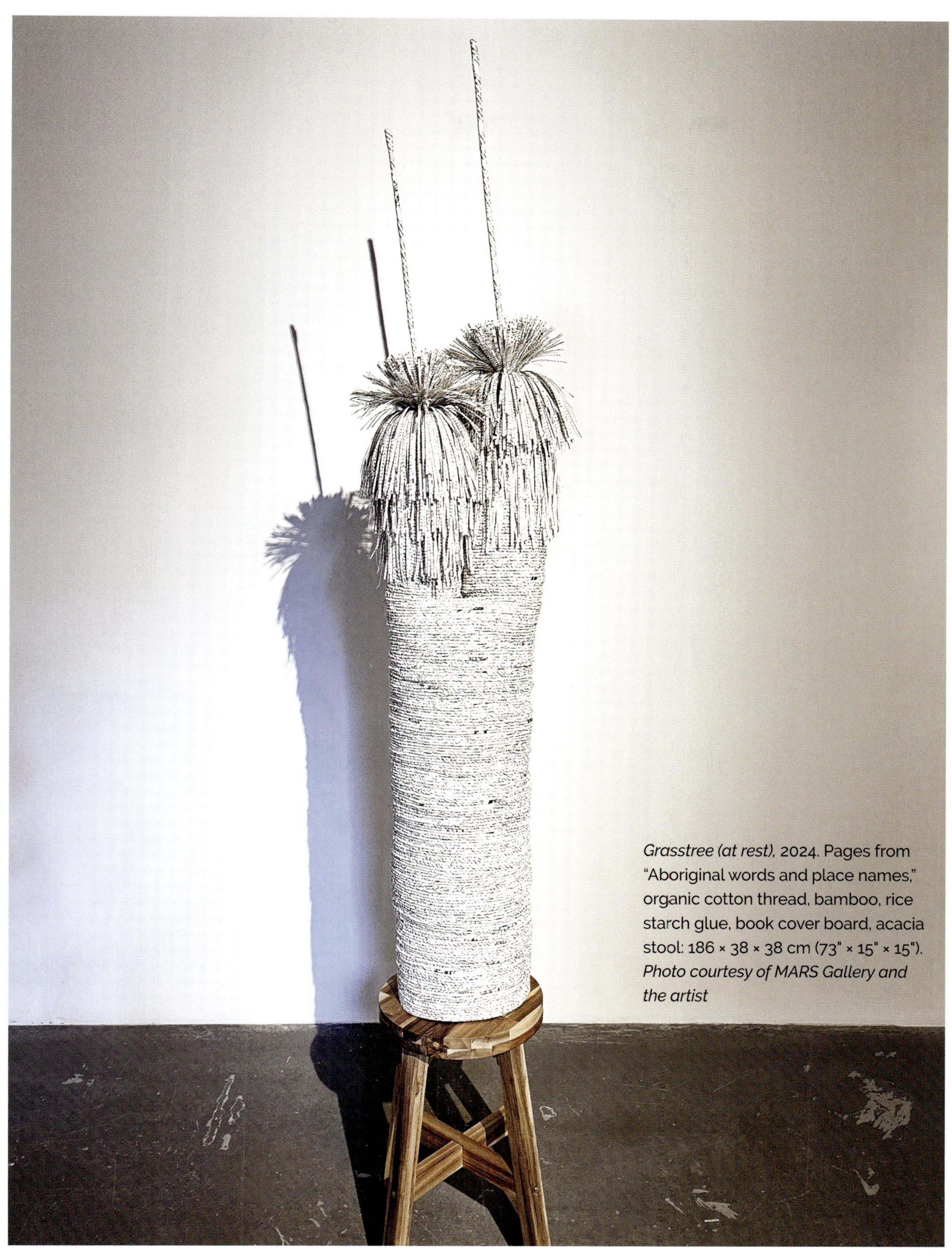

Grasstree (at rest), 2024. Pages from "Aboriginal words and place names," organic cotton thread, bamboo, rice starch glue, book cover board, acacia stool; 186 × 38 × 38 cm (73" × 15" × 15"). *Photo courtesy of MARS Gallery and the artist*

Alice FOX

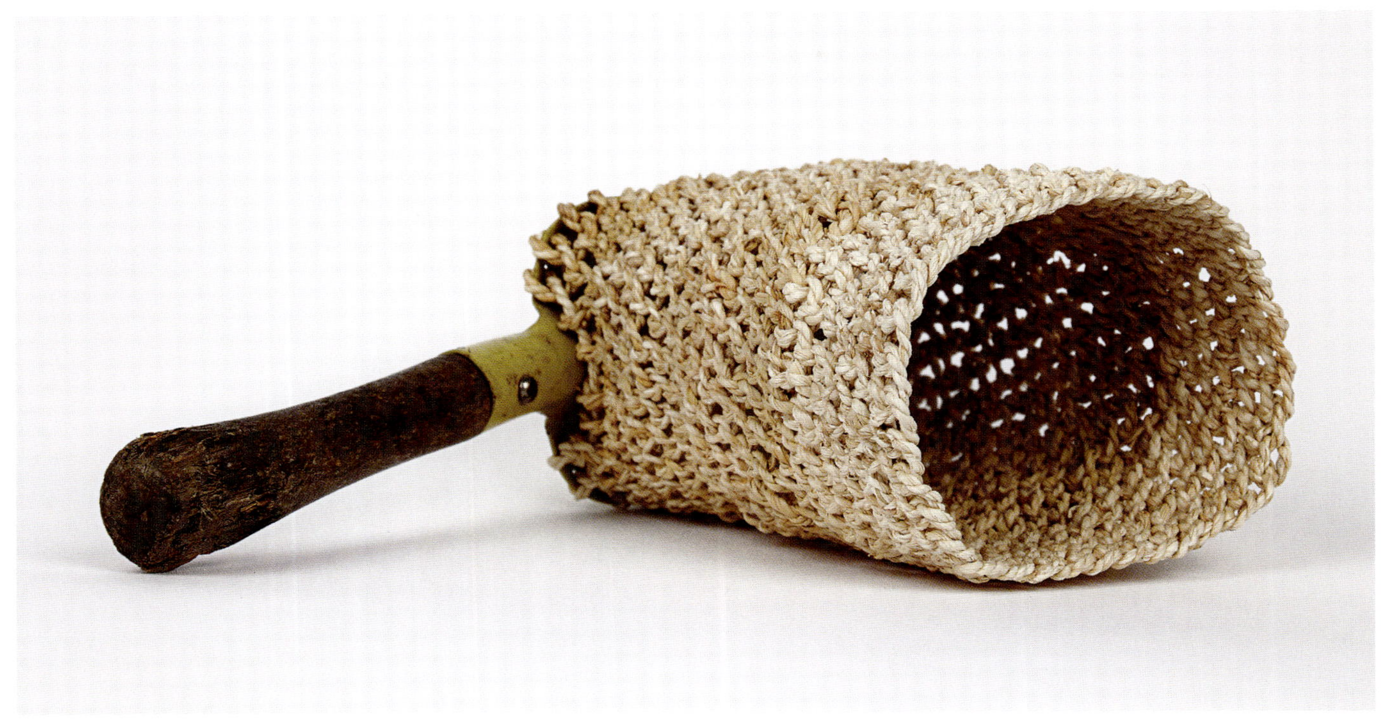

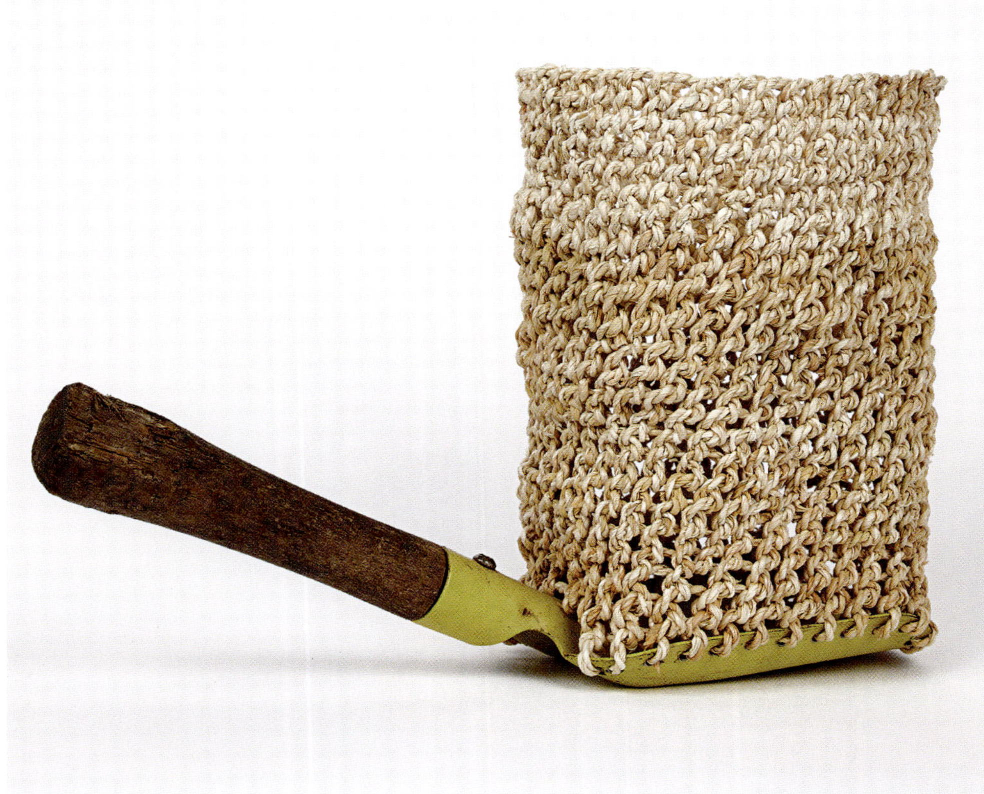

Hybrid 4, 2021. Yellow trowel, sweetcorn: 21 × 6 × 13 cm (8" × 2" × 5"). *Photos courtesy of David Lindsay*

Hybrid 4 (side view).

OPPOSITE: *Hybrid 7*, 2023. Scraper, beech, bindweed: 30 × 13 × 17 cm (11" × 5" × 6"). *Photo courtesy of David Lindsay*

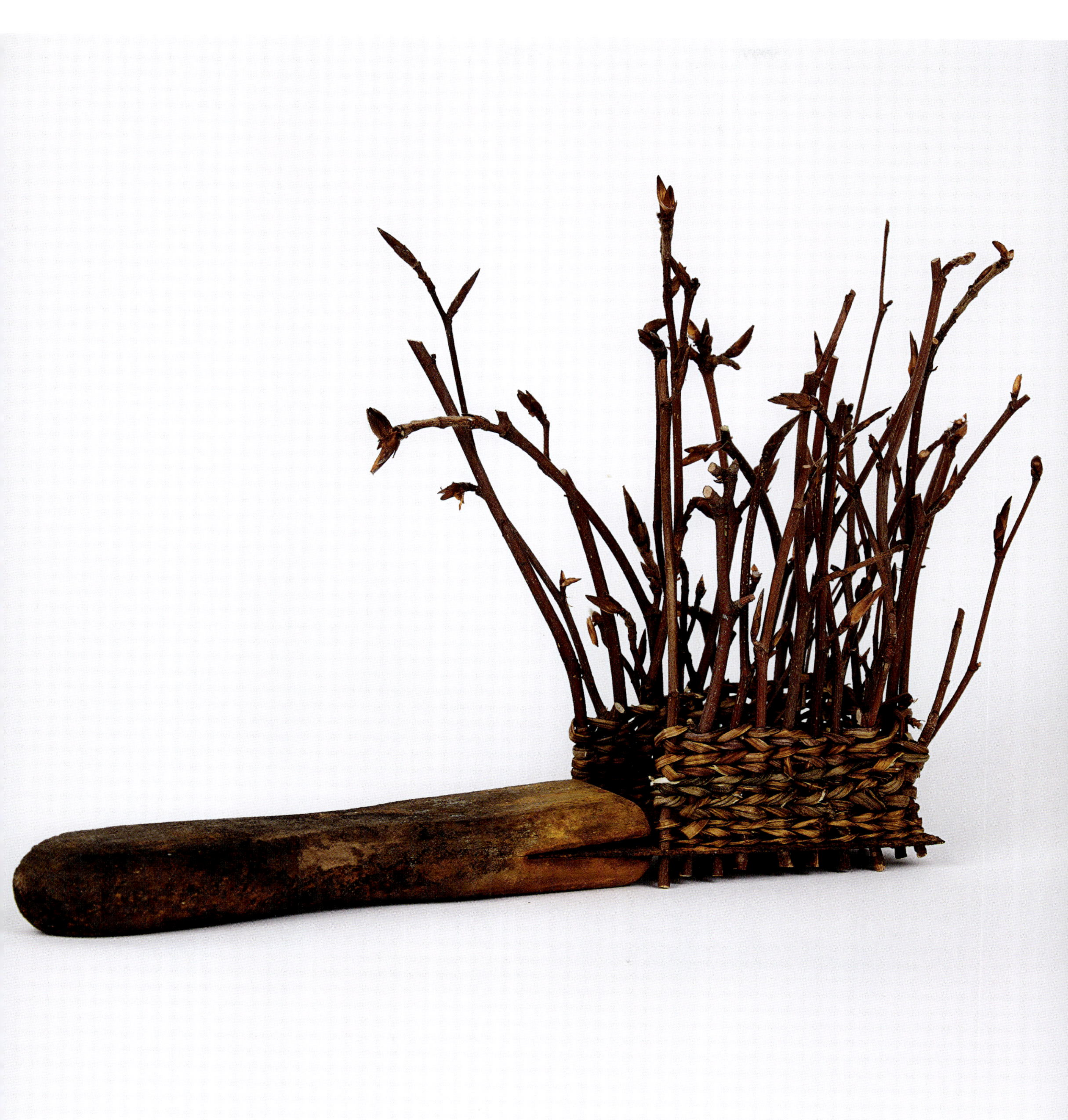

Laura LIO

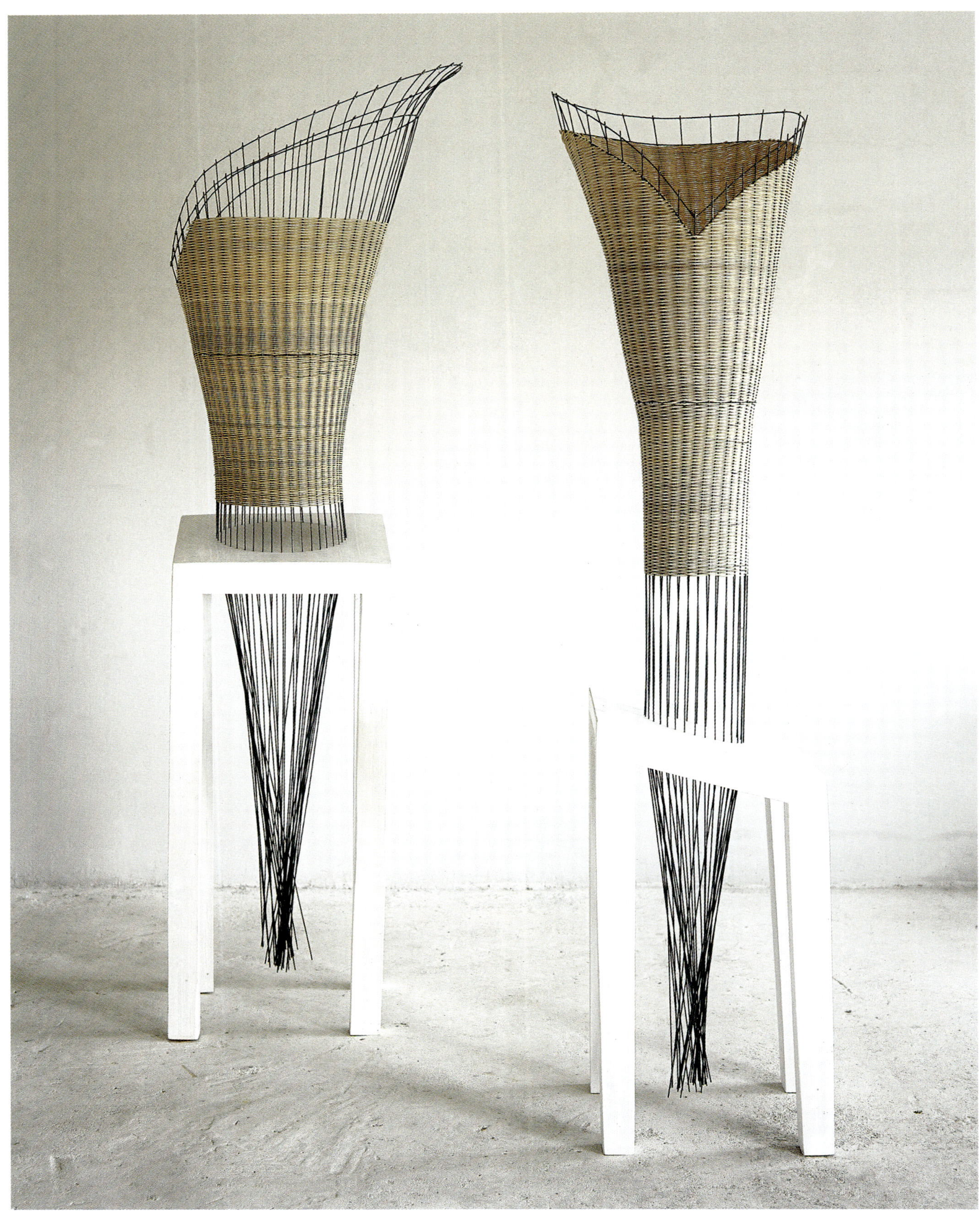

OPPOSITE; *Untitled,* 2001. Wood, iron rod, rattan: 221 × 70 × 55 cm (87" × 27" × 21"), 203 × 80 × 50 cm (80" × 31" × 19"). *Photo courtesy of the artist*

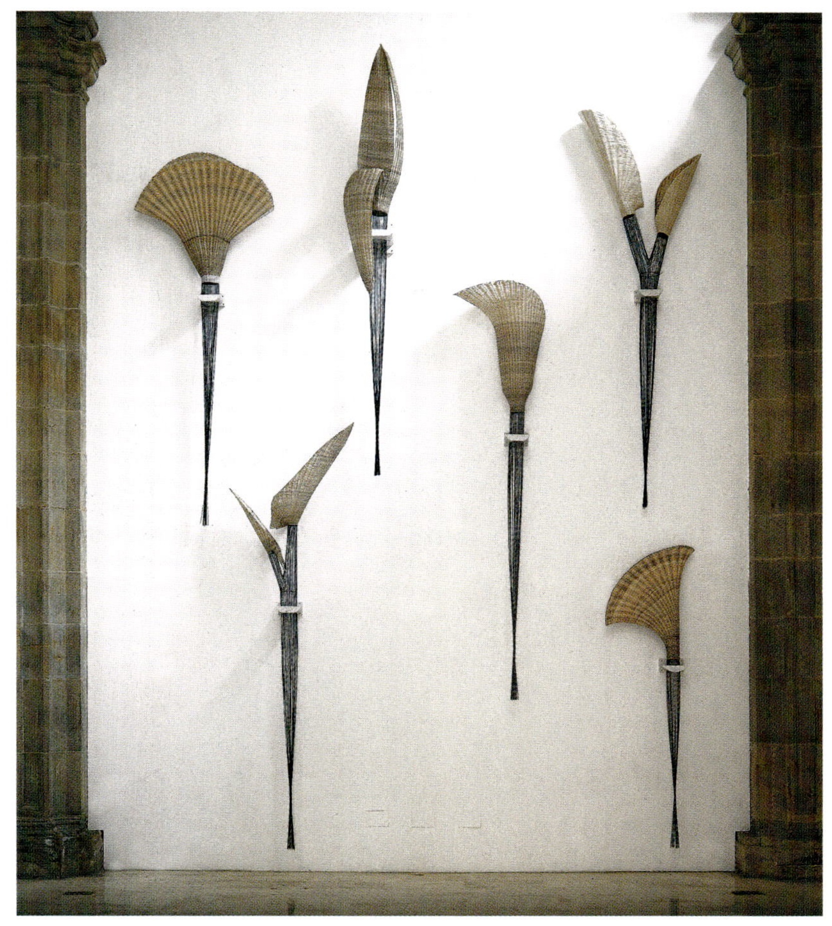

Untitled, 2003. Iron rod, rattan, wood: 300 × 112 × 25 cm (118" × 44" × 10"), 310 × 90 × 30 cm (122" × 35" × 12"), 335 × 45 × 55 cm (132" × 17" × 21"), 330 × 60 × 50 cm (130" × 24" × 19"), 330 × 110 × 50 cm (130" × 43" × 19"), 240 × 80 × 25 cm (94" × 31" × 9"). *Photo courtesy of the artist*

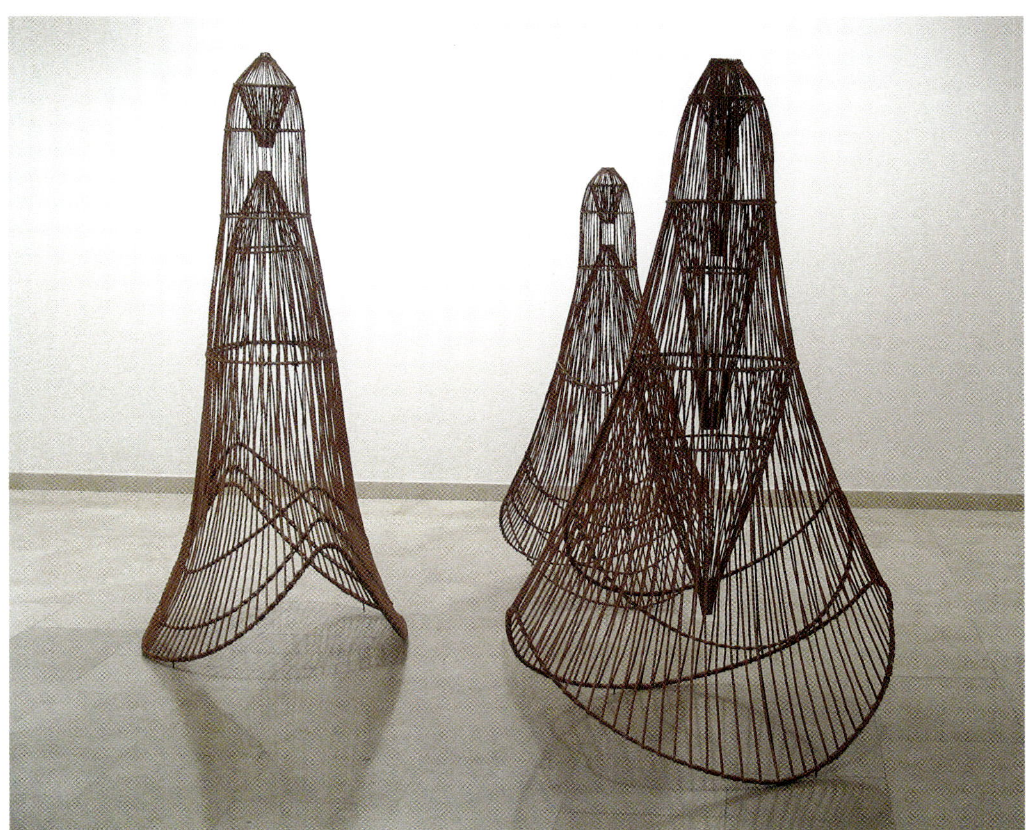

Untitled, 2007. Wicker: 194 × 300 × 300 cm (76" × 118" × 118"). *Photo courtesy of the artist*

Josep MERCADER

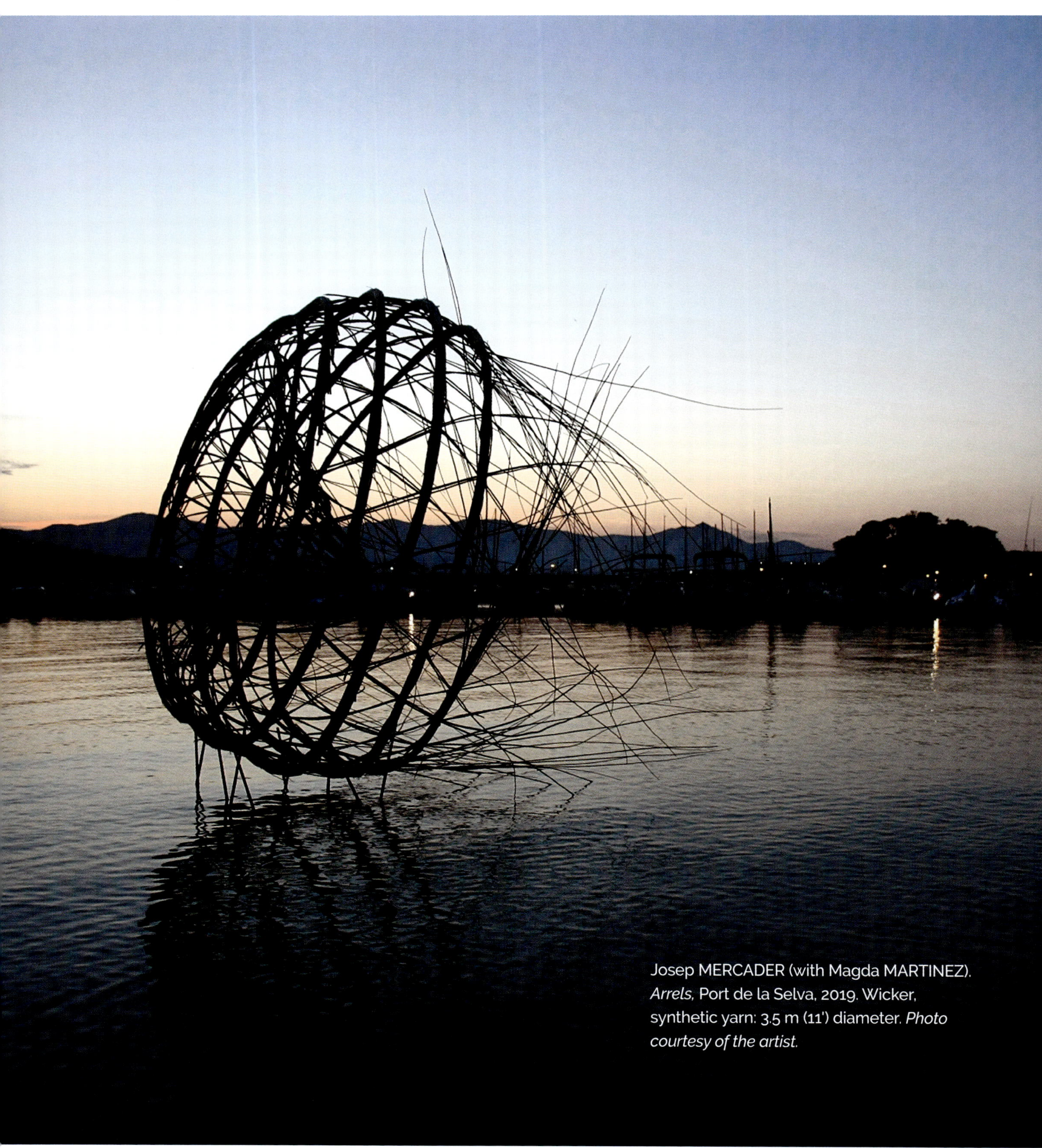

Josep MERCADER (with Magda MARTINEZ). *Arrels,* Port de la Selva, 2019. Wicker, synthetic yarn: 3.5 m (11') diameter. *Photo courtesy of the artist.*

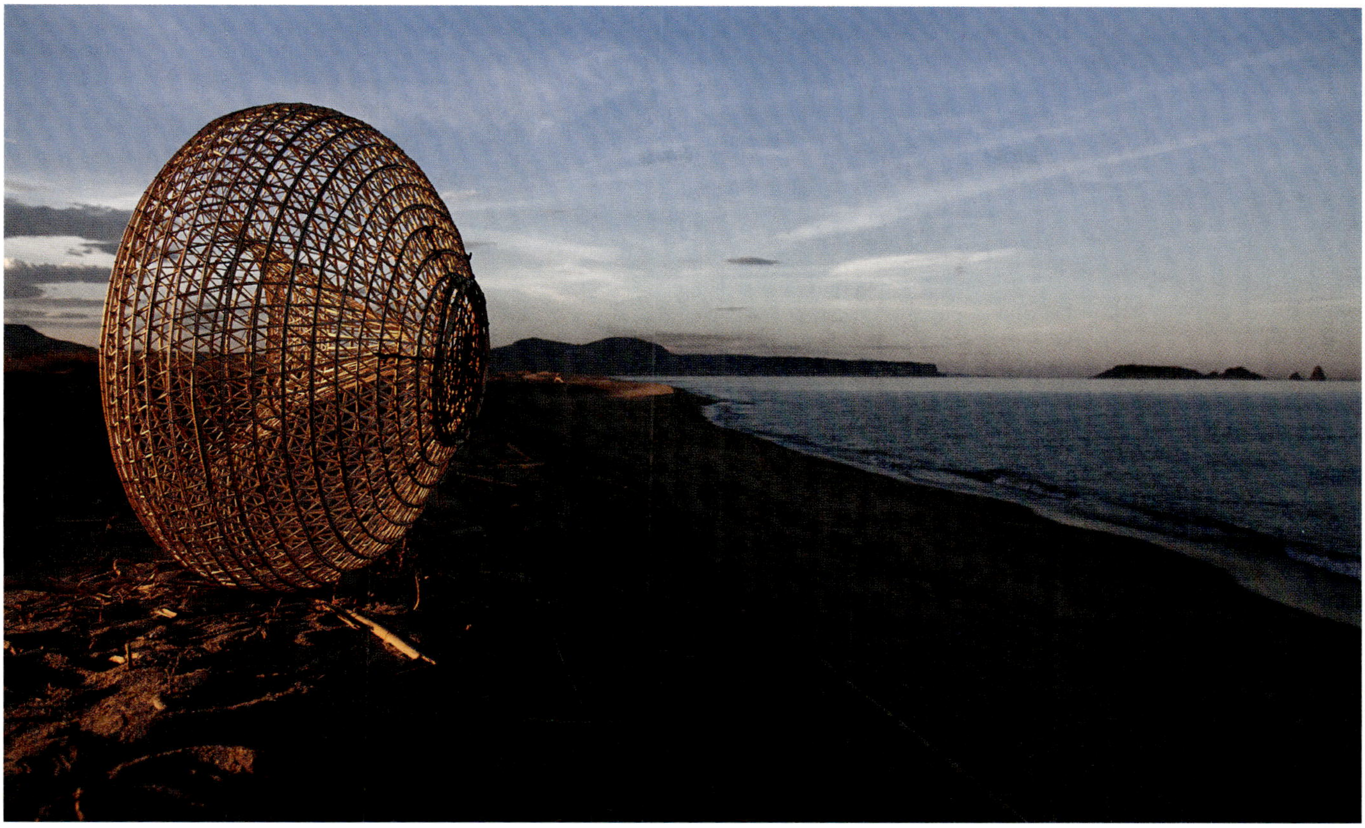

Garota, Pals, 2015. Wicker, synthetic yarn: 1 m (3') diameter.
Photos courtesy of the artist

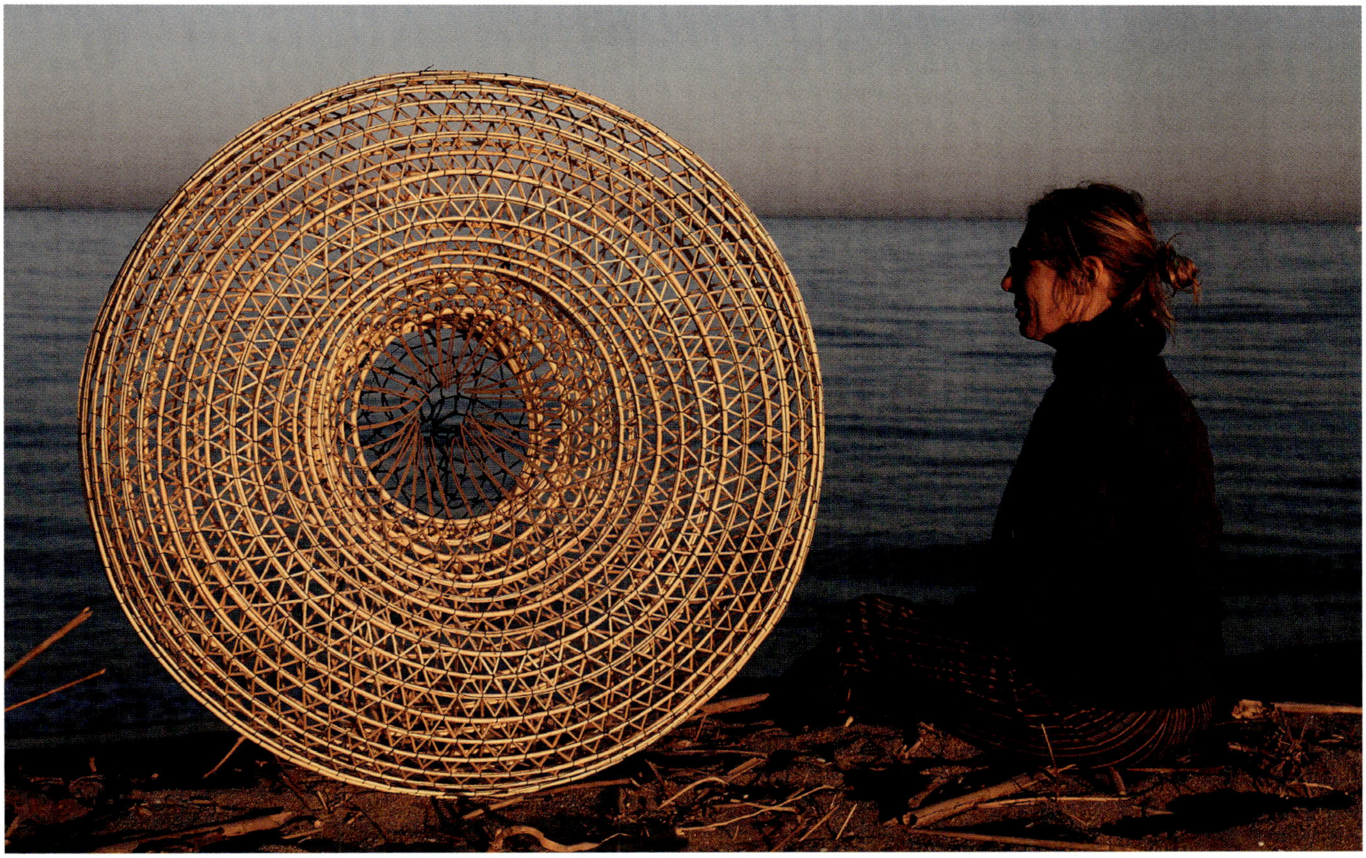

Haruko SUGAWARA

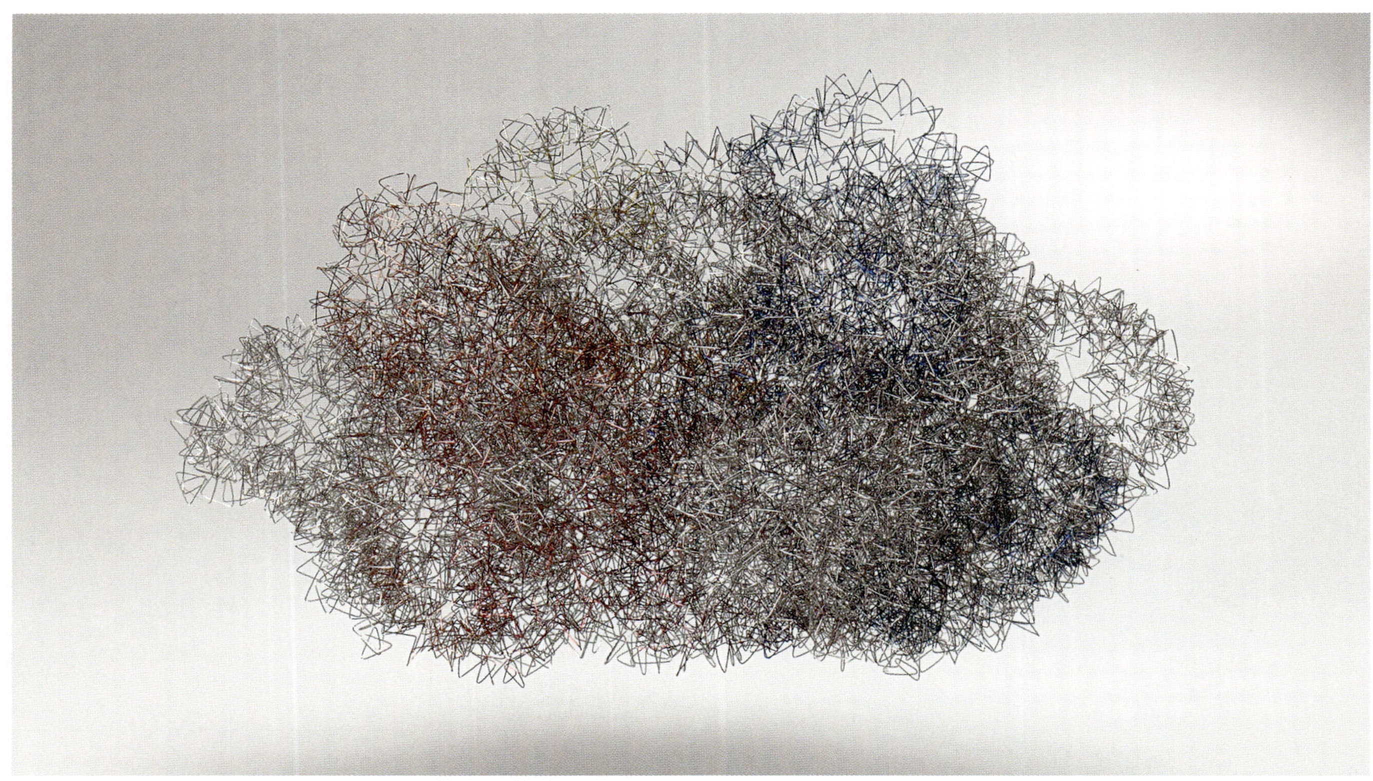

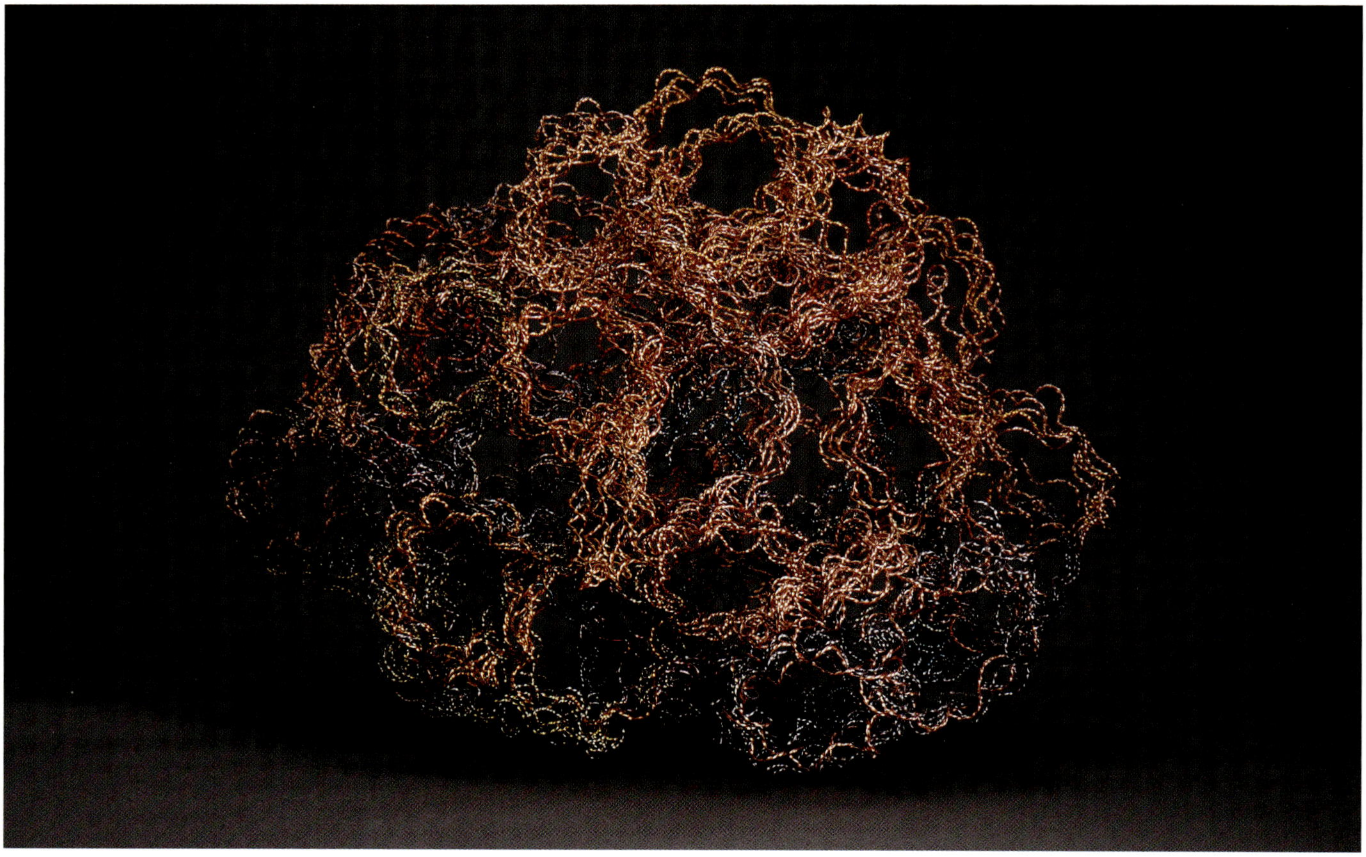

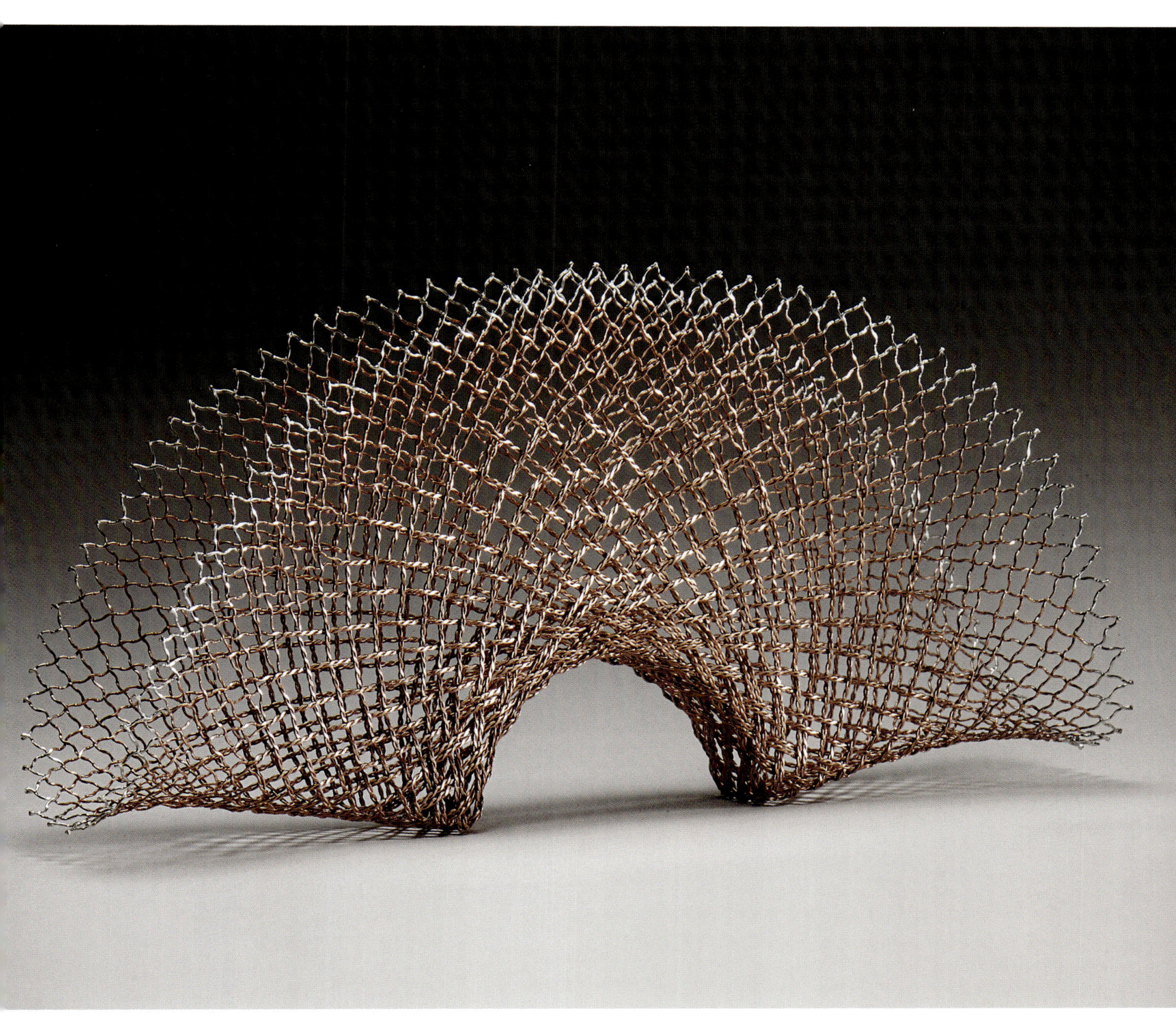

OPPOSITE, TOP: *Sunset Cloud I*, 2016. Stainless steel: 20 × 30 × 17 cm (8" × 12" × 7"). *Photo courtesy of Studio Sky*

OPPOSITE, BOTTOM: *Sunset Cloud II*, 2017. Copper: 25 × 35 × 25 cm (10" × 14" × 10"). *Photo courtesy of Studio Sky*

Unleashed Shape, 2014. Copper: 43 × 20 × 10 cm (17" × 8 " × 4"). *Photo courtesy of Studio Sky*

Pat HICKMAN

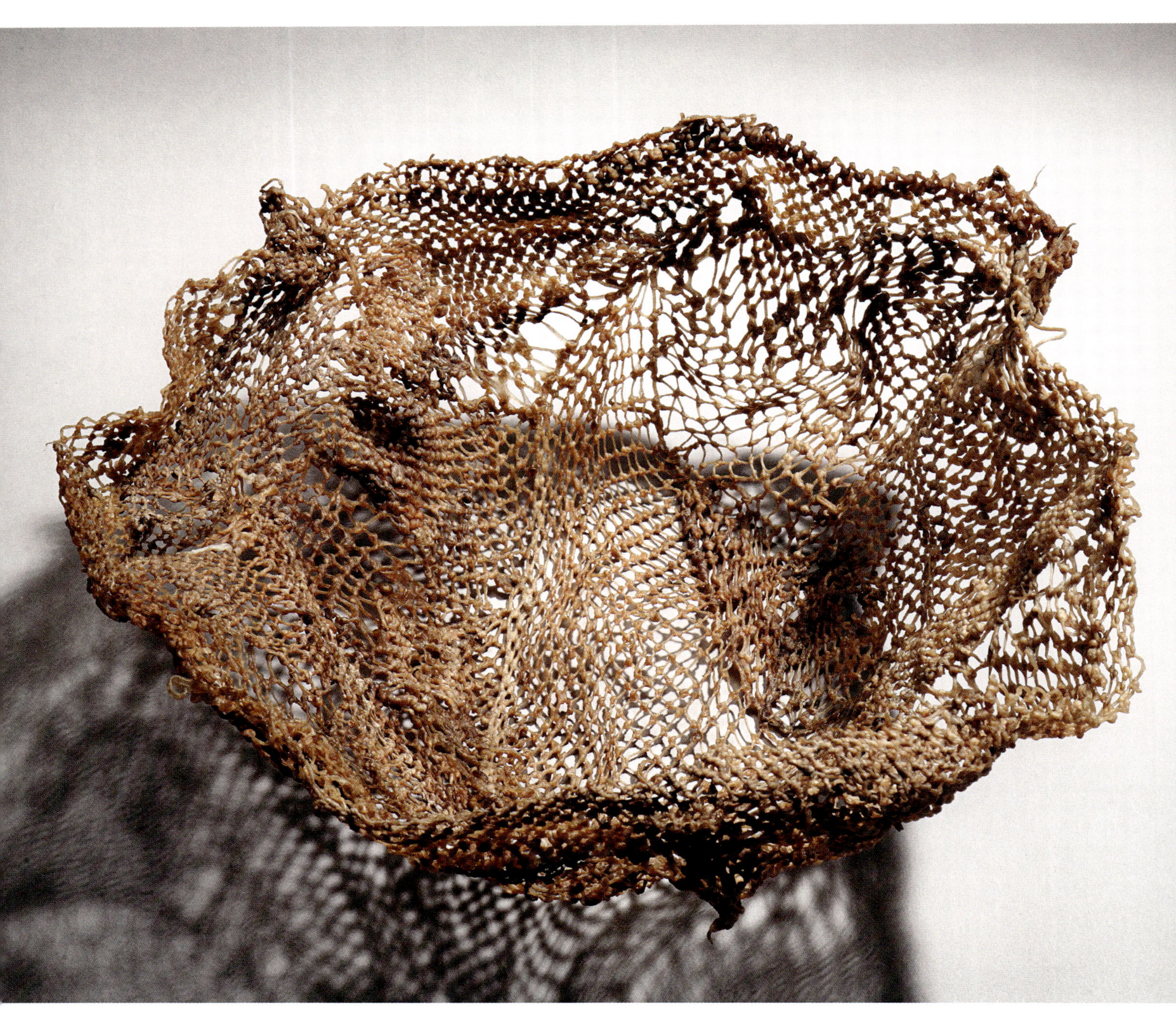

Winnow, 2023. Skin membrane (hog casings): 24 × 45 × 45 cm (9.5" × 18" × 18"). *Photo courtesy of George Potanovic, Jr.*

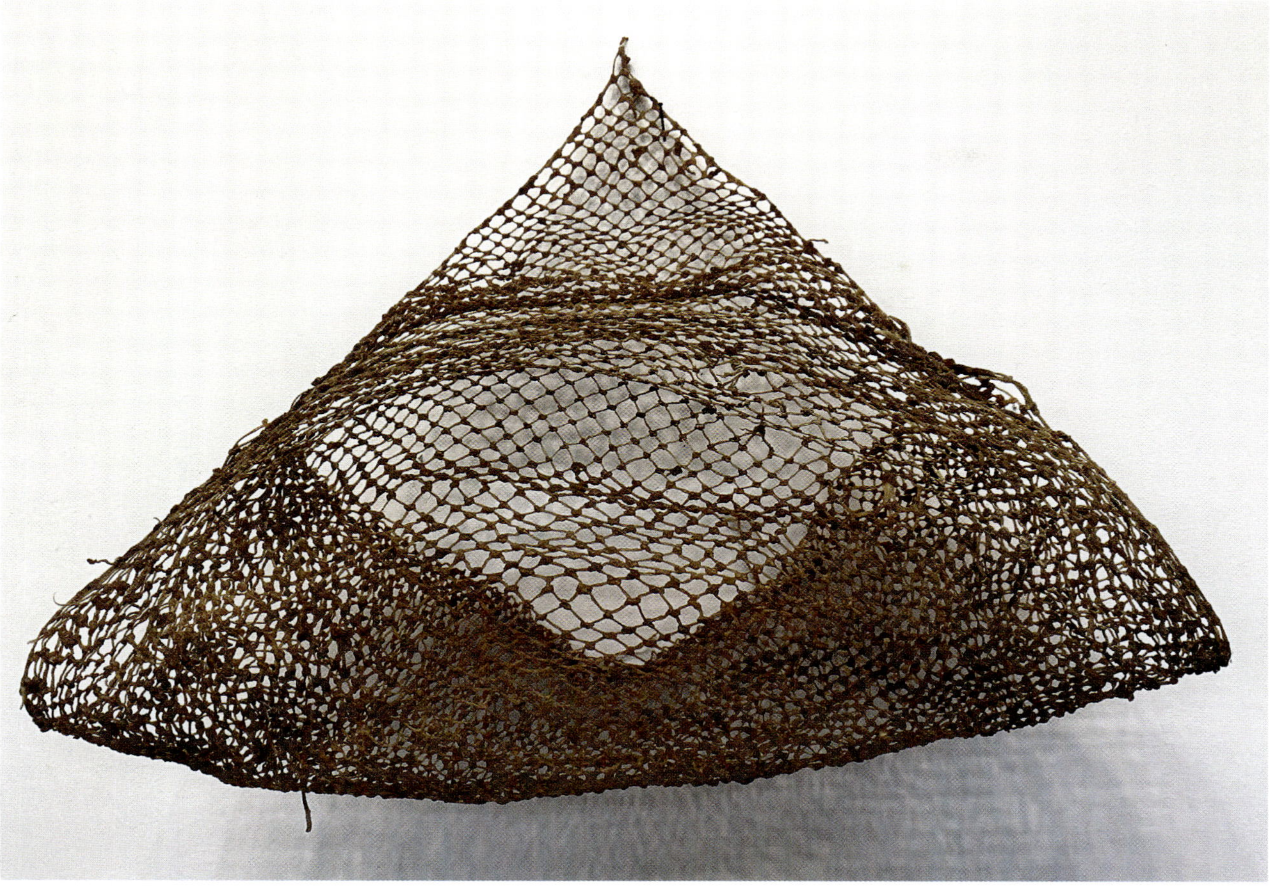

Holding, 2023. Skin membrane (hog casings): 55 × 68 × 26 cm (22" × 27" × 10.5"). *Photo courtesy of George Potanovic, Jr.*

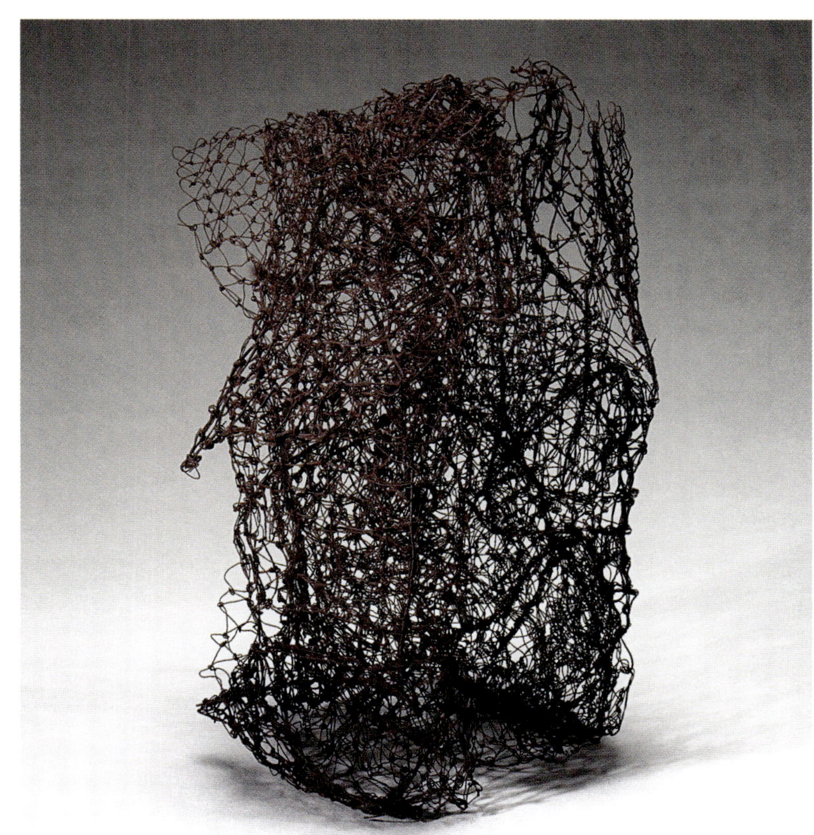

Concentration, 2005.Steel: 32 × 21 × 19 cm (12.5" × 8.25" × 7.5"). *Photo by Hal Lum courtesy of the artist*

Kazue HONMA

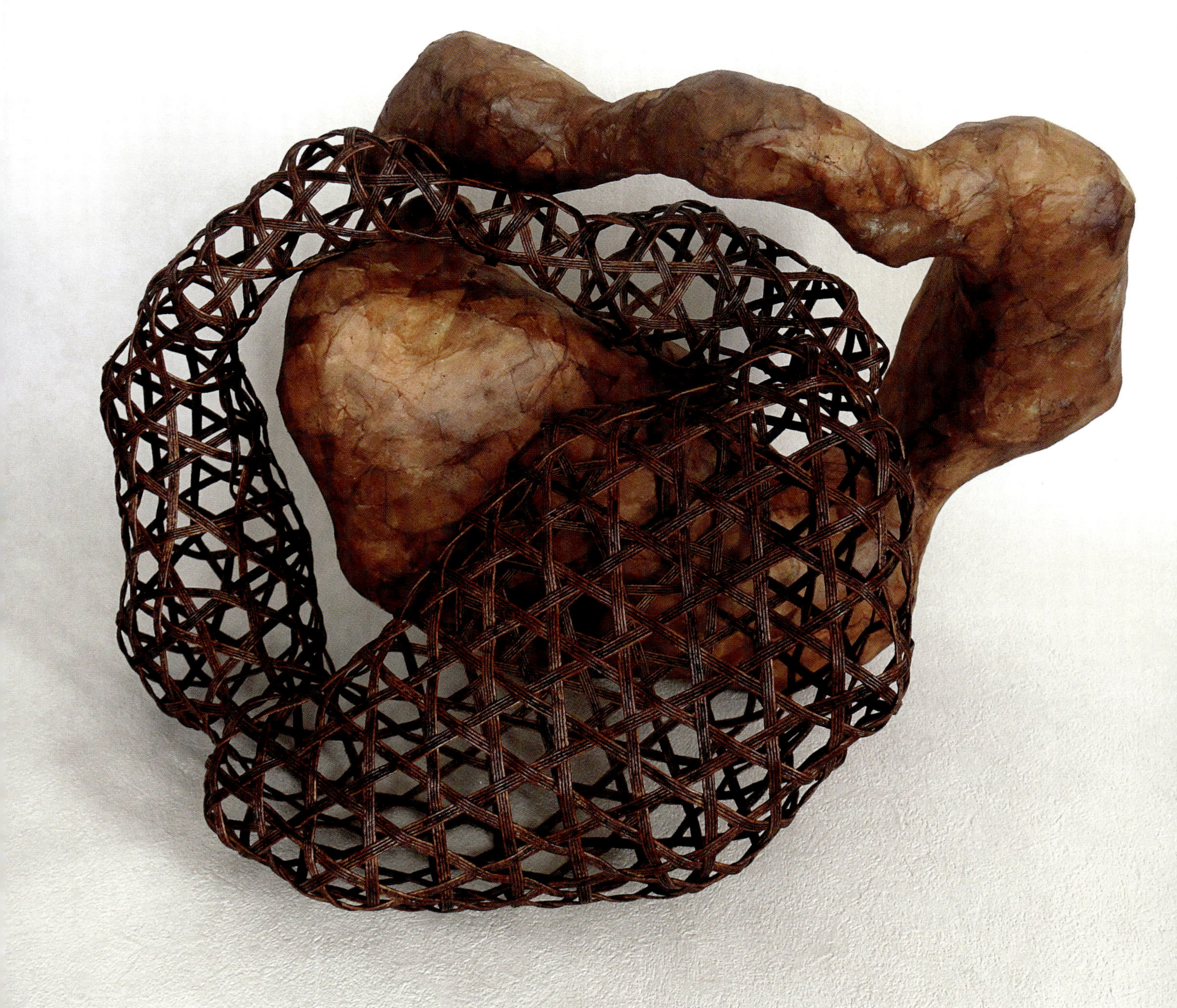

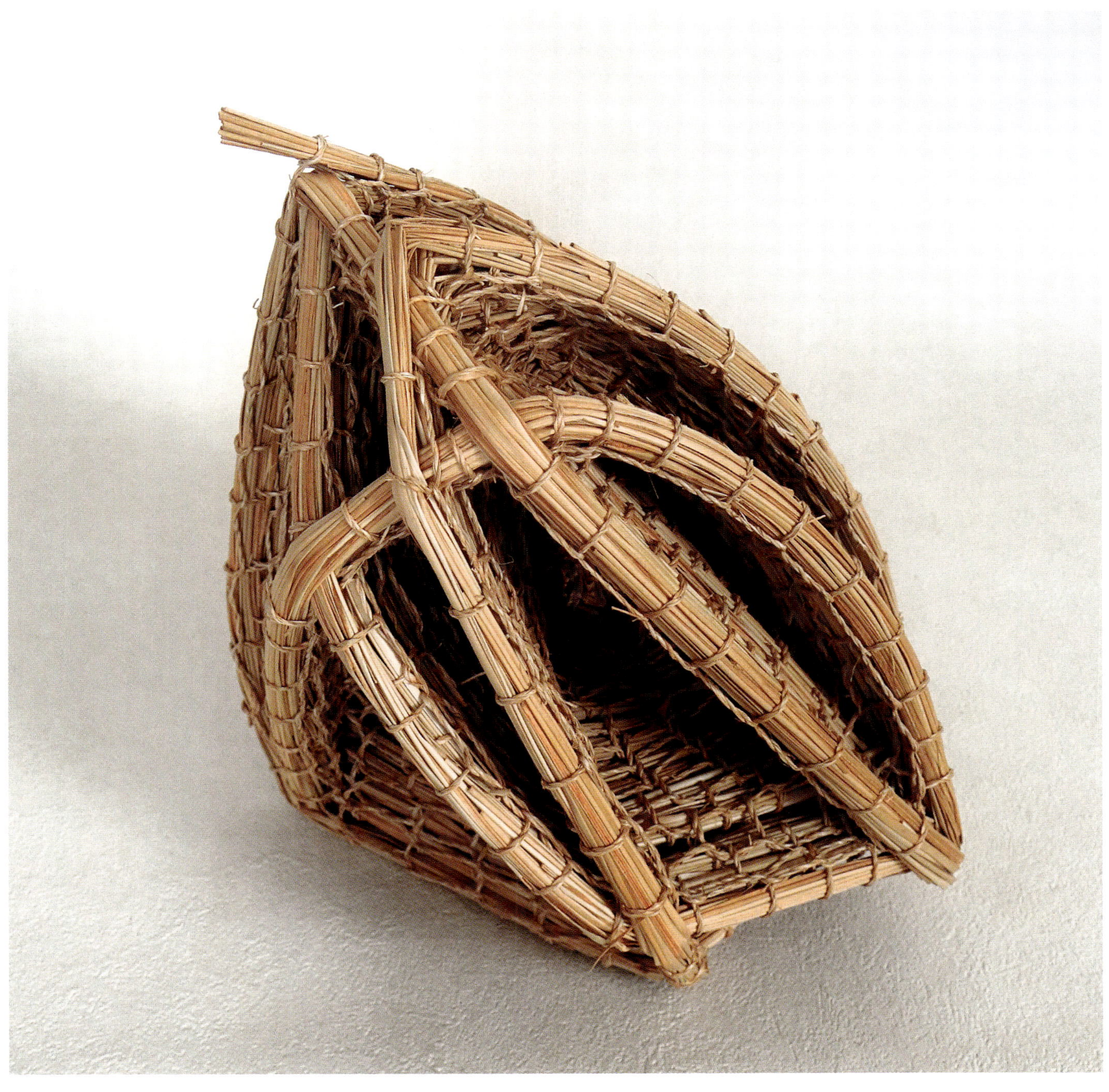

OPPOSITE: *Chiral-E*, 2014. Paper band, paper, persimmon tannin: 30 × 40 × 50 cm (11" × 15" × 19"). *Photo courtesy of the artist*

One Stroke Coiling-3, 2021. Shell ginger: 16 × 22 × 26 cm (6" × 8" × 10"). *Photo courtesy of the artist*

Karen **GOSSART** and Corentin **LAVAL**

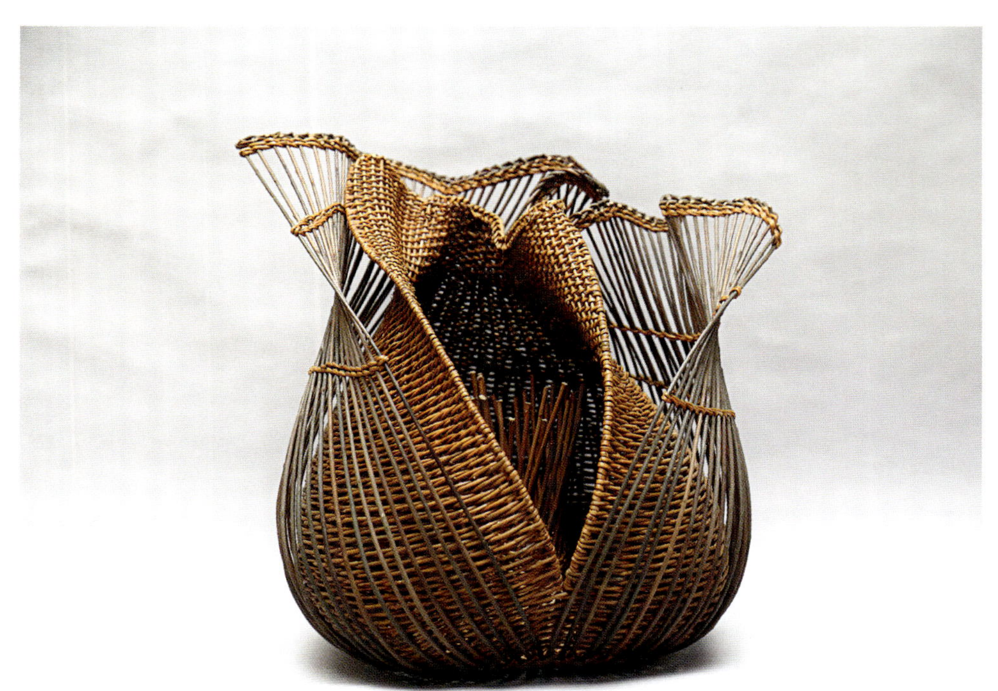

Découverte Épicarpe serie, 2021. Brown willow: 55 × 55 × 47 cm (21" × 21" × 18"). *Photo courtesy of Oseraie de l'Ile*

Bonsaï, 2019. Brown willow: 65 × 105 × 100 cm (25" × 41" × 39"). *Photo courtesy of Oseraie de l'Ile*

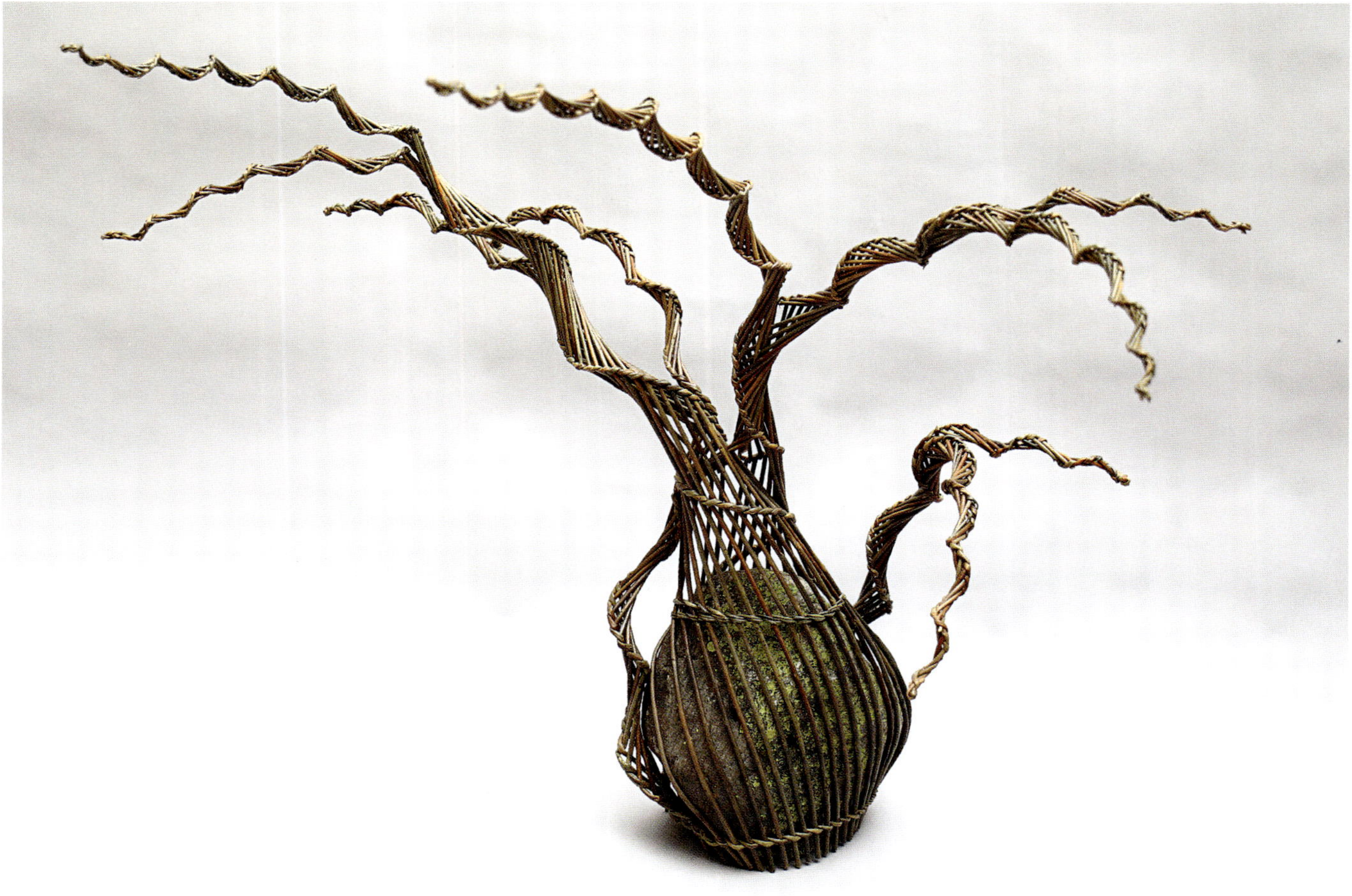

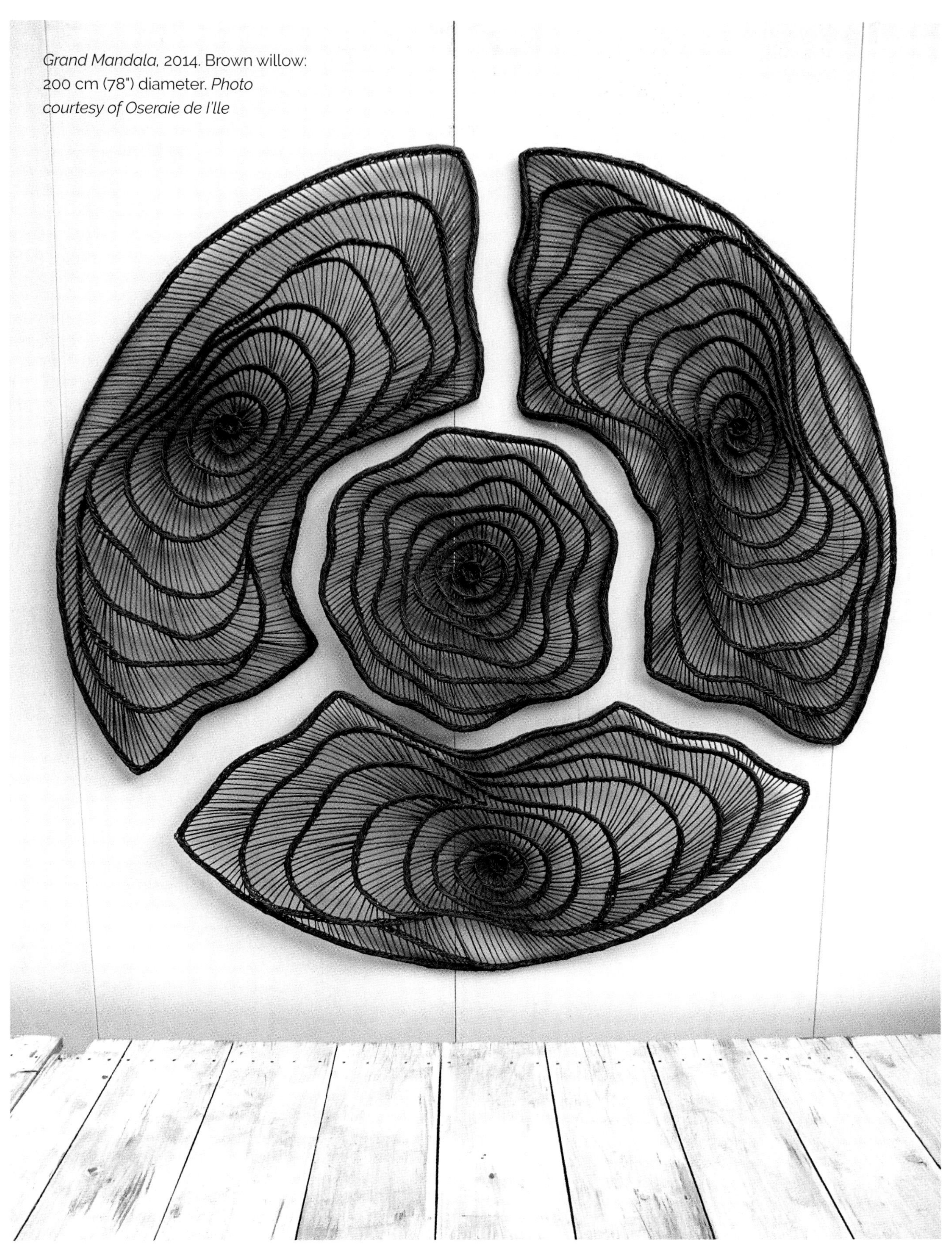

Grand Mandala, 2014. Brown willow: 200 cm (78") diameter. *Photo courtesy of Oseraie de l'Ile*

Dan COOPEY

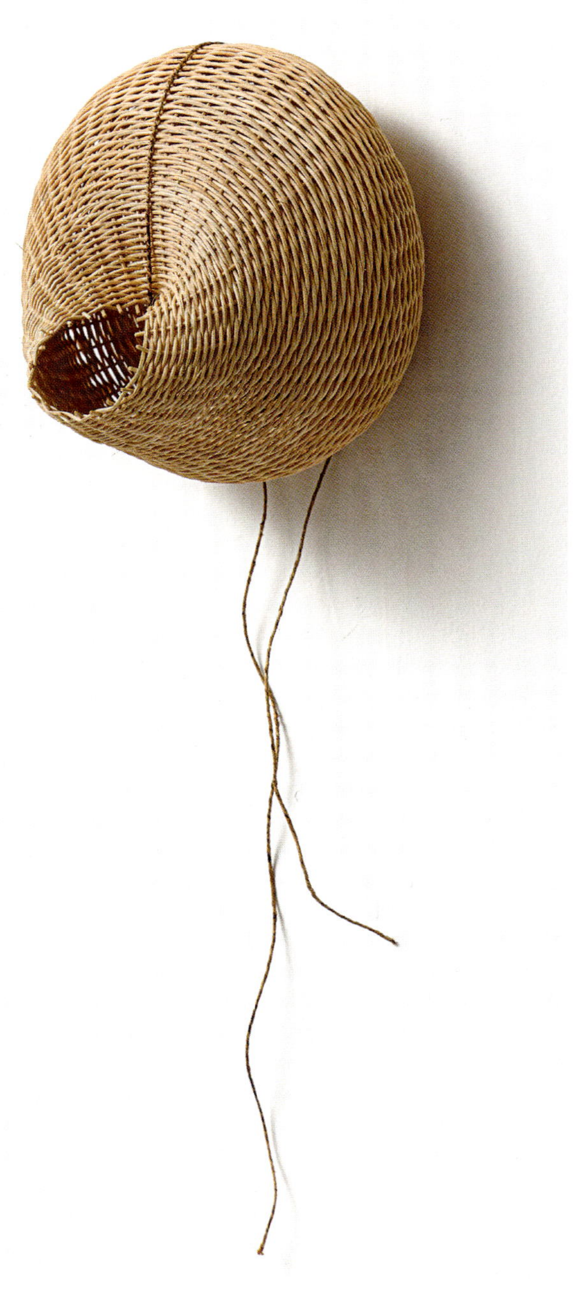

shell, 2023. Rattan: 54 × 22 × 22 cm (21" × 8" × 8"). *Photo courtesy of the artist*

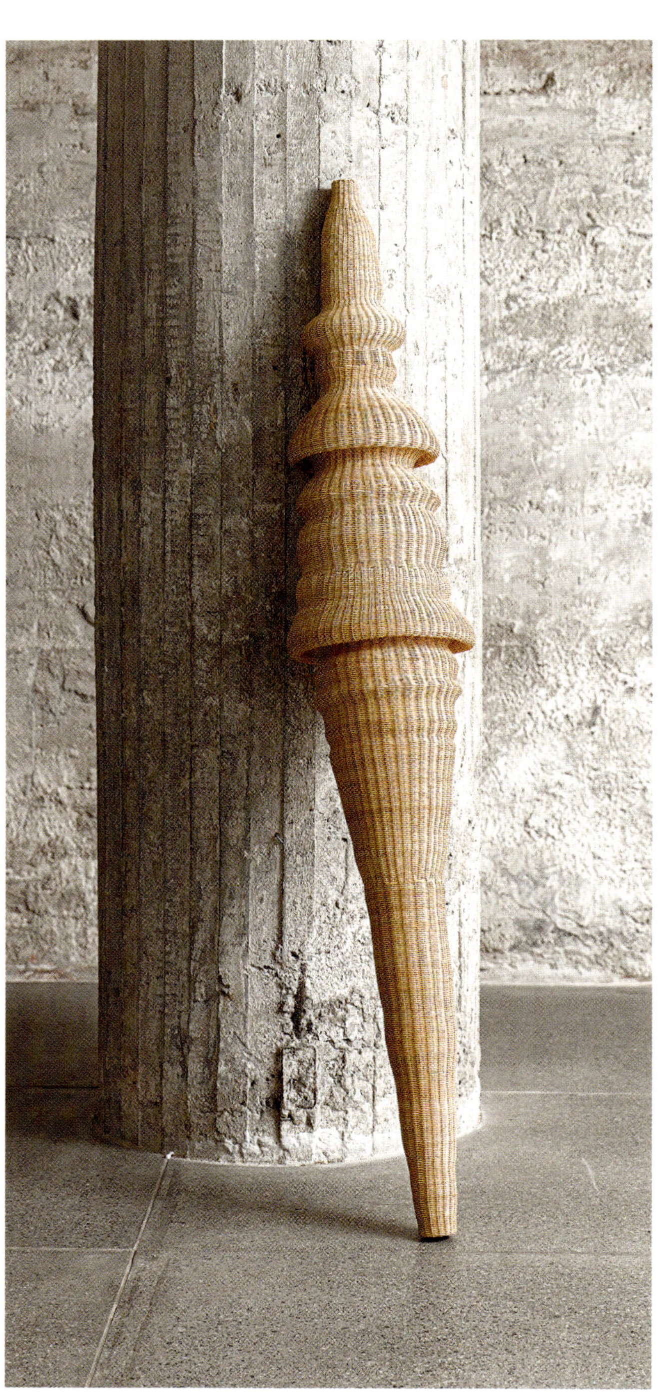

the double, 2023. Rattan, iron, chewing gum: 173 × 30 × 30 cm (68" × 11" × 11"). *Photo courtesy of the artist*

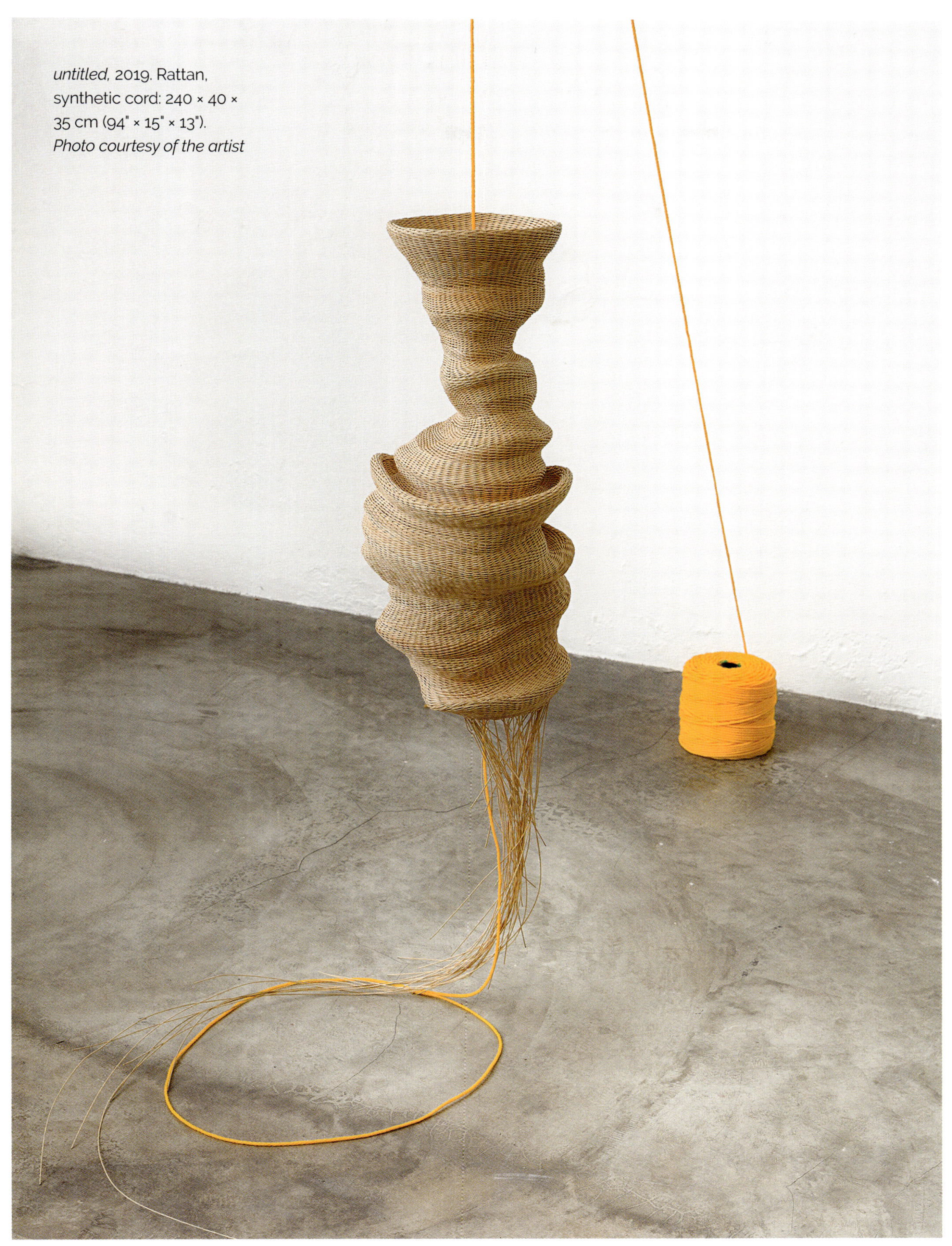

untitled, 2019. Rattan, synthetic cord: 240 × 40 × 35 cm (94" × 15" × 13"). *Photo courtesy of the artist*

Ferne JACOBS

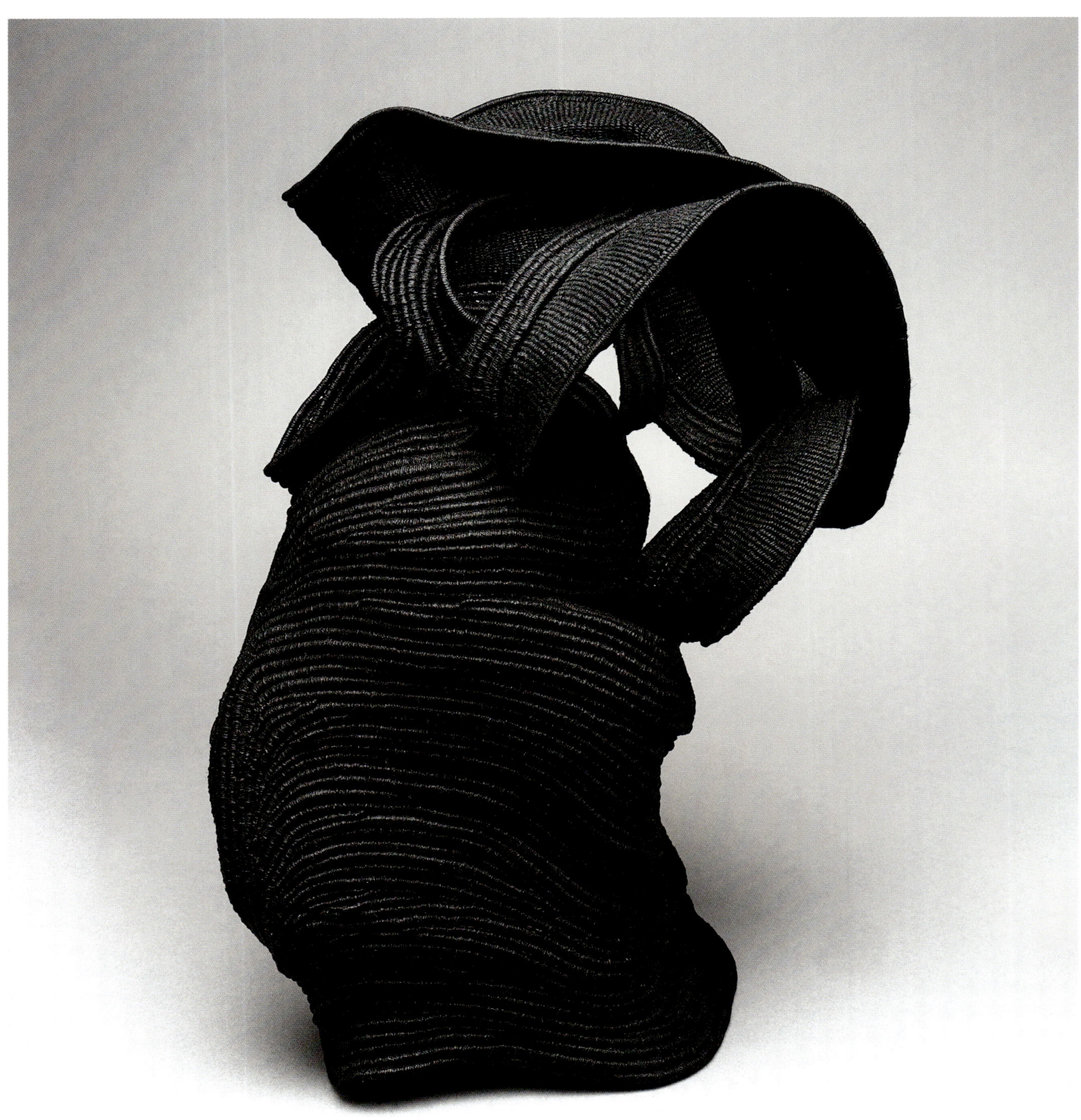

Figure/Head, 2020. Waxed linen thread: 33 × 17 × 22 cm (13" × 7" × 9"). *Photo courtesy of Bernard Wolf*

OPPOSITE: *Flight*, 2011. Waxed linen thread: 40 × 50 × 33 cm (16" × 20" × 13"). *Photo courtesy of Susan Einstein*

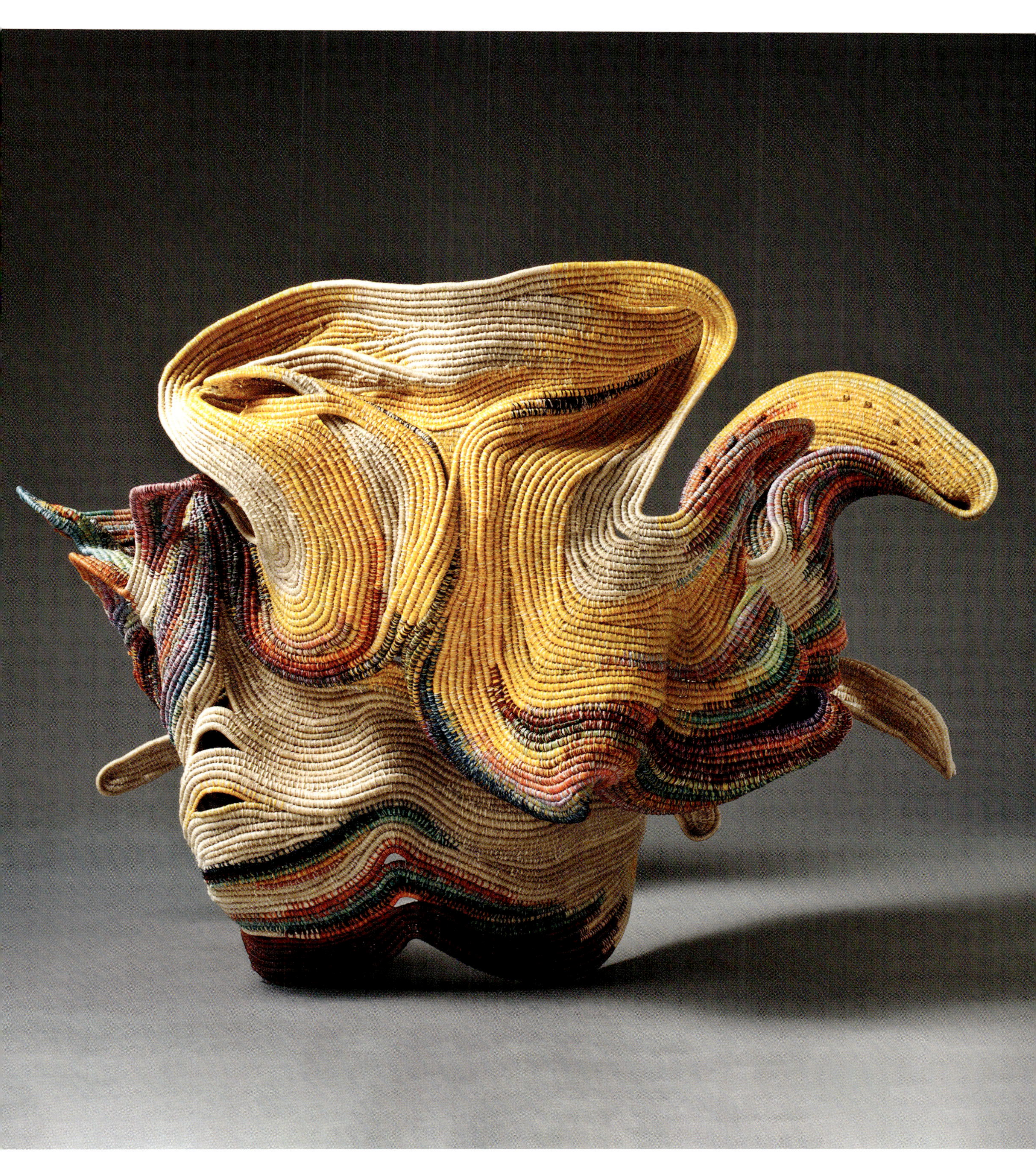

Doug JOHNSTON

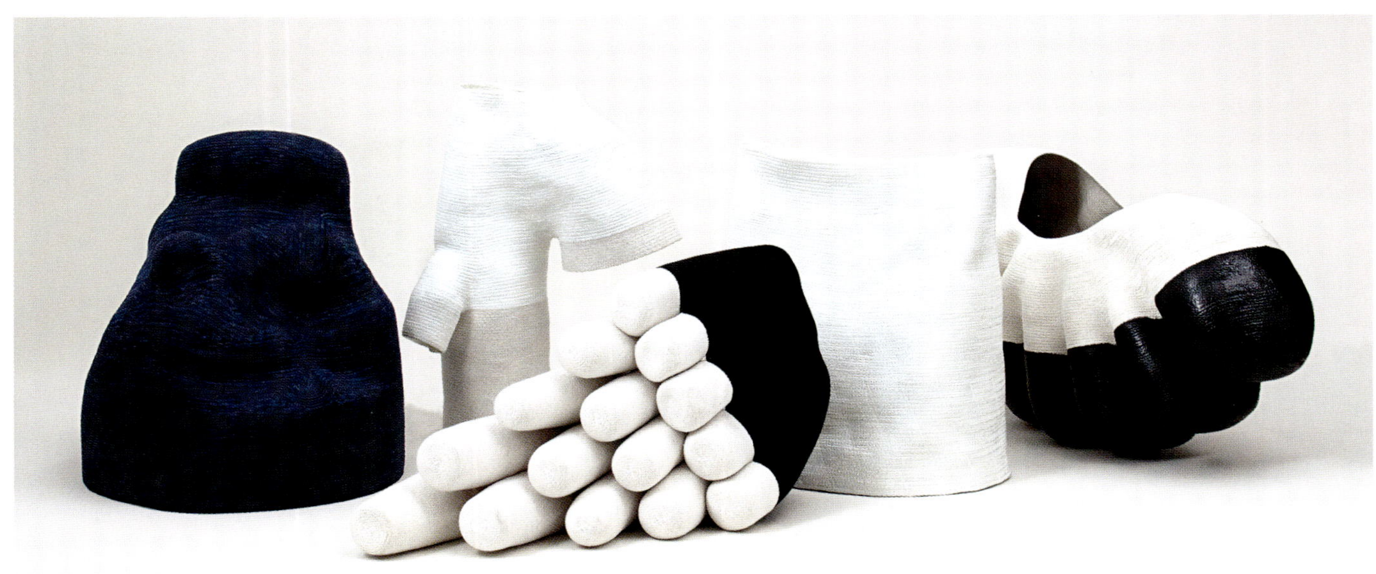

Group of coiled cord vessels including *Tripplehorn, Murzu, Double Pail, Torse,* and *Coyote*, 2017. Cotton cord and polyester sewing thread: various dimensions. *Photo courtesy of the artist*

Group of coiled cord pieces including *Untitled (Navy Shroud), Font, 15-hump Vessel, Half a Pillow,* and *7-hump Vessel,* 2015. Nylon and cotton cord, nylon sewing thread, polyurethane resin, lighting components: various dimensions. *Photo courtesy of the artist*

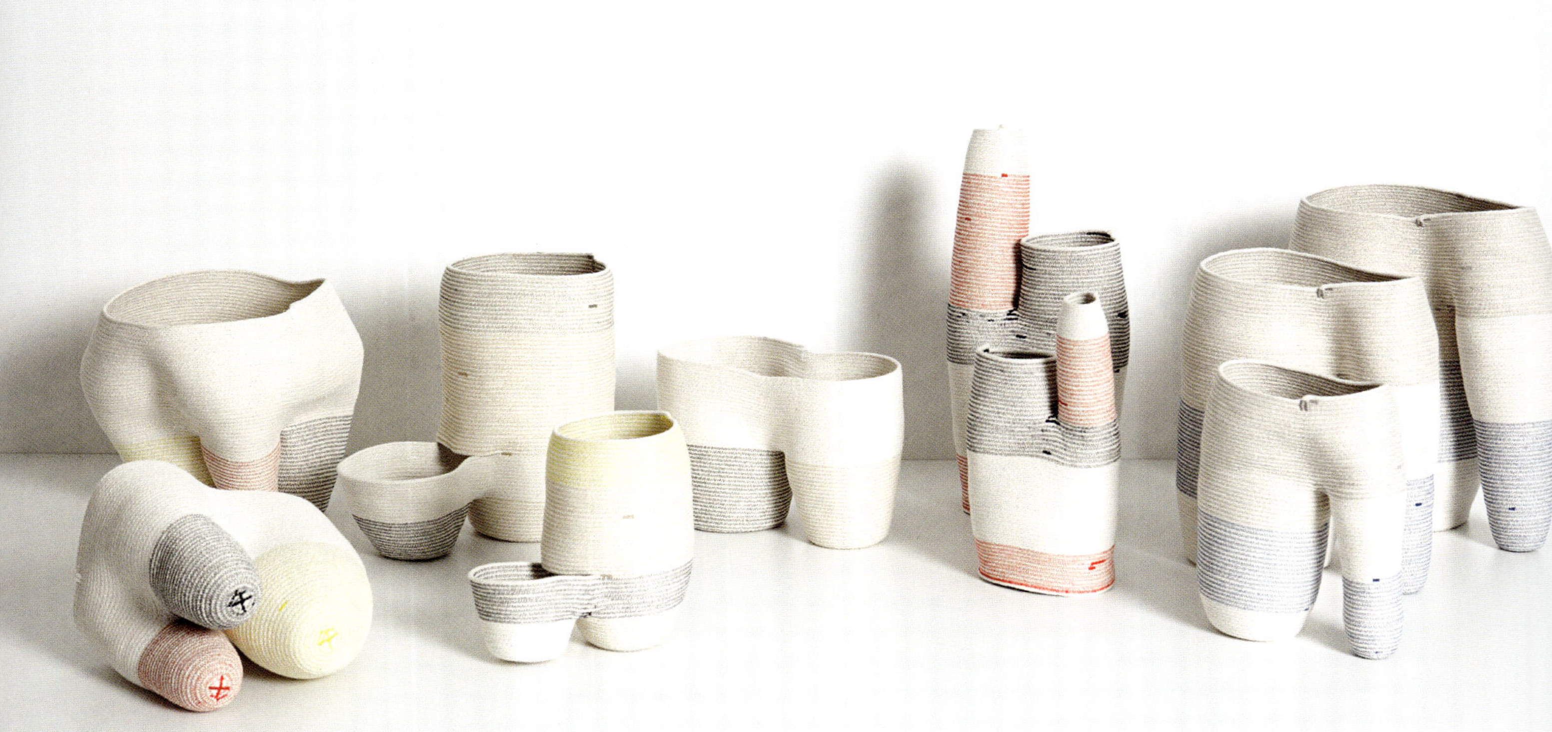

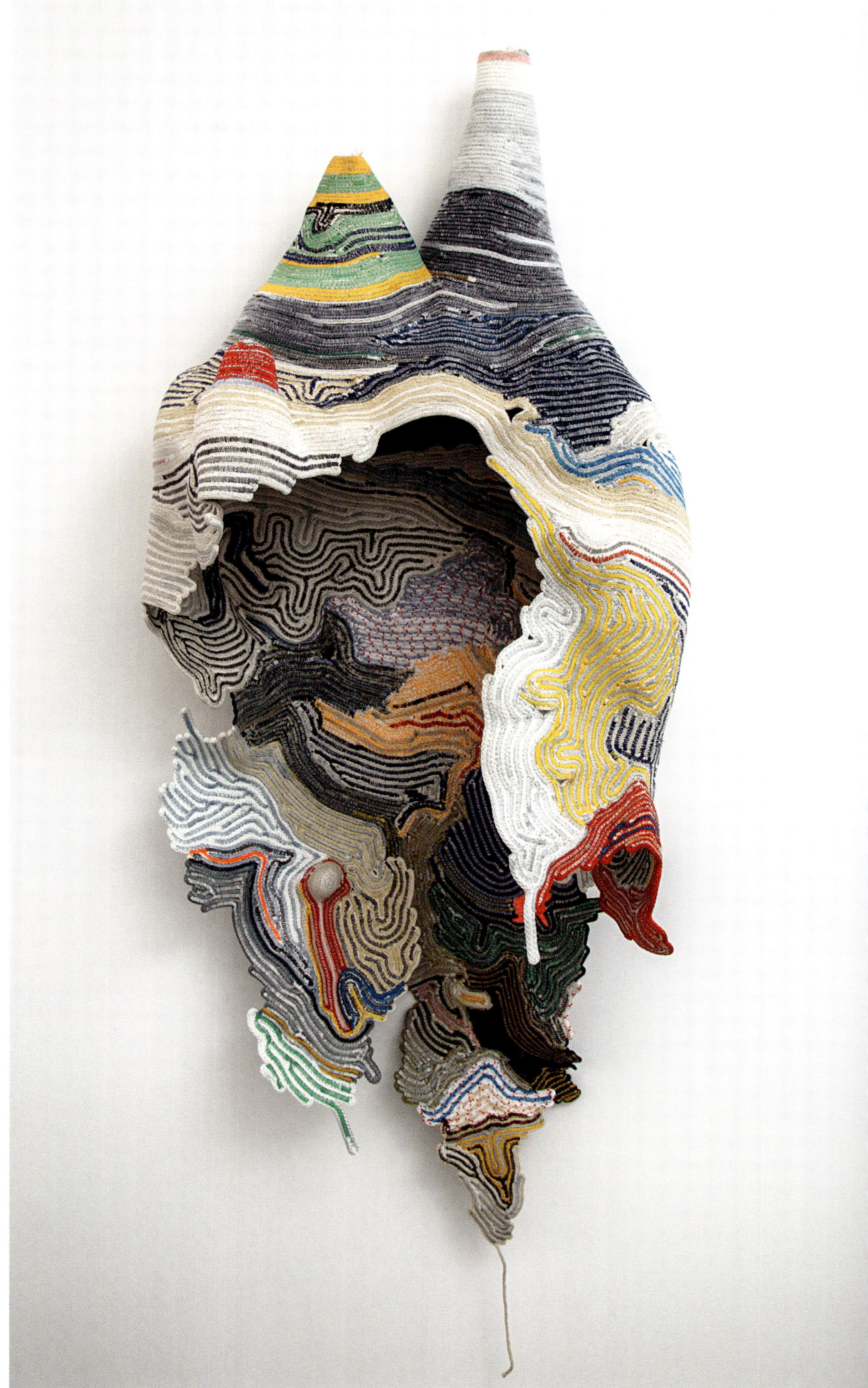

Baby's Breath, 2021. Cotton and nylon cord, nylon and polyester sewing thread: 172 × 71 × 40 cm (68" × 28" × 16"). *Photo courtesy of the artist*

Giuse MAGGI

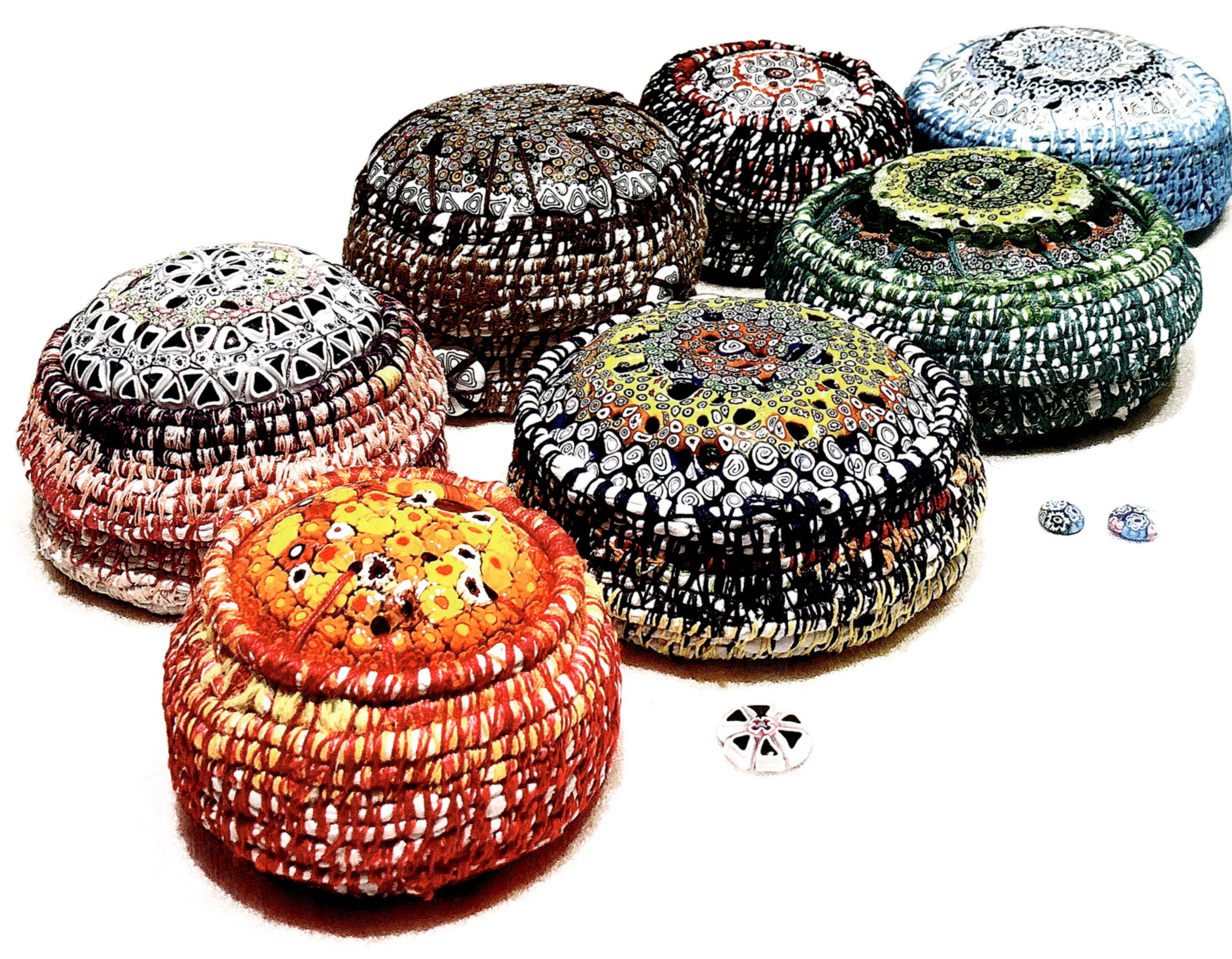

Mounds Series, Boxes, 2021. Kiln-formed murine glass, cotton fabric, cotton thread: various dimensions. *Photo courtesy of the artist*

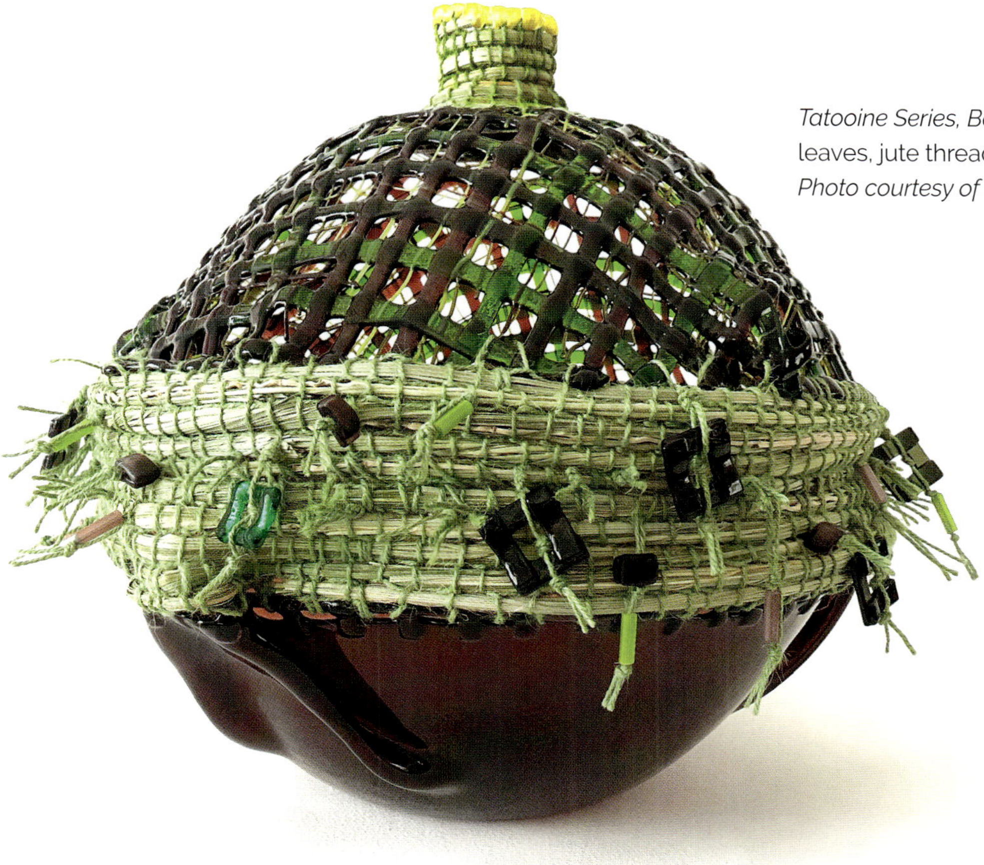

Tatooine Series, Bottle, 2020. Kiln-formed glass, palm leaves, jute thread, satin ribbon: 40 × 45 cm (15" × 17"). *Photo courtesy of the artist*

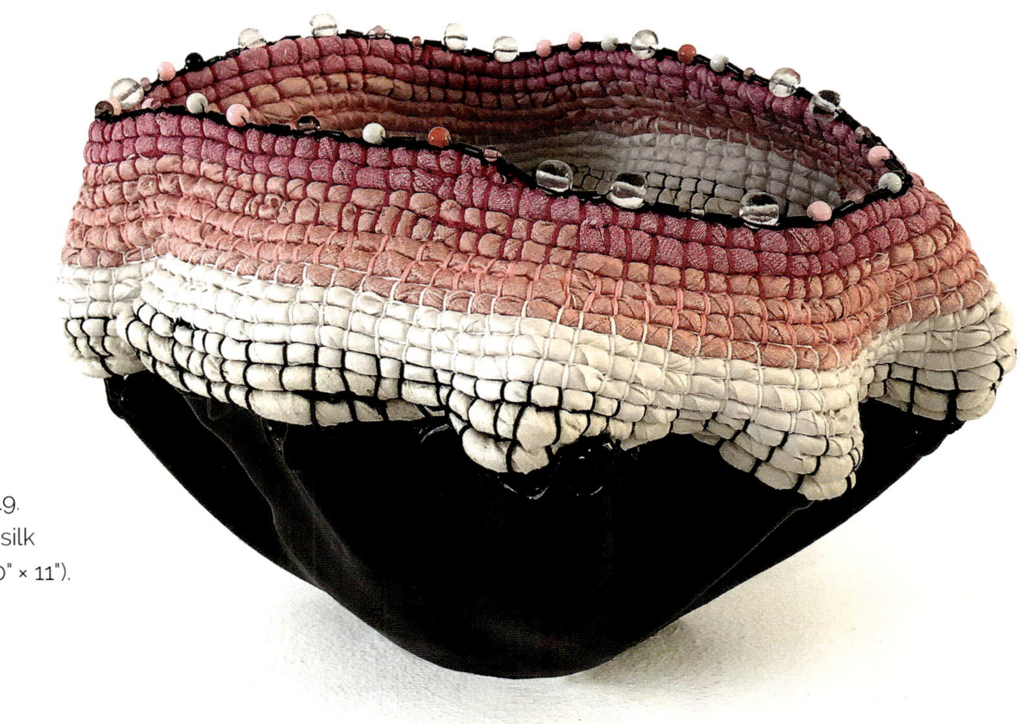

Haute Couture Series, Vessel, 2019. Kiln-formed glass, glass beads, silk fabric, jute thread: 25 × 28 cm (10" × 11"). *Photo courtesy of the artist*

Lois WALPOLE

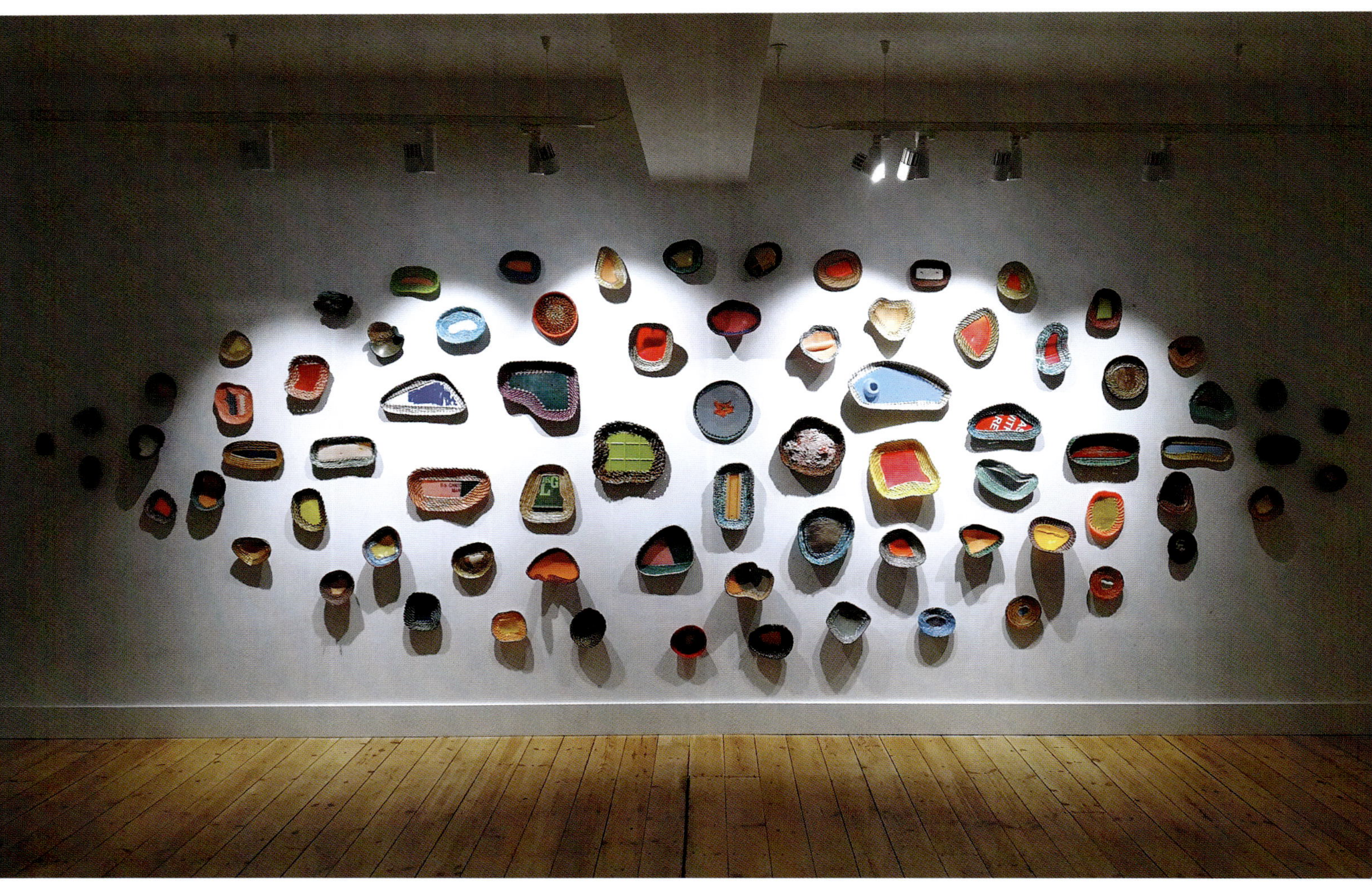

North Atlantic Drift, 2019. Found and gathered materials: 5.5 m (18') wide. *Photos courtesy of the artist*

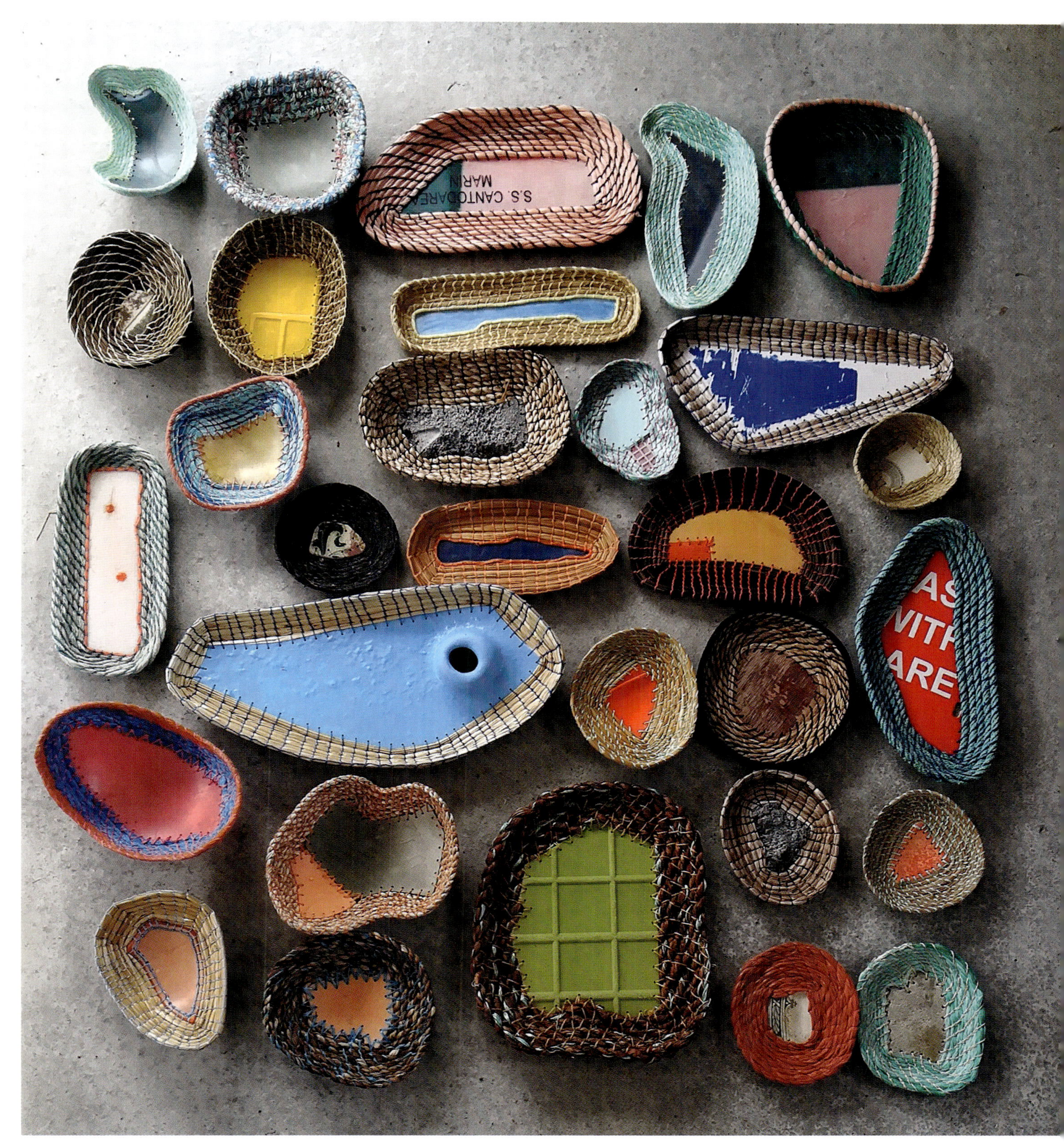

North Atlantic Drift (detail), installation 2021.

José Santiago PÉREZ

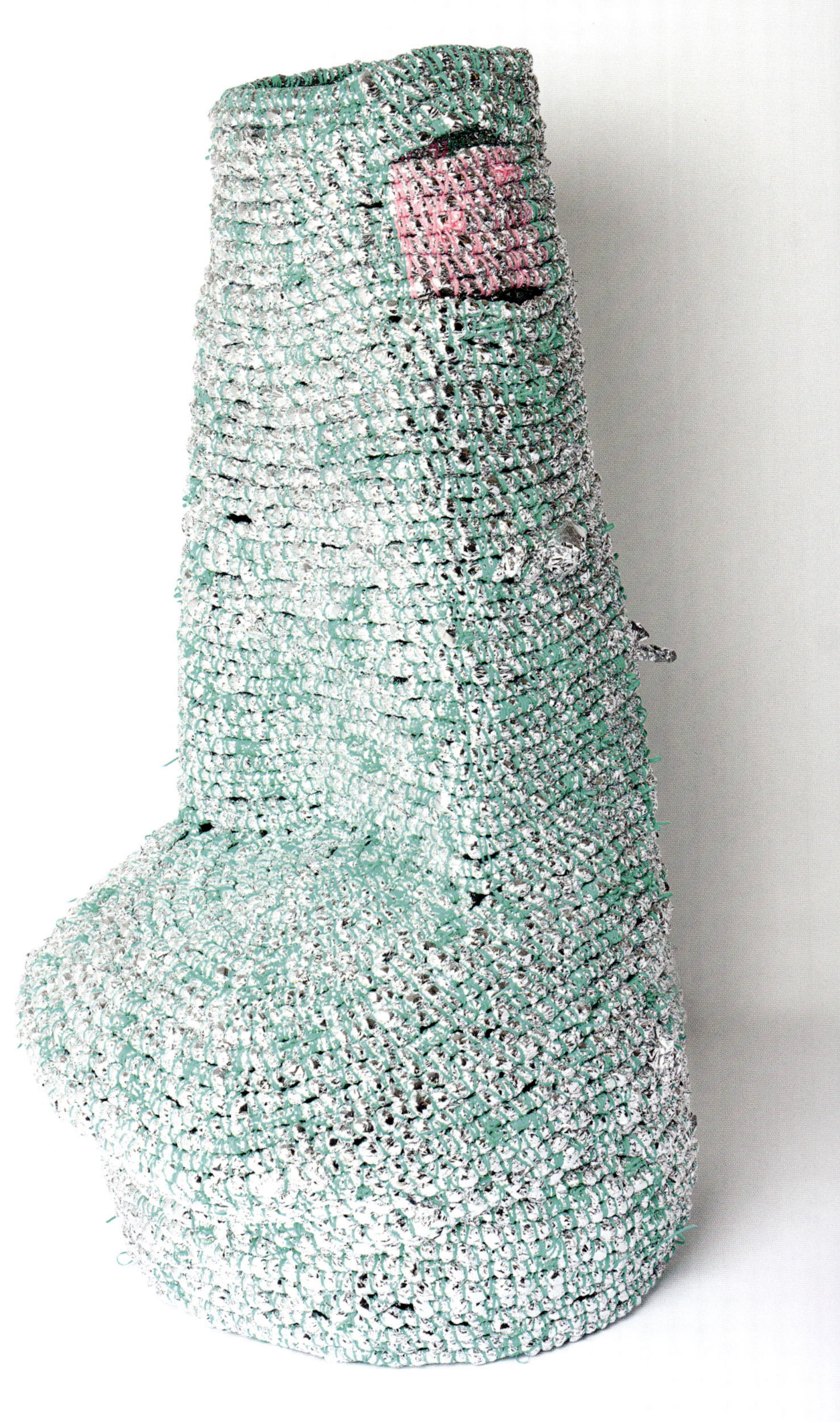

Unburden (so you may ease), 2020. Mylar emergency blankets, craft lacing; 79 × 110 cm (31" × 43.5"). *Photo courtesy of Aiyo Cheboi*

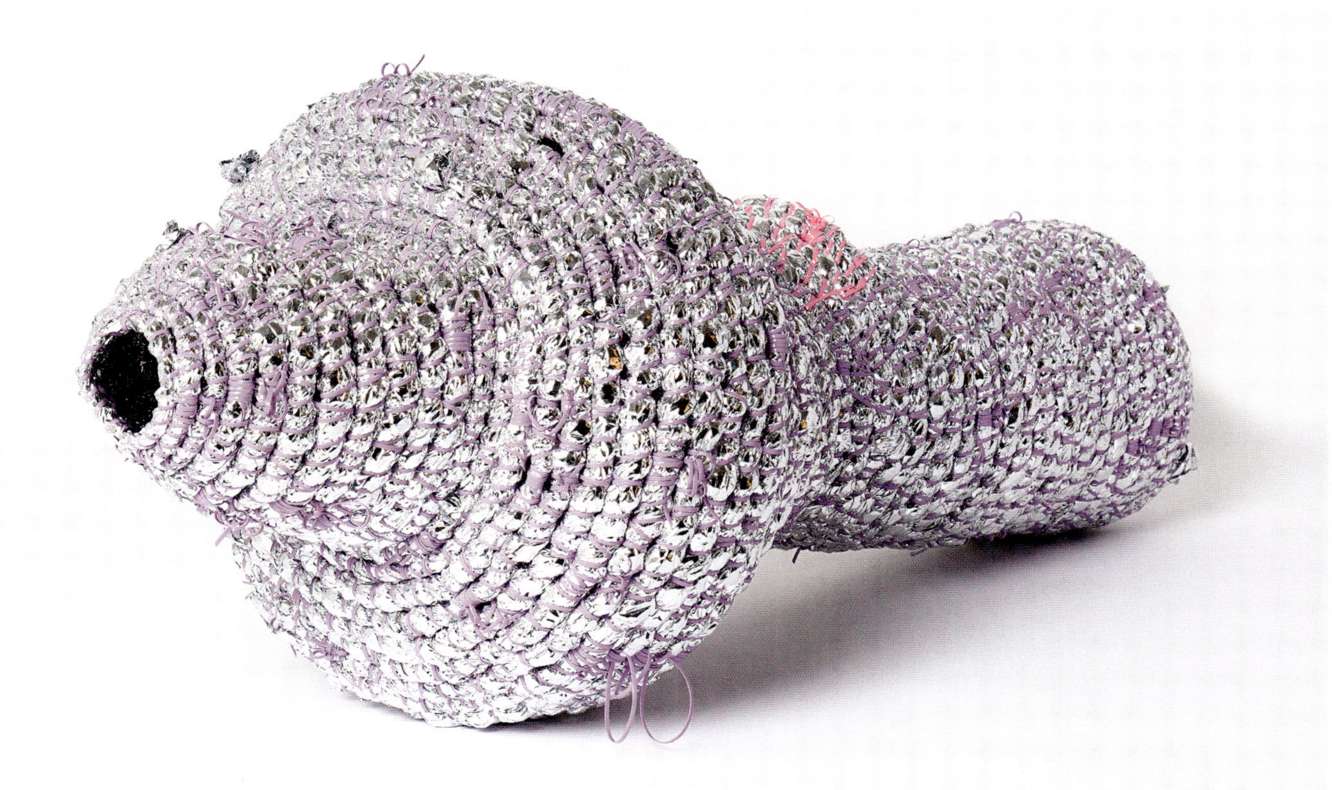

Unburden (so you may release), 2020. Mylar emergency blankets, craft lacing: 91 × 35 × 40 cm (36" × 14" × 16"). *Photo courtesy of Aiyo Cheboi*

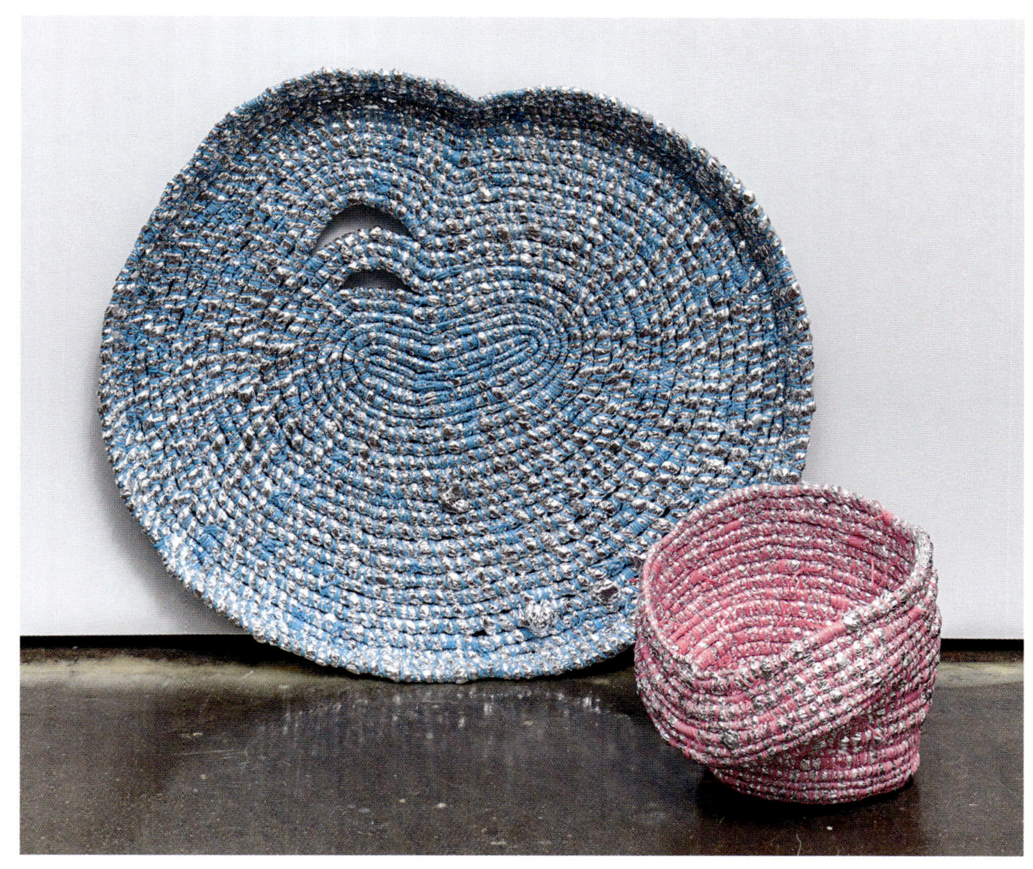

Unburden (so you may continue), 2020. Mylar emergency blankets, craft lacing: 79 × 7 × 68 cm (31" × 3" × 27") and 30 × 25 cm (12" × 10"). *Photo courtesy of Robert Chase Heishman*

Dee CLEMENTS

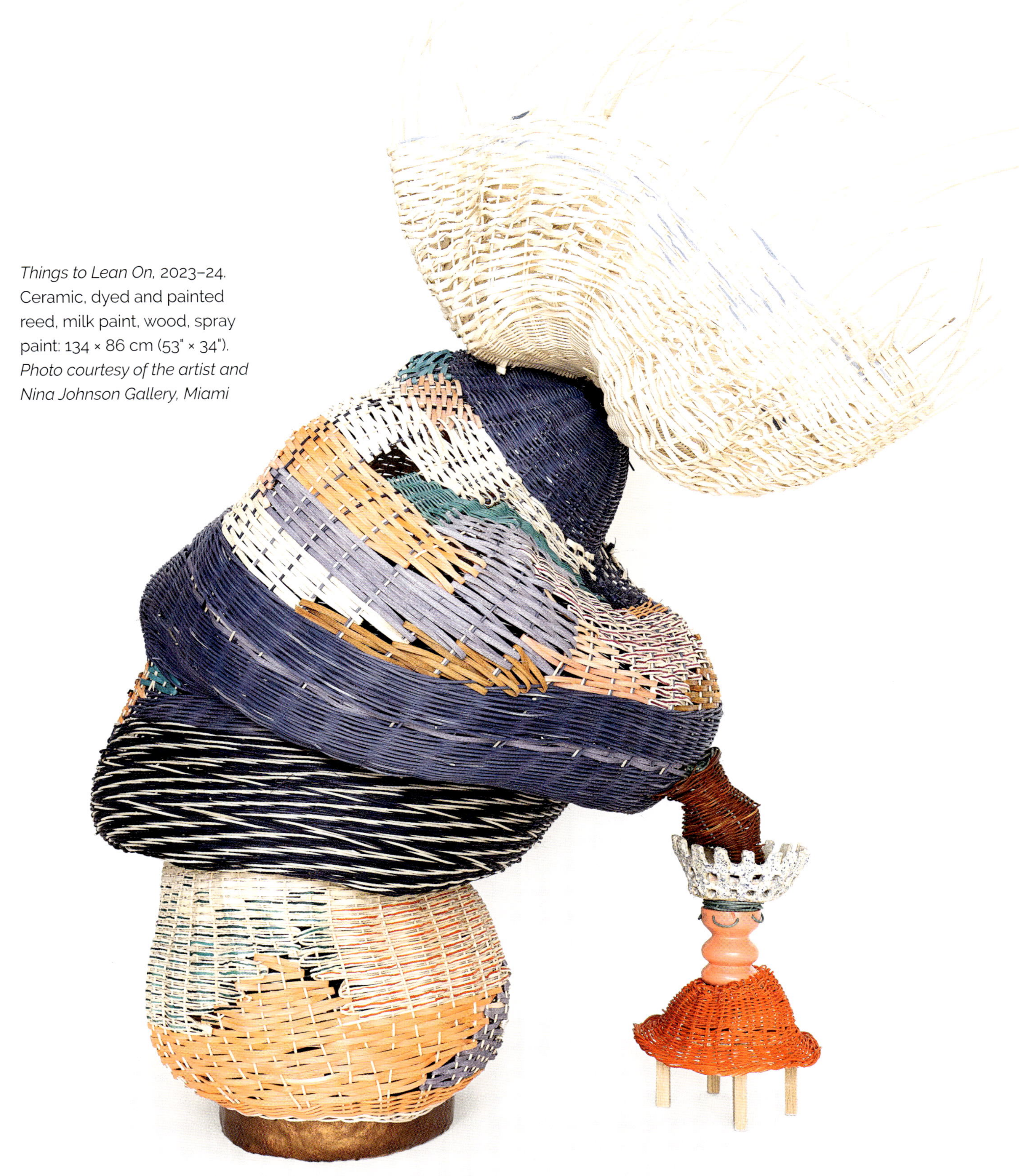

Things to Lean On, 2023–24. Ceramic, dyed and painted reed, milk paint, wood, spray paint: 134 × 86 cm (53" × 34"). *Photo courtesy of the artist and Nina Johnson Gallery, Miami*

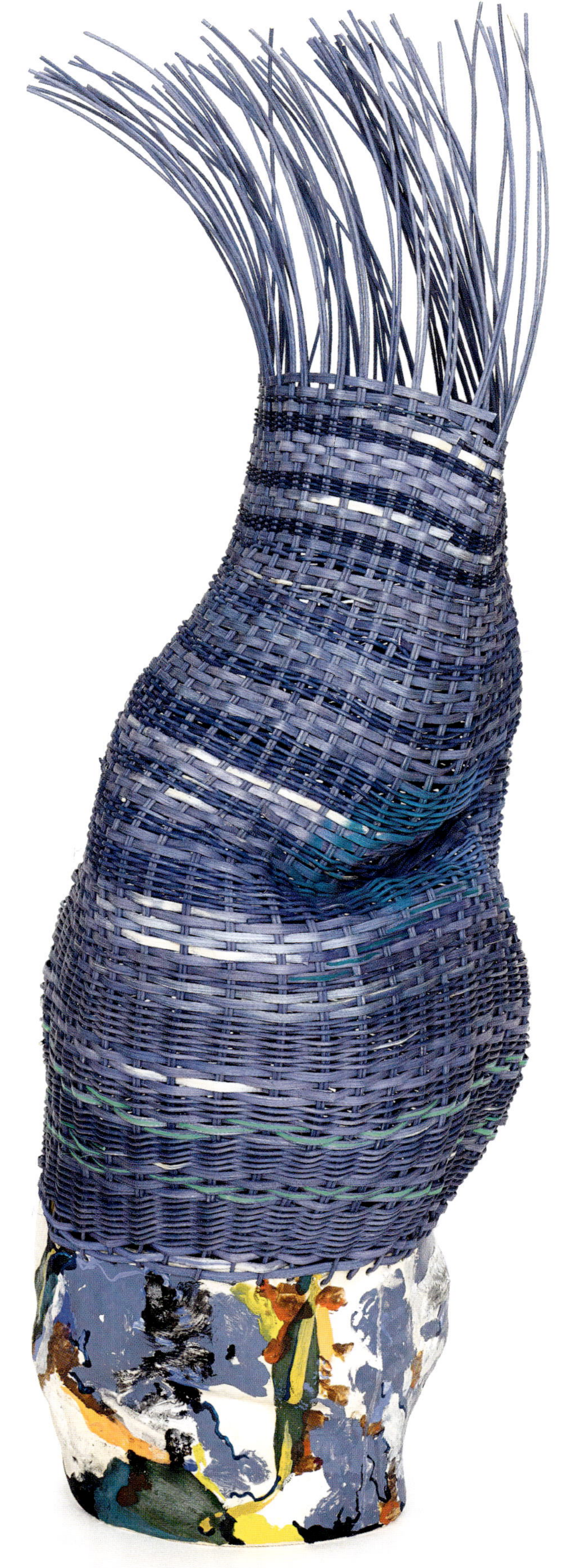

Permission to Disappear, The Tallest Girl in the Room, 2023–24. Ceramic, dyed reed, gouache paint: 111 × 45 cm (44" × 18"). *Photo courtesy of the artist and Nina Johnson Gallery, Miami*

Stéphanie **JACQUES**

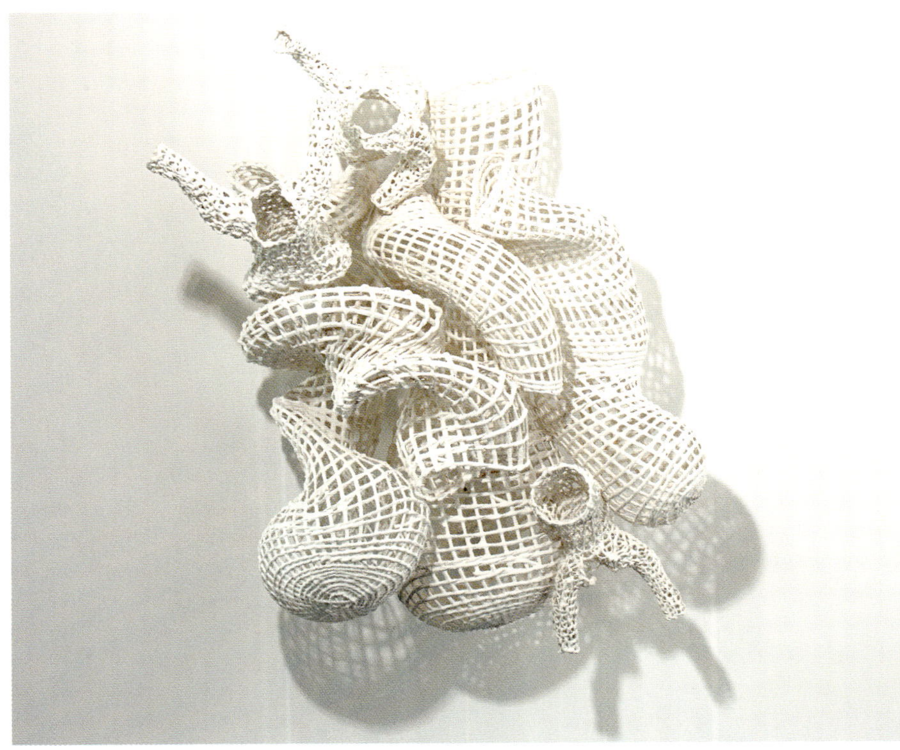

Chute/Fall, 2014. Willow, gesso, thread: 31 × 73 × 47 cm (12" × 28" × 18"). *Photo by Jean-Pierre Ruelle, courtesy of Ester Verhaeghe Art Concepts*

OPPOSITE: *Ce qu'il en reste XII / What remains XII*, 2023. Willow, gesso, thread: 193 × 52 × 25 cm (76" × 20" × 10") (left), 150 × 68 × 45 cm (59" × 26" × 17") (right). *Photo courtesy of the artist*

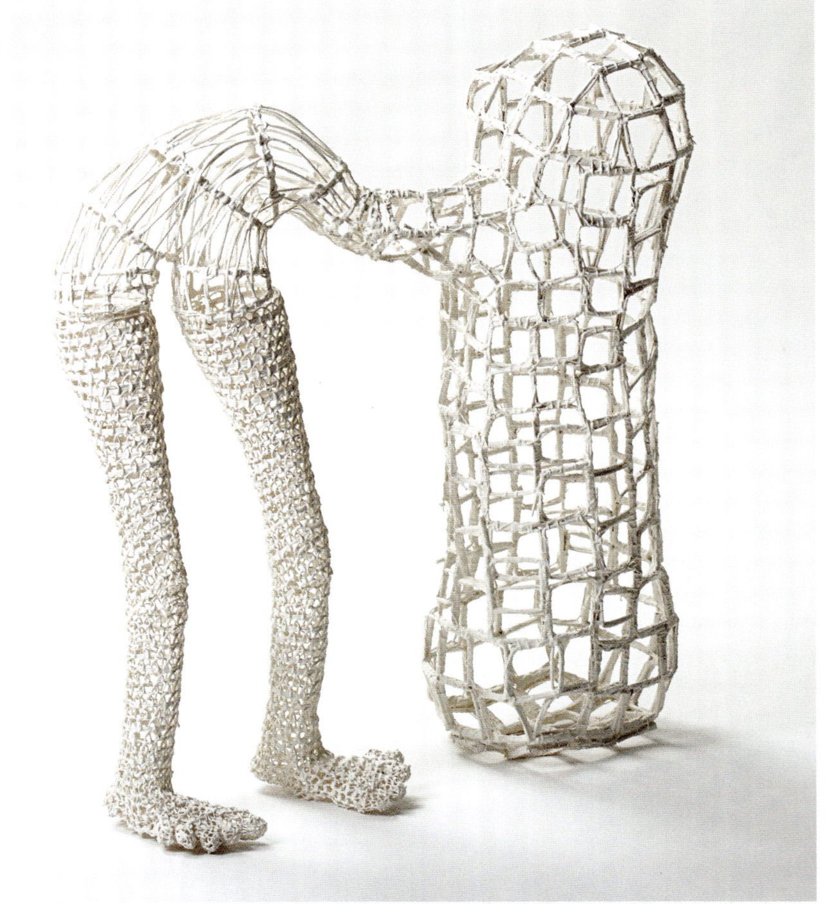

Ce qu'il en reste III / What remains III, 2015. Willow, gesso, thread: 69 × 60 × 30 cm (27" × 23" × 18"). *Photo by Patricia Mathieu, courtesy of browngrotta arts*

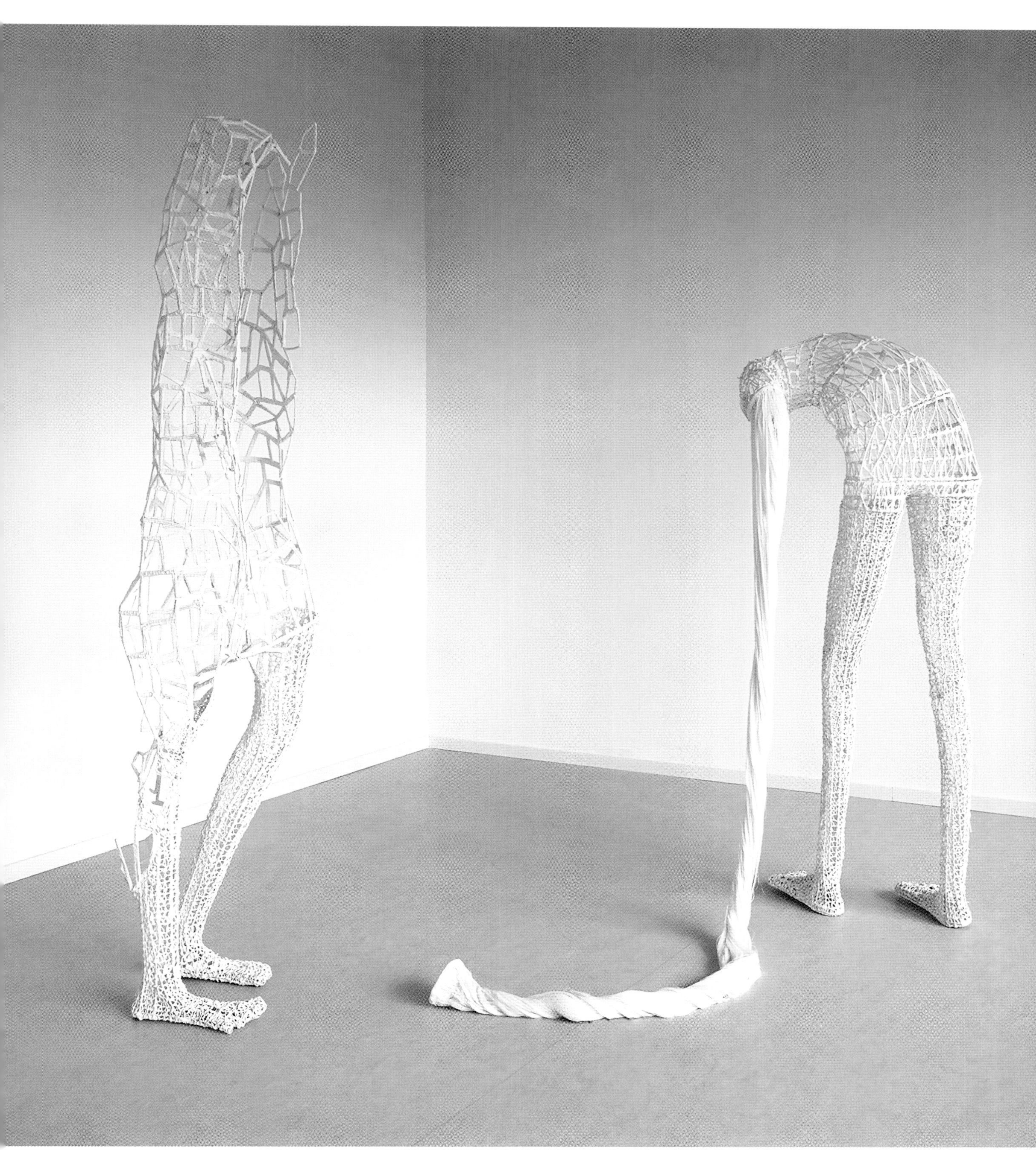

Kim AH SAM

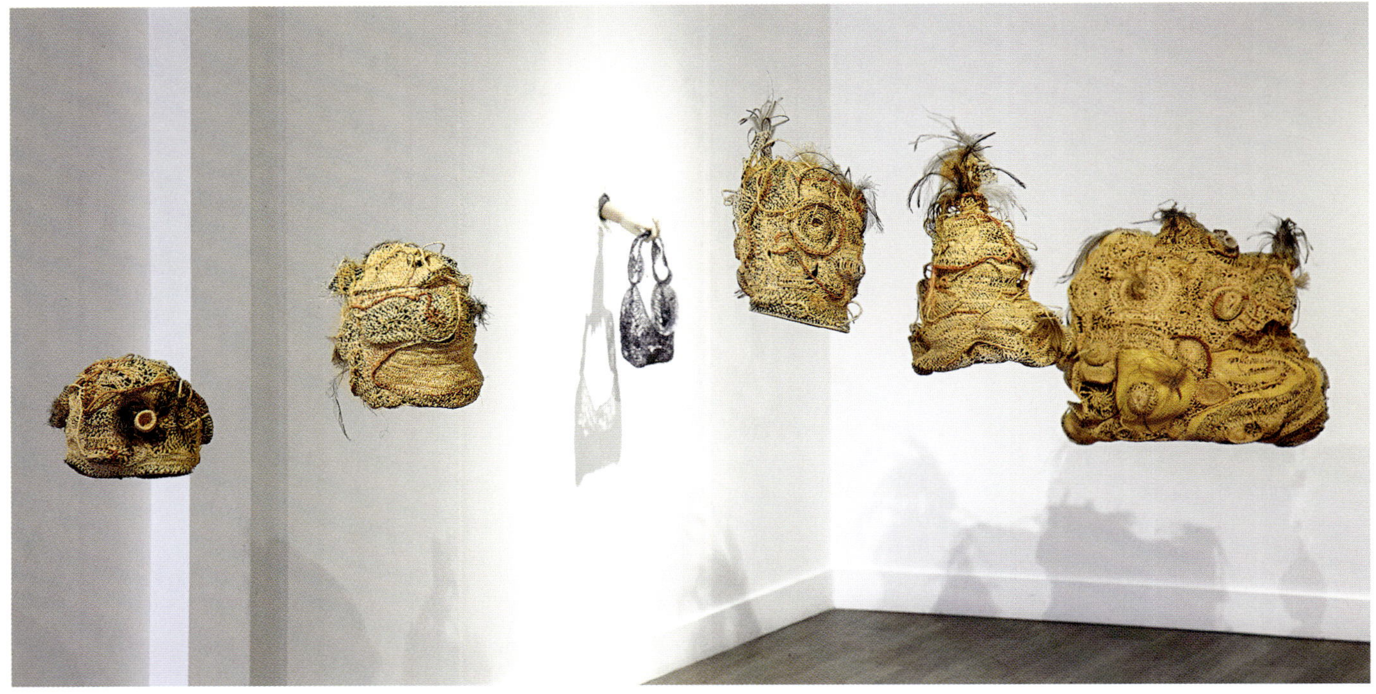

not knowing what you know, 2022. Repurposed rope, raffia, bamboo, feathers: dimensions variable. Group of five woven mask sculptures. *Photos courtesy of Vivien Anderson Gallery, Australia*

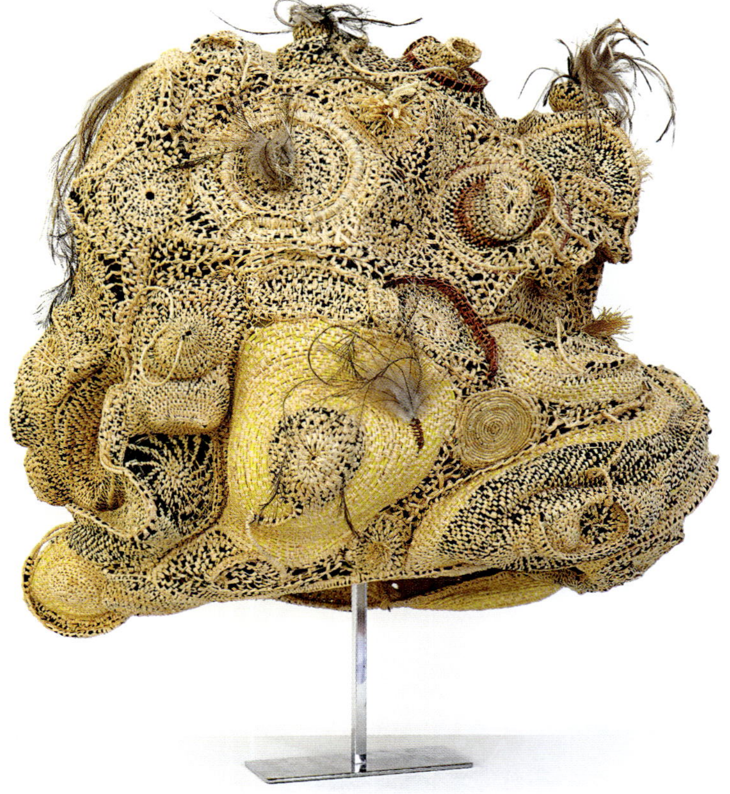

not knowing what you know (detail), 54 × 63 × 59 cm (21" × 24" × 23").

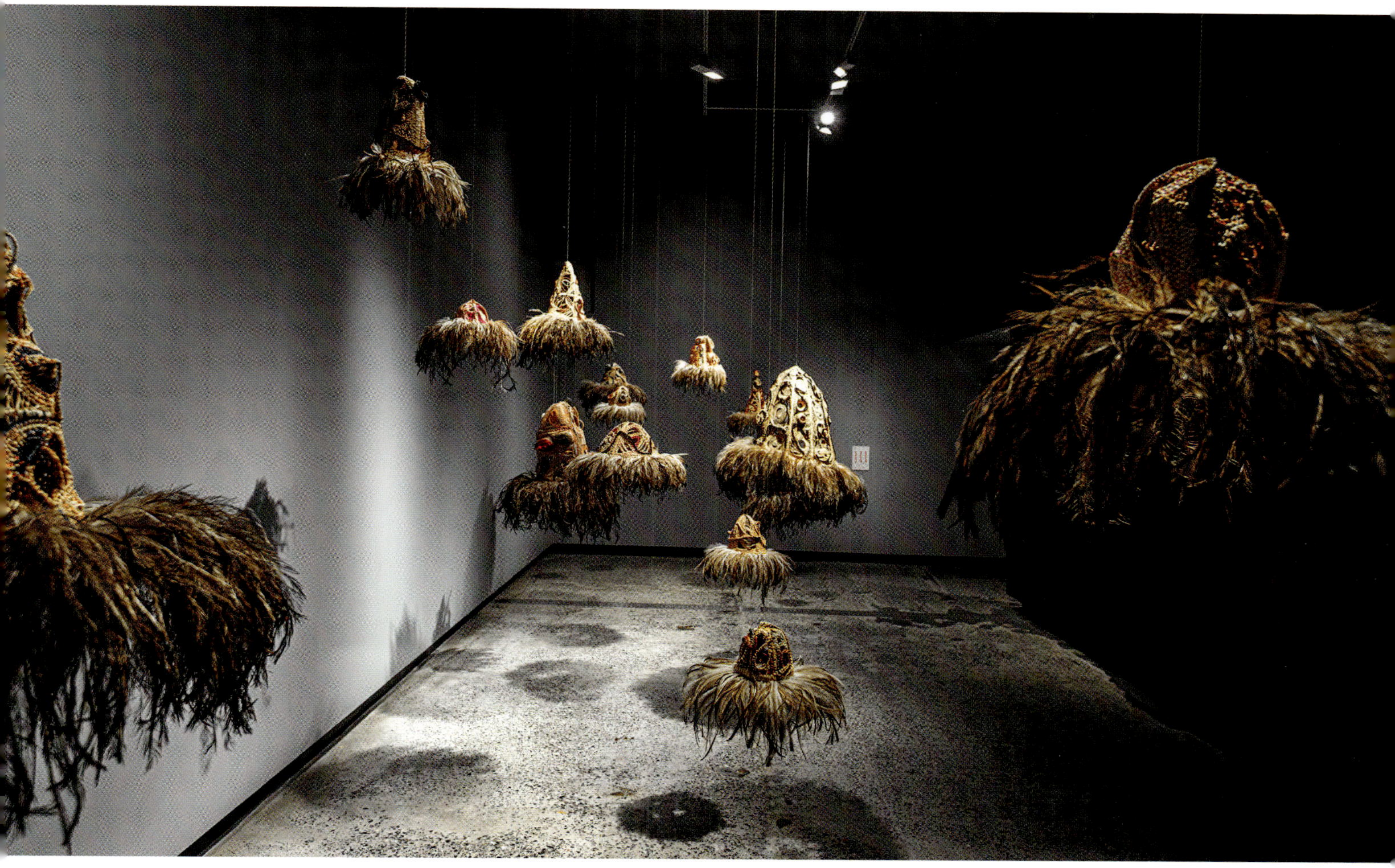

it's not only me, 2023. Repurposed twine, raffia, wire, bamboo, emu feathers: dimensions variable. Group of fourteen woven sculptures. *Photos courtesy of Vivien Anderson Gallery, Australia*

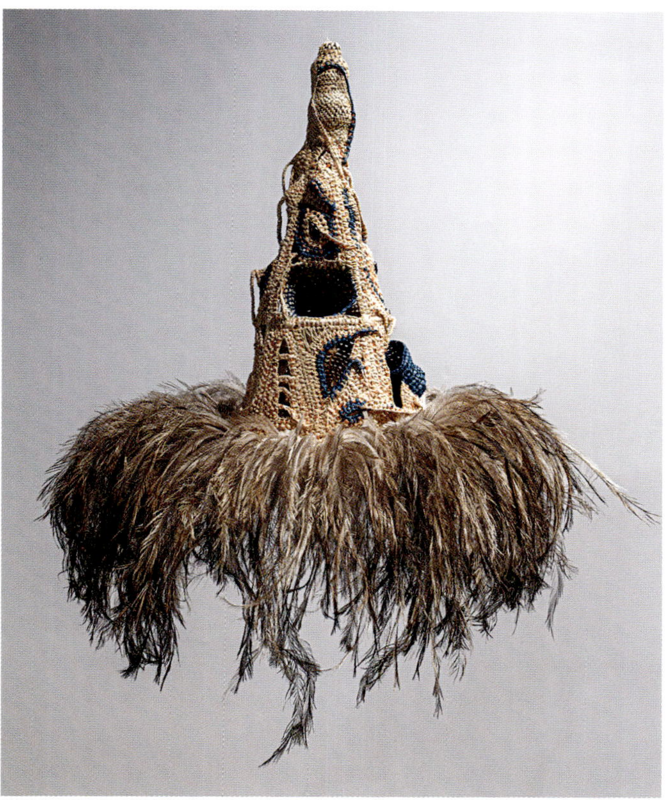

it's not only me (detail), 2023.

Lisa TELFORD

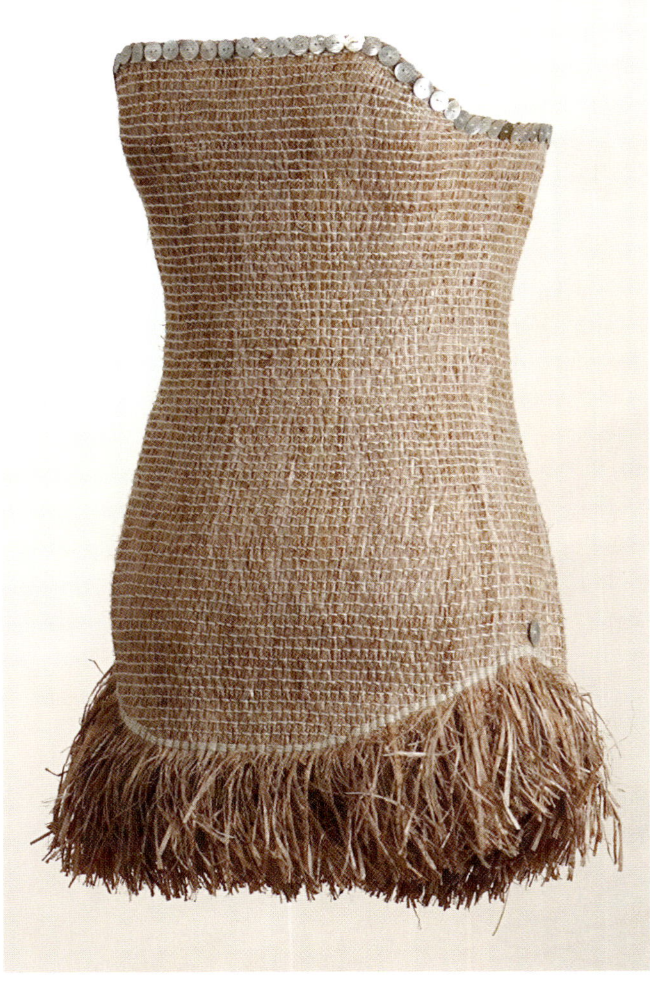

Moon Warrior, 2005. Red cedar bark cordage, abalone buttons: 63 × 35 × 22 cm (25" × 14" × 9"). Collection of Arizona State University Art Museum, Tempe; gift of Sara and David Lieberman. *Photo courtesy of the museum*

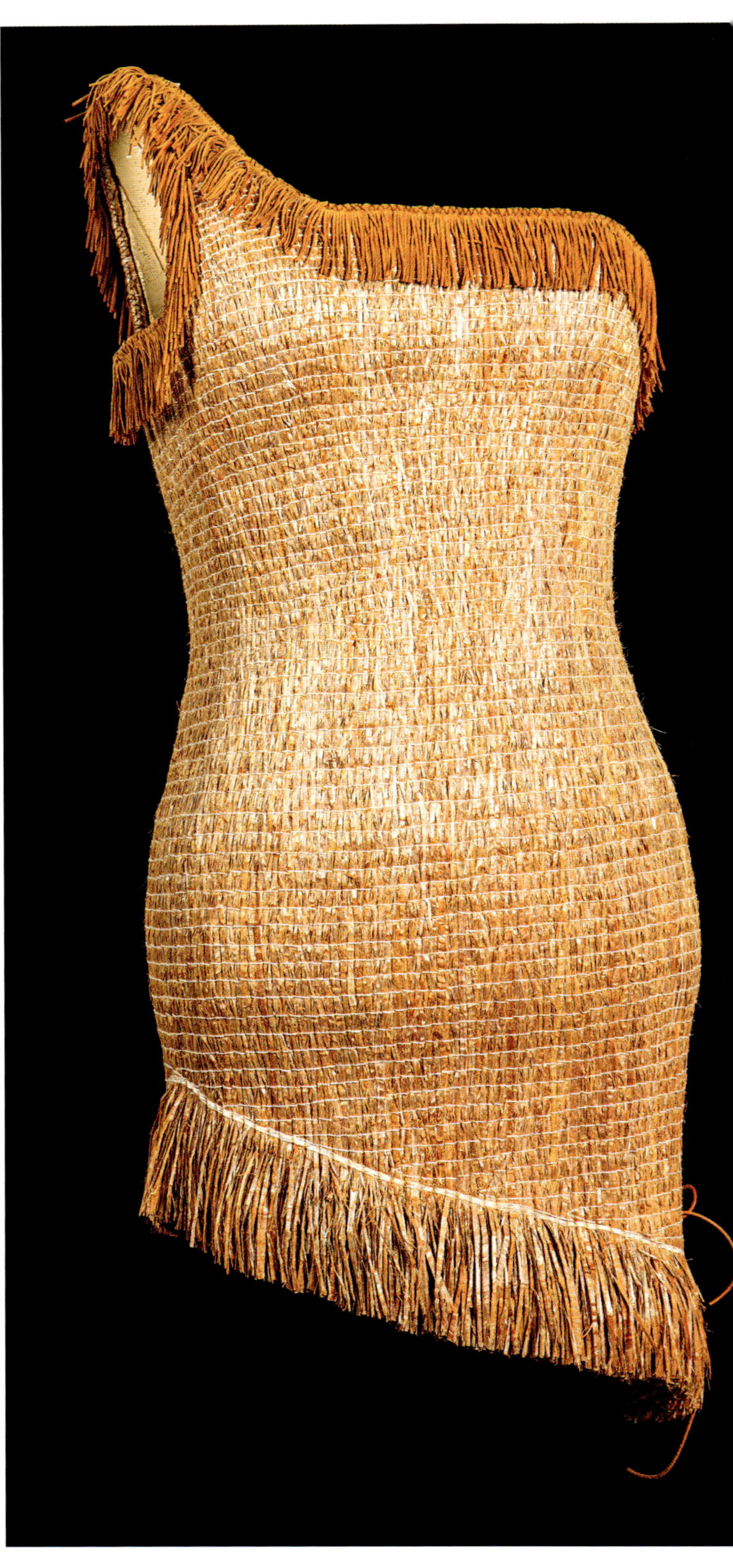

PochaHaida, 2014. Red cedar bark, cordage, cloth: 89 × 34 × 30 cm (35" × 13.5" × 12"). Collection of the Burke Museum of Natural History and Culture, Seattle, catalog number 2014-50/1. *Photo courtesy of the museum*

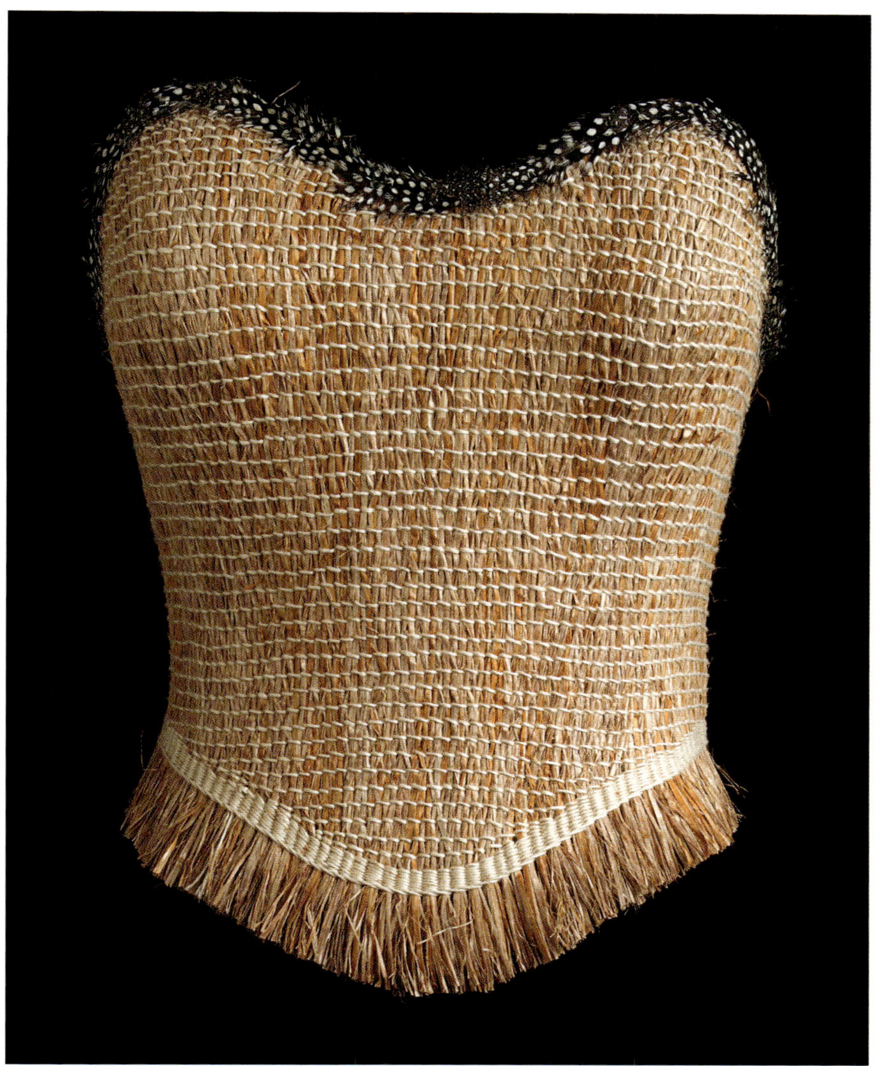

Night on the Village, 2004. Red cedar bark, guinea feathers, carved bone buttons, cotton cordage: 39 × 29 × 28 cm (15.5" × 11.5" × 11"). Collection of The Heard Museum, Phoenix. *Photo by Craig Smith, courtesy of the museum*

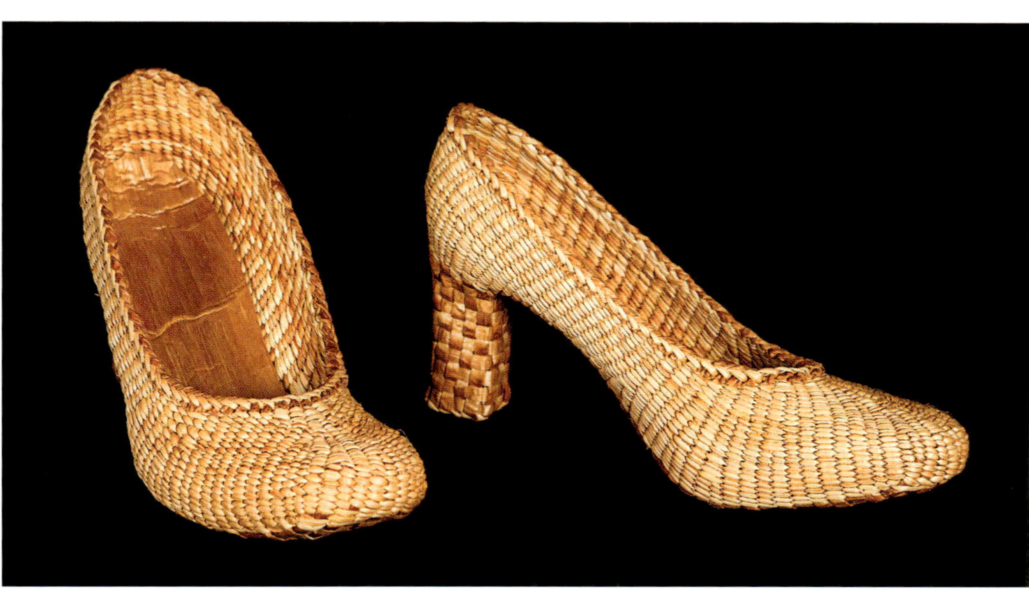

High Heels, 2007. Red cedar bark, yellow cedar bark: 23 × 8 × 13 cm (9.2" × 3.4" × 5.25"). Collection of the Burke Museum of Natural History and Culture, Seattle, catalog number 2007-7/1. *Photo courtesy of the museum*

Naomi Wanjiku **GAKUNGA**

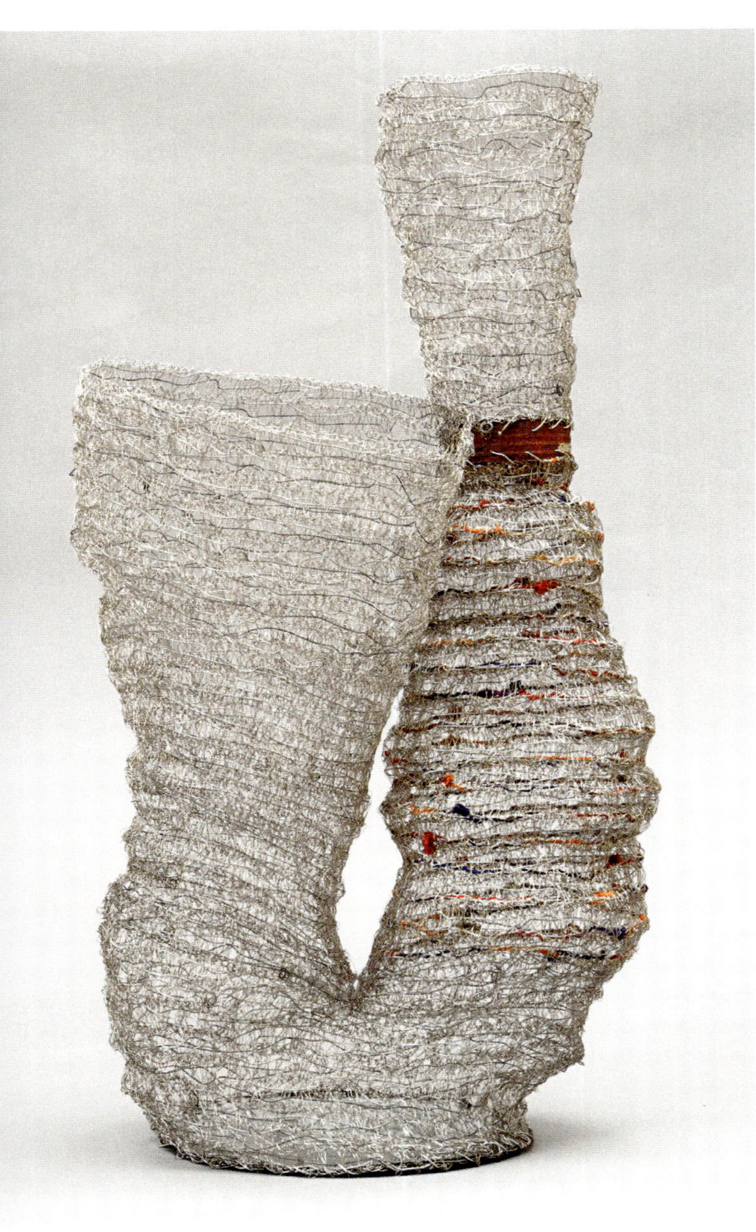

Wīnyitīrīre na Nīī / Lean on Me, 2015. Stainless steel wire, galvanized steel wire, sheet metal, yarn: 53 × 23 × 23 cm (21" × 9" × 9"). *Photo courtesy of Naomi Wanjiku Studio*

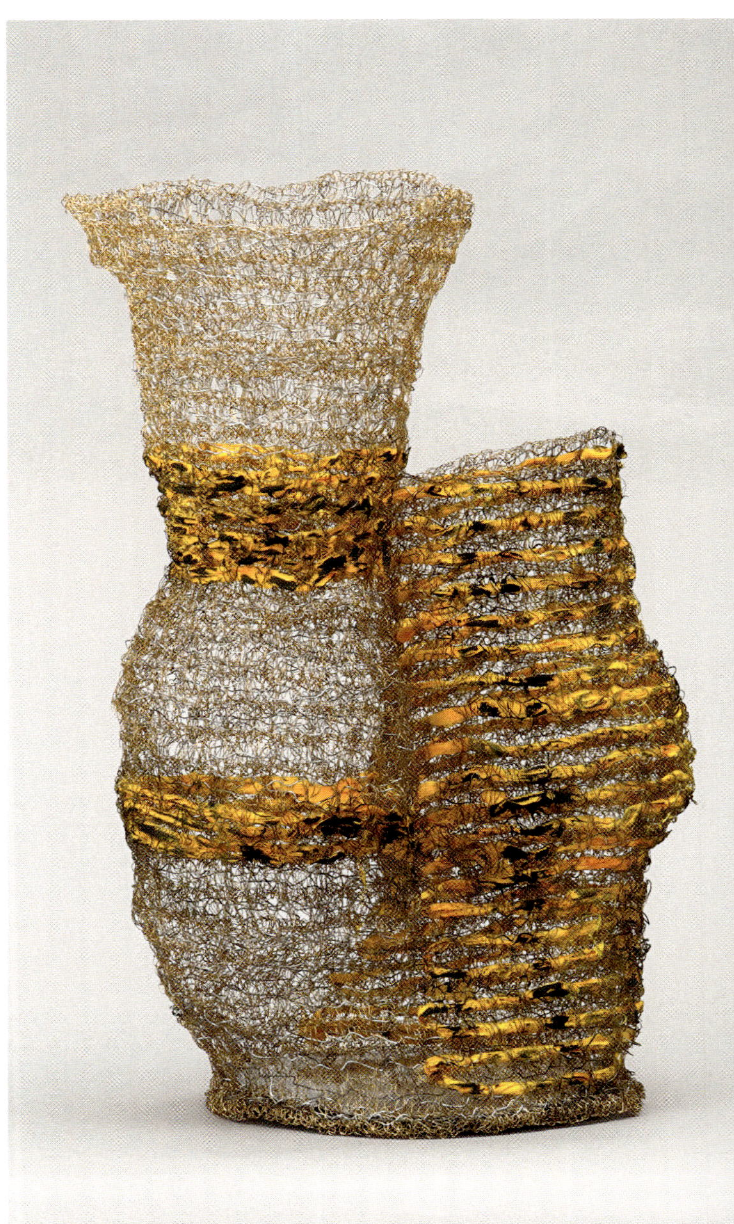

Mūtiiri/The Mentor, 2015. Stainless steel wire, galvanized steel wire, sheet metal, fabric: 43 × 28 × 28 cm (17" × 11" × 11"). *Photo courtesy of Naomi Wanjiku Studio*

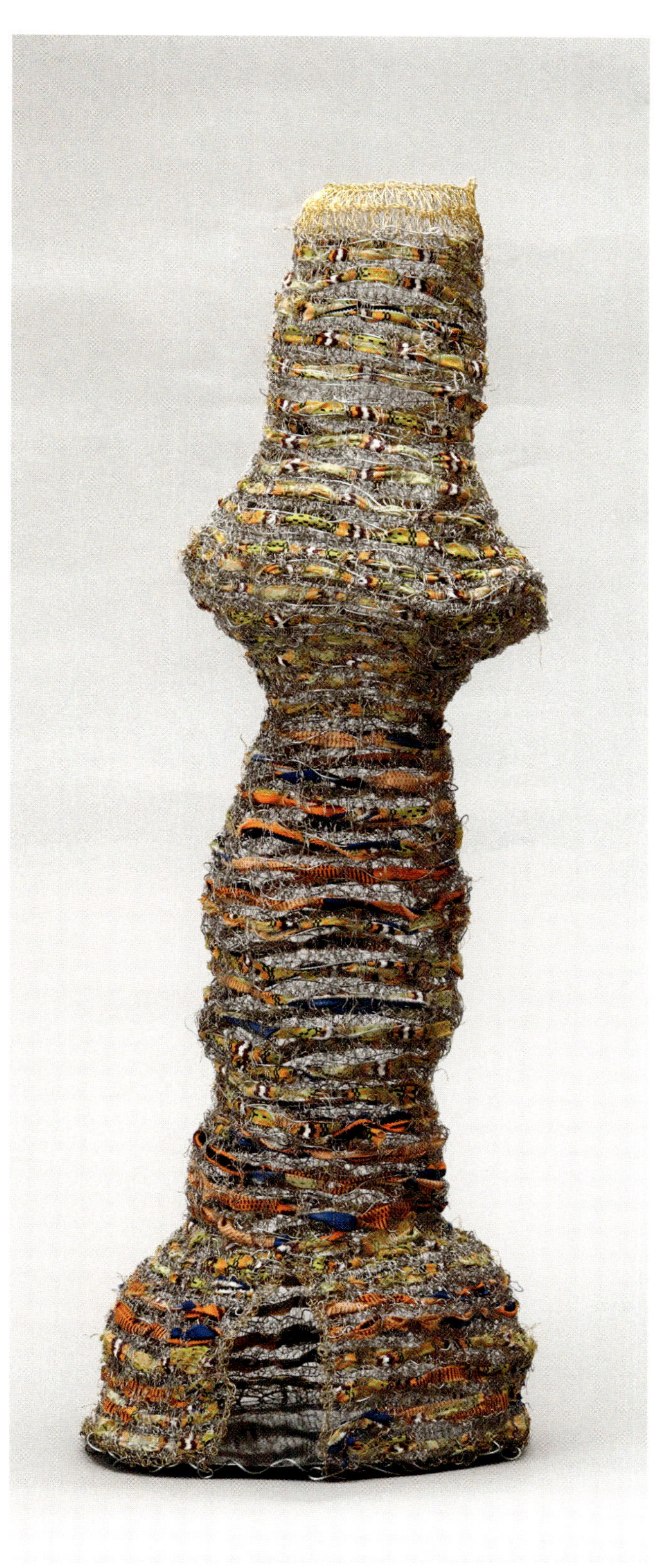

Ūtaana/Generosity, 2014. Stainless steel wire, galvanized steel wire, sheet metal, fabric: 53 × 23 × 23 cm (21" × 9" × 9"). *Photo courtesy of Naomi Wanjiku Studio*

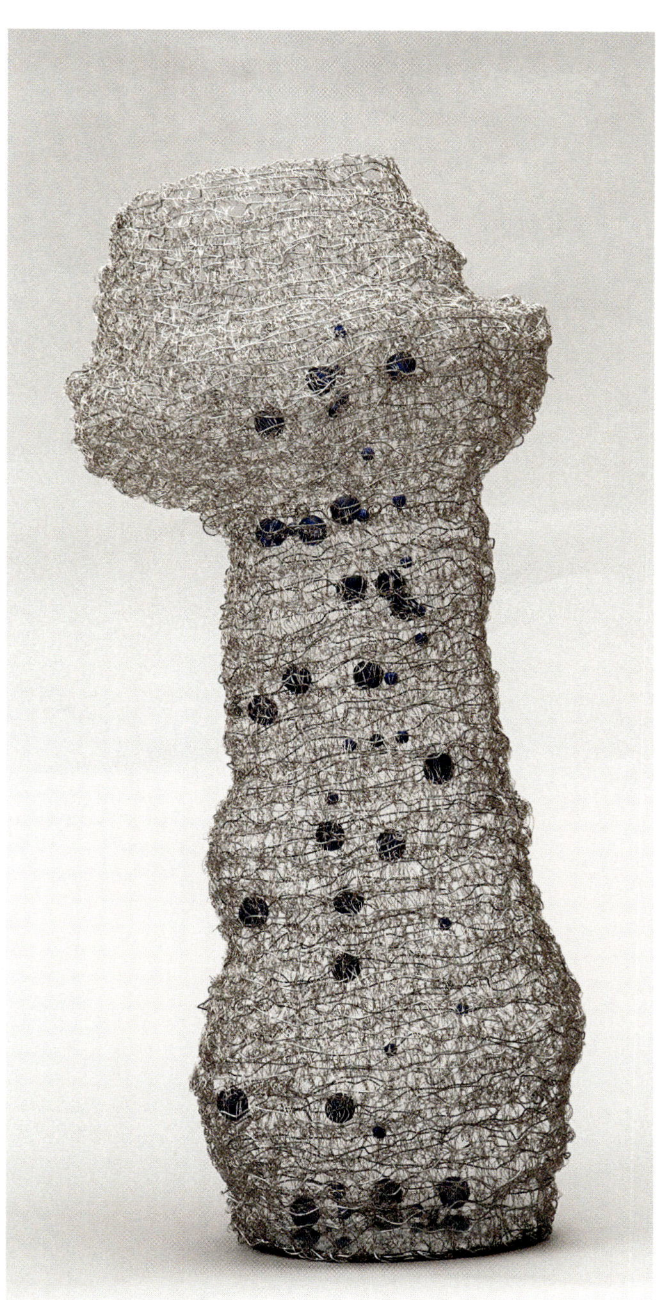

Ngatho/Gratitude, 2014. Stainless steel wire, galvanized steel wire, sheet metal, Krobo beads: 53 × 28 × 28 cm (21" × 11" × 11"). *Photo courtesy of Naomi Wanjiku Studio*

Carolina CARUBIN

Argos, 2024. Natural fibers: 40 × 100 cm (16" × 39"). *Photo by germanphotoartes, courtesy of the artist*

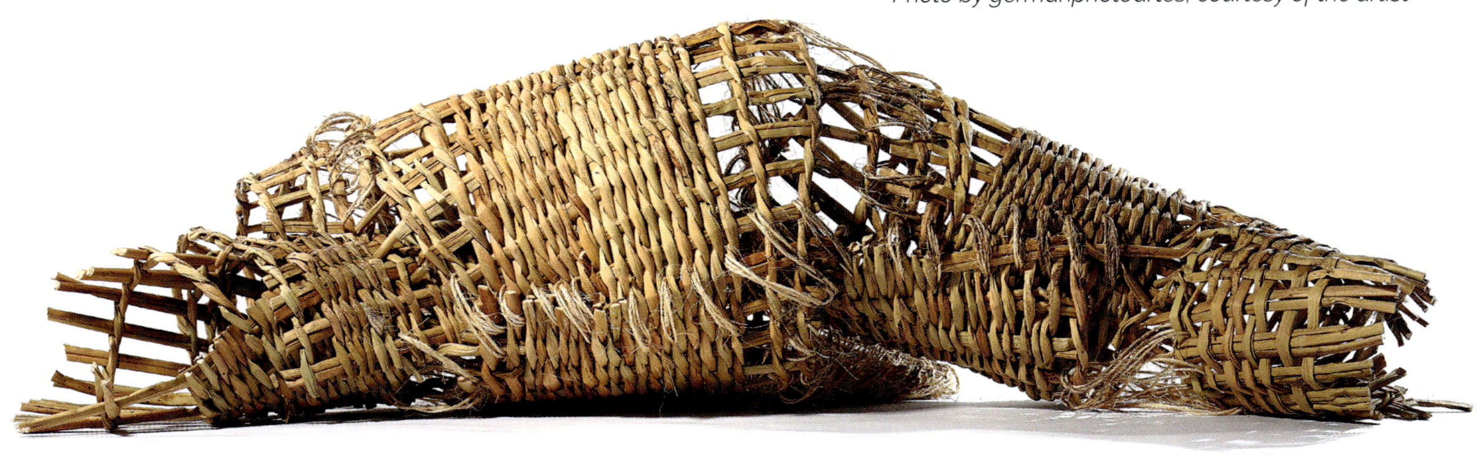

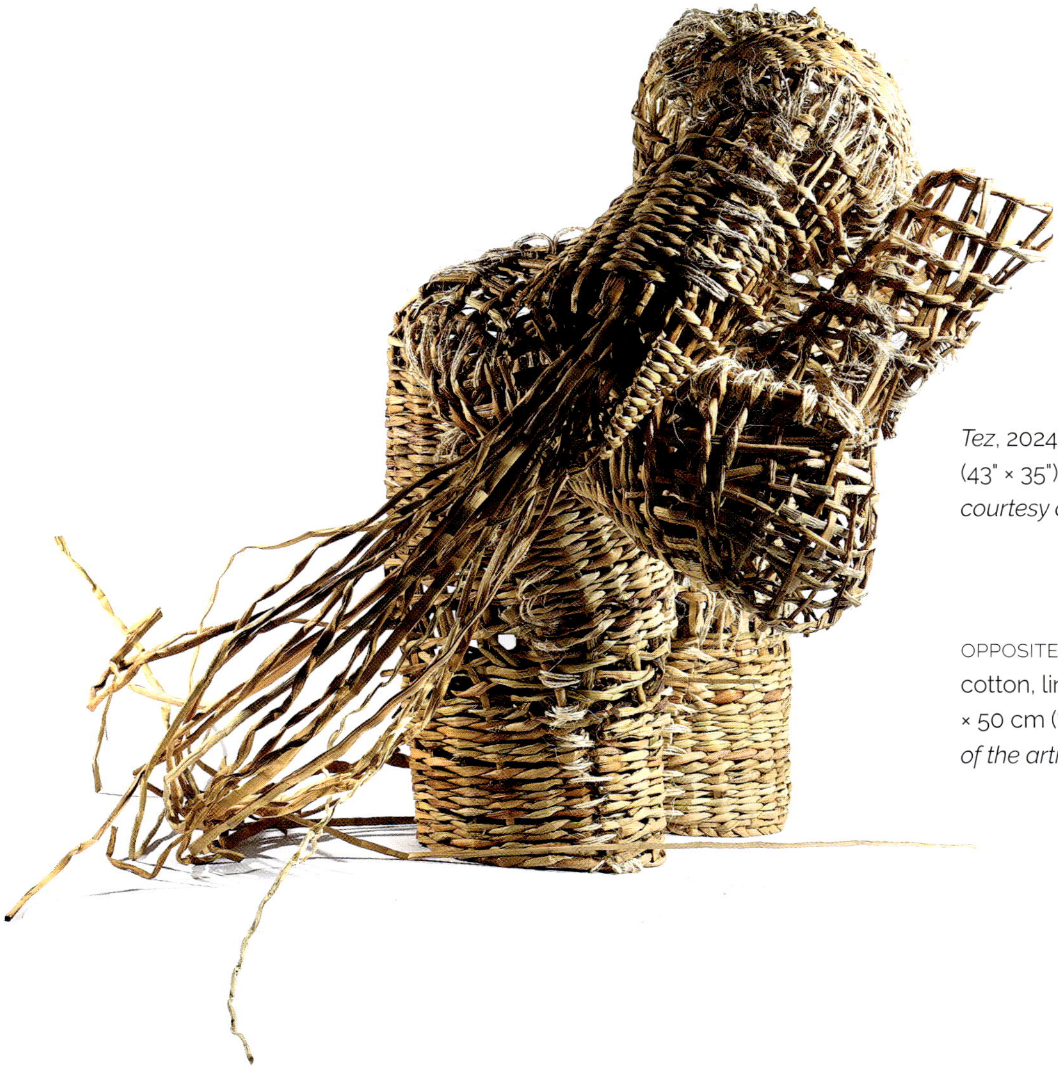

Tez, 2024. Natural fibers: 110 × 90 cm (43" × 35"). *Photo by germanphotoartes, courtesy of the artist*

OPPOSITE: *Tlön,* 2023. Reed, sisal, cotton, linen, stainless steel: 200 × 105 × 50 cm (79" × 41" × 20"). *Photo courtesy of the artist*

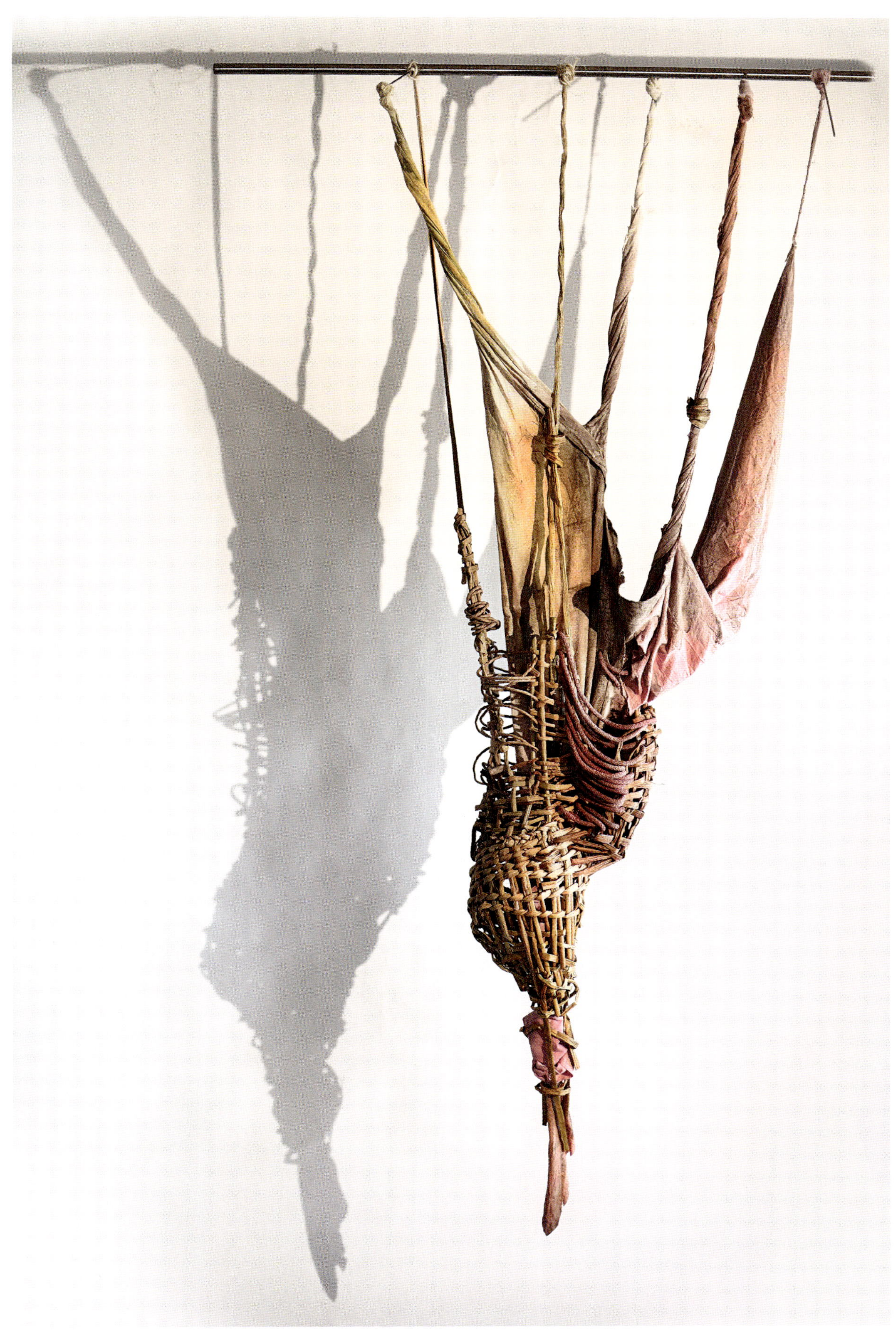

Masako **YOSHIDA**

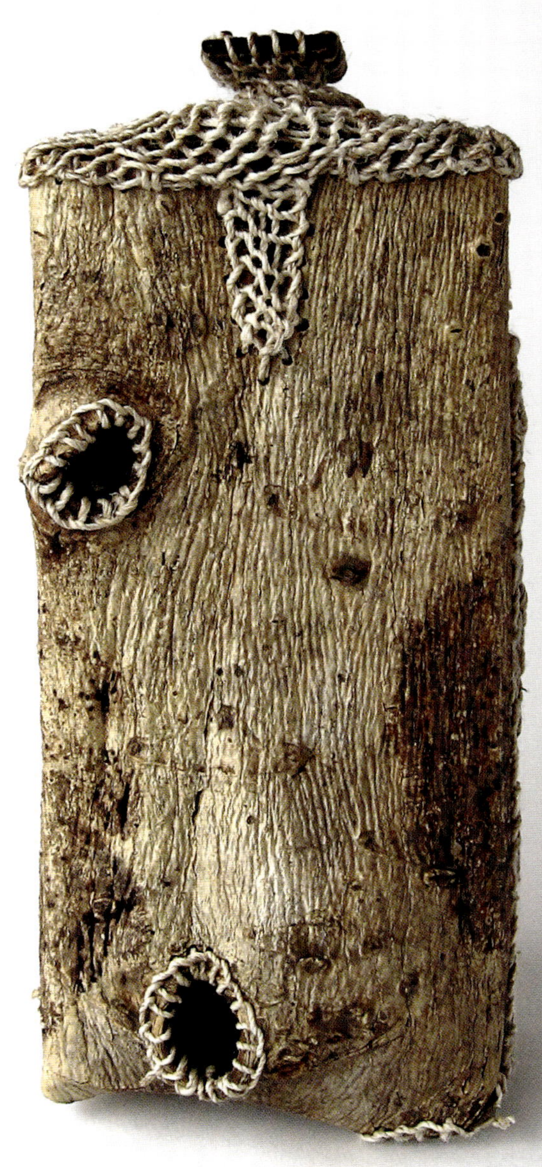

Hyoyyoko (Crikey), 2022. Walnut, rami: 20 × 10 × 10 cm (8" × 4" × 4"). *Photo courtesy of the artist*

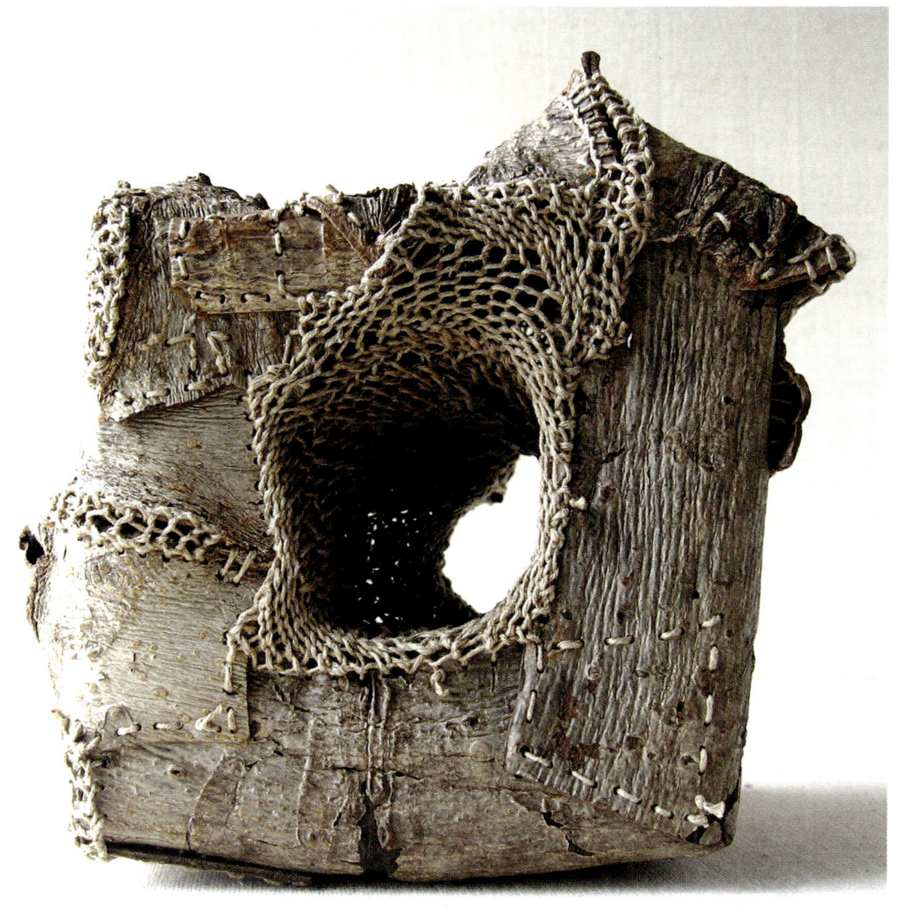

Air Hole, 2017. Walnut, flax: 20 × 18 × 20 cm (8" × 7" × 8"). Photo courtesy of the artist.

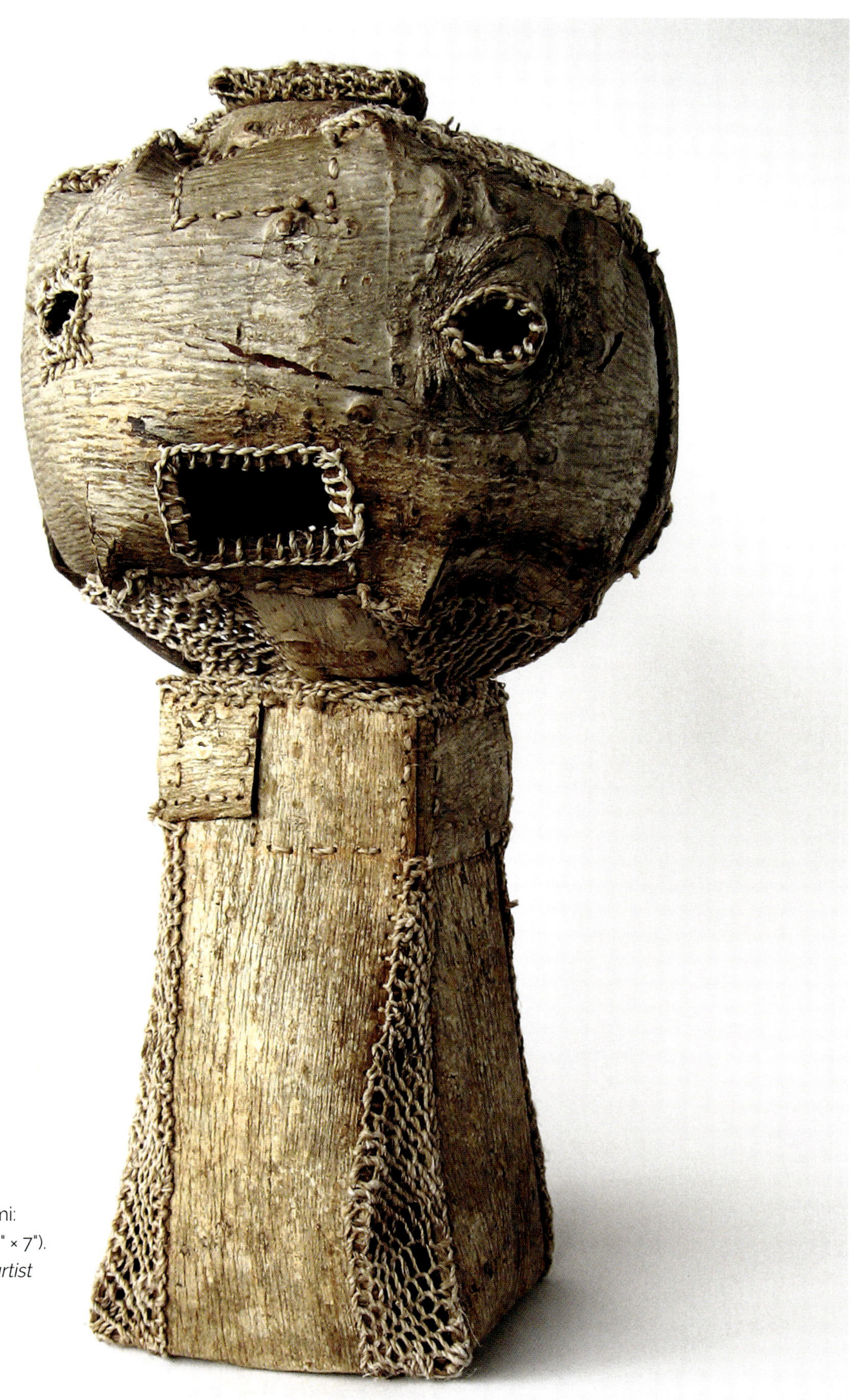

Sing, 2022. Walnut, rami:
35 × 20 × 18 cm (13" × 8" × 7").
Photo courtesy of the artist

Joe FEDDERSEN

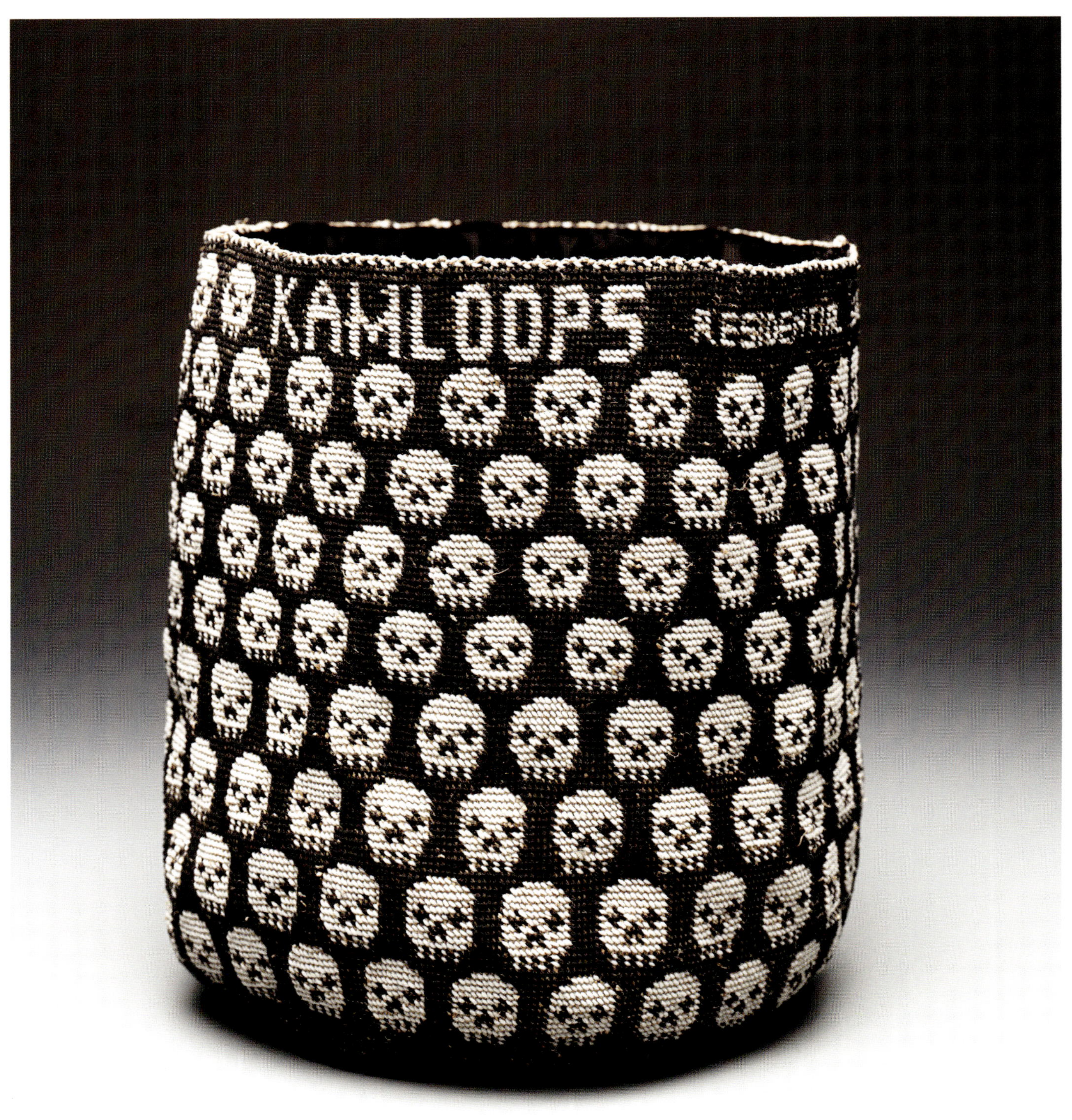

Kamloops Residential School, 2024. Waxed linen: 24 × 22 cm (9.5" × 9"). *Photos courtesy of Dean Davis Photography.*

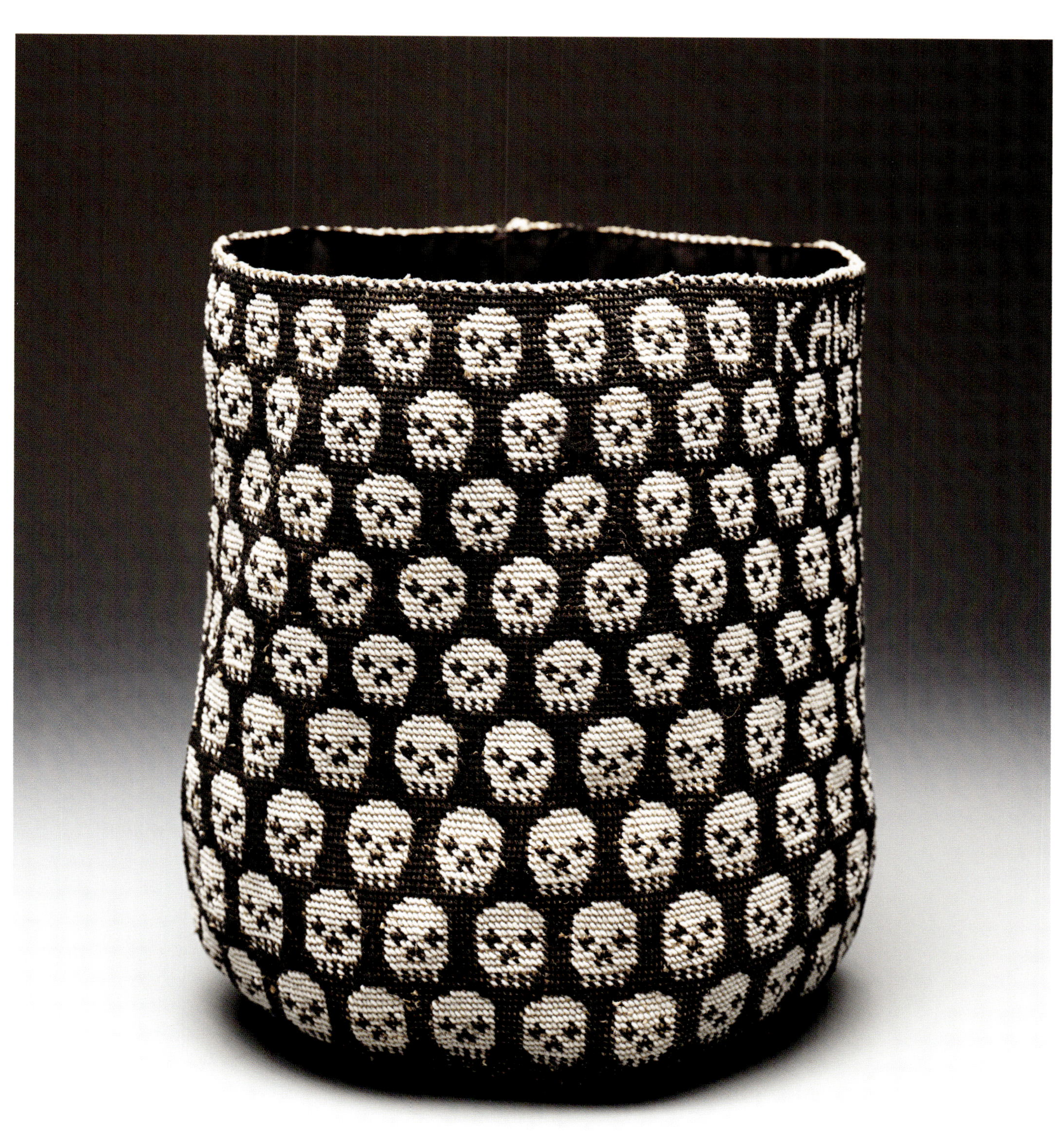

Kamloops Residential School (view 2).

Anina MAJOR

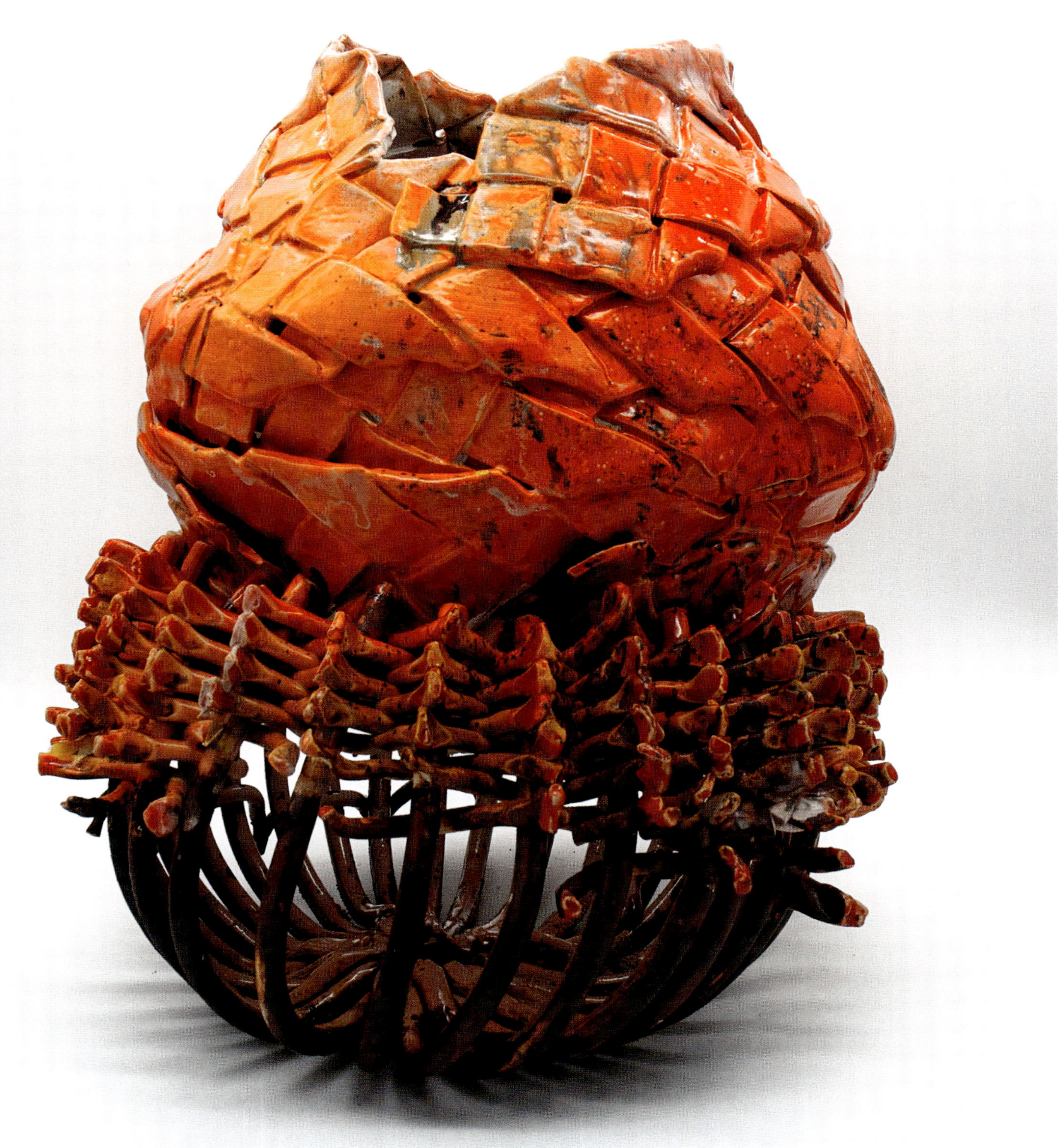

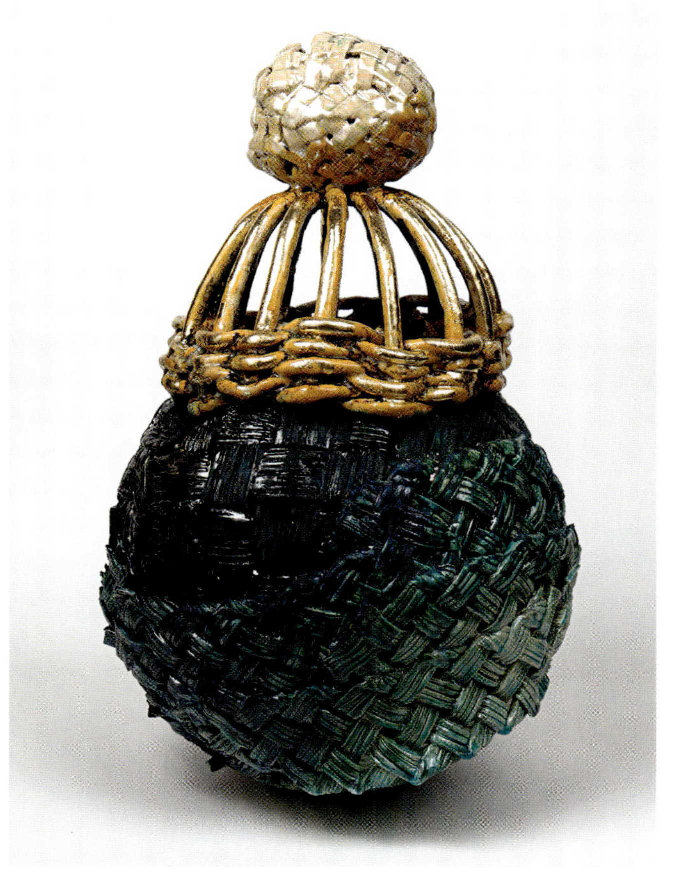

Crowning Sunshine, 2023. Glazed stoneware, glass, gold leaf: 58 × 35 cm (23" × 14") diameter. *Photo courtesy of Andrew White*

OPPOSITE: *Crawfish Armor*, 2023. Glazed stoneware: 48 × 44 × 45 cm (19" × 17.5" × 18"). *Photo courtesy of the artist*

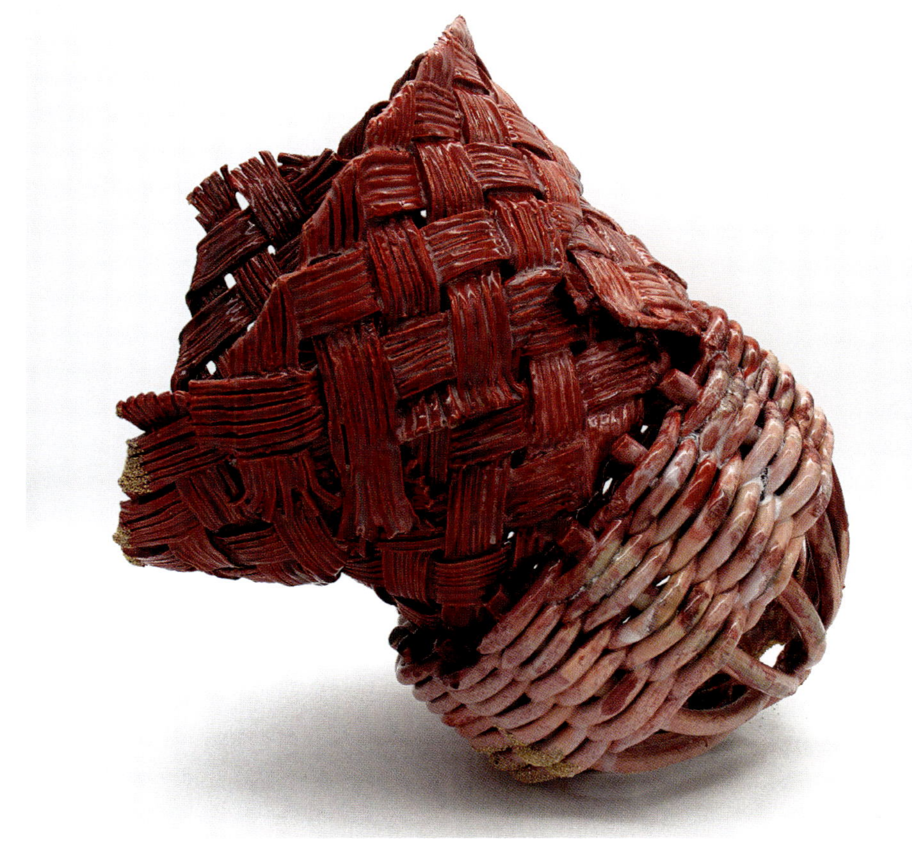

Ruby's Easter Hat, 2023. Glazed stoneware: 40 × 30 × 50 cm (16" × 12" × 20"). *Photo courtesy of the artist*

Merritt JOHNSON

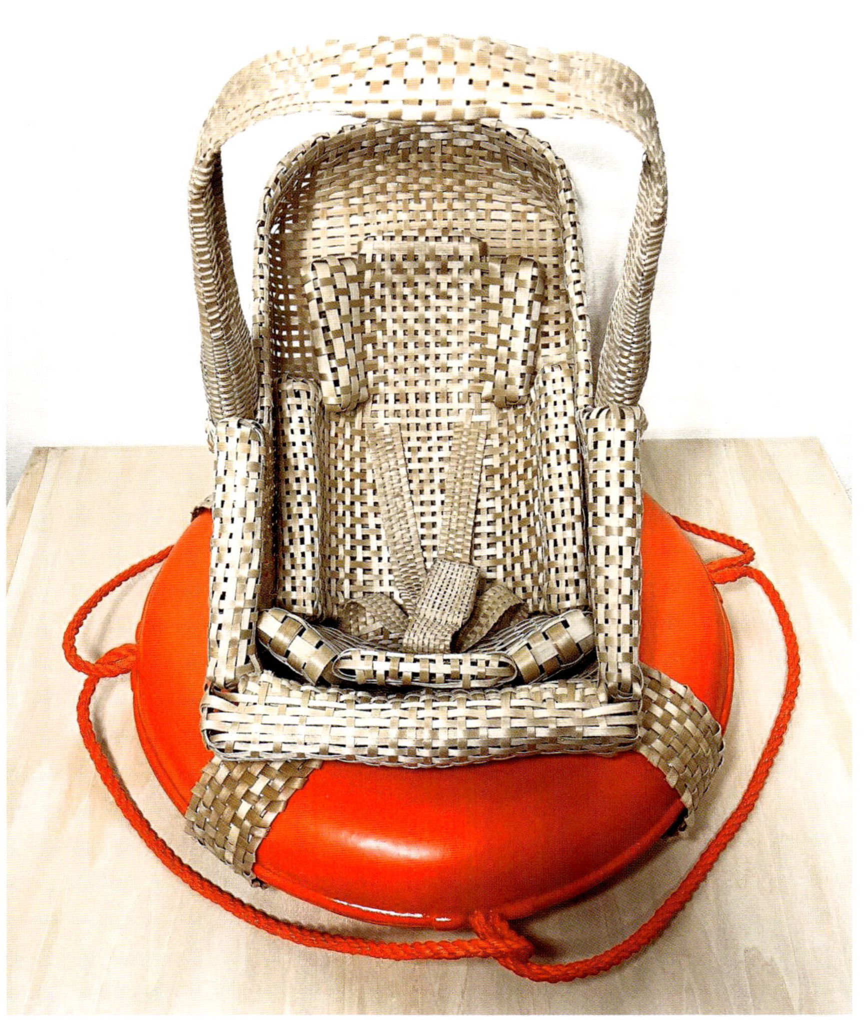

Float, 2023. Black ash, emergency life ring; life size. *Photo courtesy of the artist*

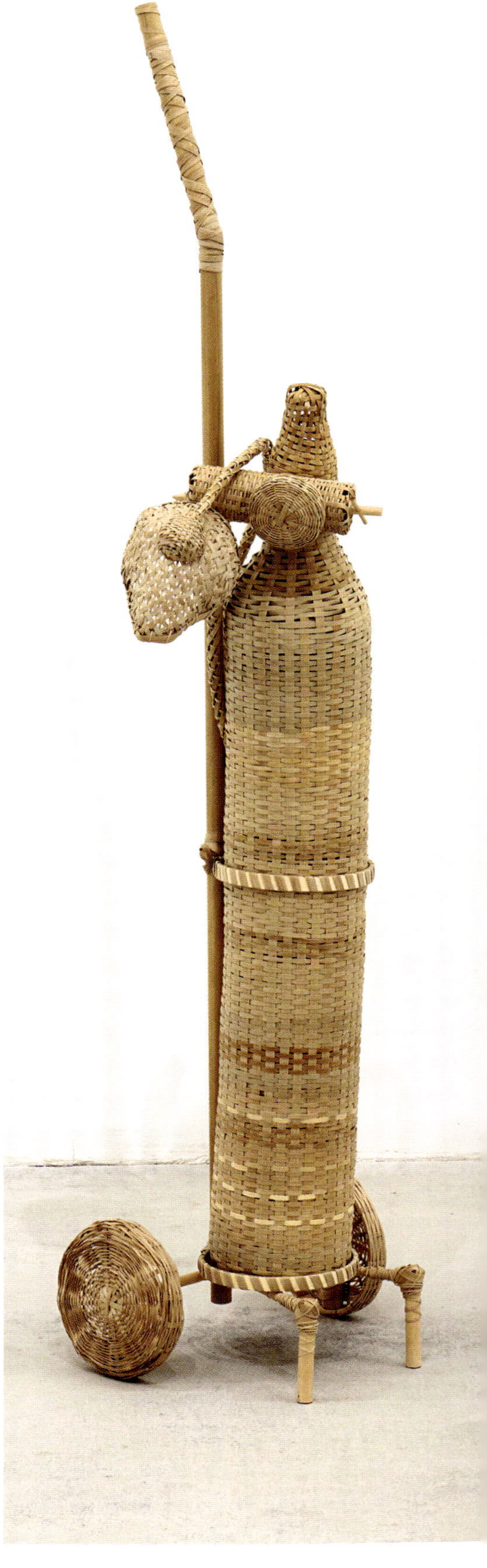

Forest Seed Basket for Present and Future Understanding, 2019. Black ash, wood, Sitka spruce seeds; life-size. *Photo courtesy of the artist*

OPPOSITE: *Weave a basket big enough to hold children, ancestors, old homes, water, food, the weight of memory, fire starter, things to wash with, pots and pans and kids toys, seeds, blankets, a sharp knife, old bones, lost teeth, shells and baby things, a tarp, medicine and a comb, strength, spare parts, extra seeds, something to dig with, rubber bands and string, needles and thread, a hammer and nails, patience, pliers and sticky things, a hatchet and bandages, extra clothes, a slingshot and stones, endurance and more bandages, ballast and floats, and leave enough cracks for things to fall through when they turn to dust*, 2023–24. Black ash, reed, palm fiber, horsehair, foam floats, pieces of life jacket, stones, tarp: 172 cm (68"). *Photo courtesy of the artist*

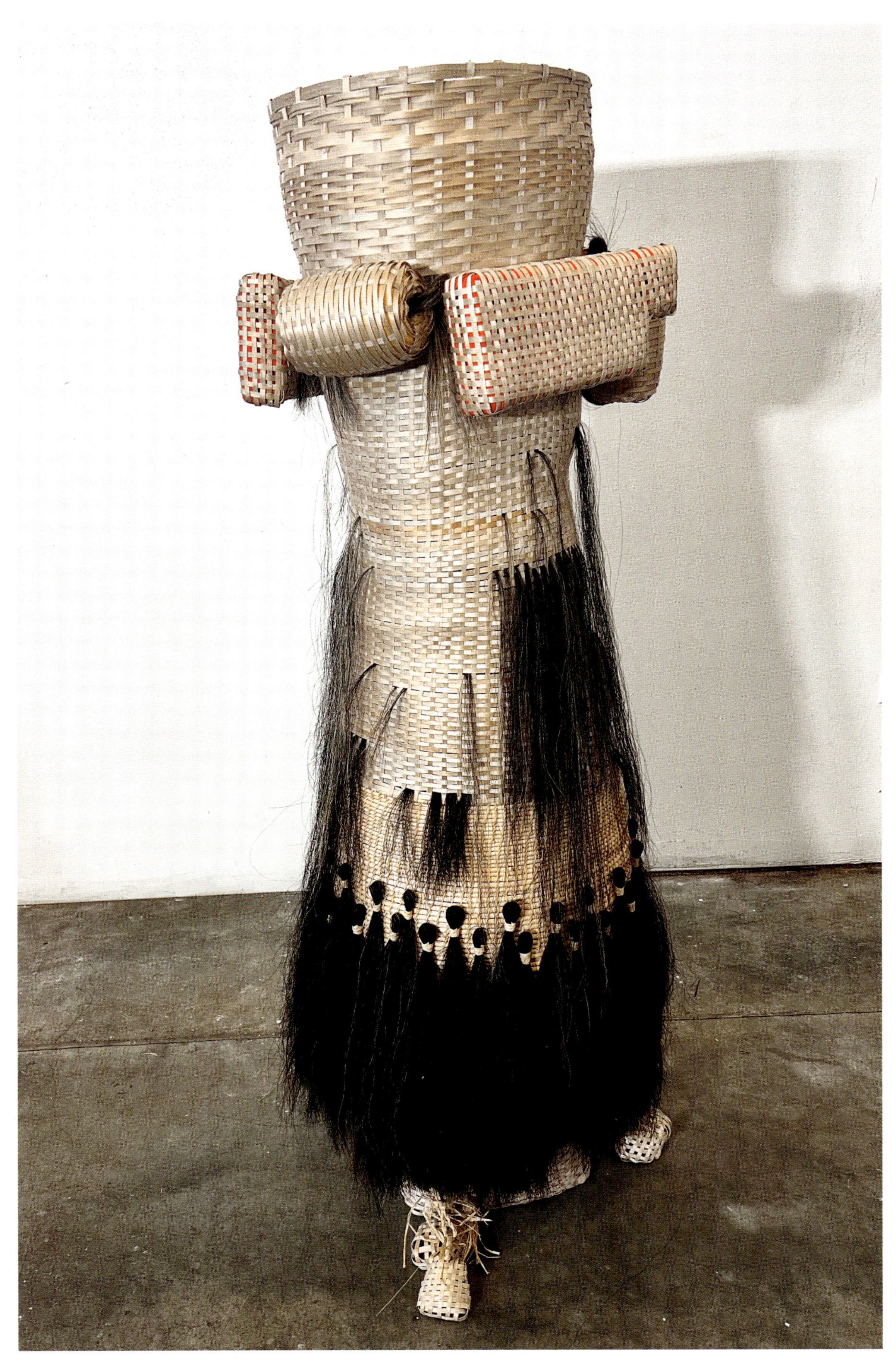

Deloss WEBBER

Old Soldiers, 2019. *Granite, rattan: 48 × 35 × 12 cm (19" × 14" × 5"), 38 × 35 × 12 cm (15" × 14" × 5"). Photo courtesy of the artist.*

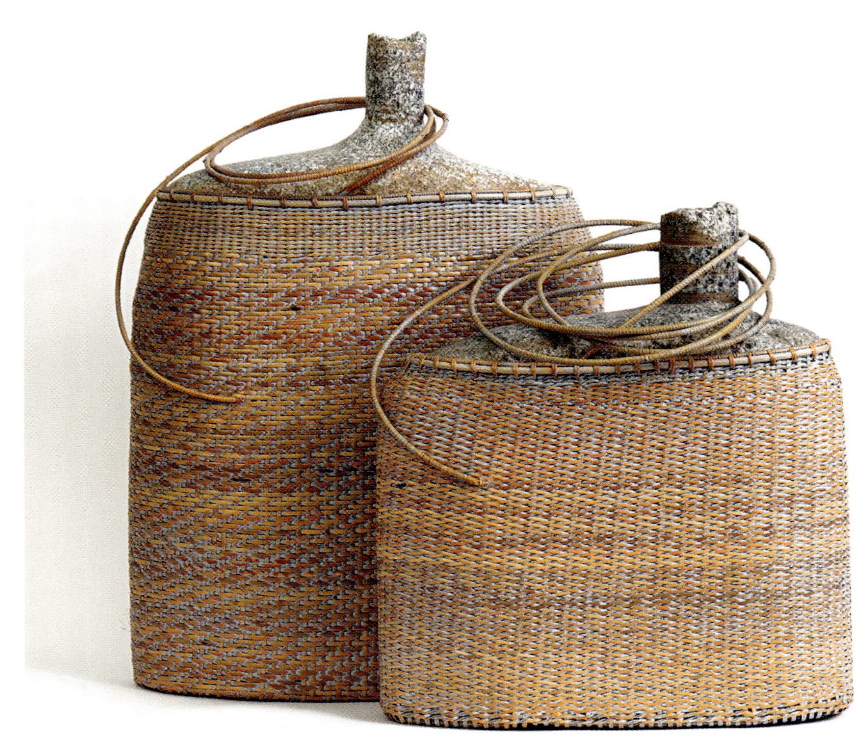

Coastal Erratics, 2024. Stone, bamboo, rattan: 43 × 40 × 38 cm (17" × 16" × 15"), 33 × 38 × 35 cm (13" × 15" × 14"). *Photo courtesy of the artist*

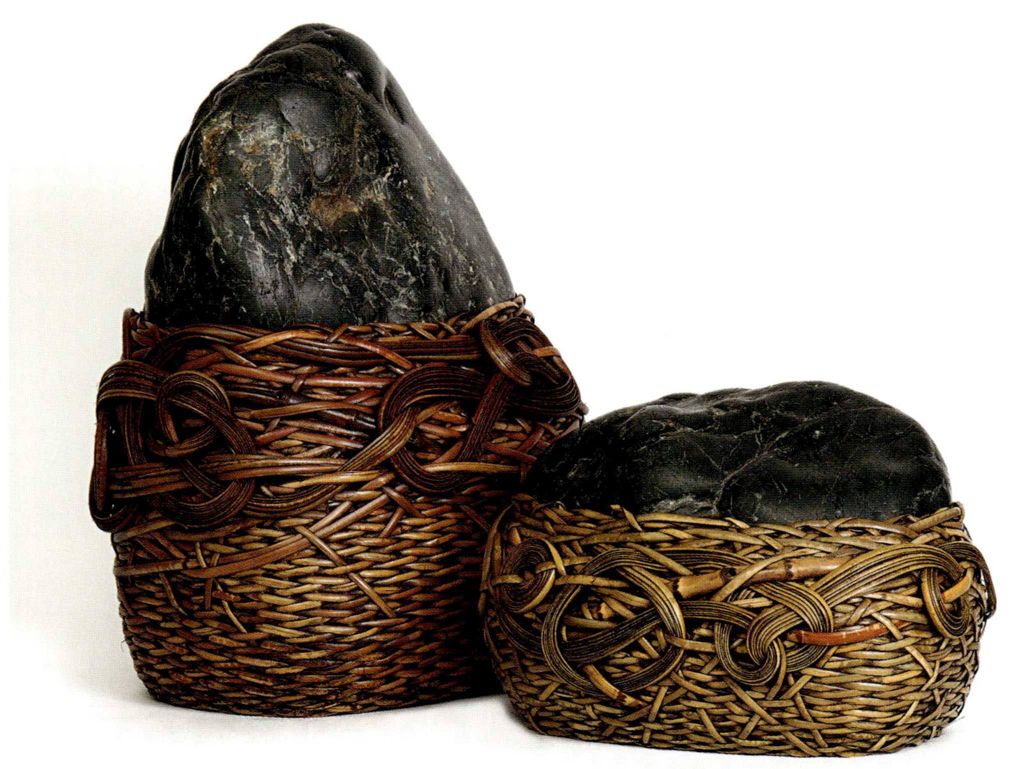

OPPOSITE: *Water Brigade*, 2024. Basalt, yellow cedar, bamboo, lacquer, rattan, kintsugi: 81 × 30 × 25 cm (32" × 12" × 10"), 78 × 30 × 25 cm (31" × 12" × 10"), 63 × 30 × 22 cm (25" × 12" × 9"). *Photo courtesy of the artist*

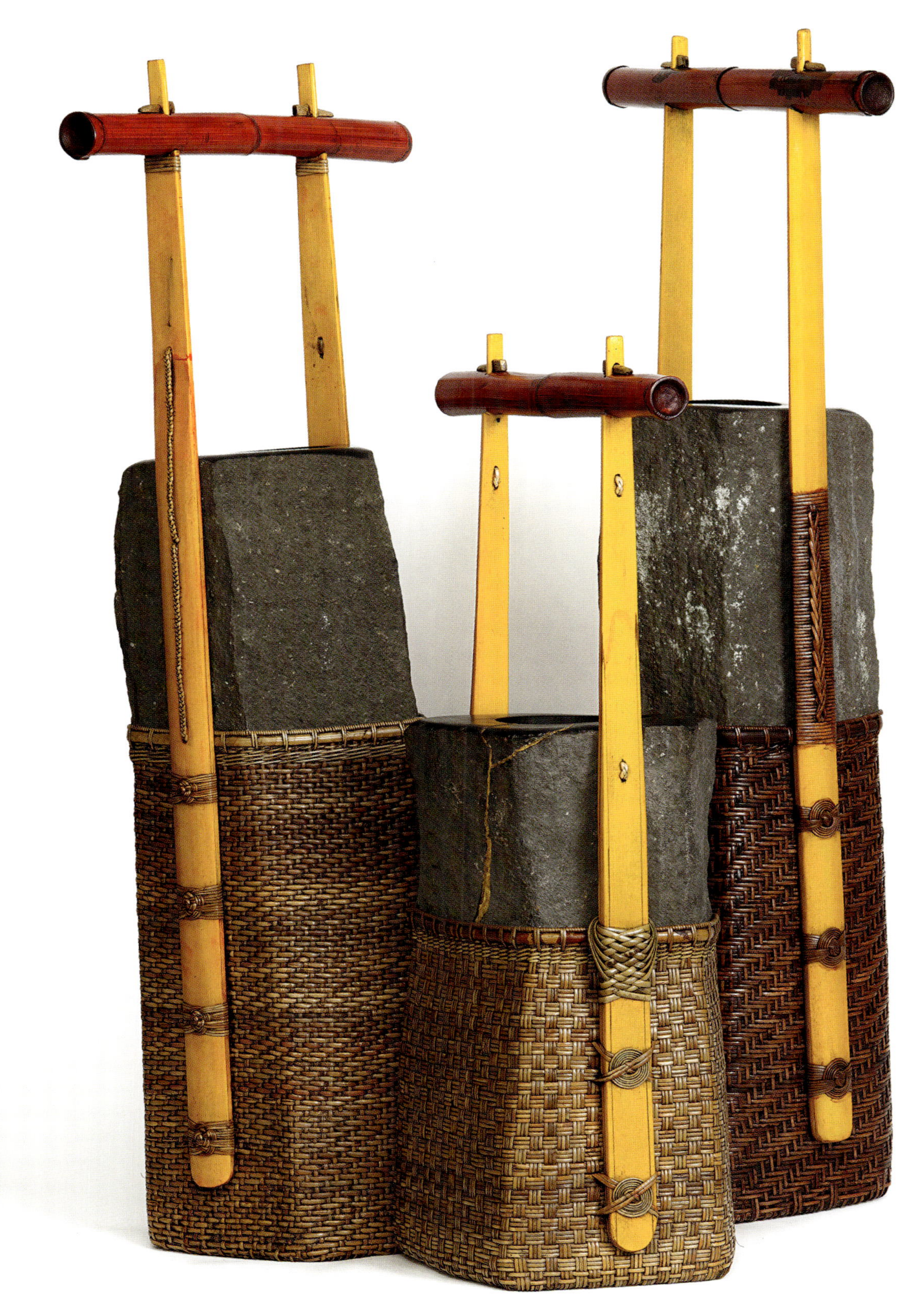

Eneida Lombe TAVARES

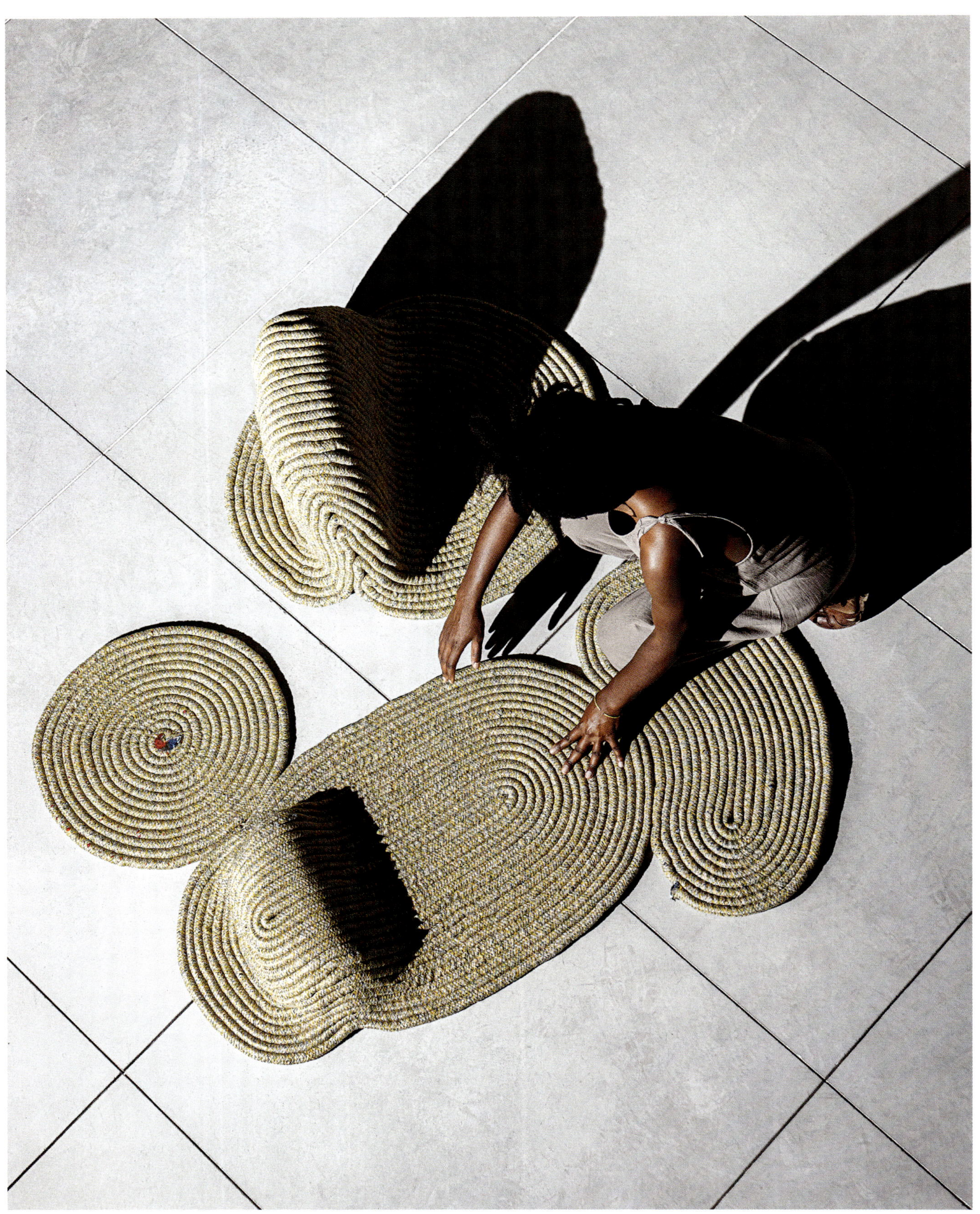

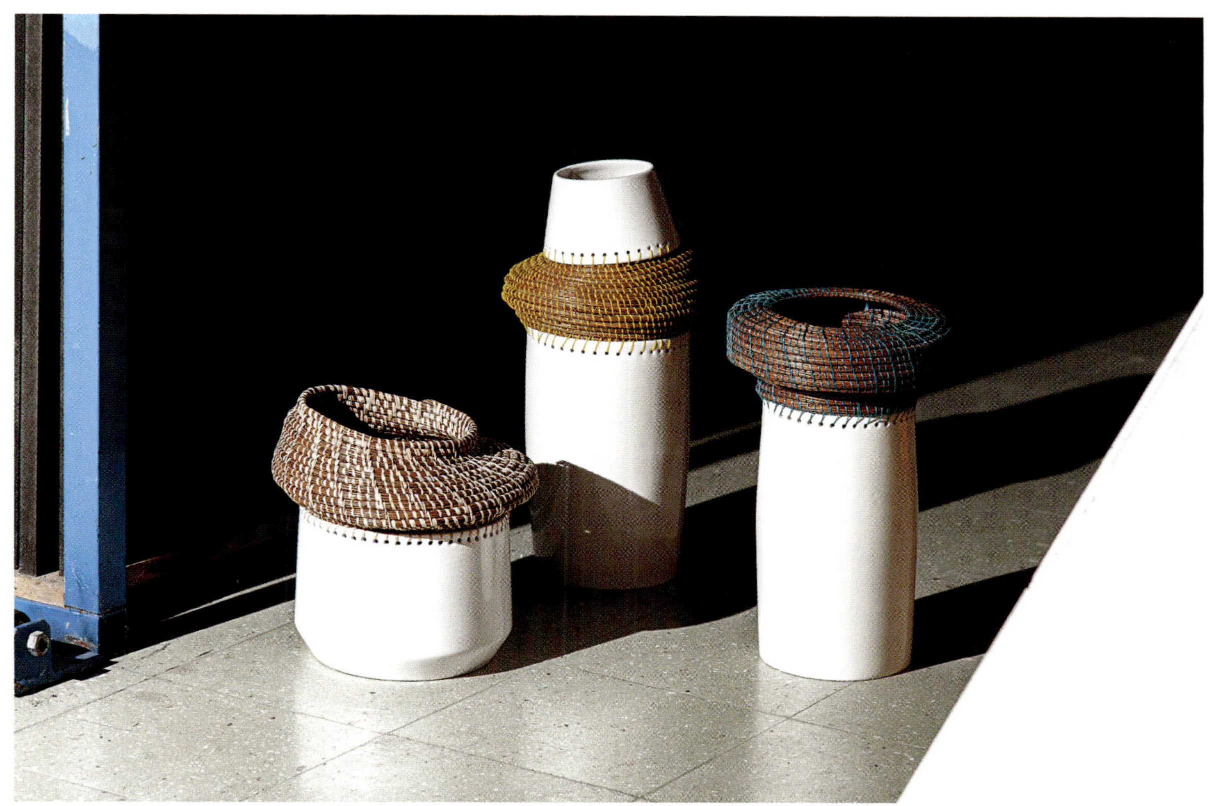

OPPOSITE: *Archipelago*, 2022. Cotton rope: dimensions variable. *Photo by Ivo Oliveira Rodrigues, courtesy of the artist*

Caruma Series, 2014–21. Earthenware, pine tree needles, raffia. Dimensions variable. *Photo by Ivo Oliveira Rodrigues, courtesy of the artist*

Caruma Yellow, 2016. Earthenware, pine tree needles, waxed thread: 20 × 20 × 39 cm (8" × 8" × 15"). *Photo by Ivo Oliveira Rodrigues, courtesy of the artist*

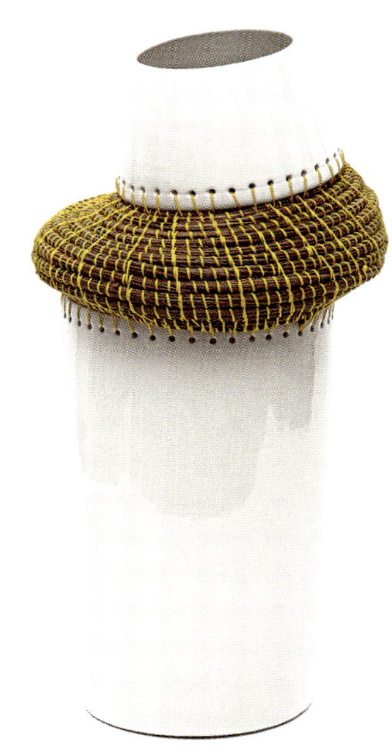

Esmé HOFMAN

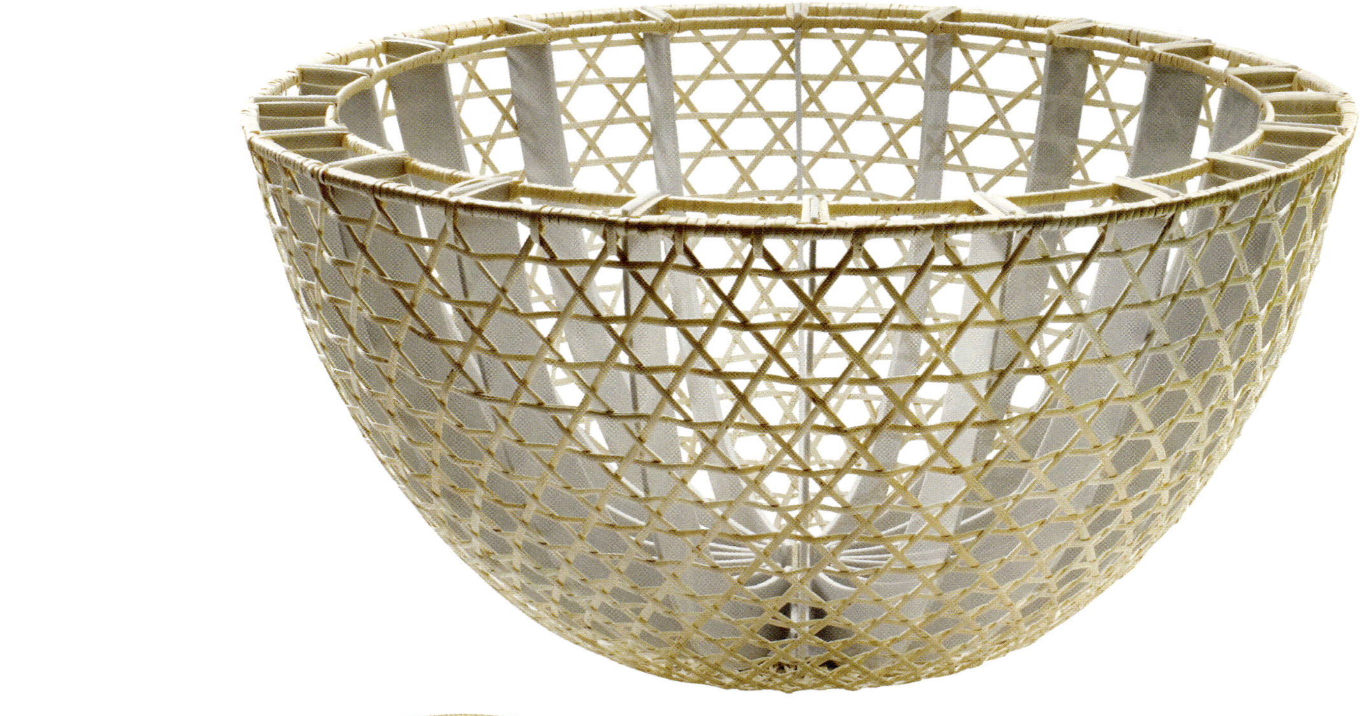

Serious Business, 2008. Willow skeins, plastic: 18 × 34 cm (7" × 13"). *Photo by te, courtesy of the artist*

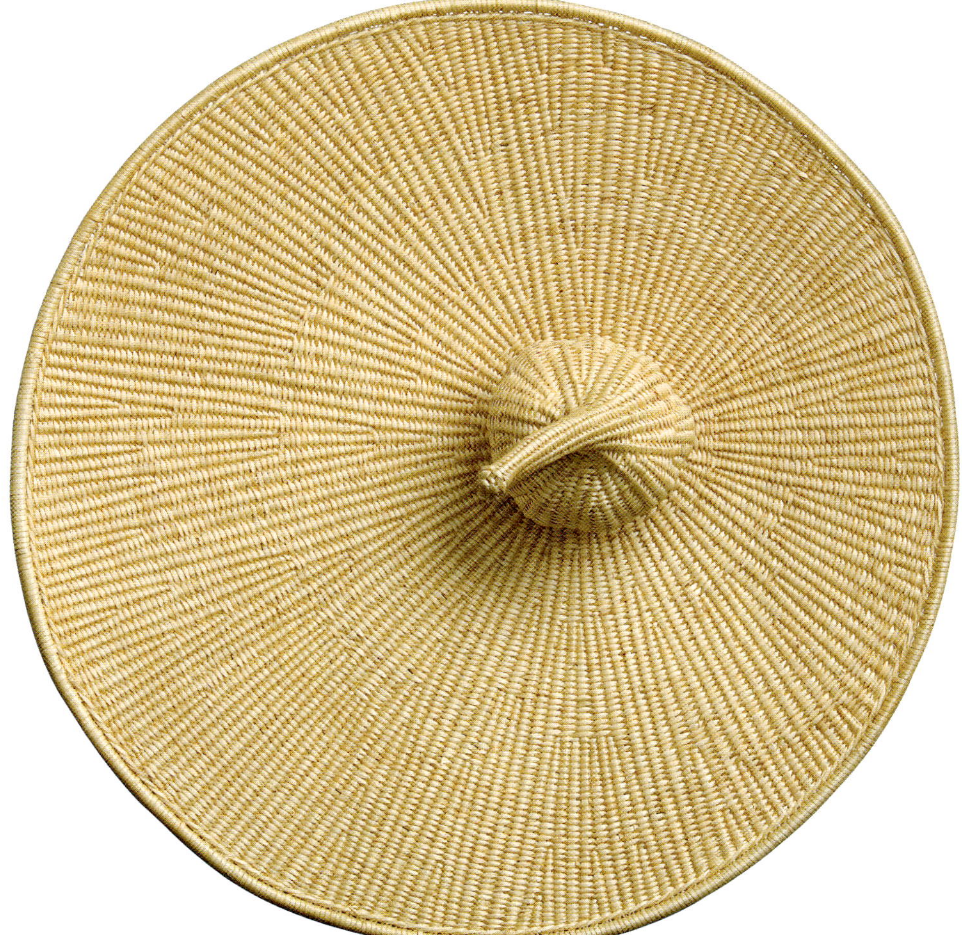

Garlic Queen, 2008. Willow skeins: 30 × 10 cm (11" × 4"). *Photo by te, courtesy of the artist*

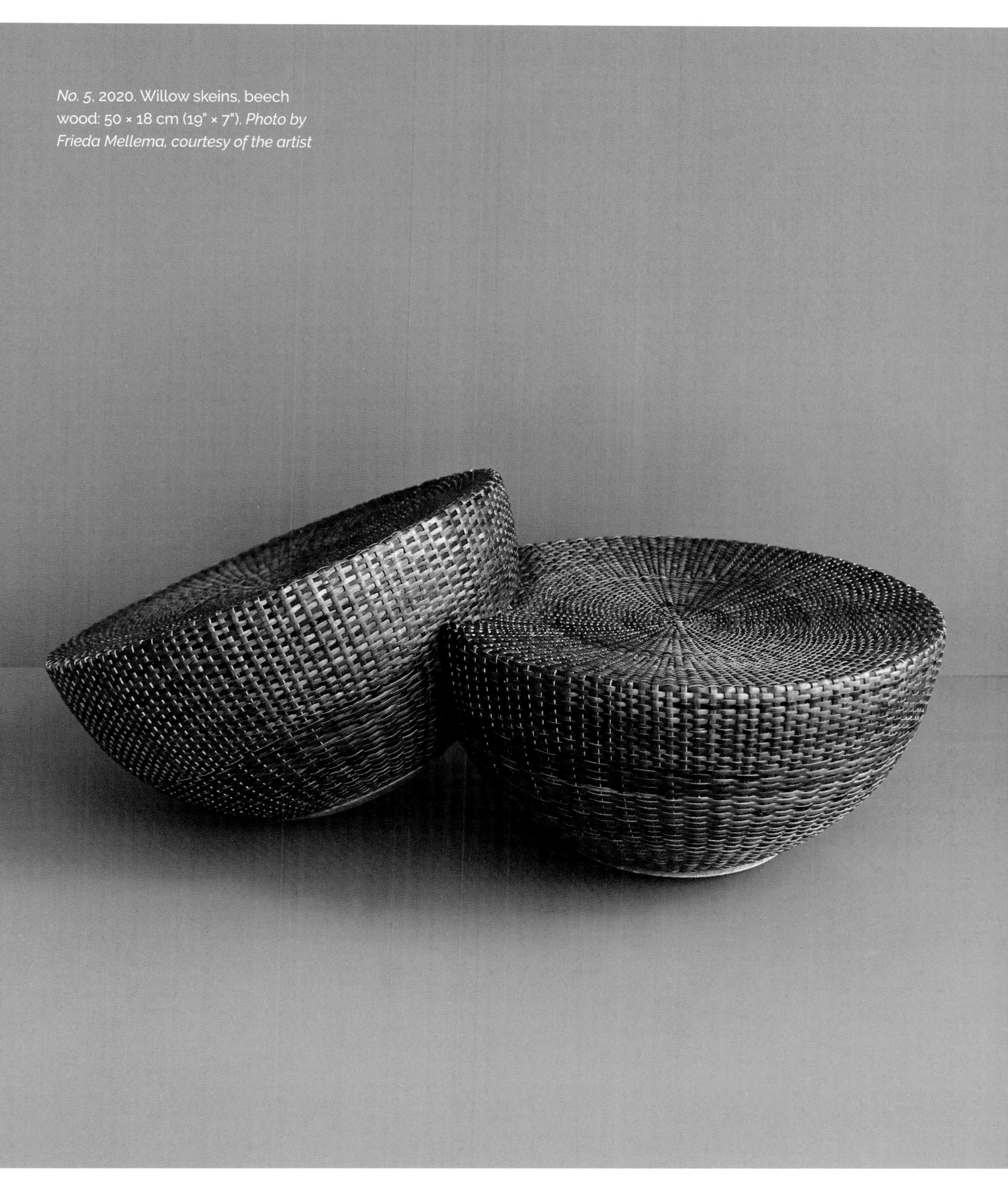

No. 5, 2020. Willow skeins, beech wood: 50 × 18 cm (19" × 7"). *Photo by Frieda Mellema, courtesy of the artist*

Hisako SEKIJIMA

Structural Discussion VI, 2016. Cedar: 38 × 29 × 9 cm (15" × 11" × 3"). *Photograph courtesy of the artist*

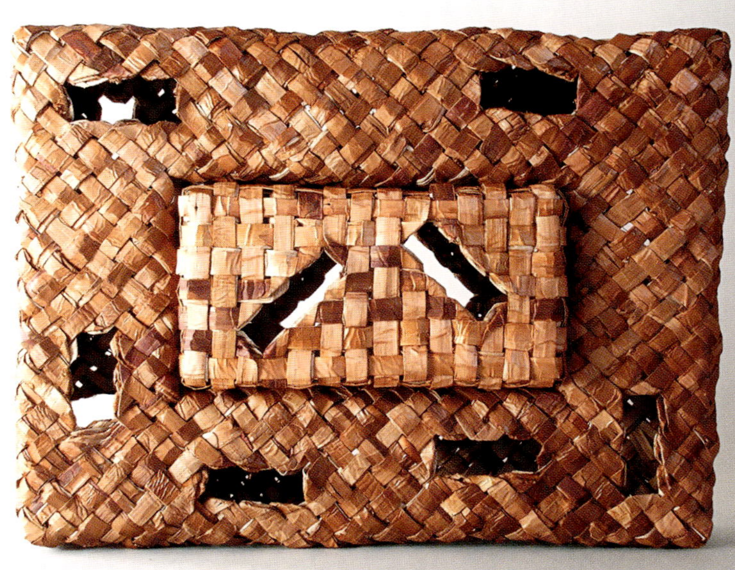

Grasp VI, 2010. Walnut: 24 × 21 × 18 cm (9" × 8" × 7"). *Photo courtesy of the artist*

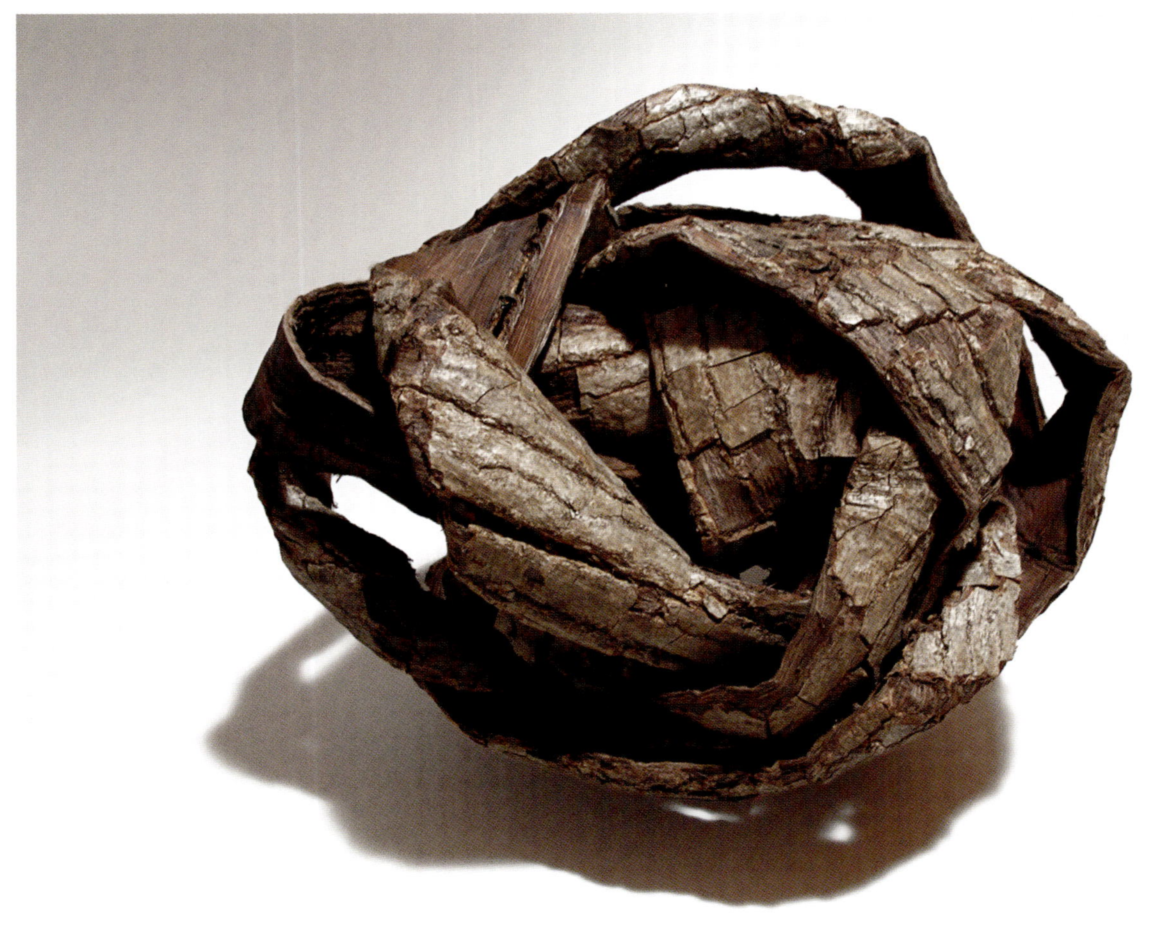

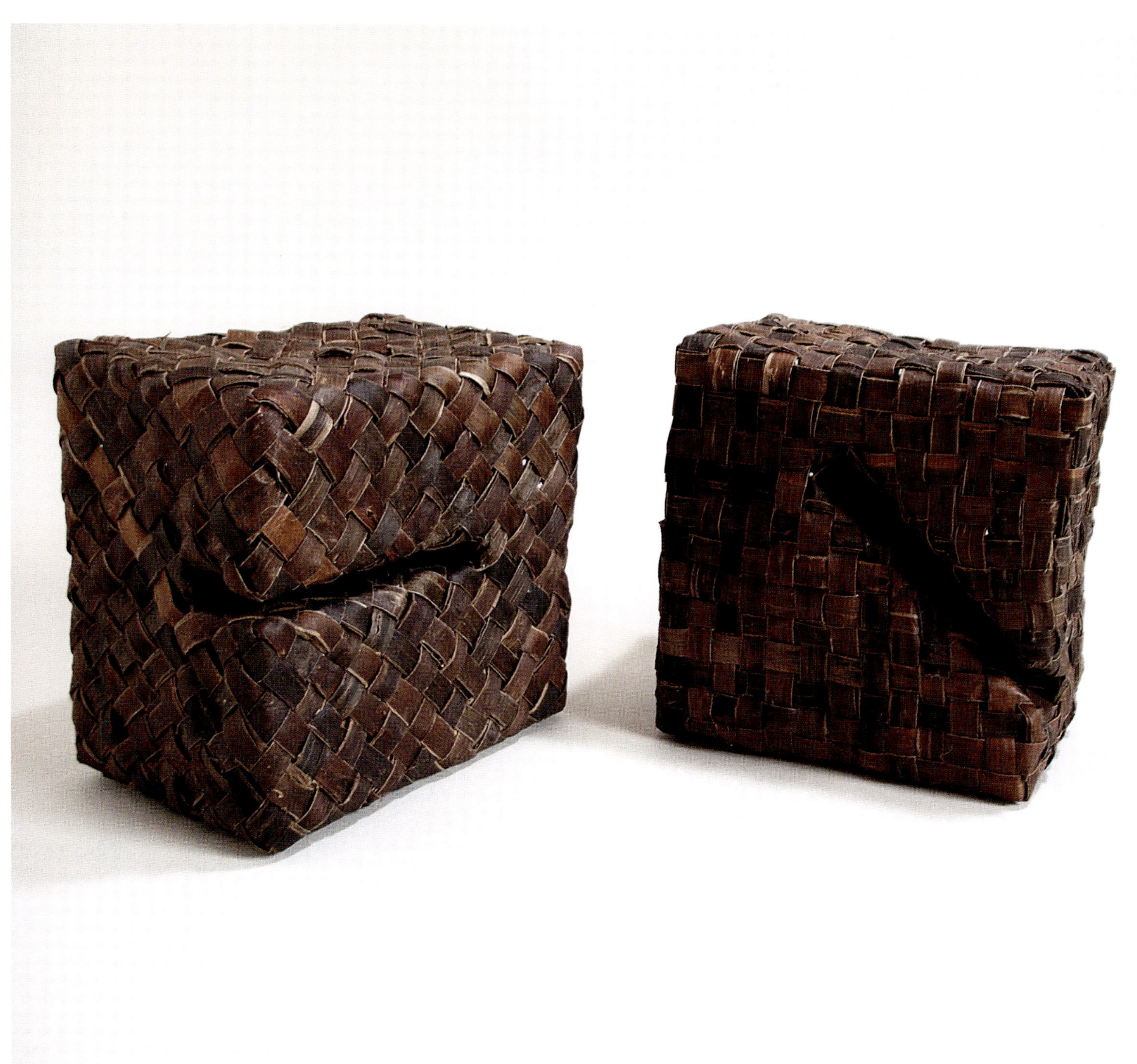

Structural Discussion, Negative, Plaited, 2018. Walnut: 18 × 14 × 20 cm (7" × 5" × 8") and *Structural Discussion, Negative, Warp/Weft Woven*, 2018. Walnut: 18 × 14 × 20 cm (7" × 5" × 8"). *Photo courtesy of the artist*

John GARRETT

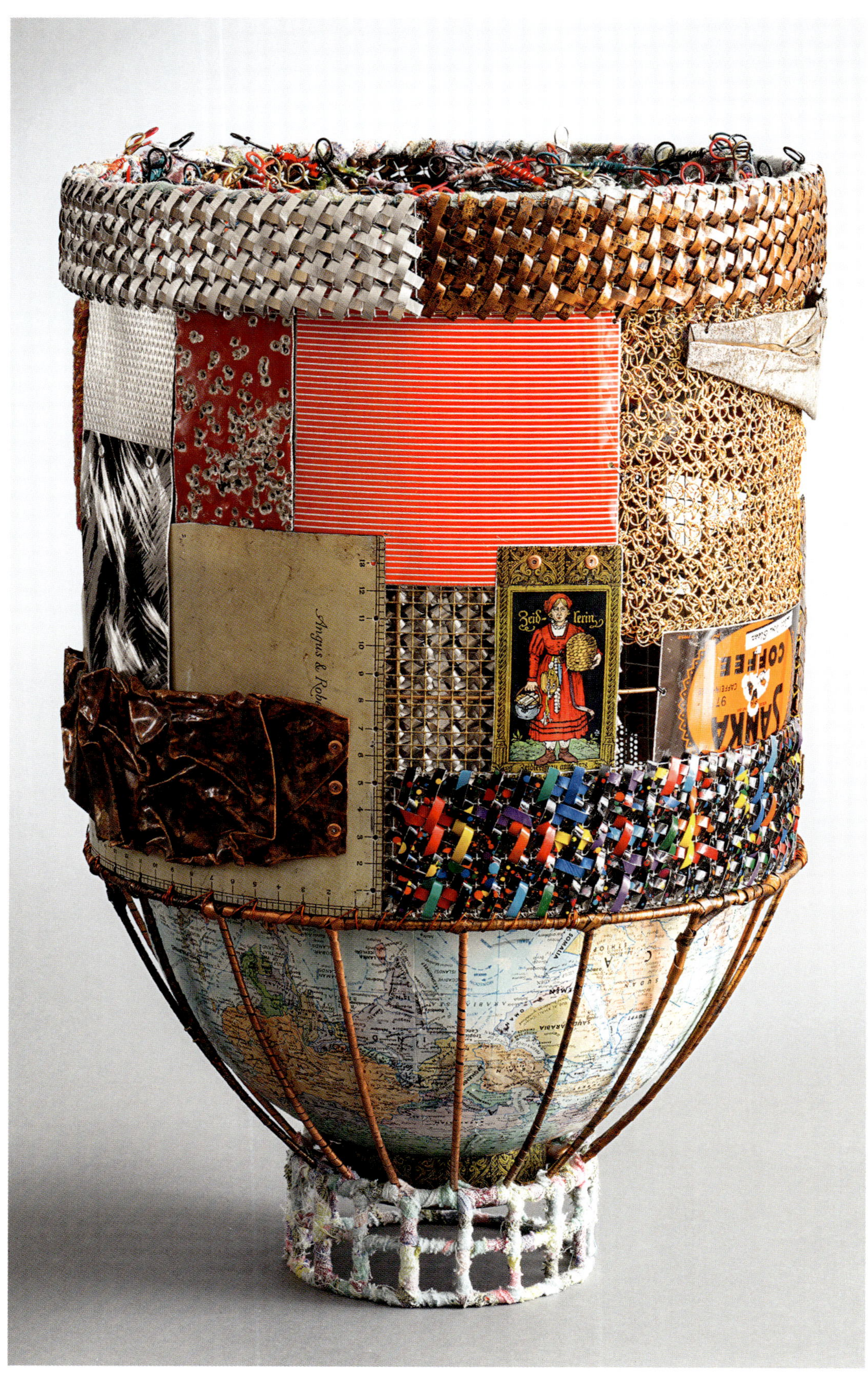

Globemaster, 2022. Steel armature, various wire grids, crocheted copper wire with brass leaf, bullet-riddled steel, perforated aluminum sheet, world globe hemisphere, fabric, printed tins, measuring tool, rebar ties, paper: 55 × 40 × 40 cm (22" × 16" × 16"). *Photo by Margot Geist, courtesy of the artist*

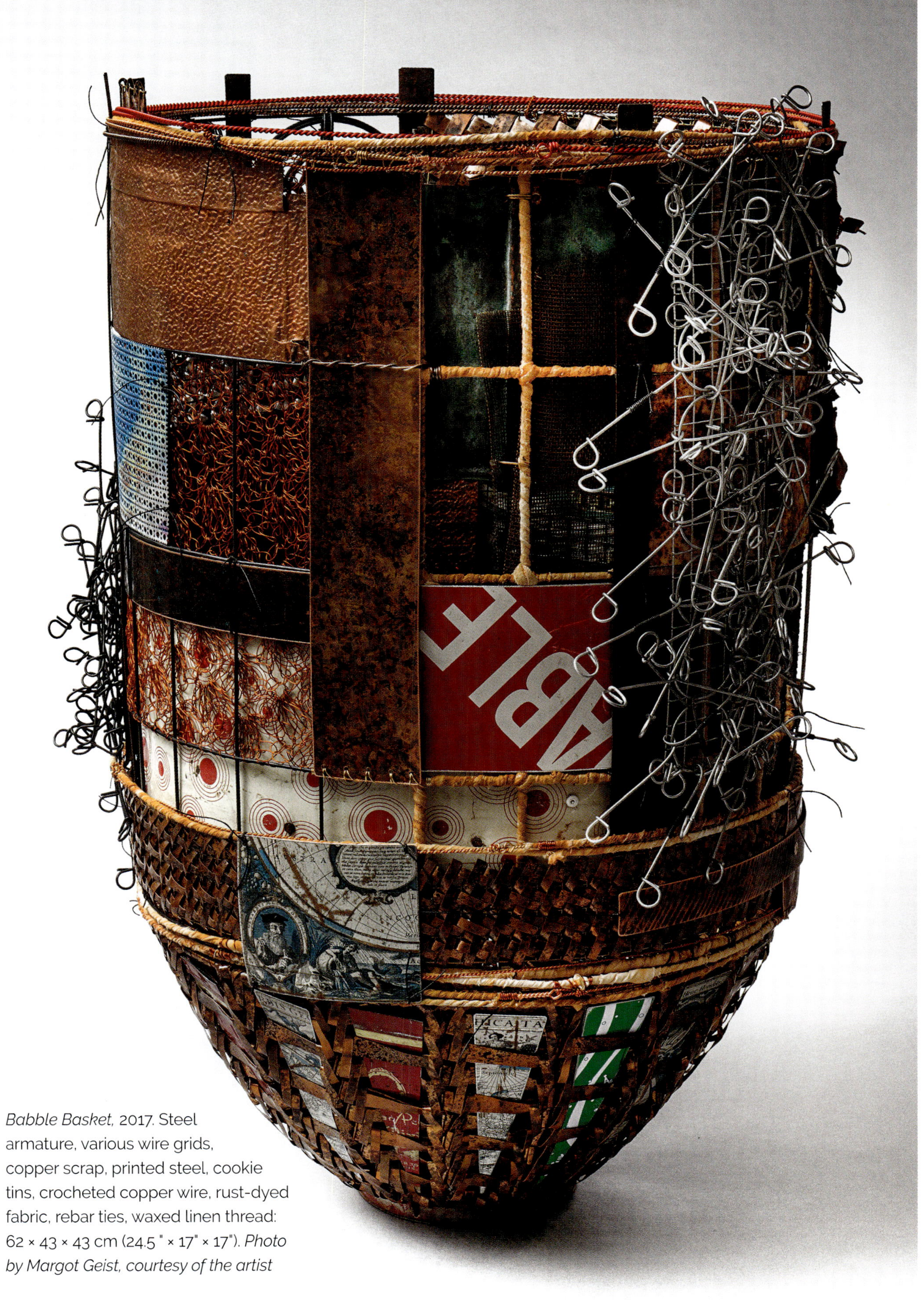

Babble Basket, 2017. Steel armature, various wire grids, copper scrap, printed steel, cookie tins, crocheted copper wire, rust-dyed fabric, rebar ties, waxed linen thread: 62 × 43 × 43 cm (24.5" × 17" × 17"). *Photo by Margot Geist, courtesy of the artist*

Gyöngy LAKY

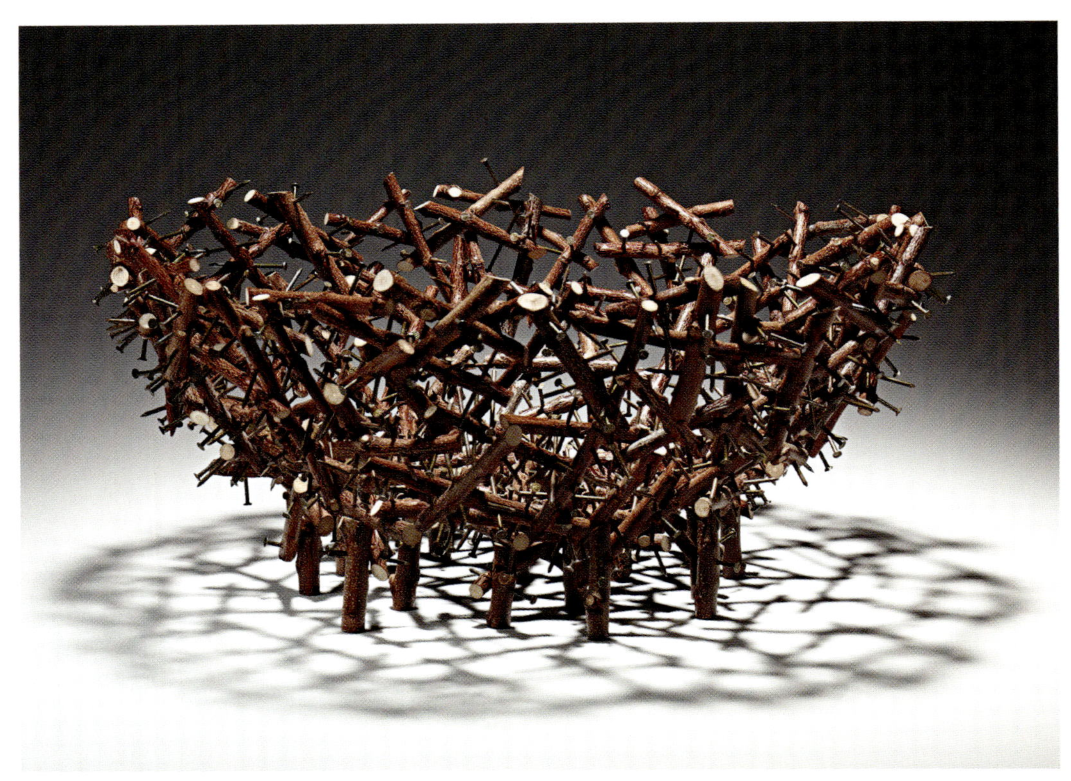

Field Notes, 2012. Apricot, vinyl-coated nails: 22 × 58 cm (9" × 23"). *Photo courtesy of M. Lee Fatherree*

Cradle to Cradle, 2007. Apple, commercial wood, screws: 39 × 76 cm (15.5" × 30"). *Photo courtesy of Ben Blackwell*

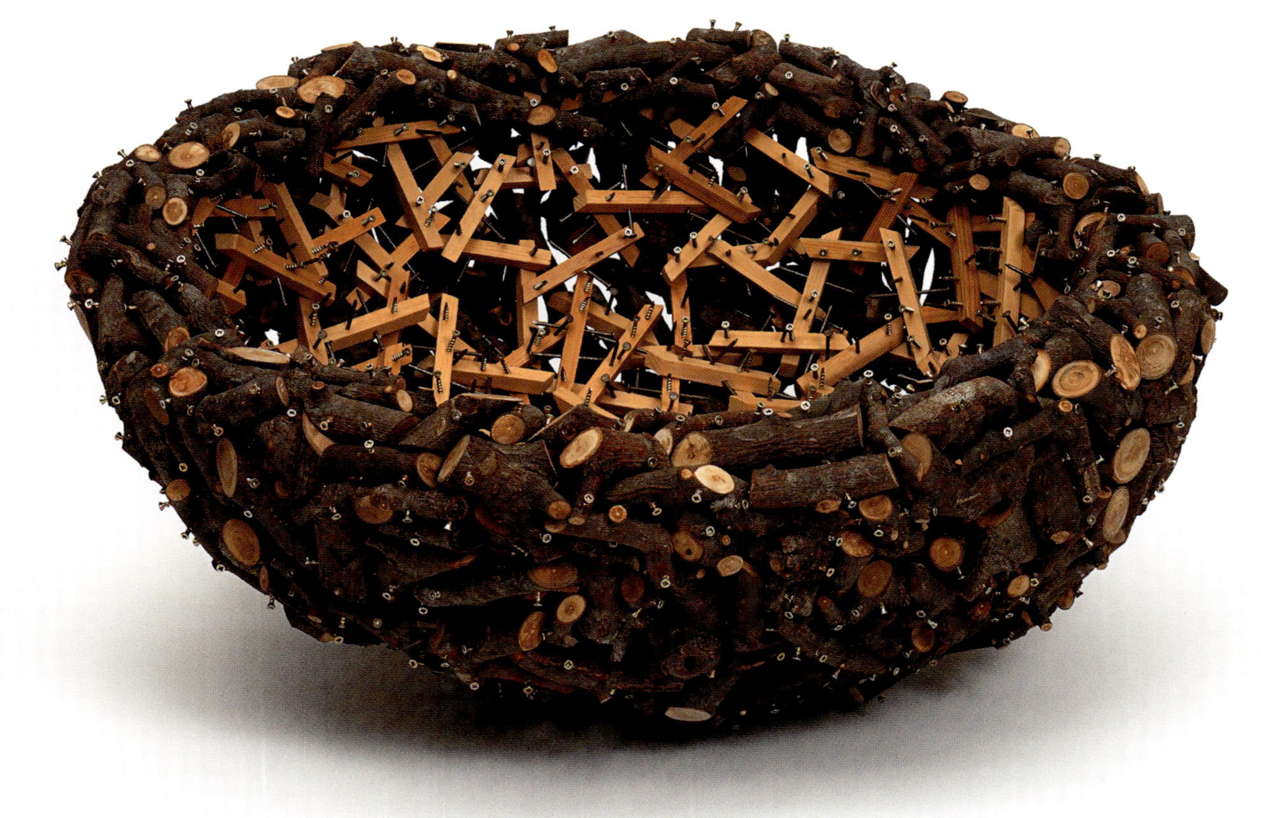

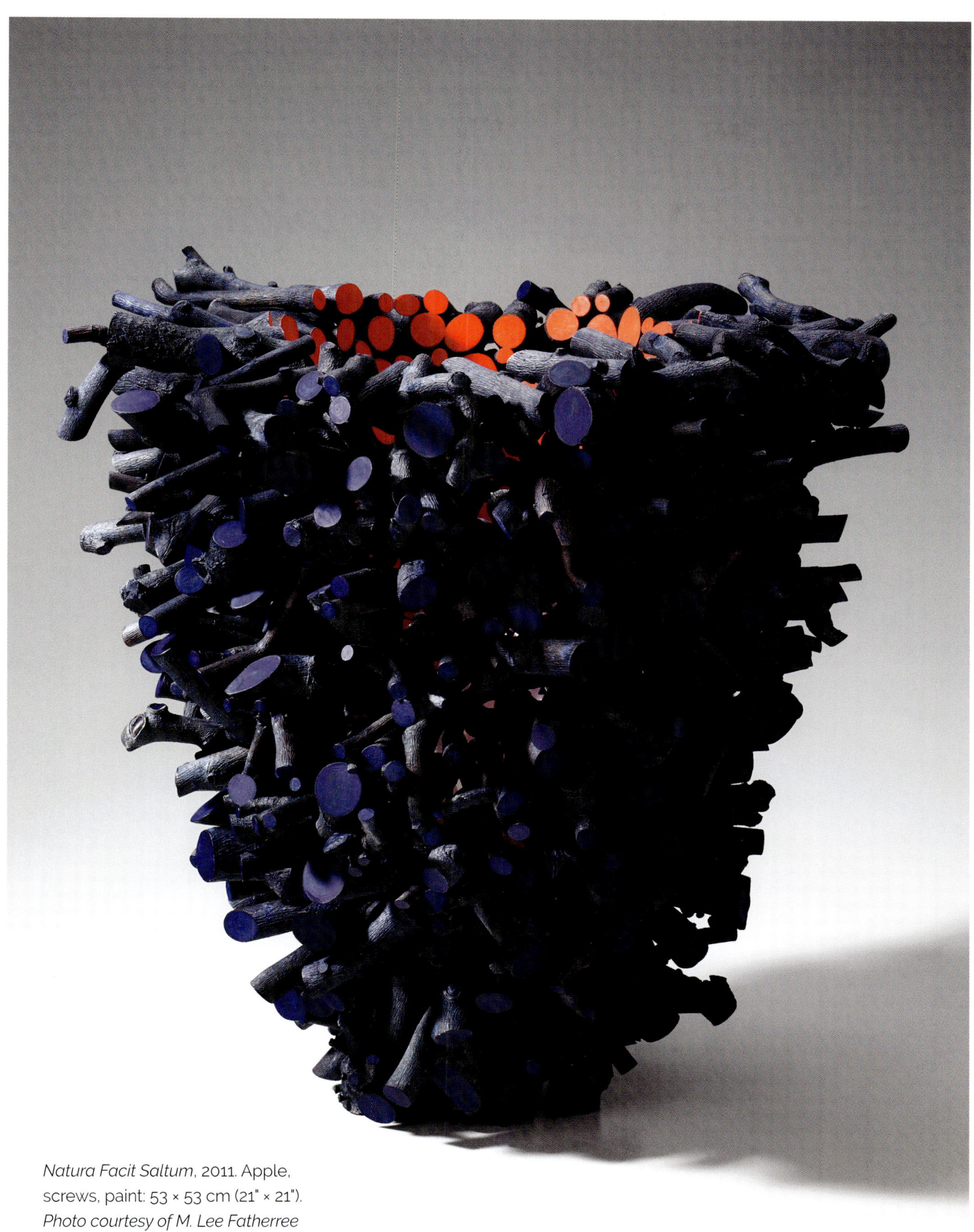

Natura Facit Saltum, 2011. Apple, screws, paint: 53 × 53 cm (21" × 21"). *Photo courtesy of M. Lee Fatherree*

Joanne LAMB

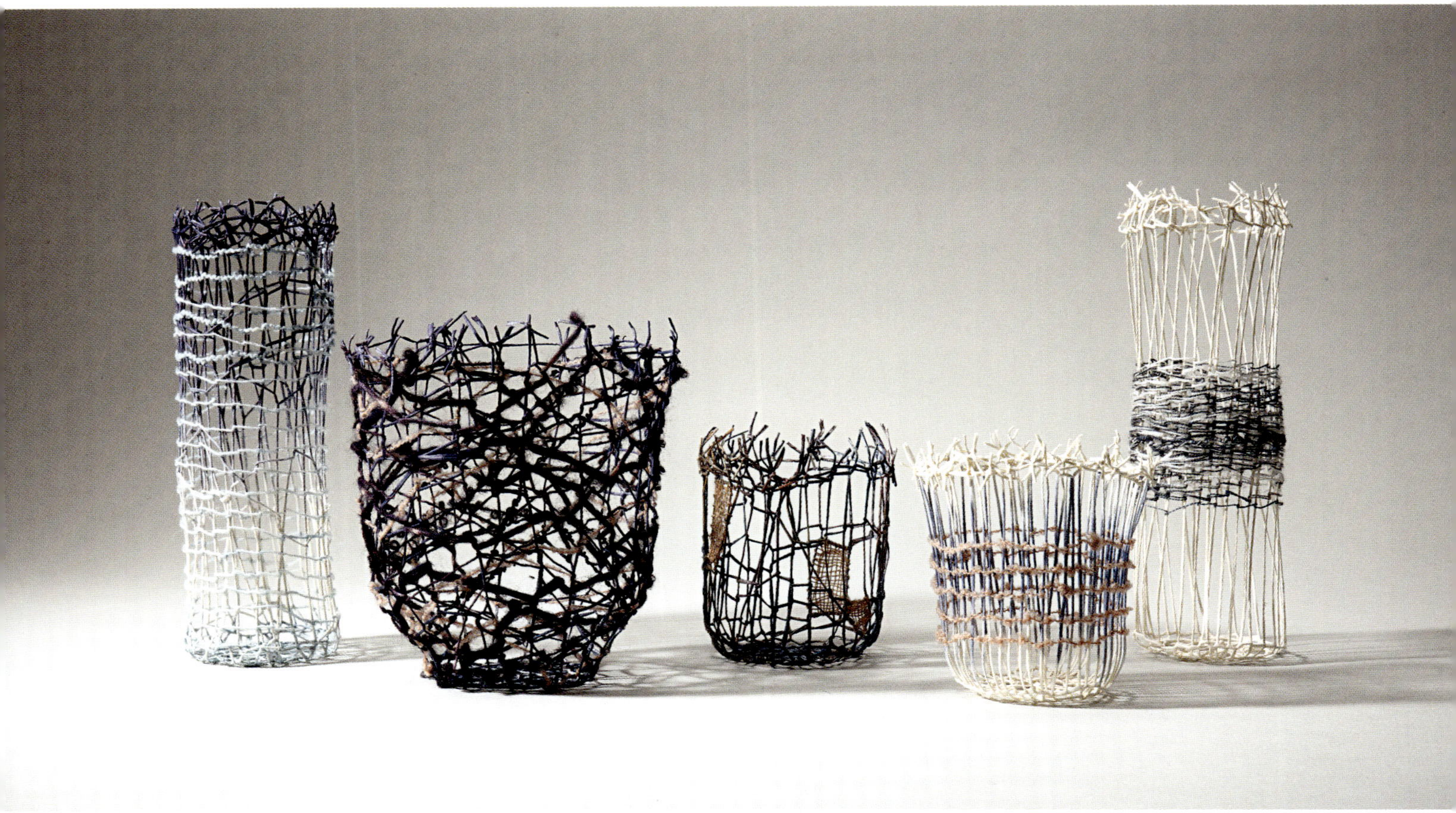

Samhain group, 2023. Tatami paper, wool, mohair, silk: 20 × 50 × 20 cm (8" × 19" × 8"). *Photo by Jan Naraine, courtesy of the artist*

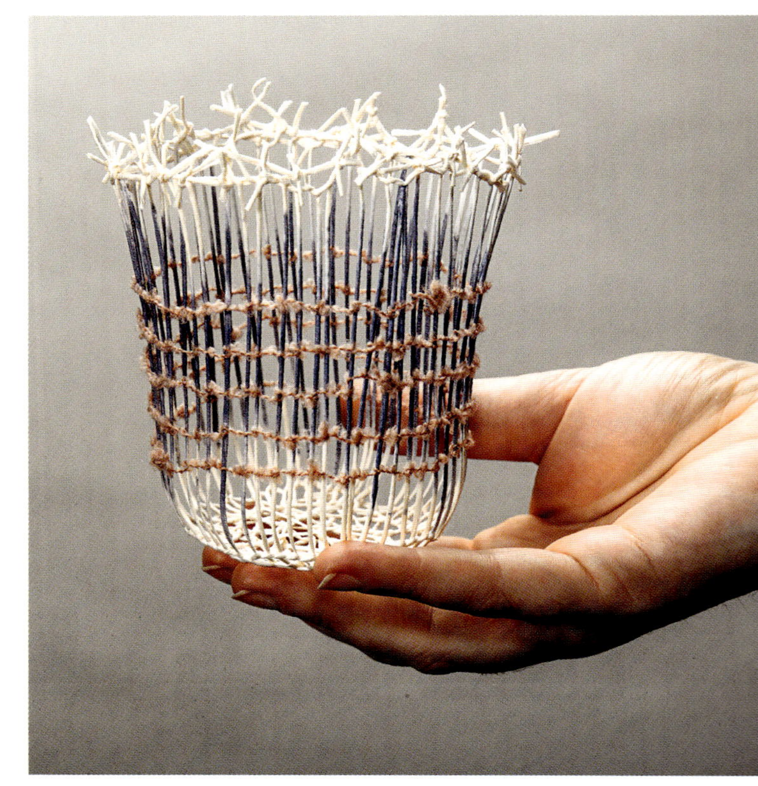

Samhain vessel, 2023. Tatami paper, wool, mohair, silk: 9 × 10 cm (3.5" × 4"). *Photo by Jan Naraine, courtesy of the artist*

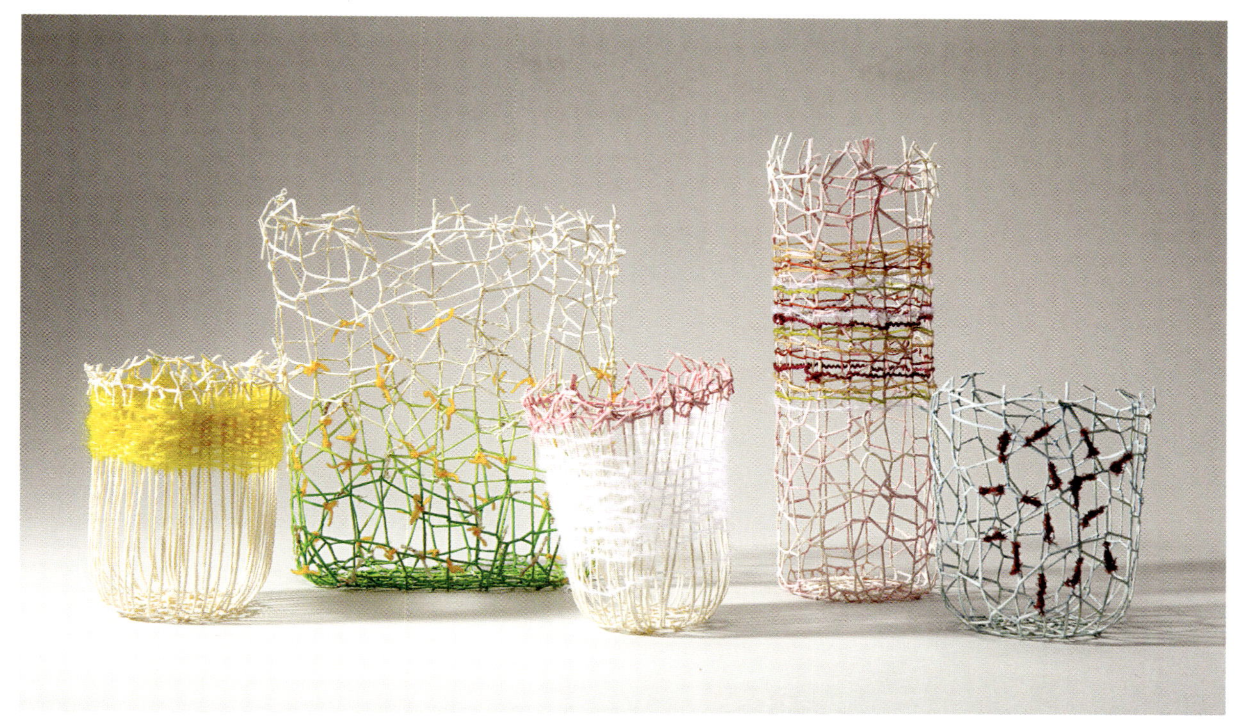

ABOVE: *Imbolc* group, 2023. Tatami paper, wool, mohair, silk: 20 × 50 × 20 cm (8" × 19" × 8"). *Photo by Jan Naraine, courtesy of the artist*

BELOW: *Bealtaine* group, 2023. Tatami paper, wool, mohair, silk: 20 × 50 × 20 cm (8" × 19" × 8"). *Photo by Jan Naraine, courtesy of the artist*

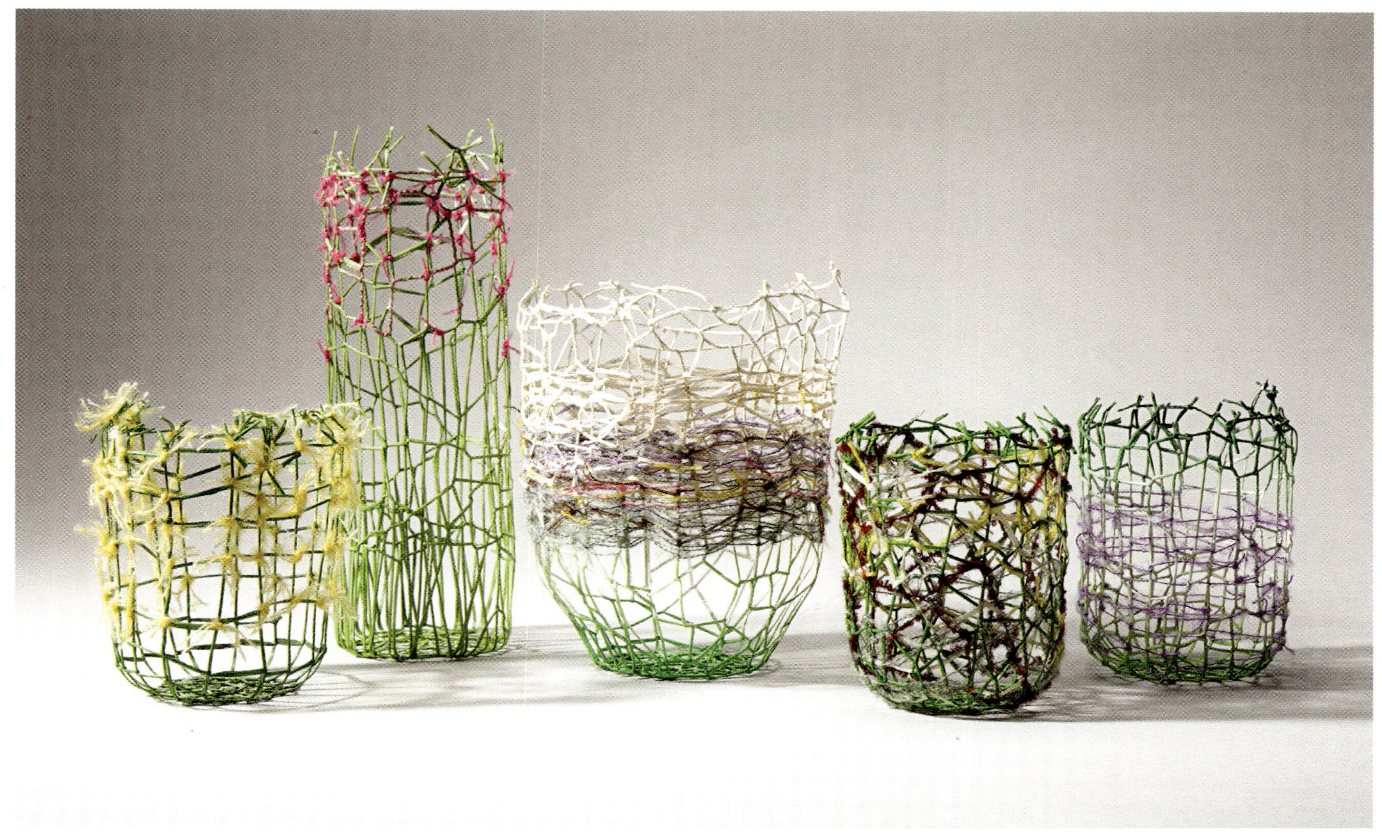

Noriko TAKAMIYA

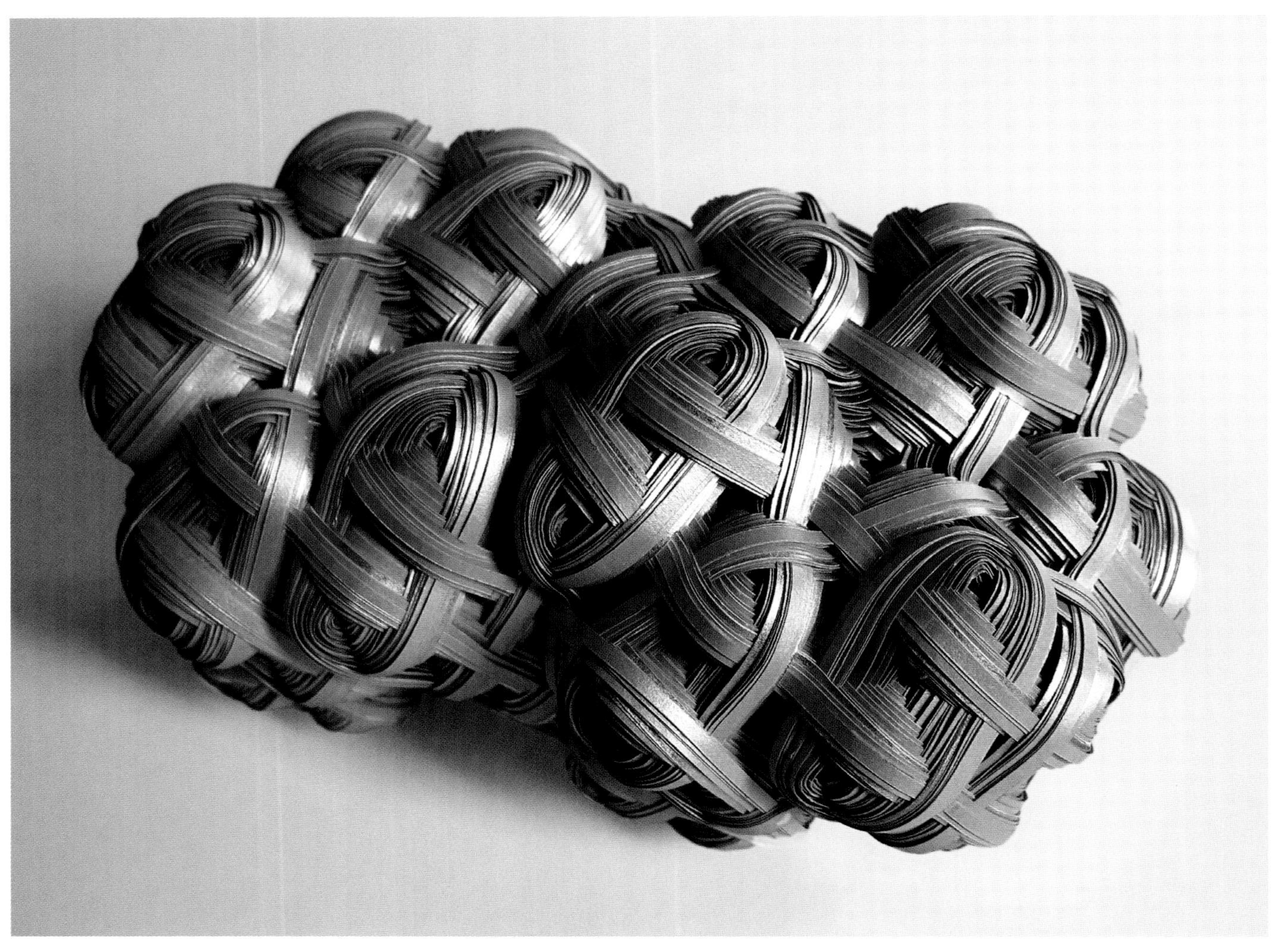

Cube Connection #16, 2018. Paper: 25 × 15 × 15 cm (10" × 6" × 6"). *Photo courtesy of the artist*

OPPOSITE: *Cube Connection #14*, 2017. Paper: 20 × 20 × 11 cm (8" × 8" × 4"). *Photo courtesy of the artist*

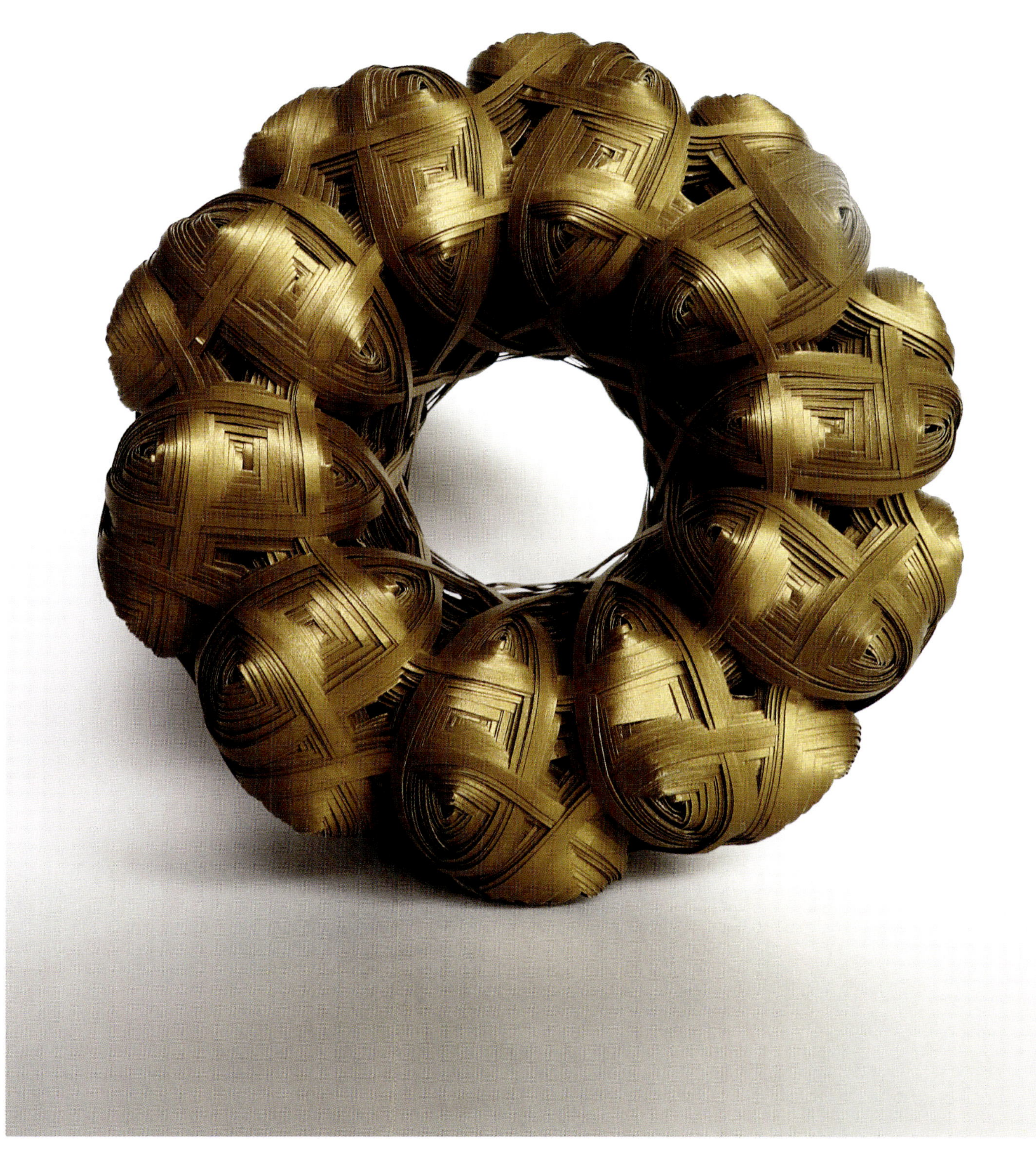

Julie Bénédicte LAMBERT

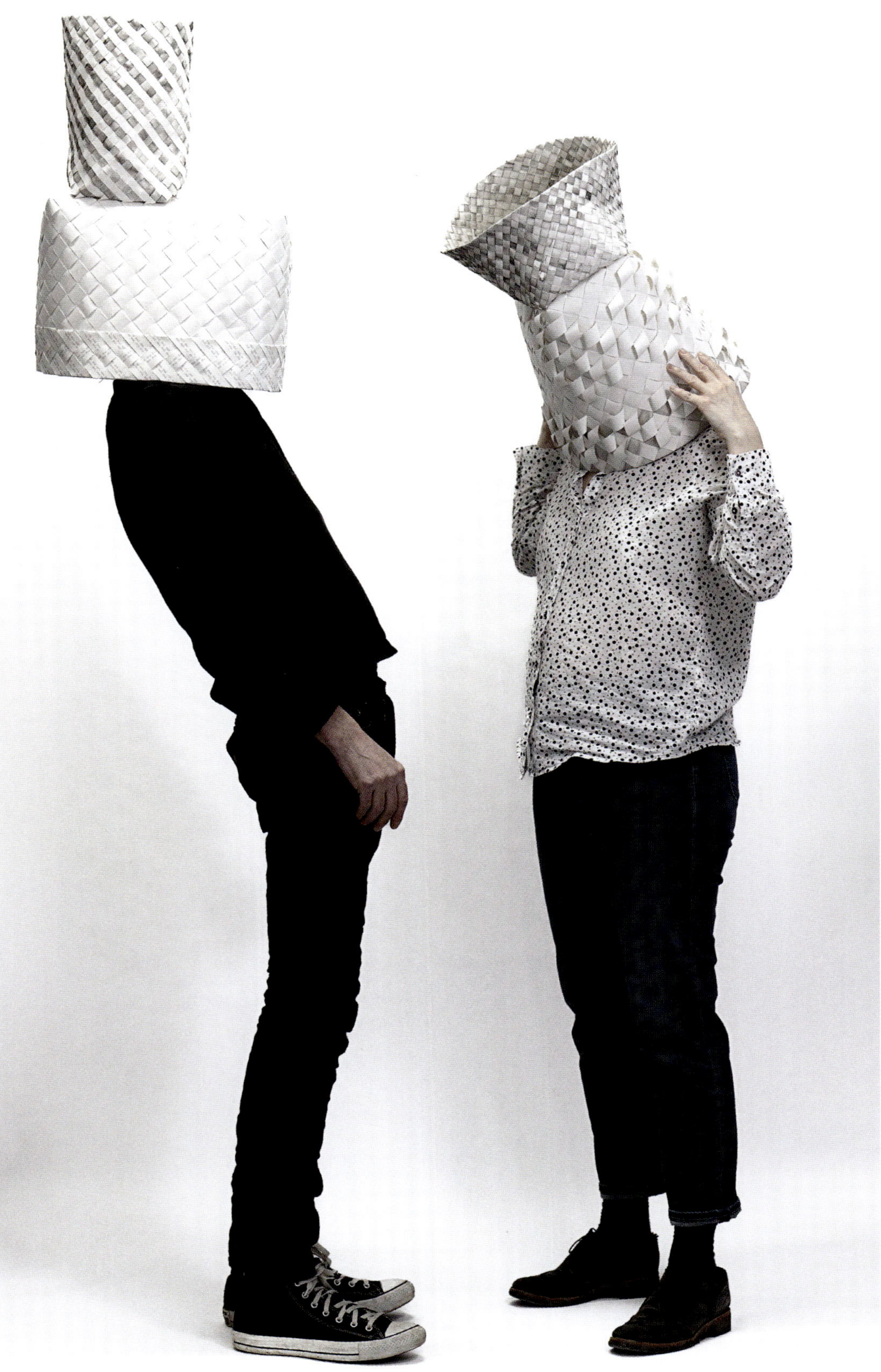

Motifs à dire. Série 2: Les greffes. [*Conversation/Text(ile) Patterns. Series 2: The grafts.*] 2023. Artisanal paper (cotton, flax, jute), industrial abaca paper, India ink: dimensions variable. *Photo by Michael Patten, courtesy of the artist*

OPPOSITE, TOP: *Motifs à dire. Série 1: Les greffes #5 écrasée.* [*Text(ile) Patterns. Series 1: the grafts #5 flatten.*] 2019. Handmade flax paper, industrial abaca paper, India ink: 33 × 27 × 2 cm (13" × 10" × 0.5"). *Photo by Bernard Dubois, courtesy of the artist*

OPPOSITE, BOTTOM: *Motifs à dire. Série 1: Les greffes, Duo #2.* [*Text(ile) Patterns. Series 1: The grafts, Duo #2.*] 2019. Handmade flax paper, industrial abaca paper, India ink: each 22 × 11 × 11 cm (8" × 4" × 4"). *Photo courtesy of the artist*

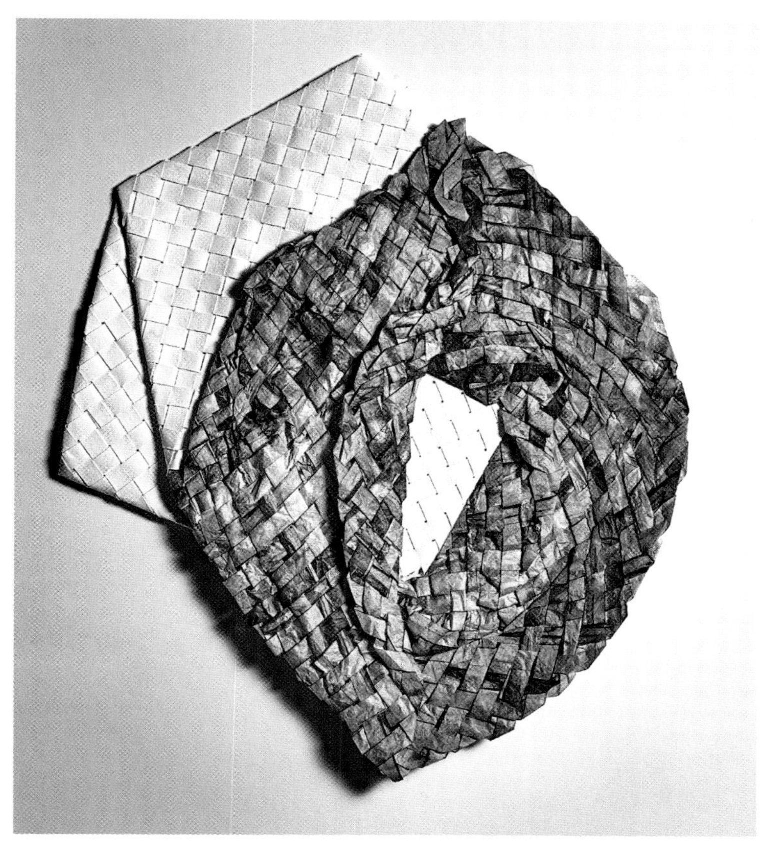

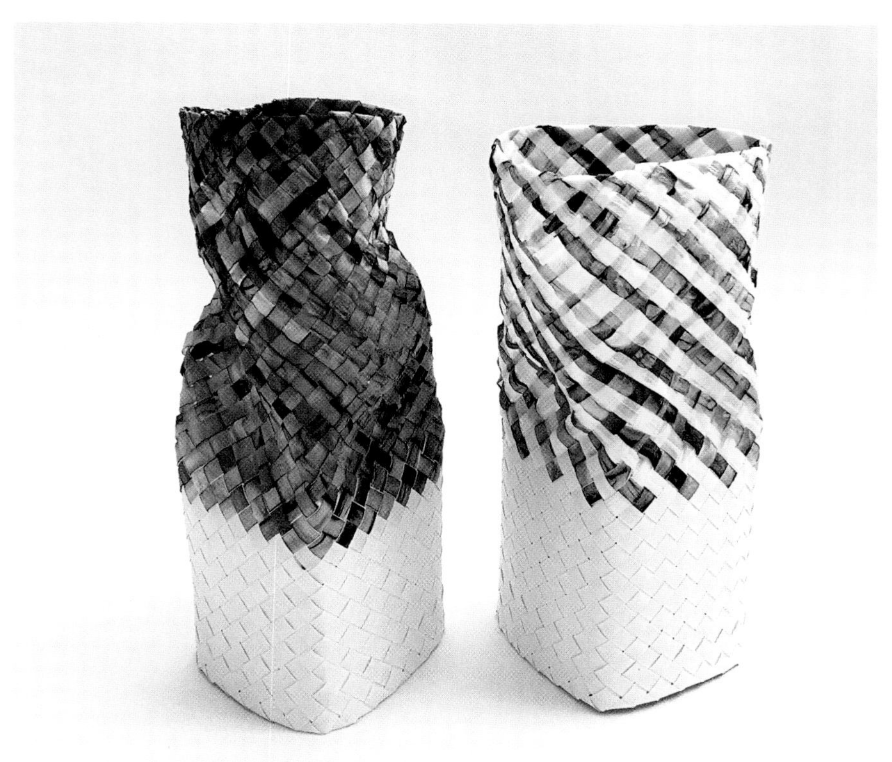

Keiji NIO

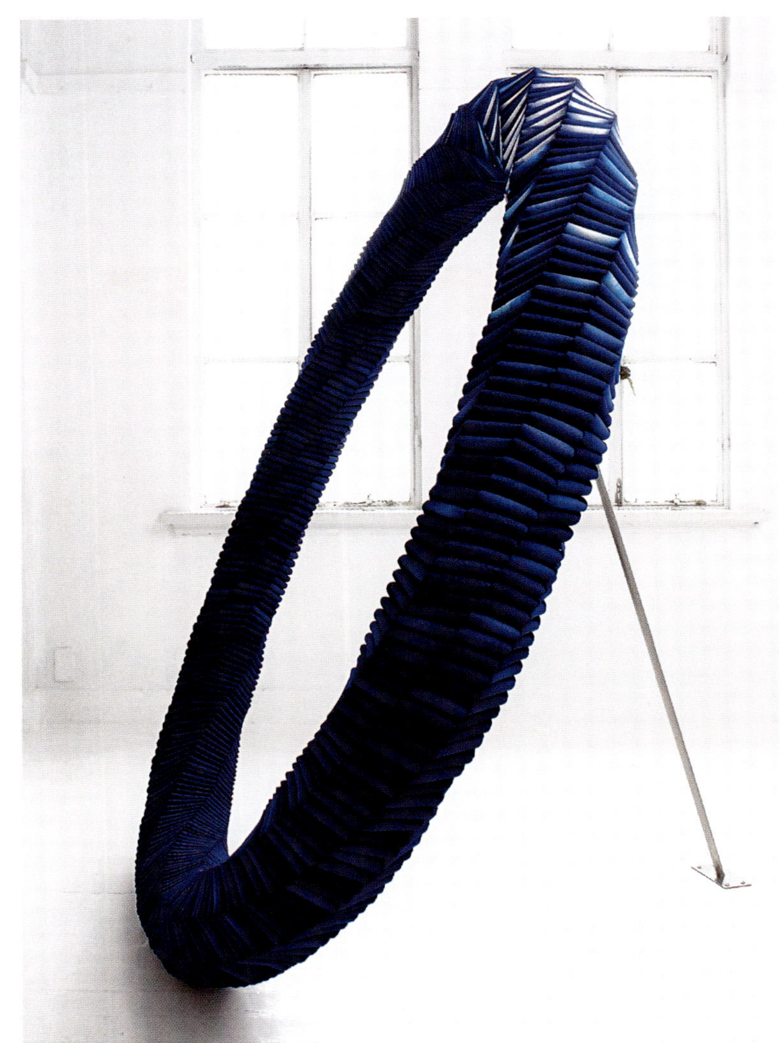

Interlacing B, 2008. Nylon: 190 × 190 × 190 cm (75" × 75" × 75"). *Photo courtesy of Nishimura*

Interlacing G, 2010. Nylon: 80 × 140 × 120 cm (31" × 55" × 47"). *Photo courtesy of Nishimura*

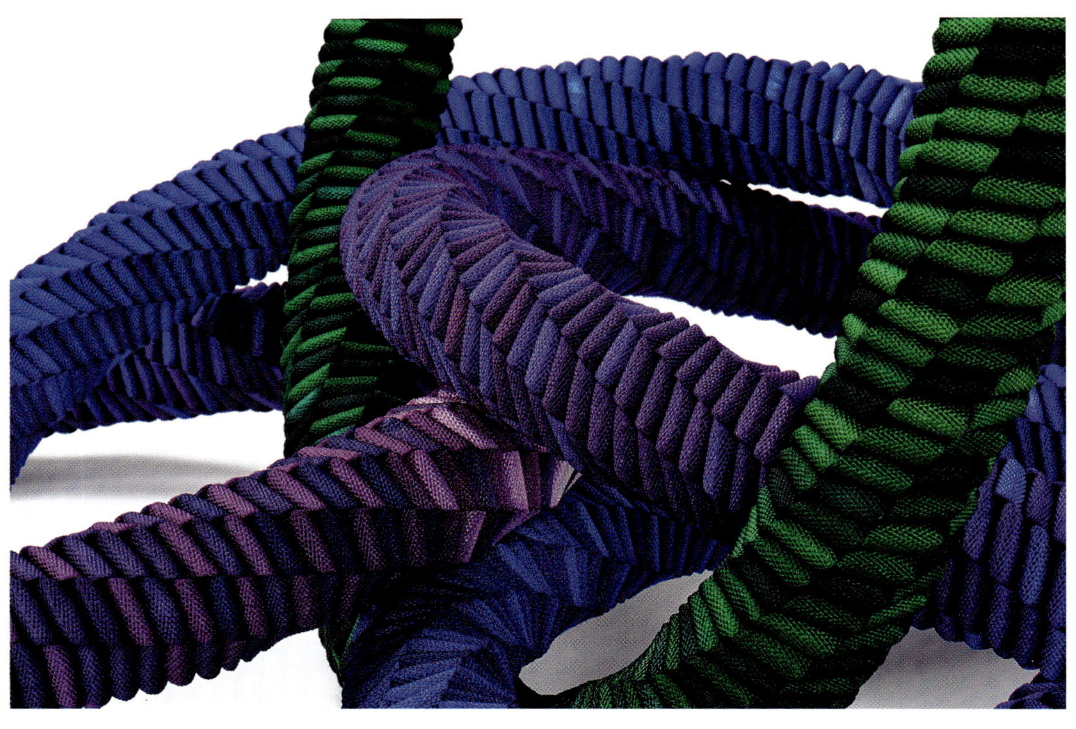

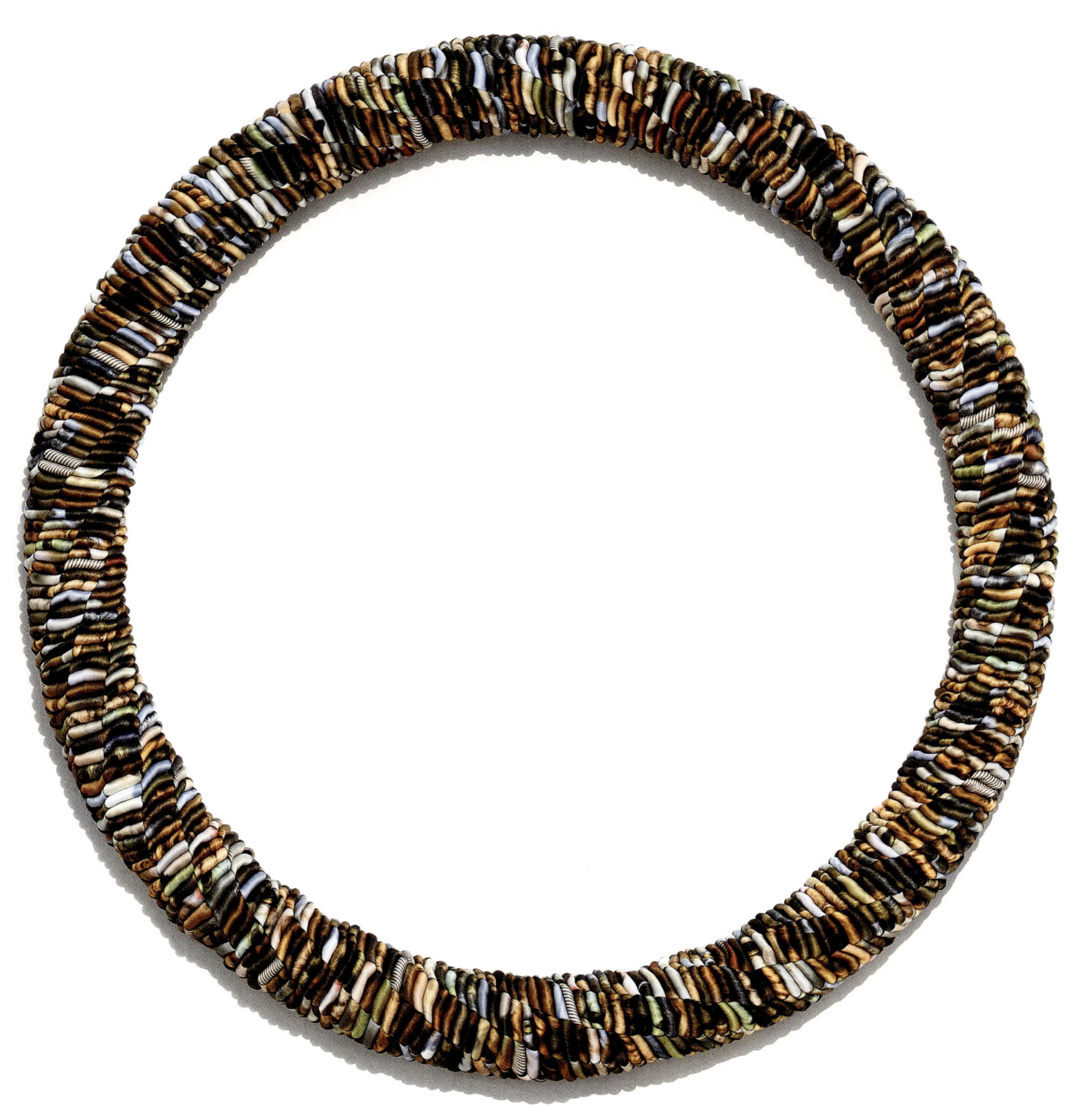

Cat Eye, 2022. Polyester:
10 × 73 × 73 cm (4" × 29" × 29"). *Photo courtesy of the artist*

Fiona GAVINO

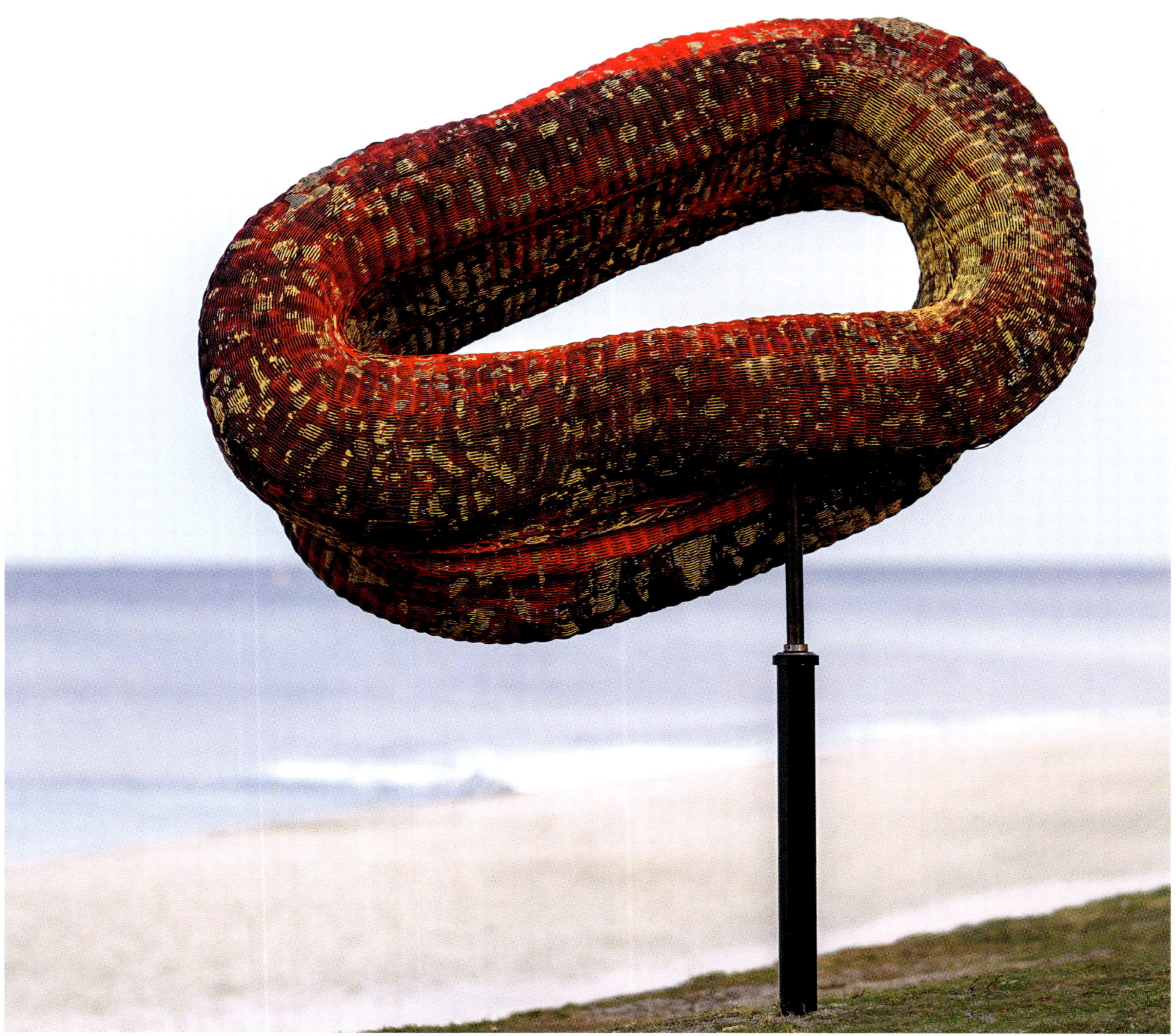

The Meditation Inhale Exhale, 2023–24. Cane, rattan, Japanese black, gold leaf, Montana resin, aerosol paint: 220 × 180 × 100 cm (86" × 70" × 39"). *Photo courtesy of Michael Goh*

OPPOSITE, TOP: *Fertility*, 2014. Cane, rattan, repurposed packing strapping: 110 × 110 × 100 cm (43" × 43" × 39"). *Photo courtesy of the artist*

OPPOSITE, BOTTOM: *tolerance, change, difference*, 2013. Cane, commercial dyes, silk, mild steel: 2 × 2 × 1 m (6' × 6' × 3'). *Photo courtesy of Jarrad Seng*

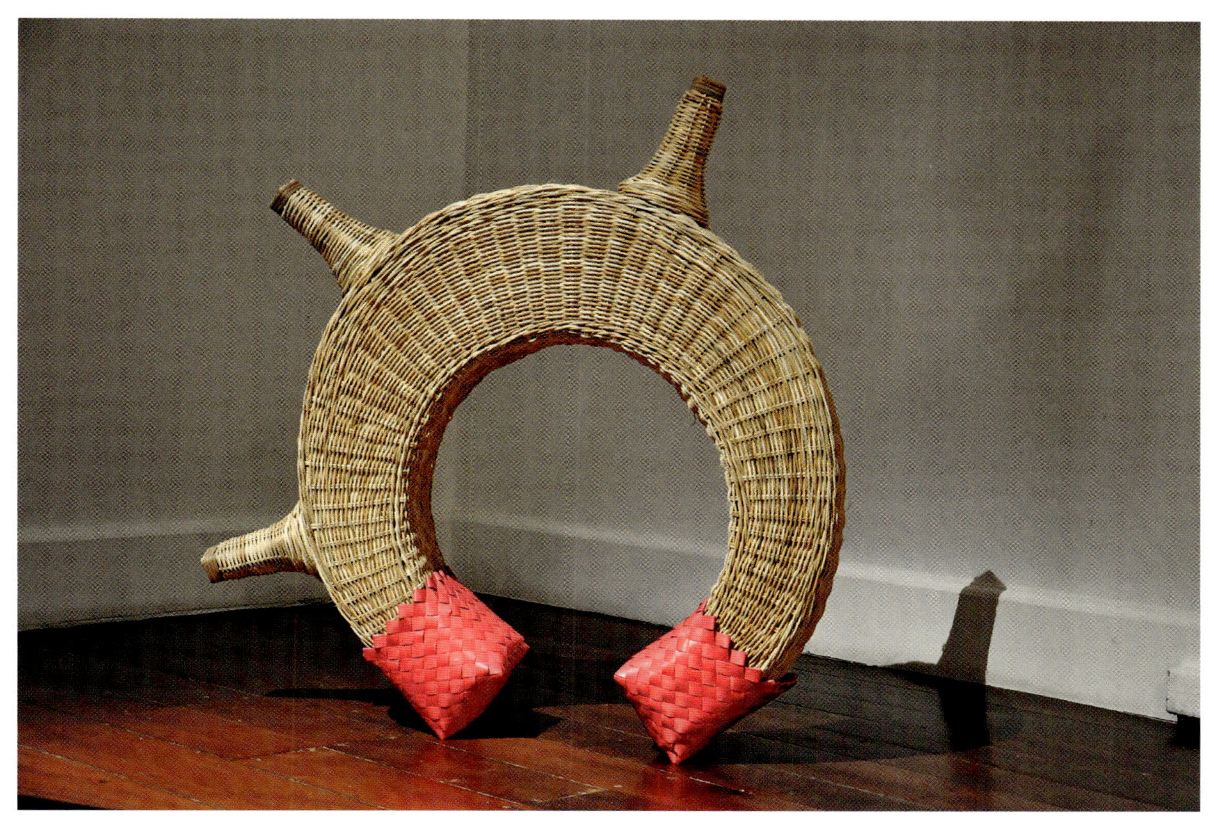

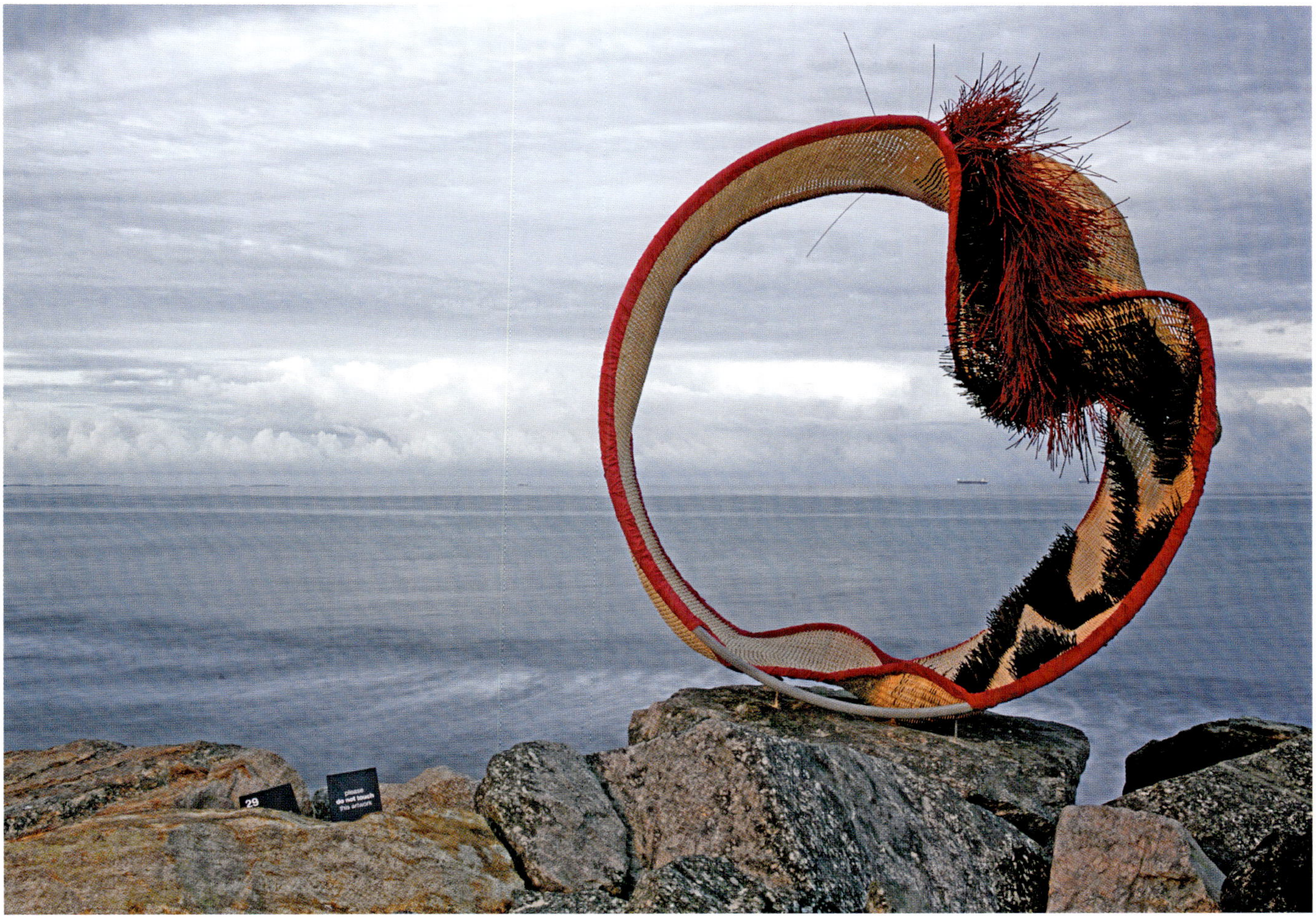

Stephen TALASNIK

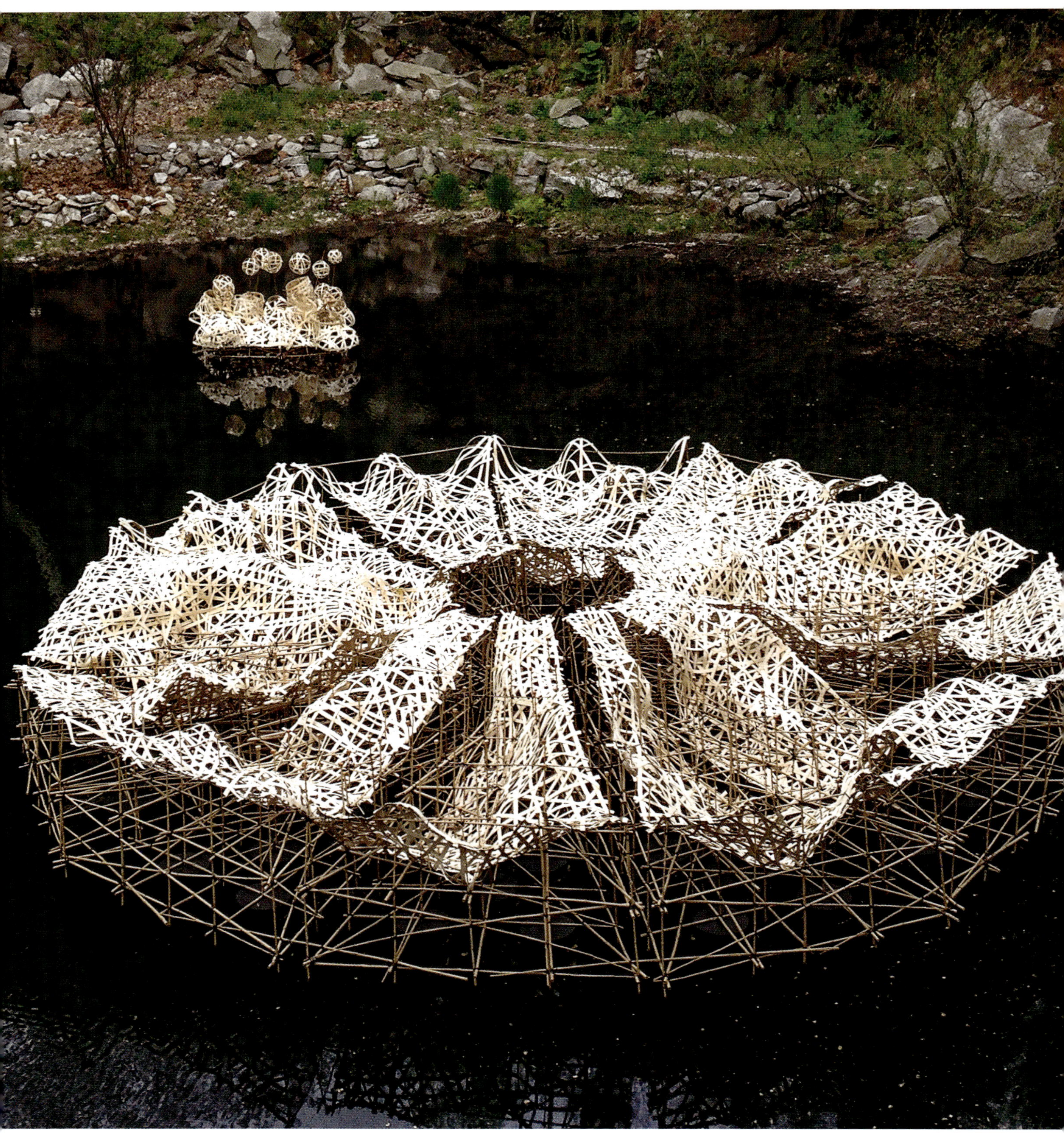

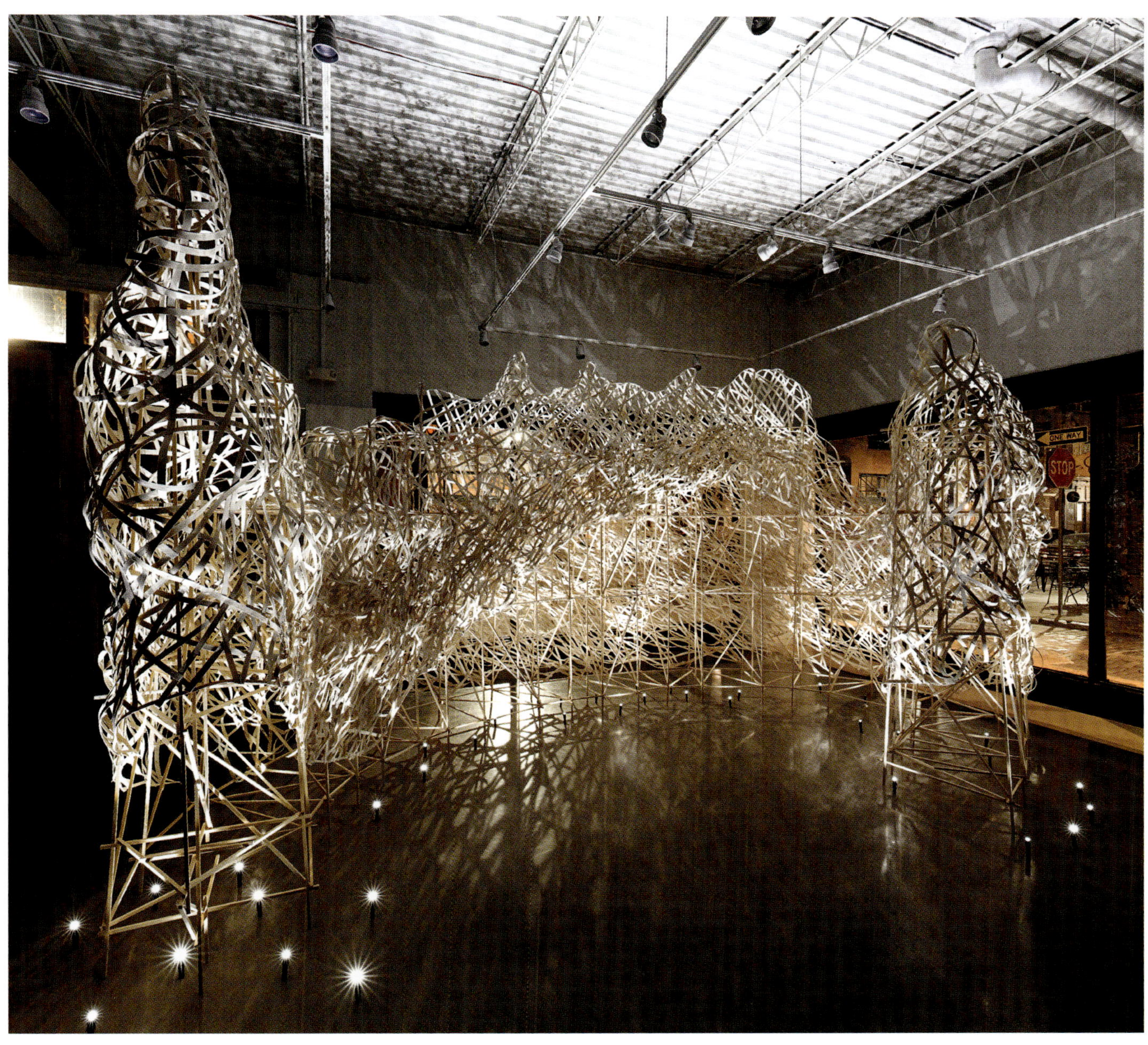

OPPOSITE: *Nimbus/Sanctuary*: an installation of Aquatic Architecture, MANITOGA / The Russel Wright Design Center, Garrison, NY, 2015. Flat reed, bamboo poles: 8 × 1 m (25' × 4'). *Photo courtesy of Don Pollard*

Glacier/FLOE: A Climate of Risk, The Fictional Archaeology of Stephen Talasnik. Museum for Art in Wood, Philadelphia, PA, 2023. Pine stick infrastructure with bamboo flat reed: 4 m × 46m^2 (12' × 500 ft^2). *Photo courtesy of Jeffery Scott French*

Shoko FUKUDA

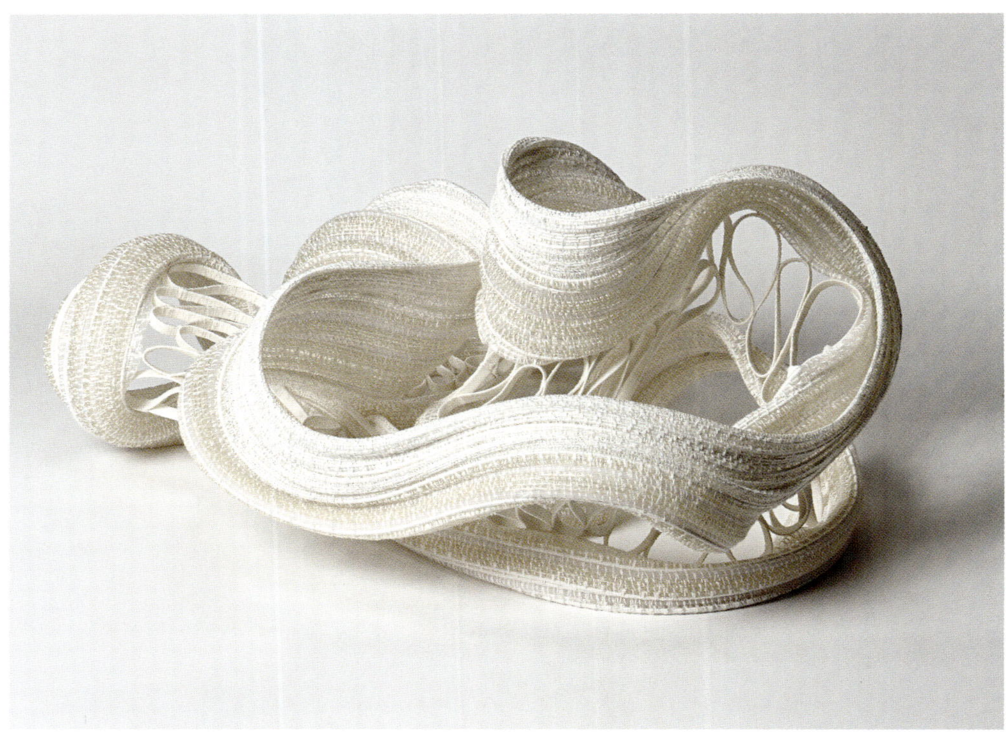

Traced Contour, 2022. Ramie, monofilament, plastic, silicone: 80 × 60 × 31 cm (31" × 23" × 12"). *Photo courtesy of Makoto Yano*

Traced Contour XIII, 2024. Ramie, plastic: 74 × 42 × 38 cm (29" × 16" × 15"). *Photo courtesy of Makoto Yano*

OPPOSITE: *Crossed Helix XIII,* 2024. Ramie, plastic: 100 × 90 × 225 cm (39" × 35" × 88"). *Photo courtesy of Makoto Yano*

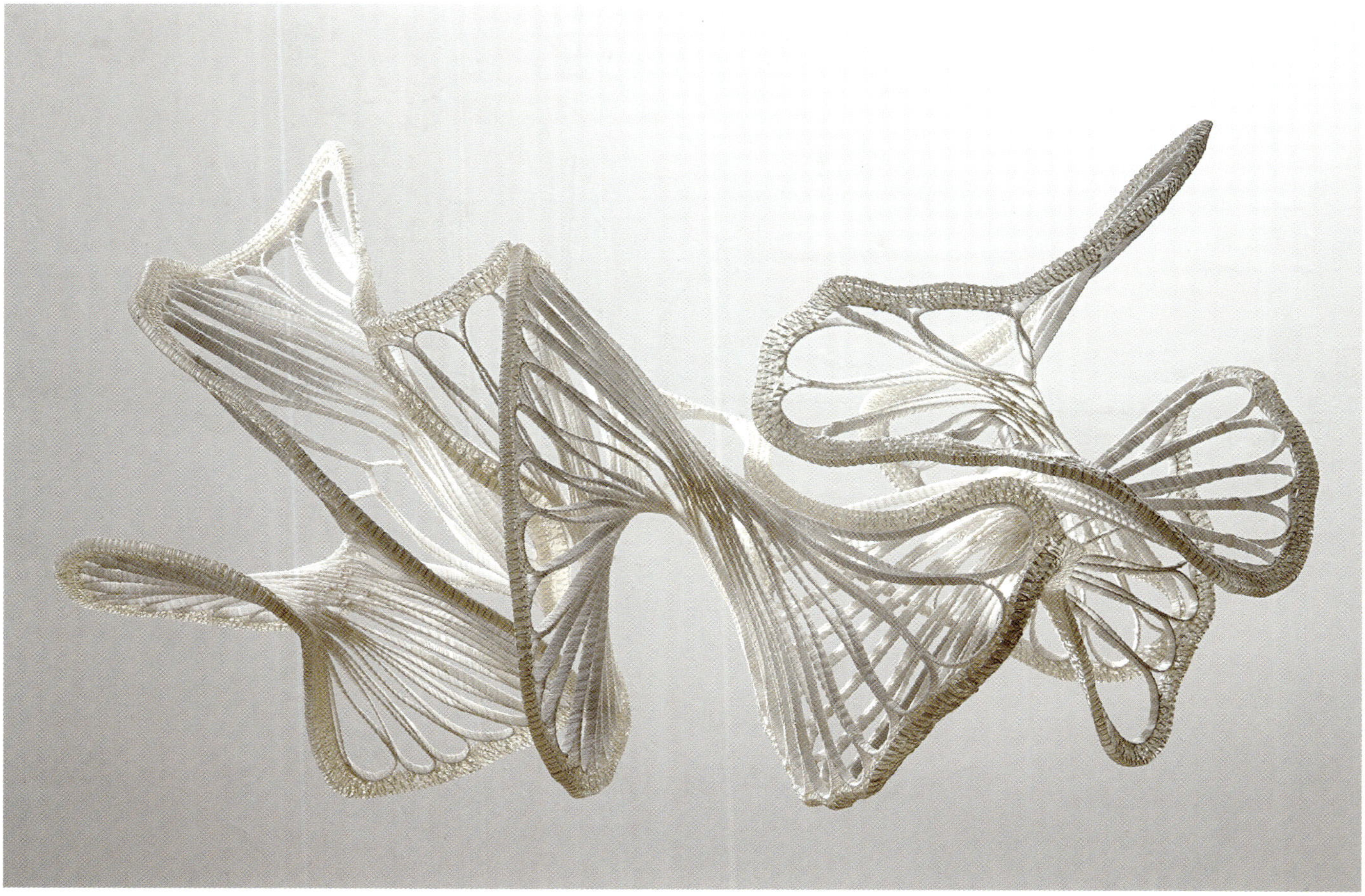

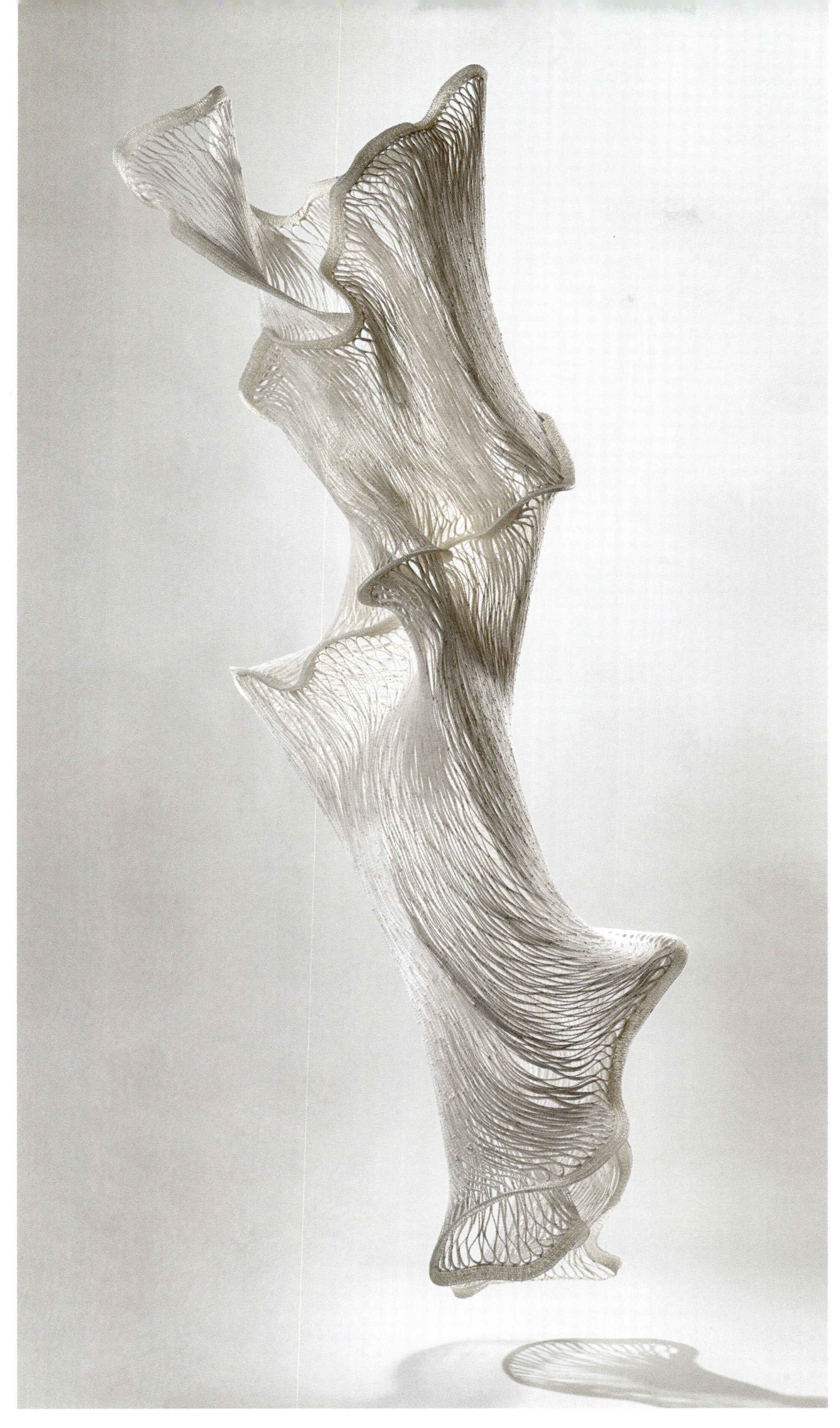

Laura Ellen **BACON**

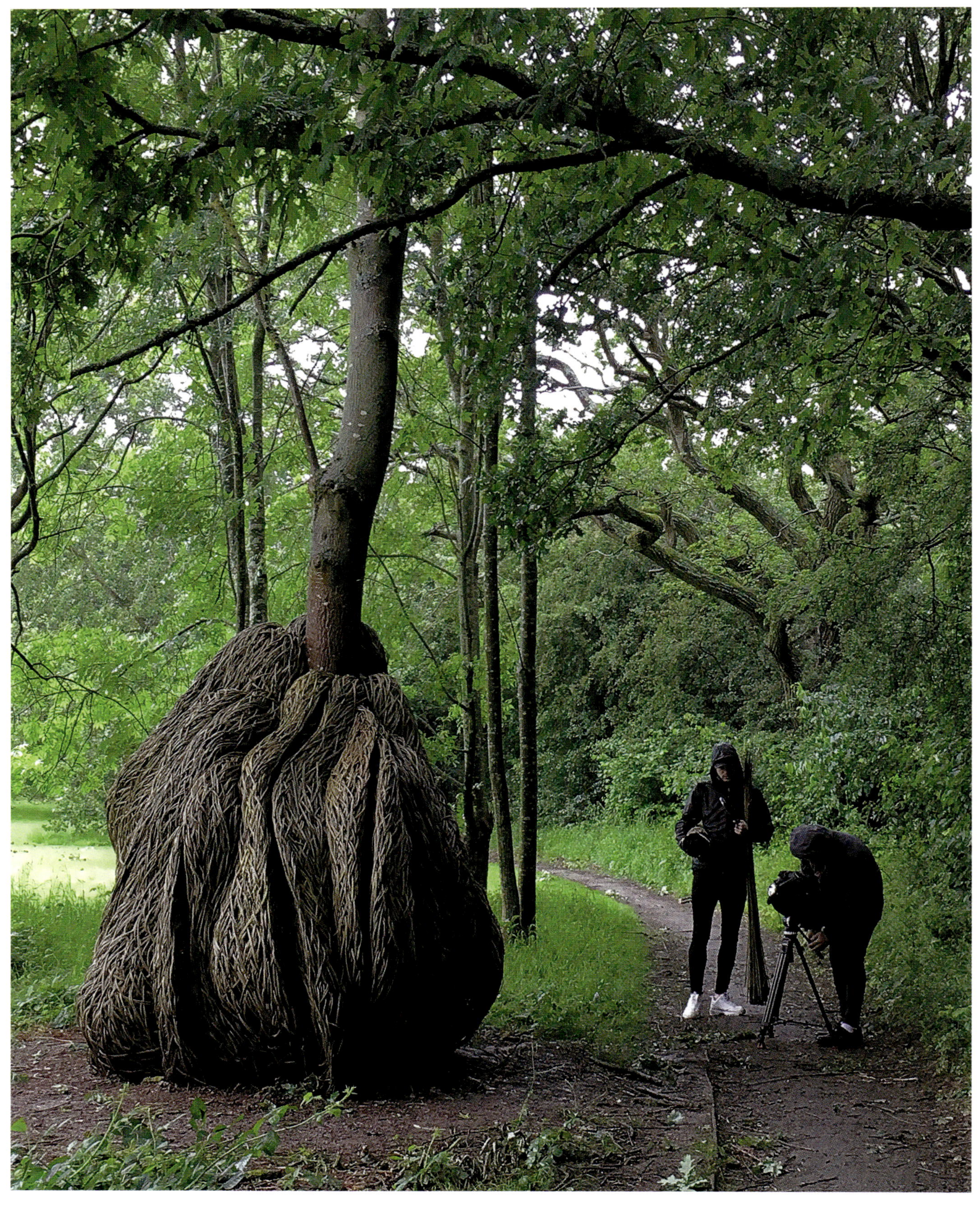

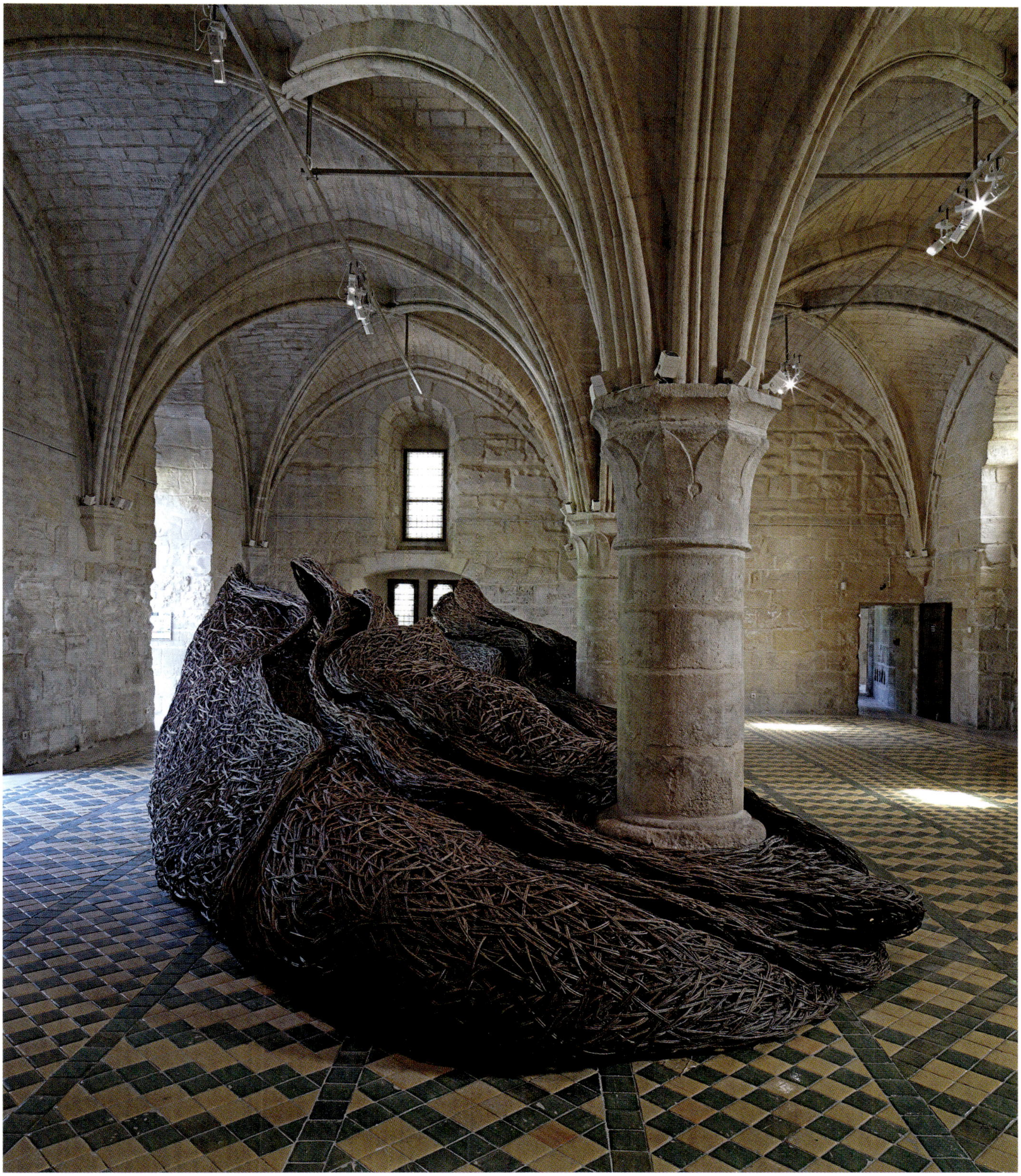

OPPOSITE: *Don't Let Go*, 2019. Installation at University of Warwick, UK. Willow. *Photo courtesy of the artist*

The Feeling Remains, 2022. Installation at Abbaye de Maubuisson, France. Willow and tree branches from the surrounding parkland. *Photo courtesy of Jean-Michel Rousvoal*

Patrick DOUGHERTY

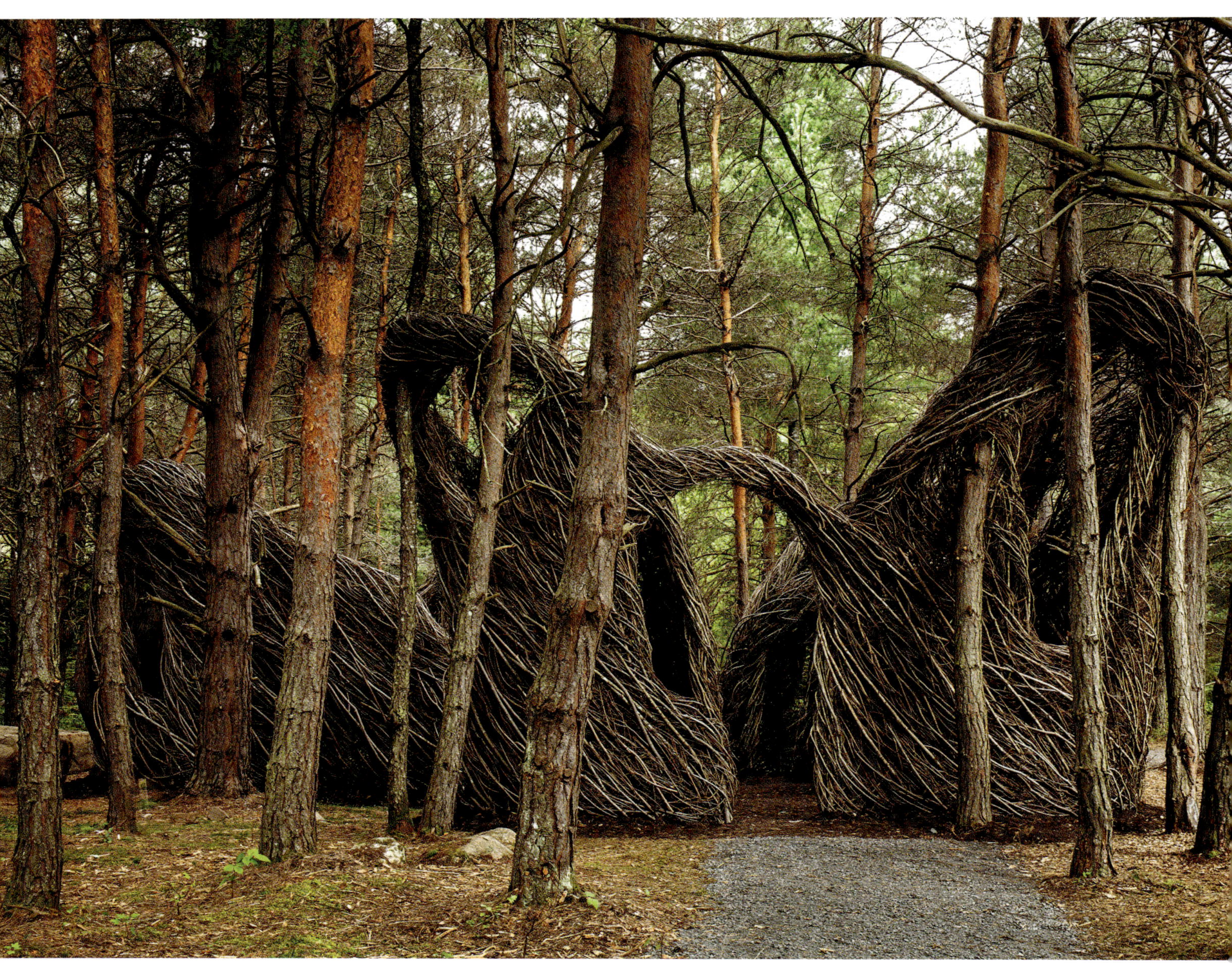

Hopscotch, 2021. Red maple and sugar maple: 9 × 15 × 4 m (30' × 50' × 15'). Installation at The W!ld Center, Tupper Lake, NY. *Courtesy of The W!ld Center*

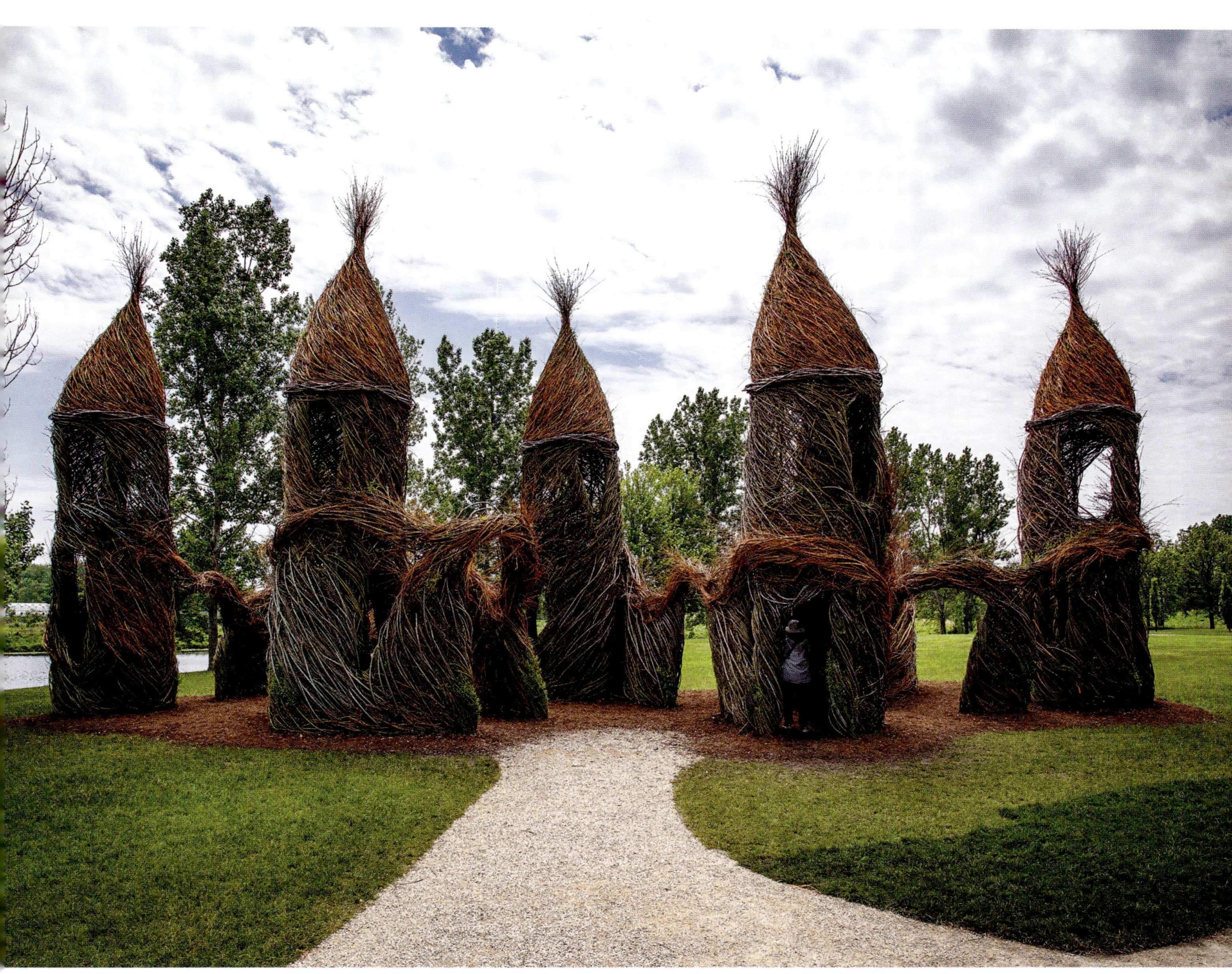

The Rookery, 2022. Willow: 18 × 9 × 6 m (60' × 30' × 21'). Installation at Chicago Botanic Garden, Glencoe, IL. *Courtesy of Chicago Botanic Garden*

Jette MELLGREN

Tunnel of Hope, Ramsau am Dachstein, Austria, 2023. Willow, iron bars: 2.5 × 2 × 16 m (8' × 6' × 52'). *Photos courtesy of the artist*

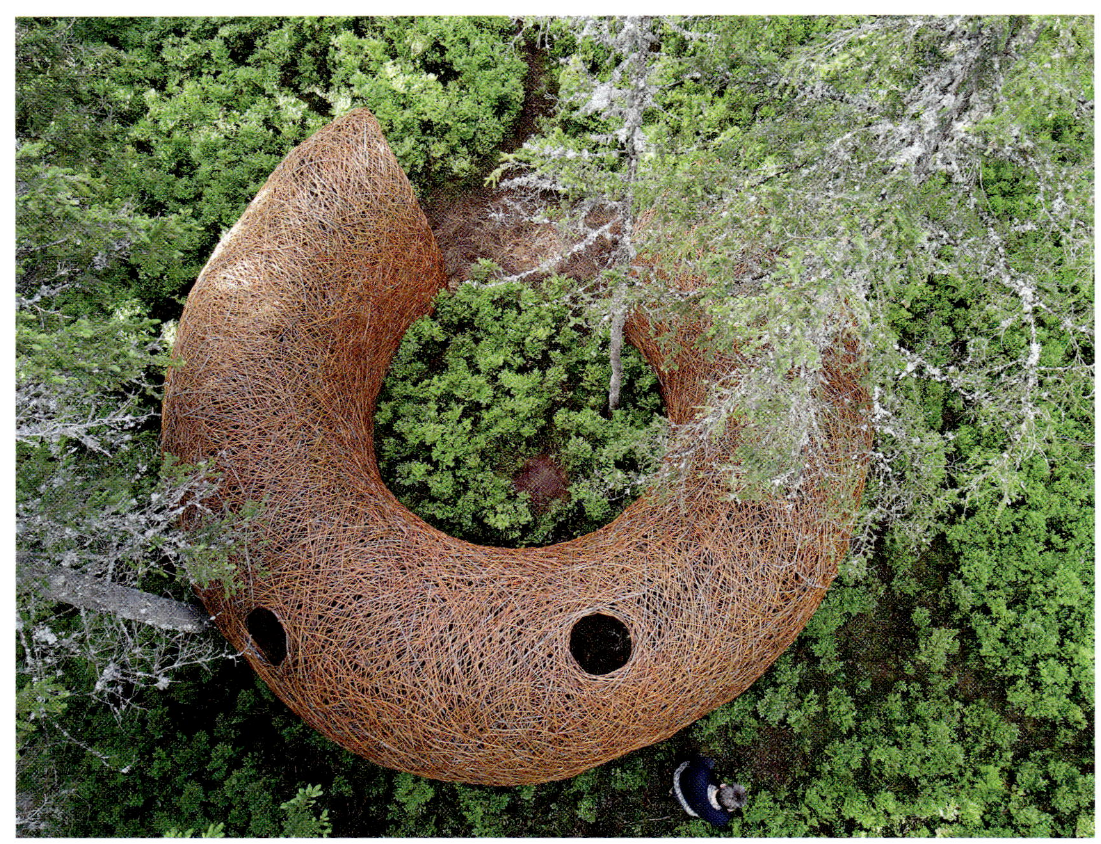

Tunnel of Hope (view 2).

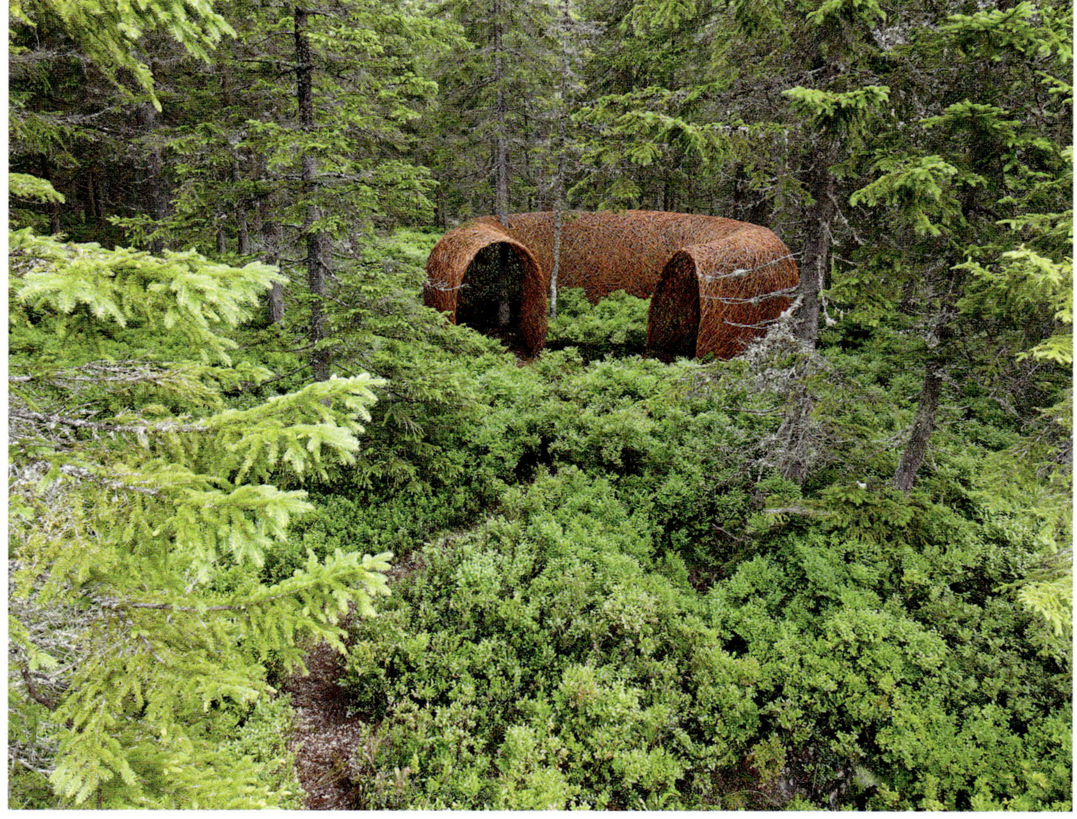

OPPOSITE: *Nesting*, Murun Sum, Khentji Aimag, Mongolia, 2018. Dried sticks found on-site: 110 cm (43") diameter. *Photo courtesy of the artist*

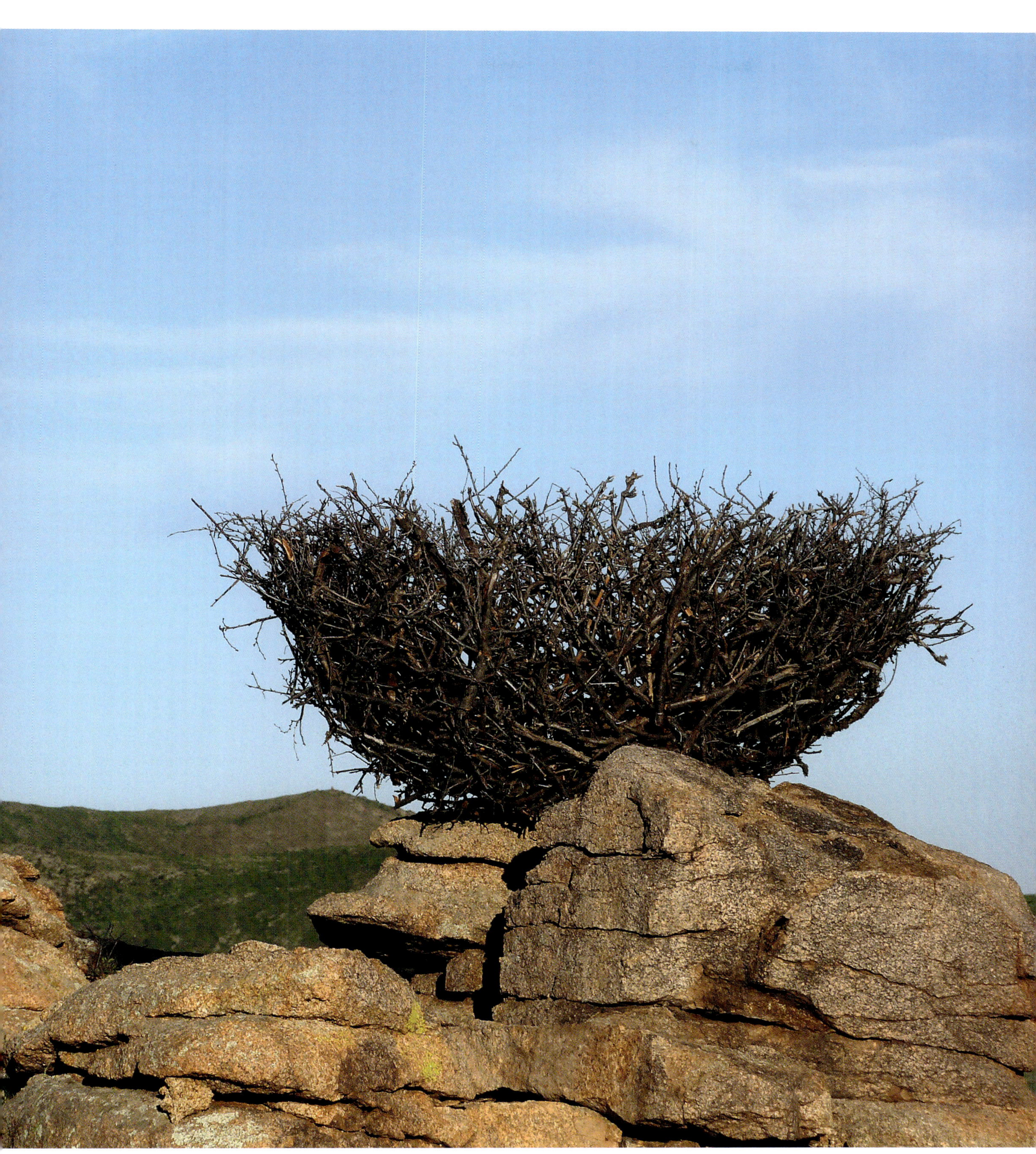

Roger RIGORTH

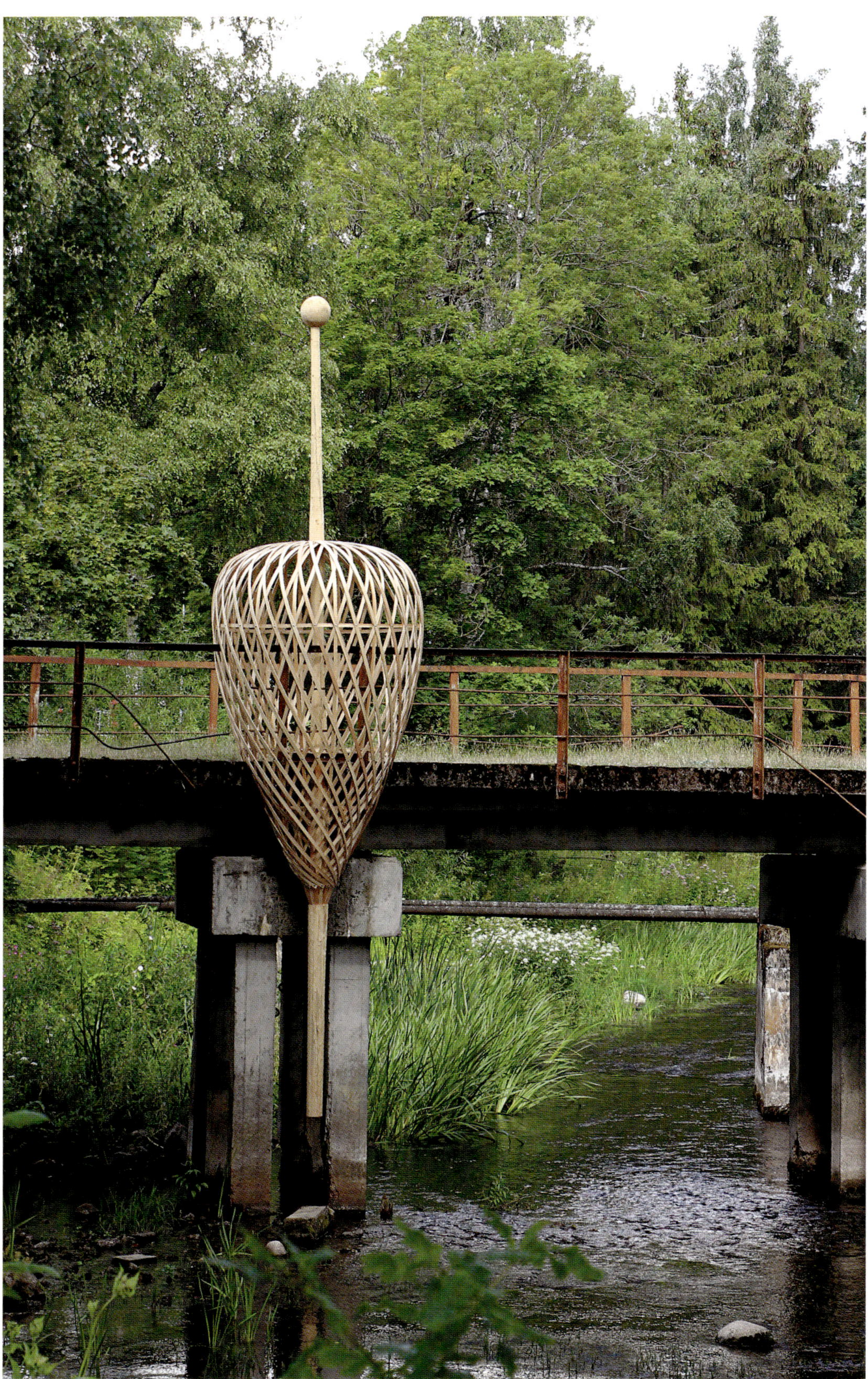

Kohila Dragon, TAKKK International Symposium of Environmental Art, Kohila, Estonia, 2022. Wood: 700 × 140 × 140 cm (275" × 55" × 55"). *Photo courtesy of the artist*

OPPOSITE: *The Giant Matador,* International Symposium "Dichter ob het land," Schokland, Holland, 2023. Harvester, steel, hay, reed: 800 × 400 × 650 cm (315" × 157" × 256"). *Photo courtesy of the artist*

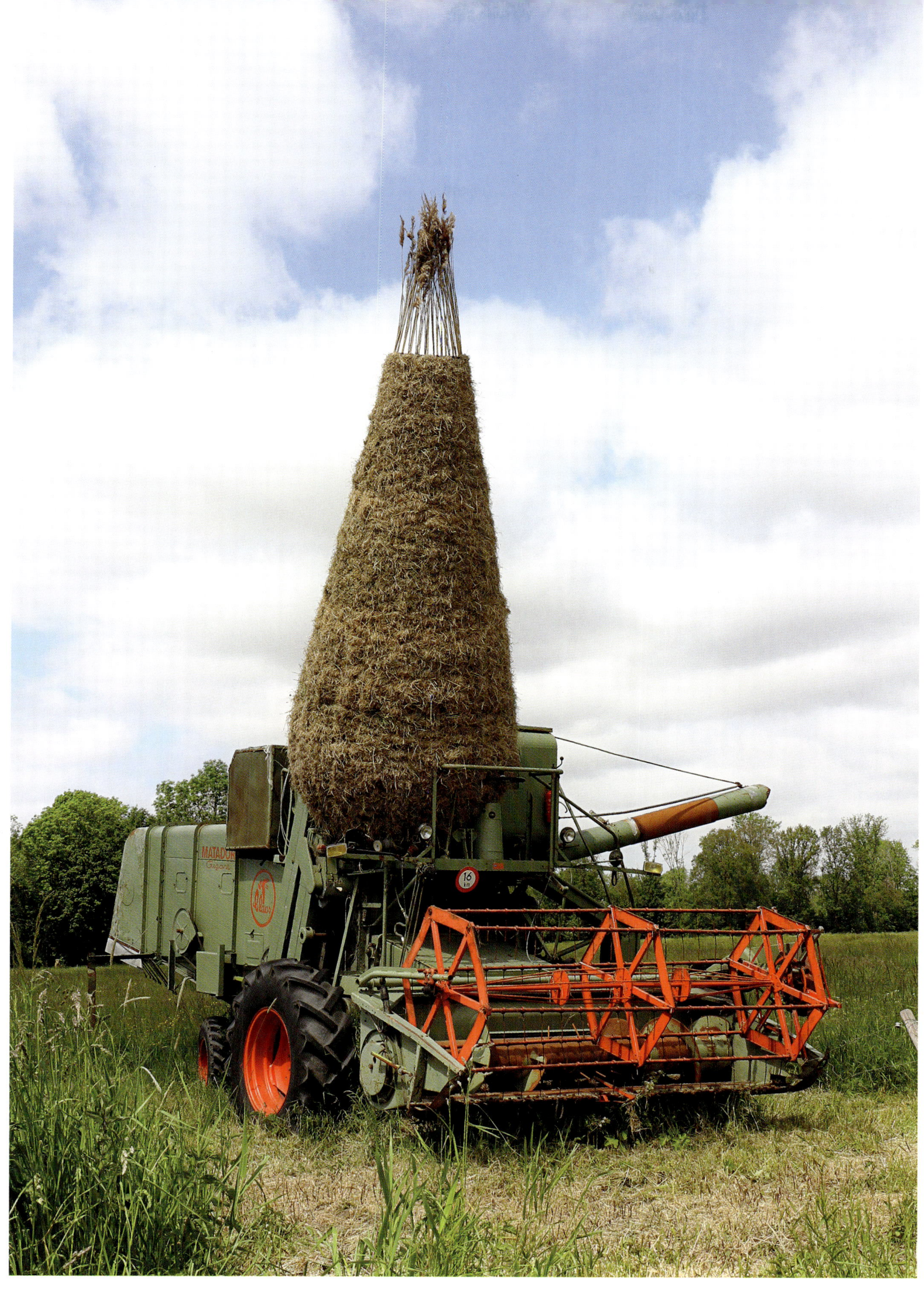

Karin VAN DER MOLEN

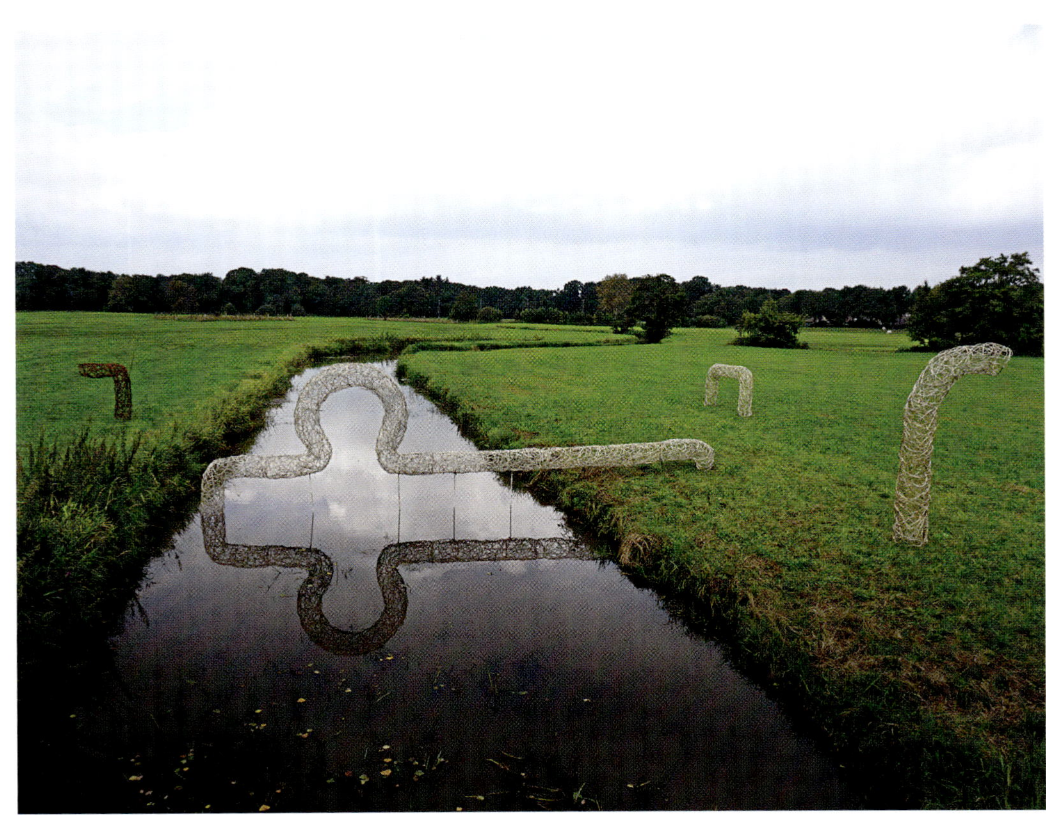

Ceci n'est pas une pipe, 2017. Steel, willow: 300 × 1,000 × 5,000 cm (118" × 394" × 1,986"). *Photo courtesy of the artist*

Cellule, 2023. Steel, willow, reeds: 250 × 275 × 150 cm (98" × 108" × 59"). *Photo courtesy of the artist*

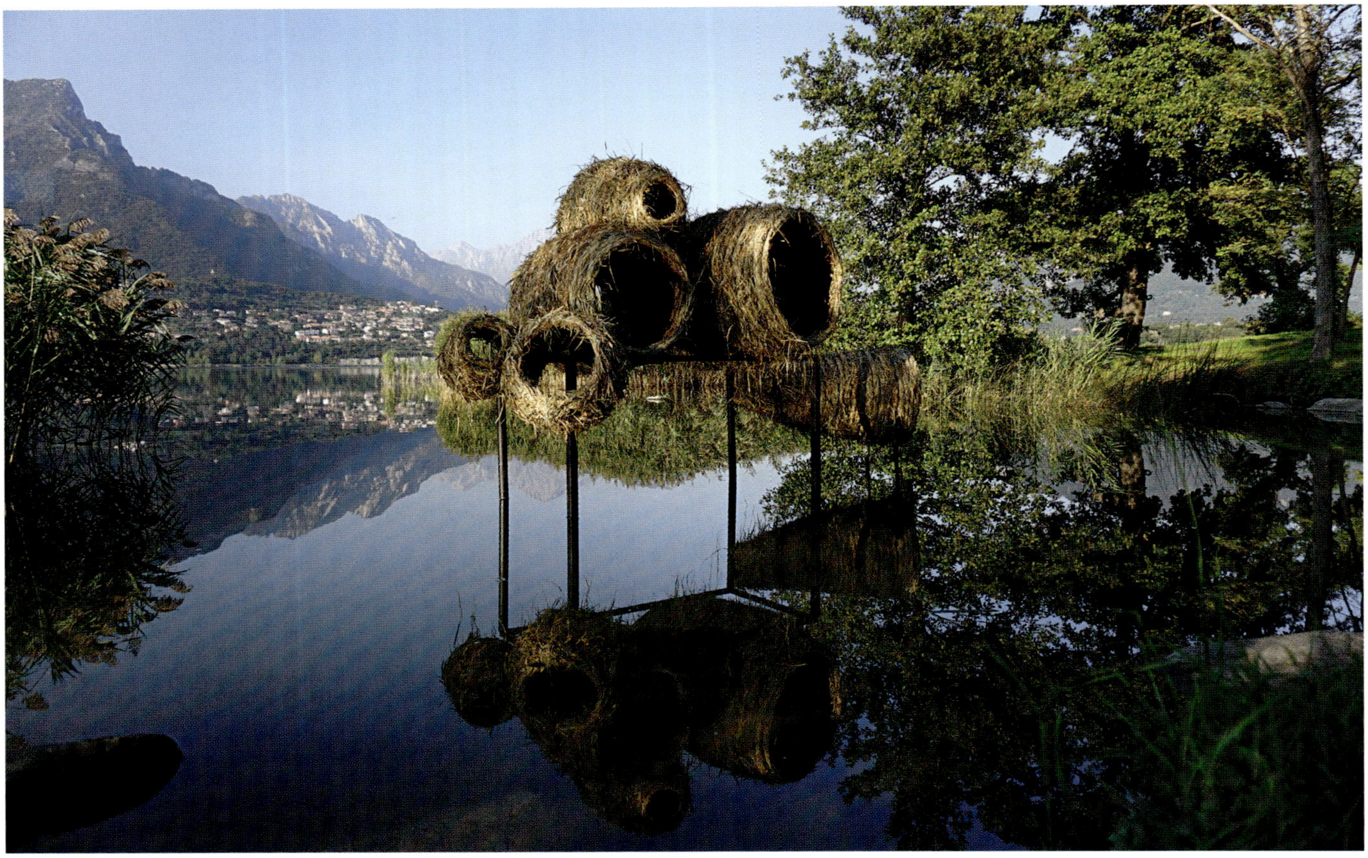

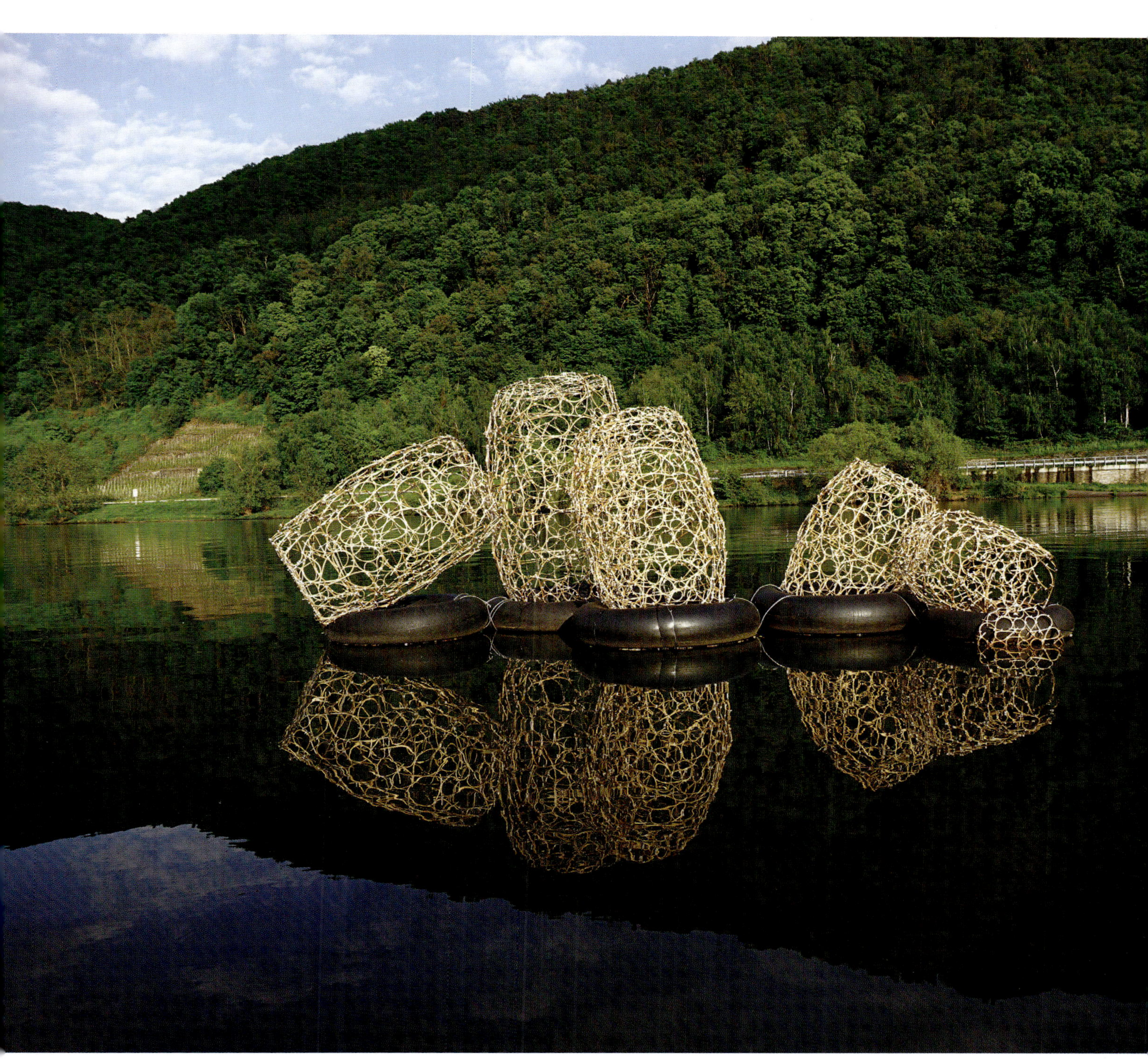

The Remains, 2022. Willow, steel, tubes: 150 × 350 × 230 cm (59" × 138" × 90"). *Photo courtesy of the artist*

Gjertrud HALS

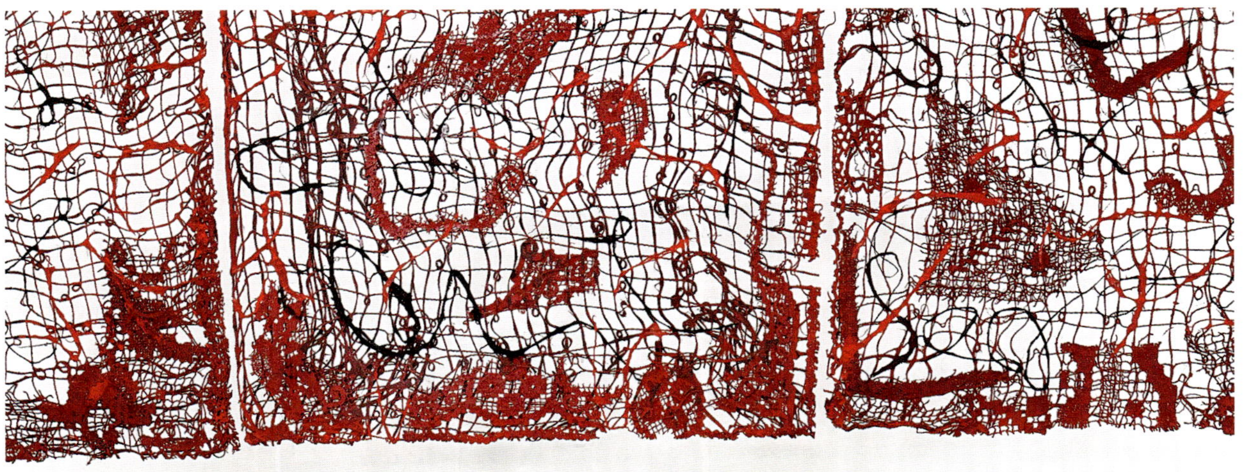

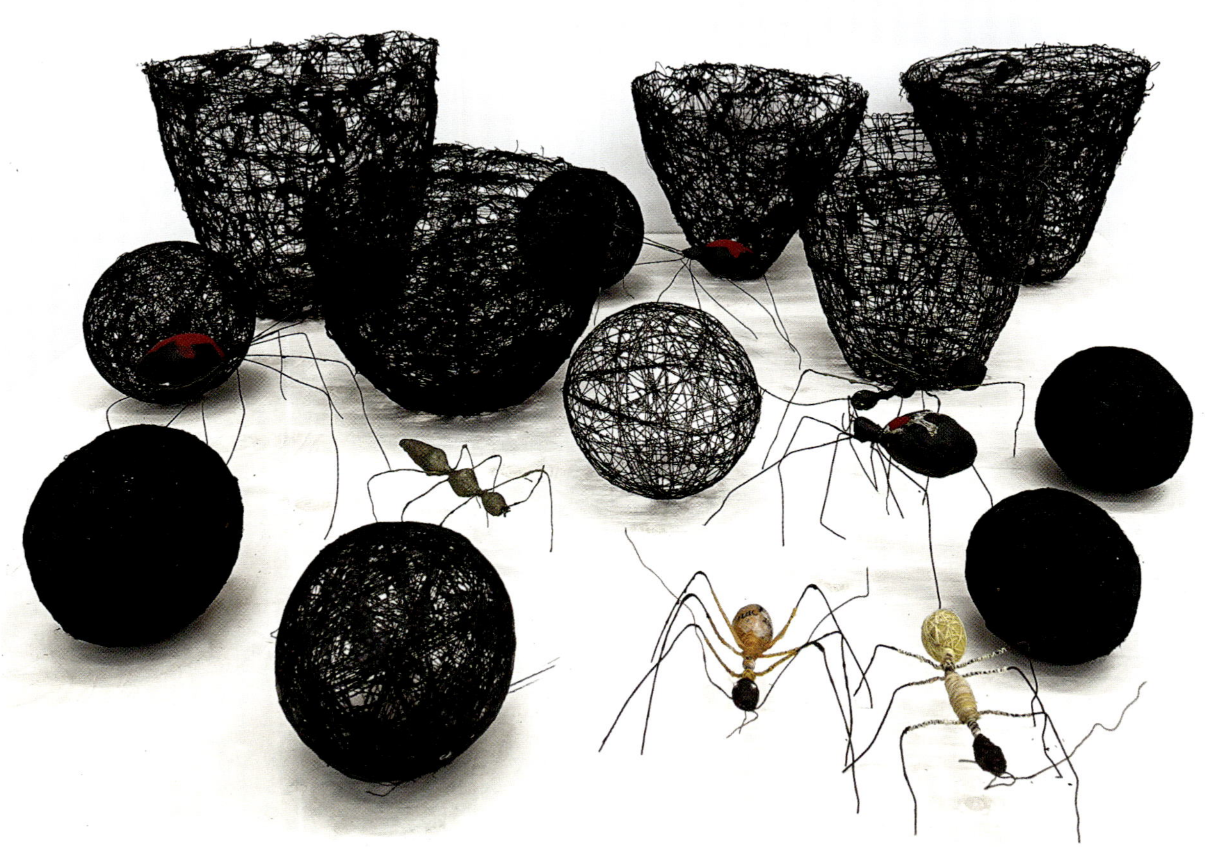

Root Baskets, 2021. Metal wire, cotton and linen thread, resin, glue, pigment: 23 × 22 cm (9" × 8")–27 × 26 cm (10.5" × 10"), balls 11 × 13 cm (4" × 5"), spiders 15 × 20 cm (6" × 7"), ants 13 × 13 cm (5" × 5"). *Agnus Dei* wall hanging above. *Photo courtesy of the artist*

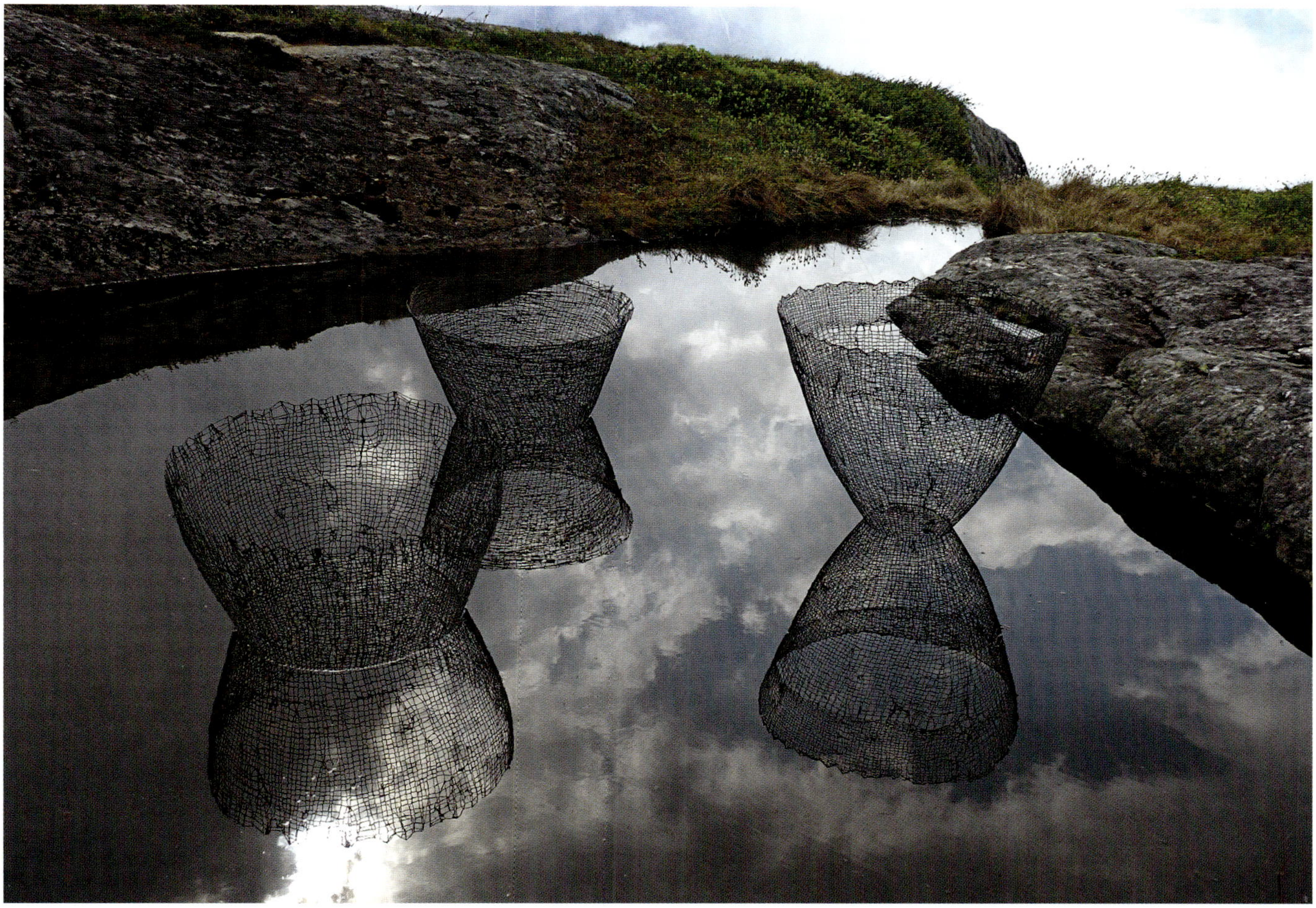

Ultima in the Mountains, 2015. Linen thread, paper pulp, resin: 95 × 87–99 × 97 cm (37" × 34"–39" × 38"). *Photo courtesy of the artist*

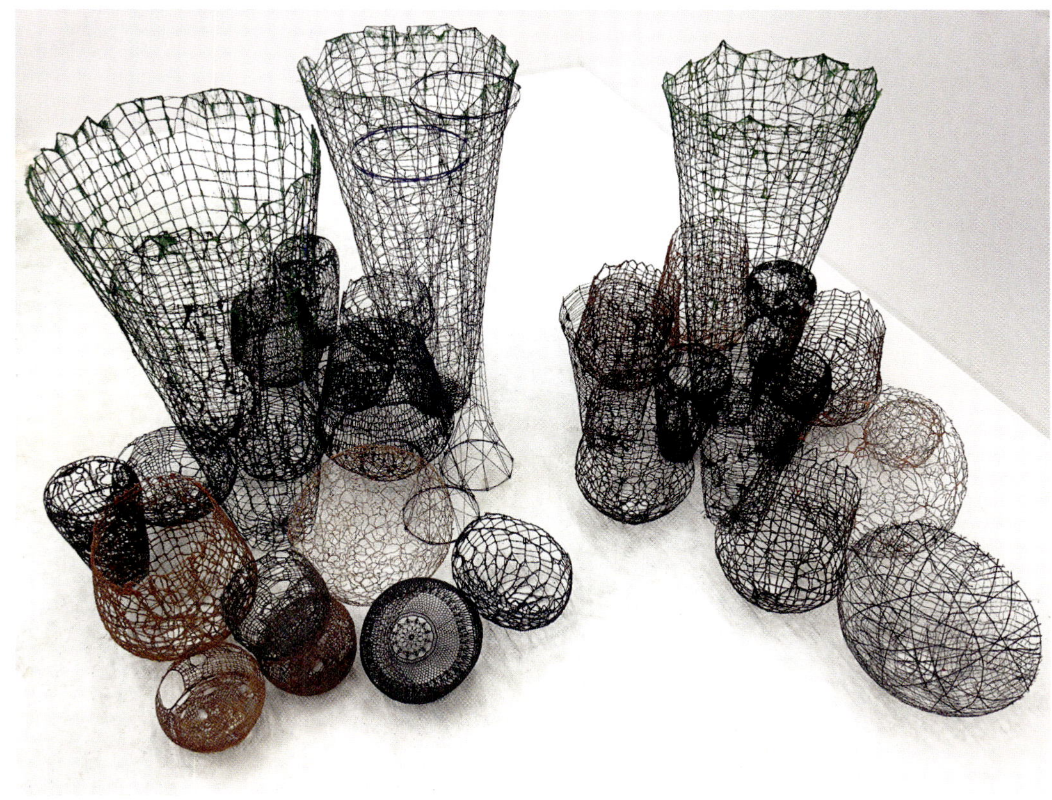

Baskets in the Studio, 2017–21. Metal wire, roots and twigs, paper pulp, cellulose glue, cotton and linen threads, resin, pigment: 23 × 22–120 × 65 cm (9" × 8"–47" × 25"). *Photo courtesy of the artist*

Cheng-Tsung **FENG**

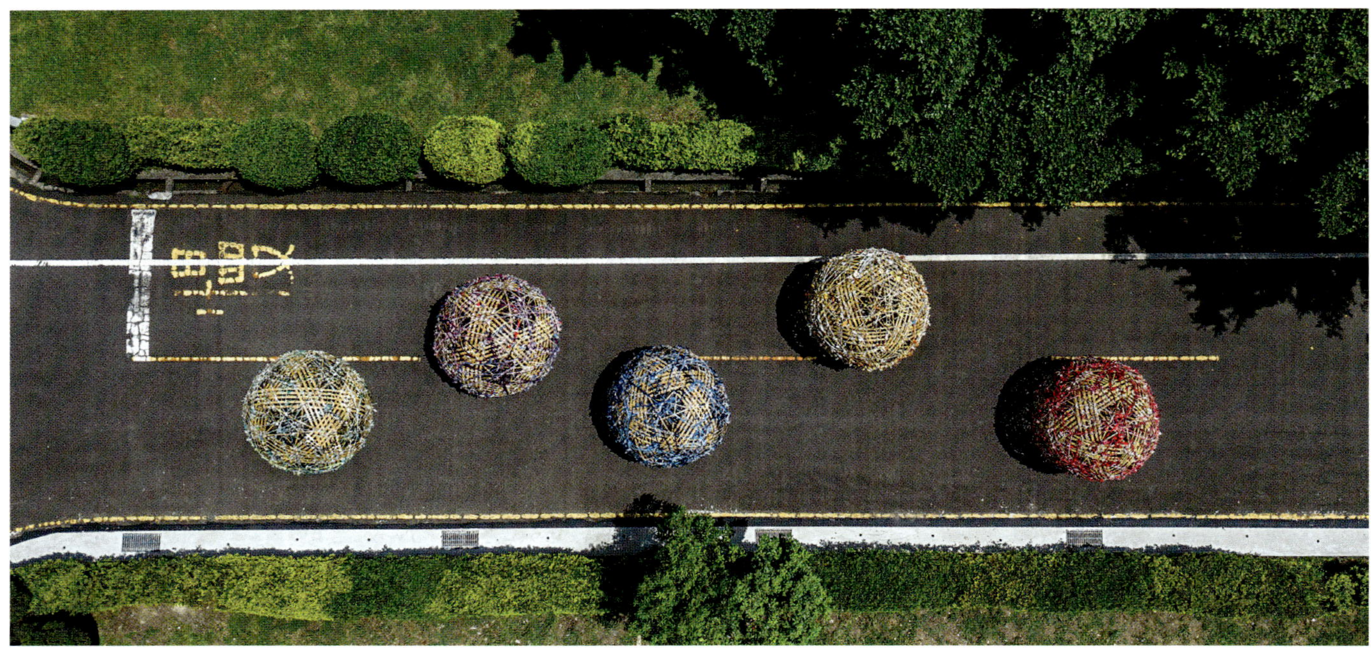

Rolling Plan, 2020. Rattan, recycled clothing: dimensions variable. *Photos by Po Han Chen, courtesy of the artist*

Rolling Plan (detail).

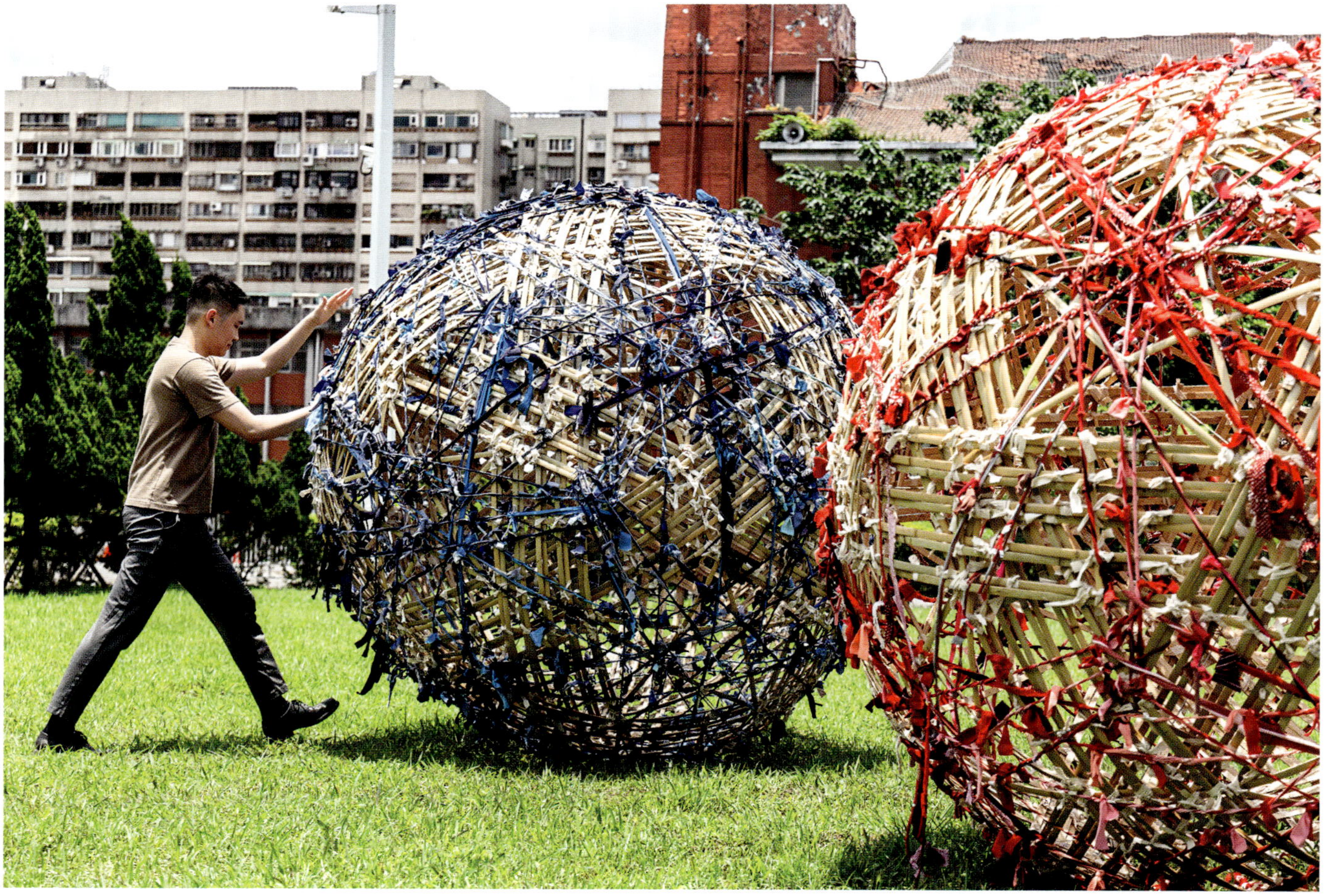

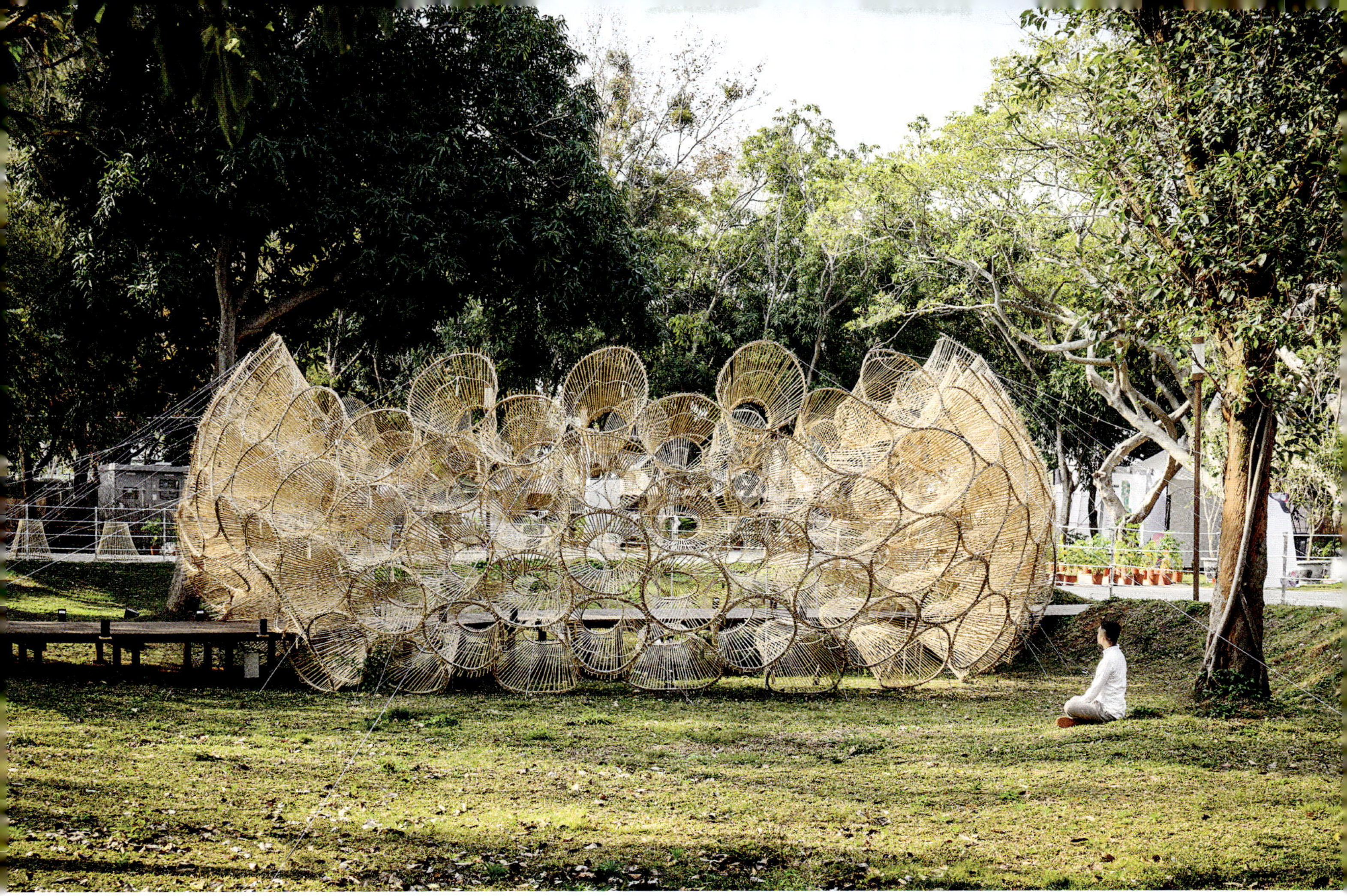

Fish Trap House IV Houli, 2020. Bamboo, rattan, stainless steel: 600 × 1,200 × 1,200 cm (236" × 472" × 472"). *Photos by Yi-Hsien Lee, courtesy of the artist*

Fish Trap House IV Houli (detail).

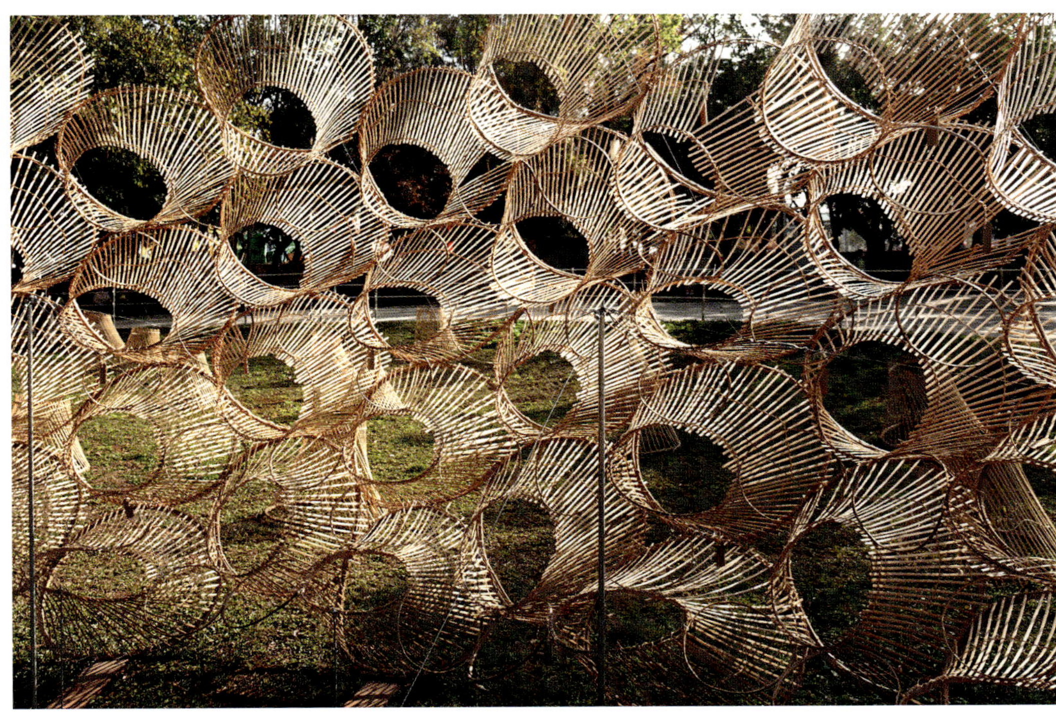

Leeroy NEW

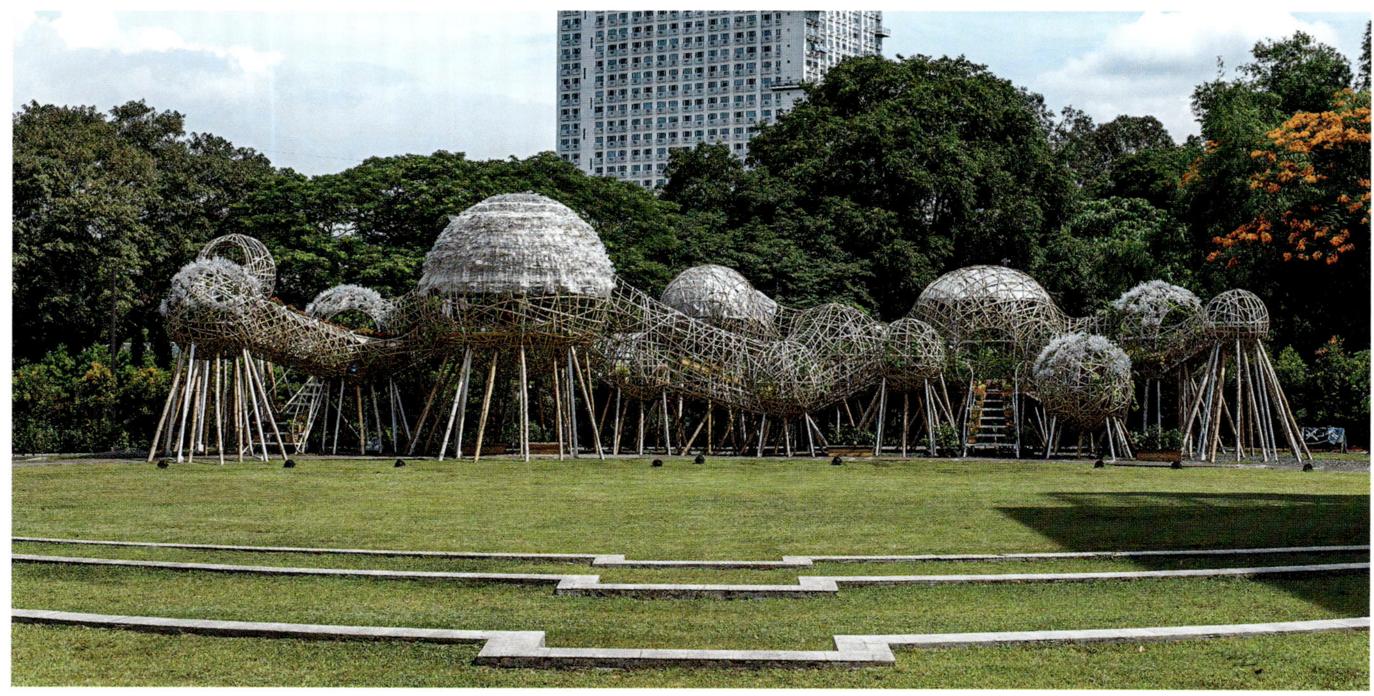

Mebuyan Colony, Arete, Ateneo De Manila University, 2022. Bamboo, found materials: 7 × 25 m (23' × 82'). *Photos courtesy of ADMU and the artist*

Mebuyan Colony (detail).

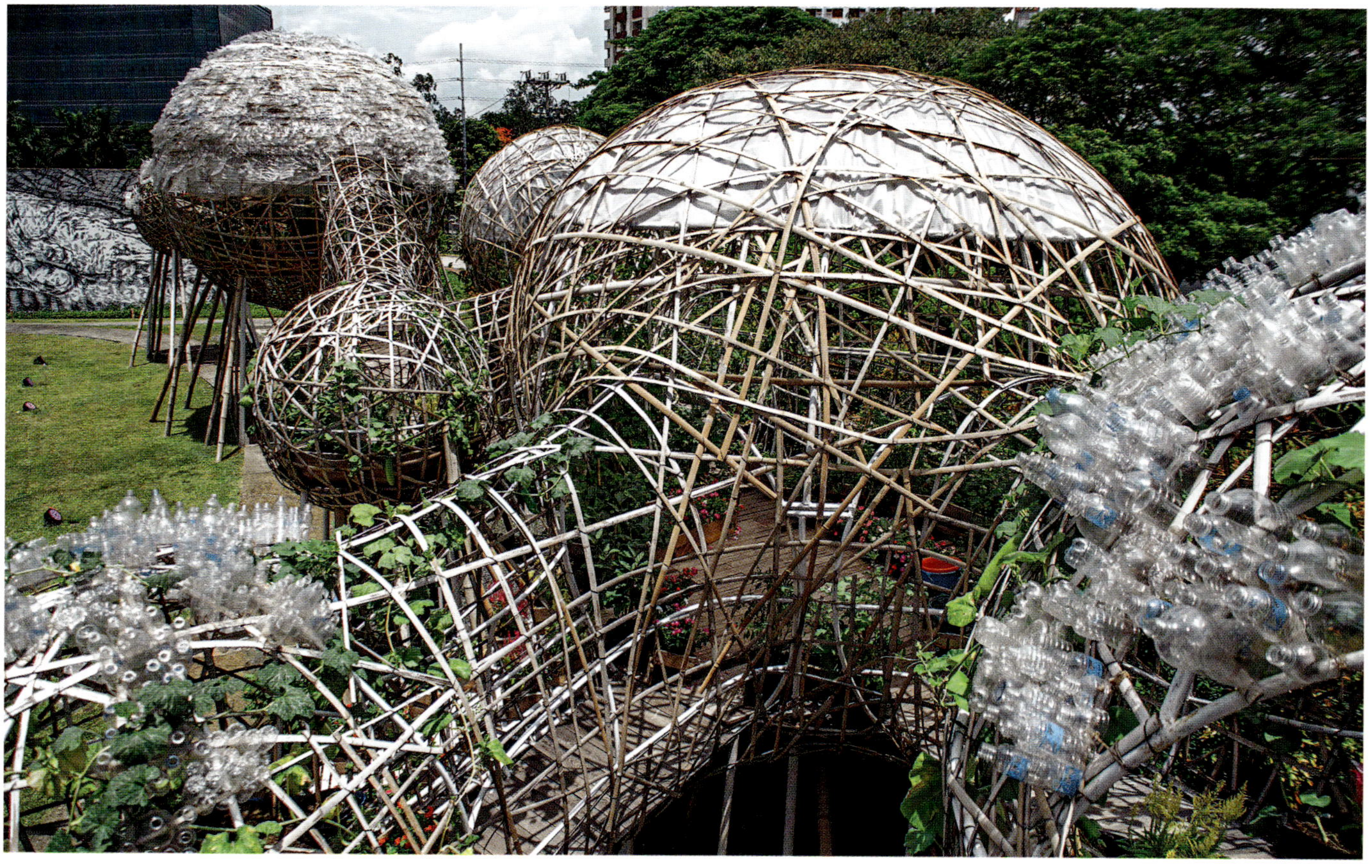

The Arks of Gimokudan, Somerset House, London, 2022. Bamboo, found materials: dimensions variable. *Photos by Ben Queenborough, courtesy of Somerset House*

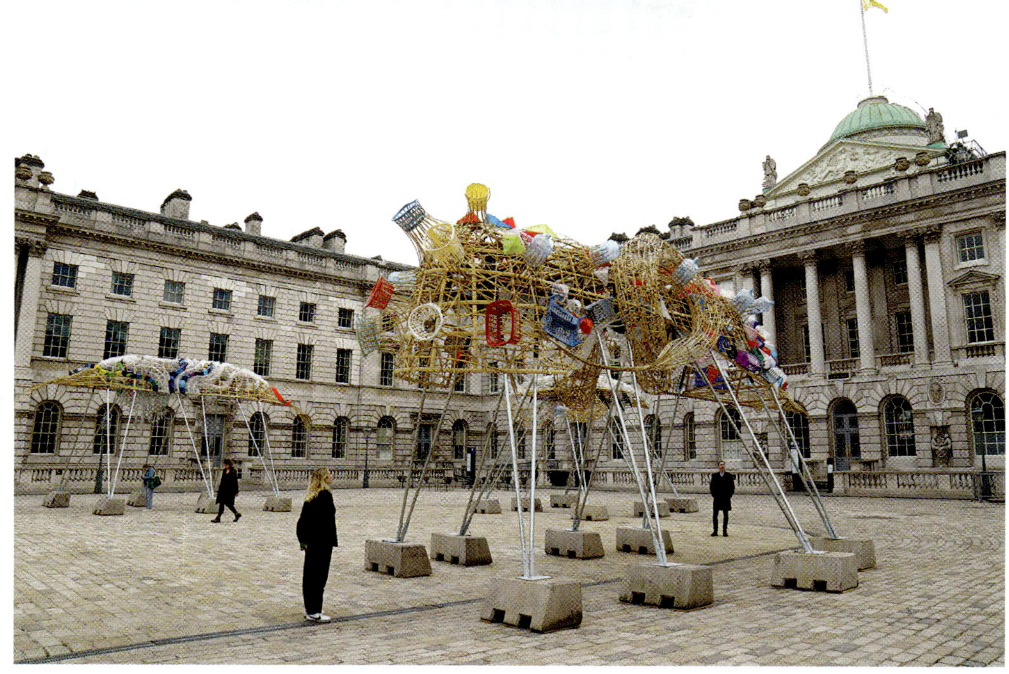

The Arks of Gimokudan (detail).

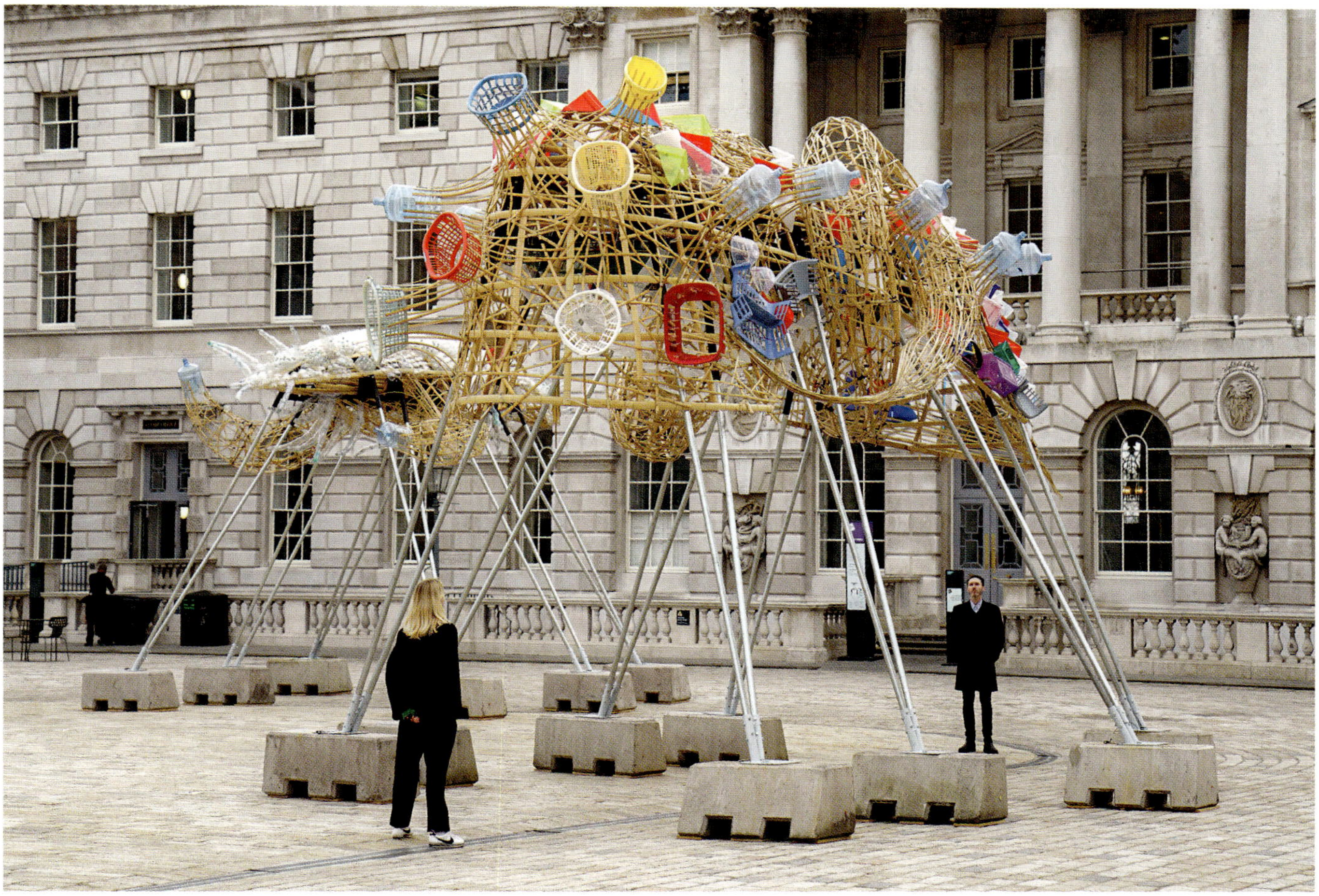

LEE Kuei-Chih

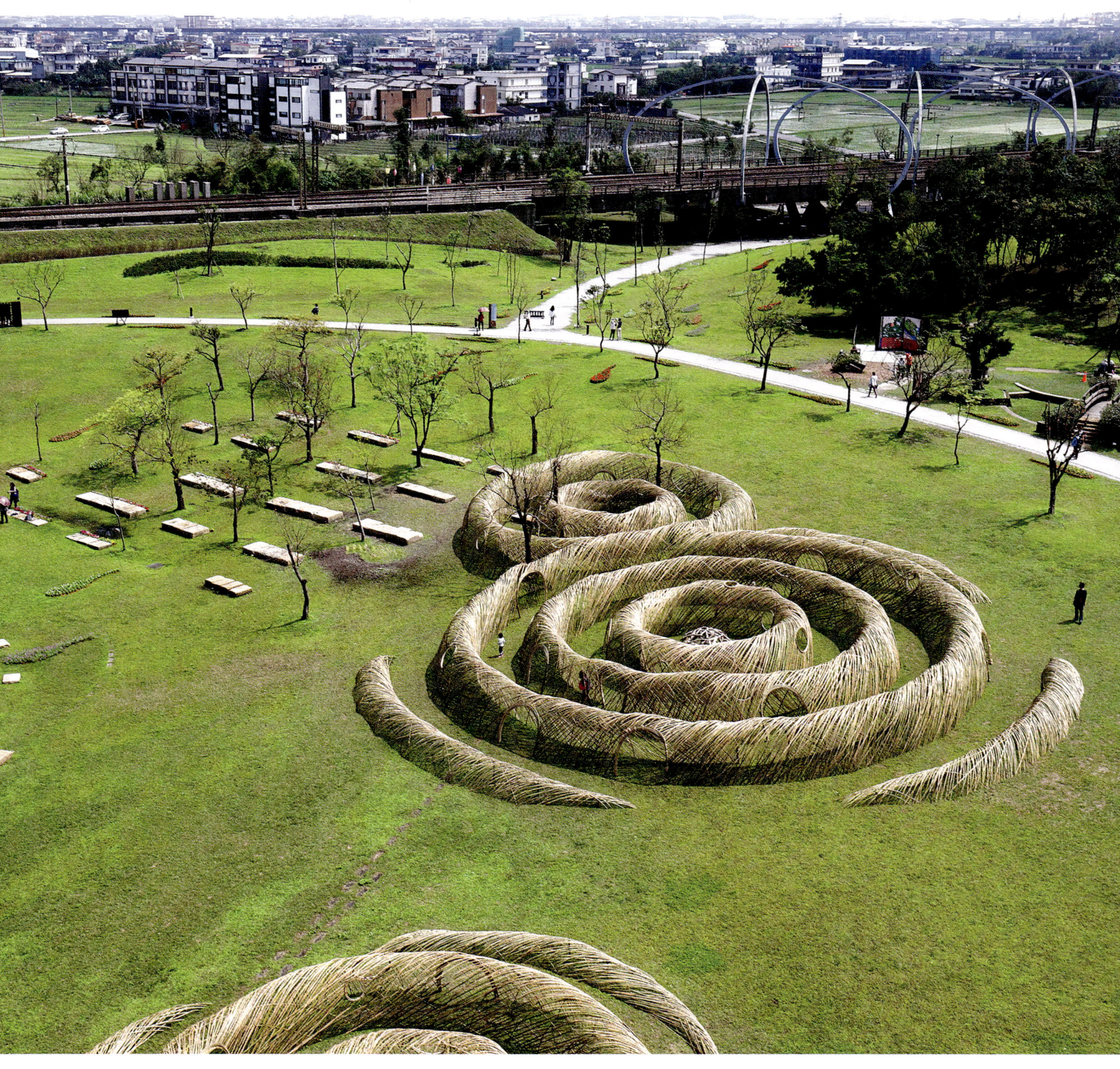

The Ripple Maze, 2017. Bamboo, driftwood: 65 × 45 × 2.5 m (213' × 147' × 8'). *Photo courtesy of the artist*

OPPOSITE, TOP: *Chenglong Shelter*, 2018. Bamboo, branches, driftwood, oystershell, sisal rope: 20 × 18 × 4 m (65' × 59' × 13'). *Photo courtesy of the artist*

OPPOSITE, BOTTOM: *Transition*, 2020. Steel bar, driftwood, bamboo, marine waste, cloth rope: 30 × 16 × 4 m (98' × 52' × 13'). *Photo courtesy of the artist*

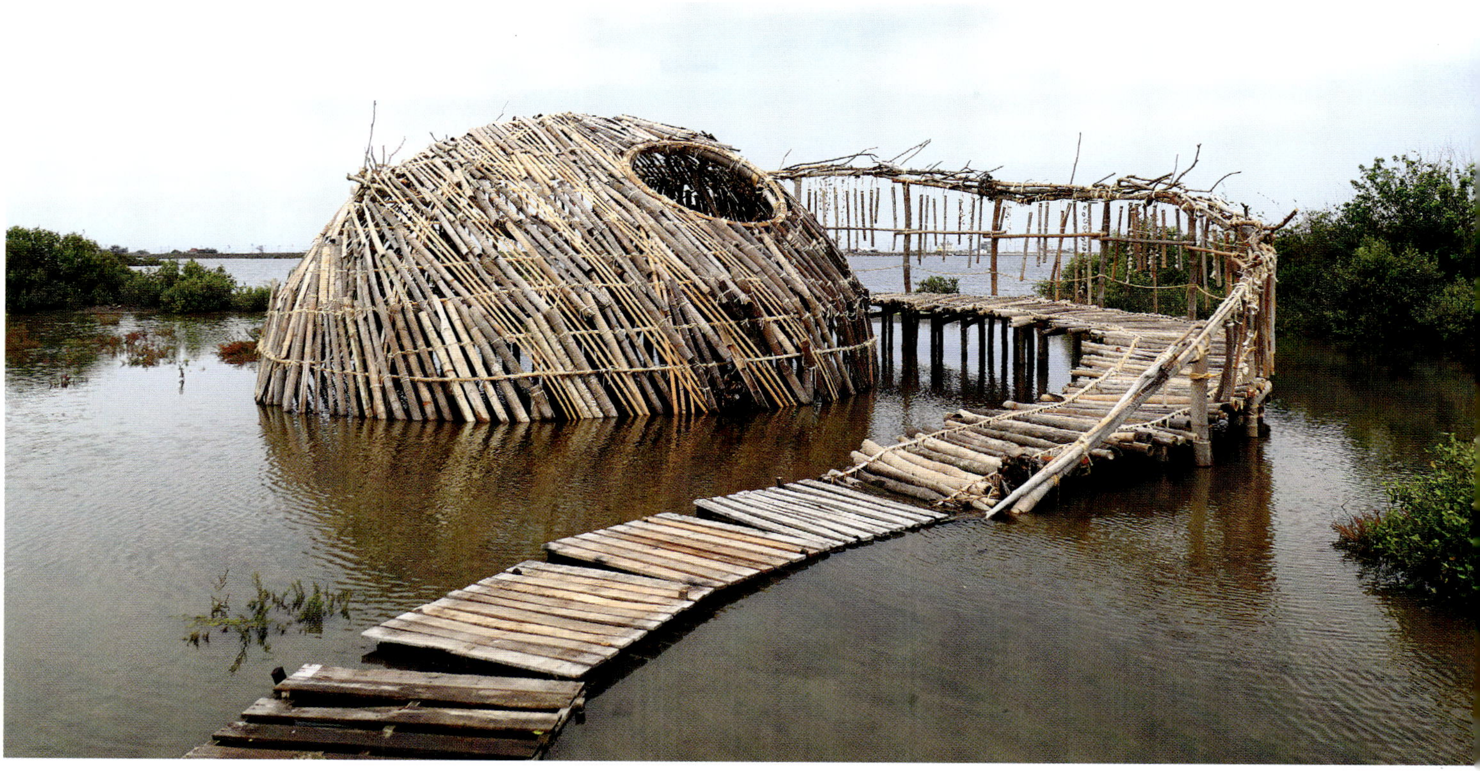

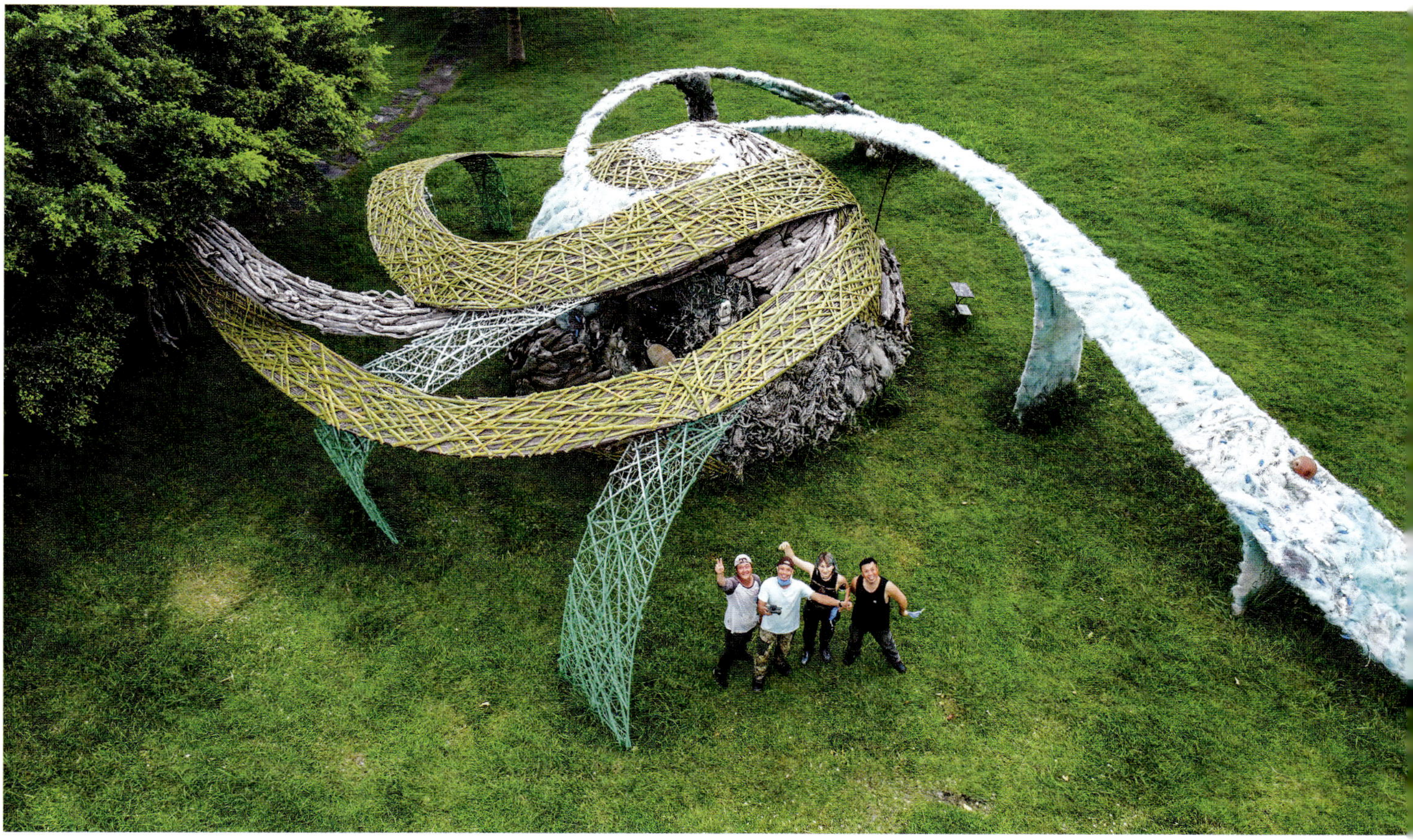

Edgardo **MADANES**

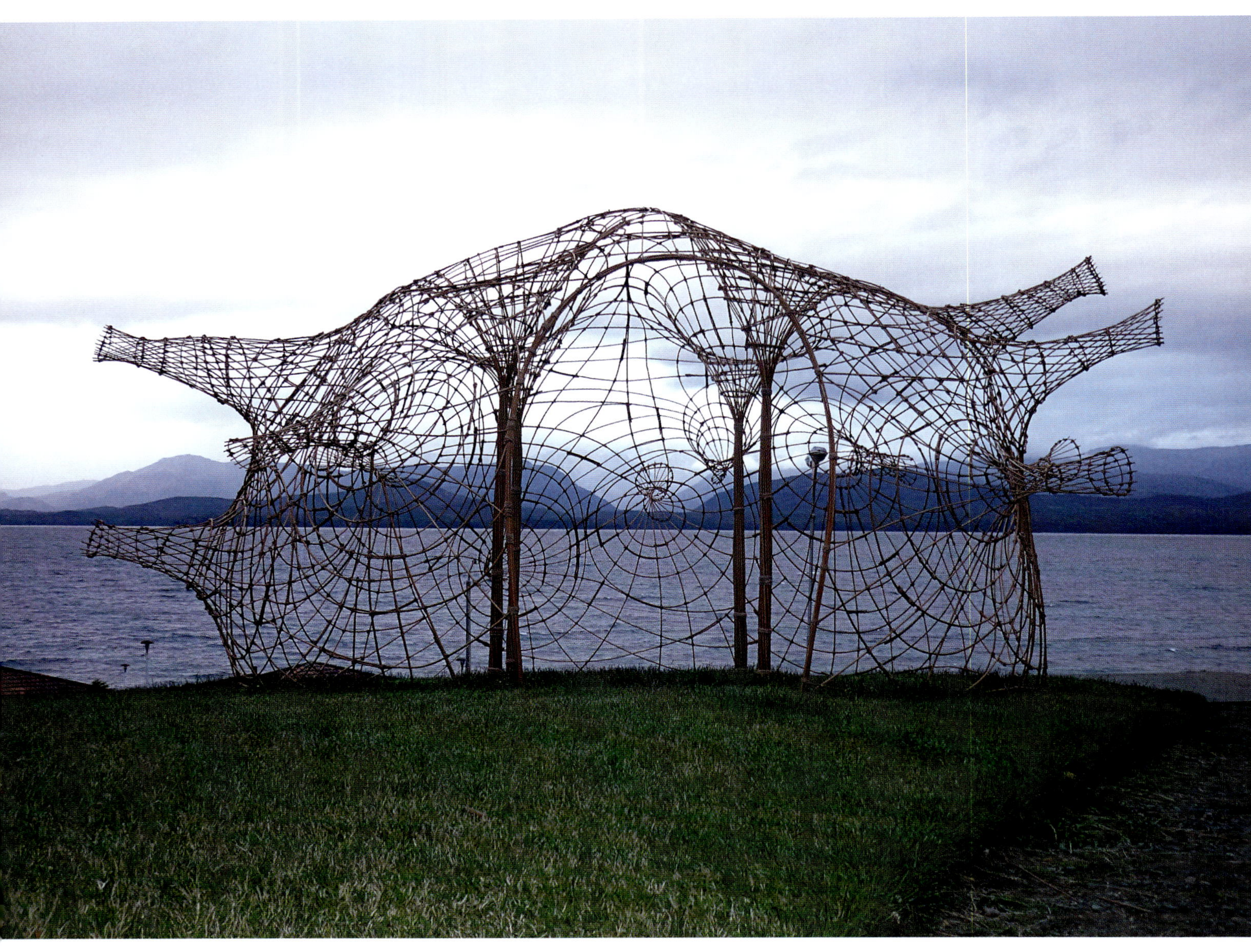

Mirador, 2014. Willow wicker: 3 × 6 m (10' × 19'). *Photo courtesy of the artist*

OPPOSITE: *Proyecto para las nubes*, 2020. Willow wicker, rope, silo, text, lights: 13 × 8 m (42' × 26'). *Photo courtesy of Federico Kremenchuzky*

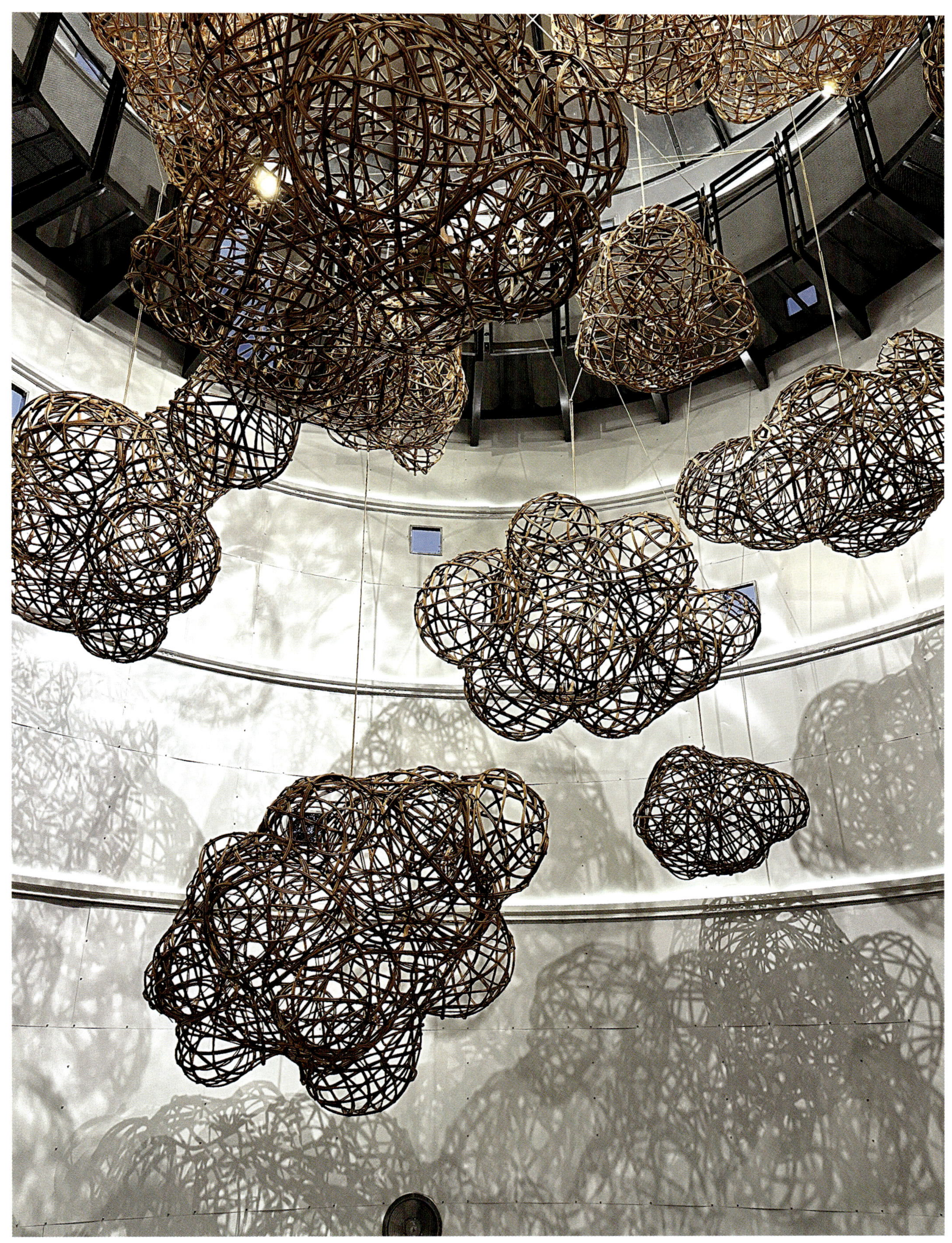

Asim WAQIF

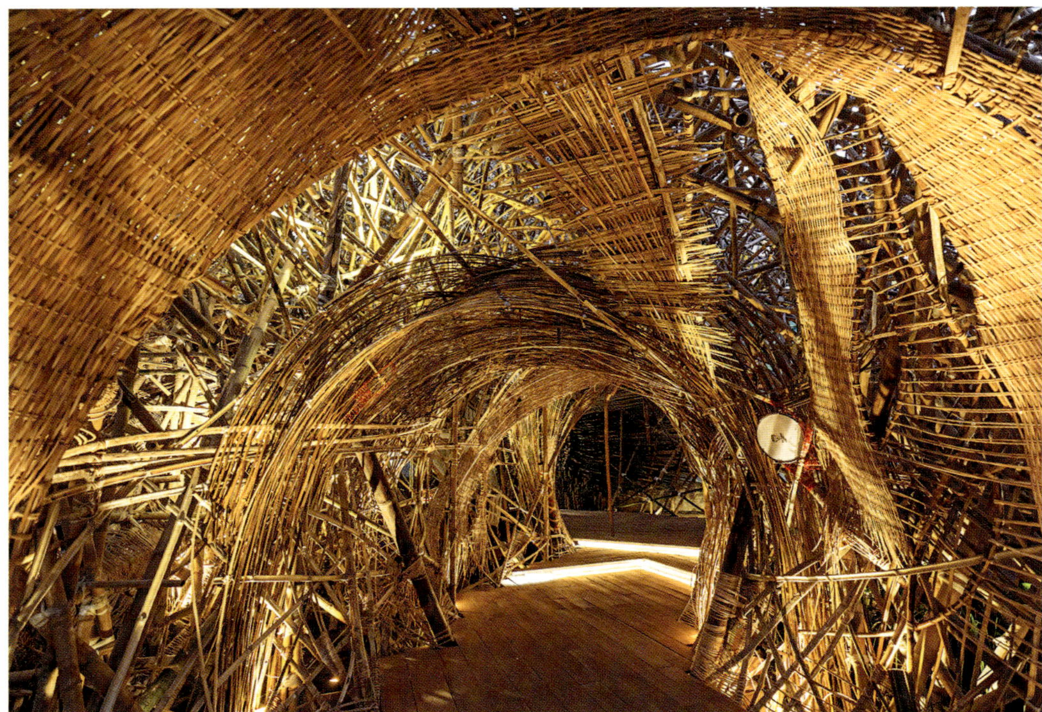

লয় *Loy* (entrance view), 2019. Bamboo, cane, cloth, rope, with interactive electronic and acoustic system. Durga Puja Pandal commissioned by Arjunpur Amra Sabai Club, Kolkata. Asim Waqif in collaboration with Ashhar Farooqui, Anpu Varkey, Harry Samson, Hoang Quyet, Shantanu Heisnam, Nadeem Waqif, Pradeep Patra, and Khokon Da and his team of bamboo and cane artisans. *Photos by Vivian Sarky, courtesy of the artist*

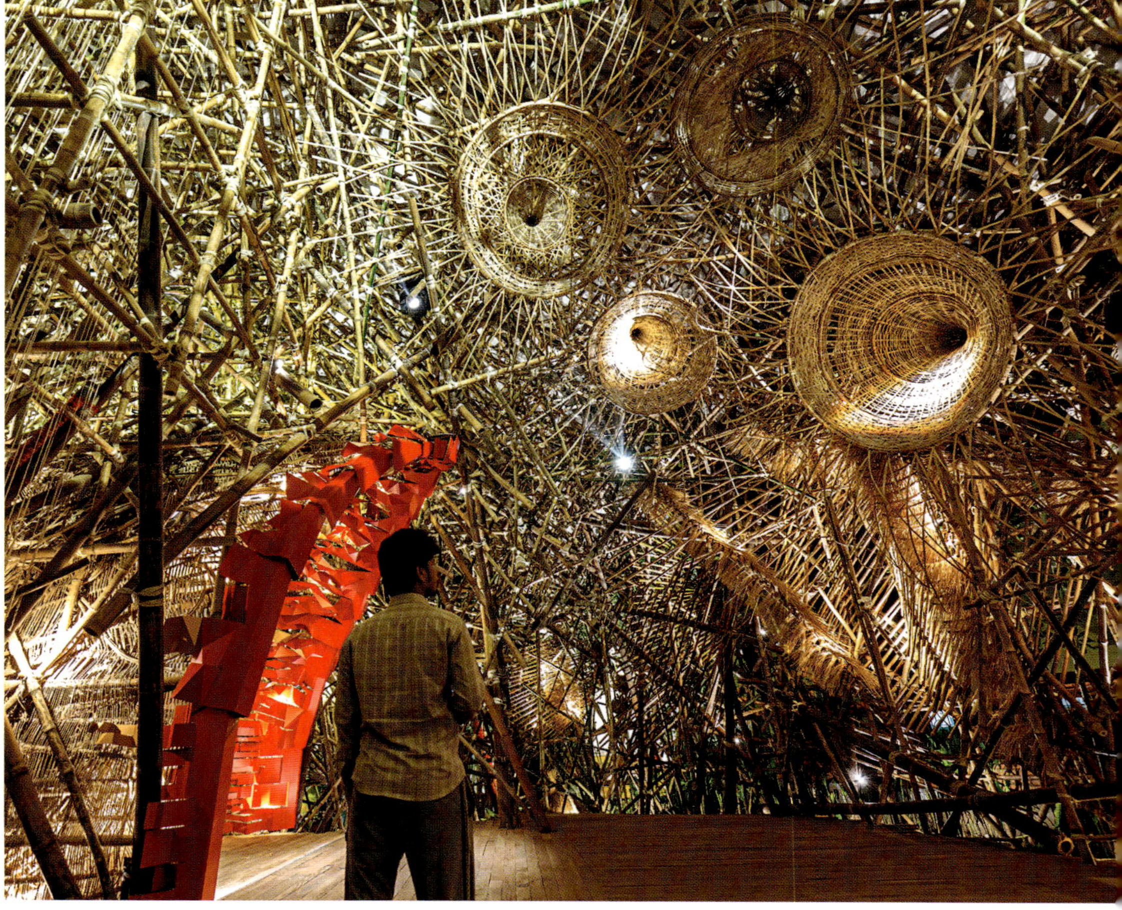

লয় *Loy* (interior view).

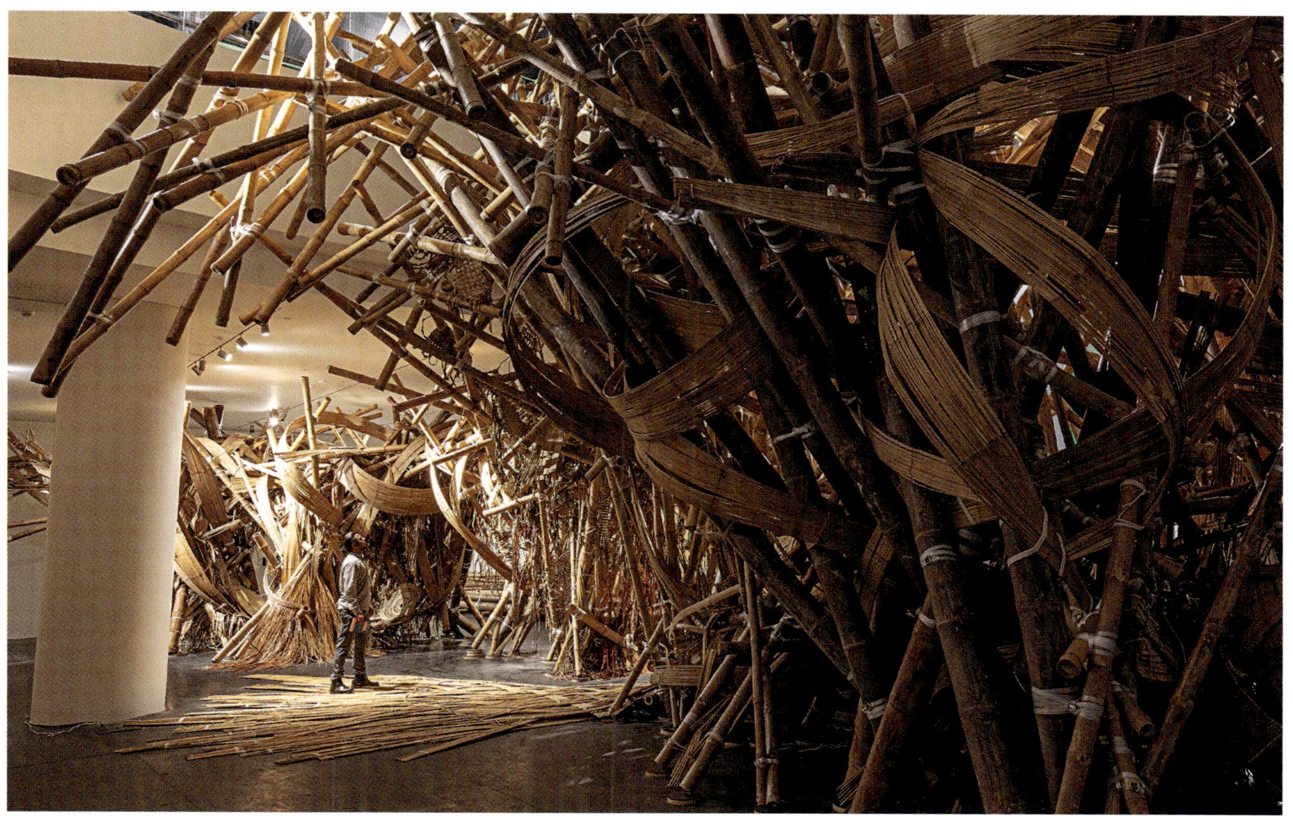

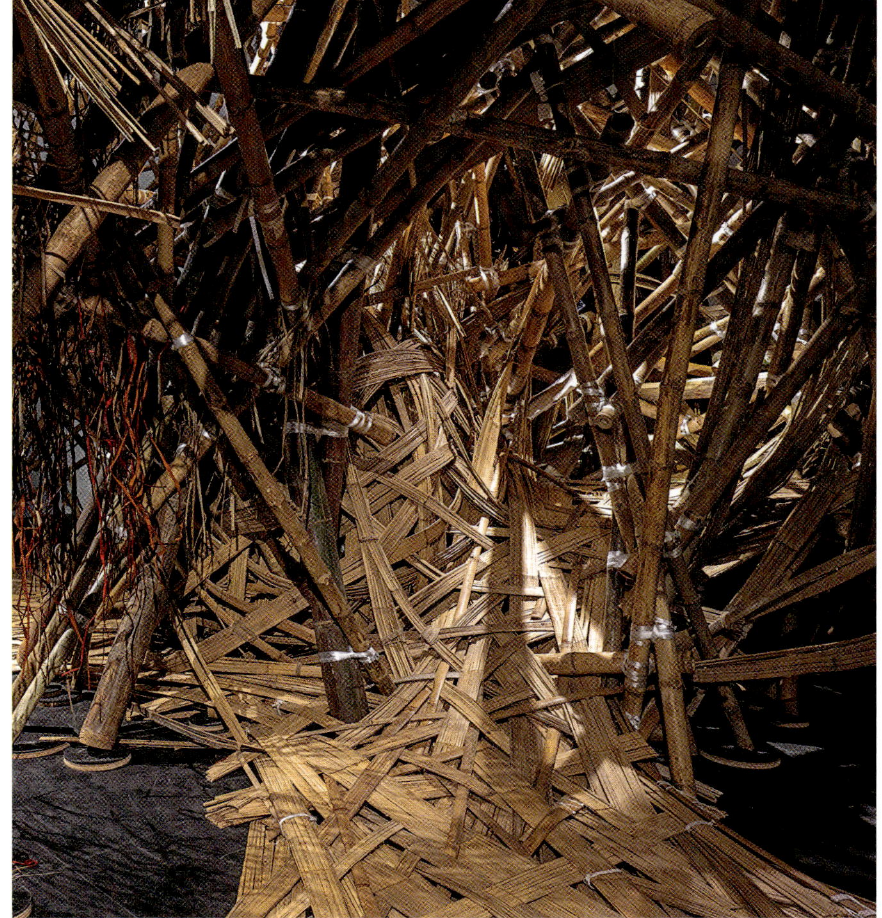

चाल *Chaal* چال (detail), 2024. Bamboo, cane, screw pine weaving, reed weaving, various ropes and cords; embedded with an interactive electronic and acoustic system. Specific installation at Nita Mukesh Ambani Cultural Centre, Mumbai. Asim Waqif in collaboration with Shantanu Heisnam, Udit Mittal, Harry Samson, Subhadeep Biswas, Aman Jagwani, Hemant Sreekumar, and Ajmal Islam and his team of bamboo and cane artisans. *Photos courtesy of Nita Mukesh Ambani Cultural Centre*

चाल *Chaal* چال (detail).

Lucia **LOREN**

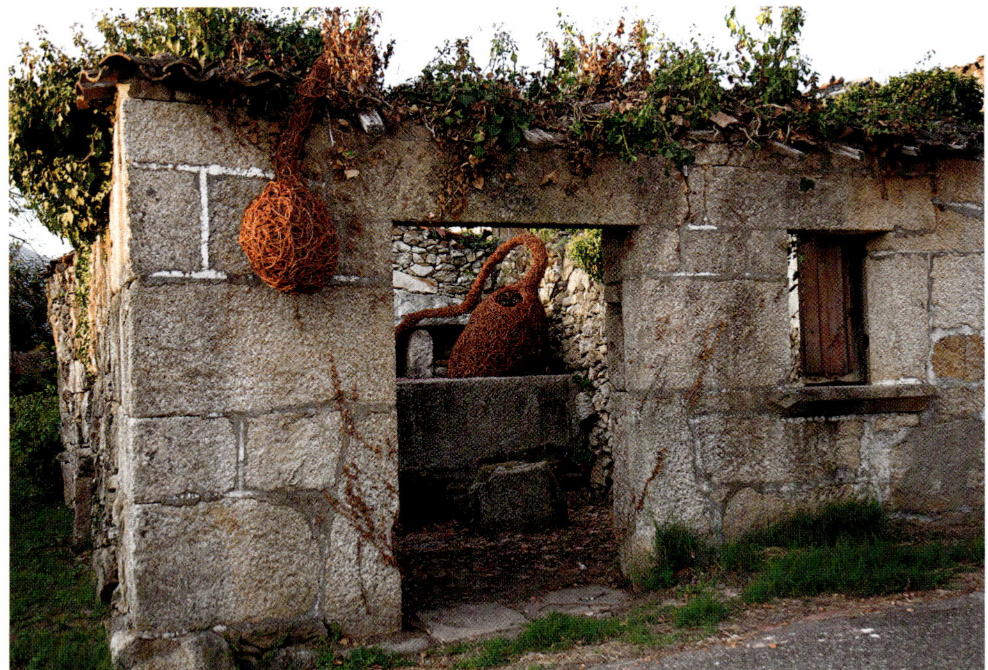

Lagar [Galicia, Spain], 2023. Wickerwork: dimensions variable. *Photo courtesy of the artist*

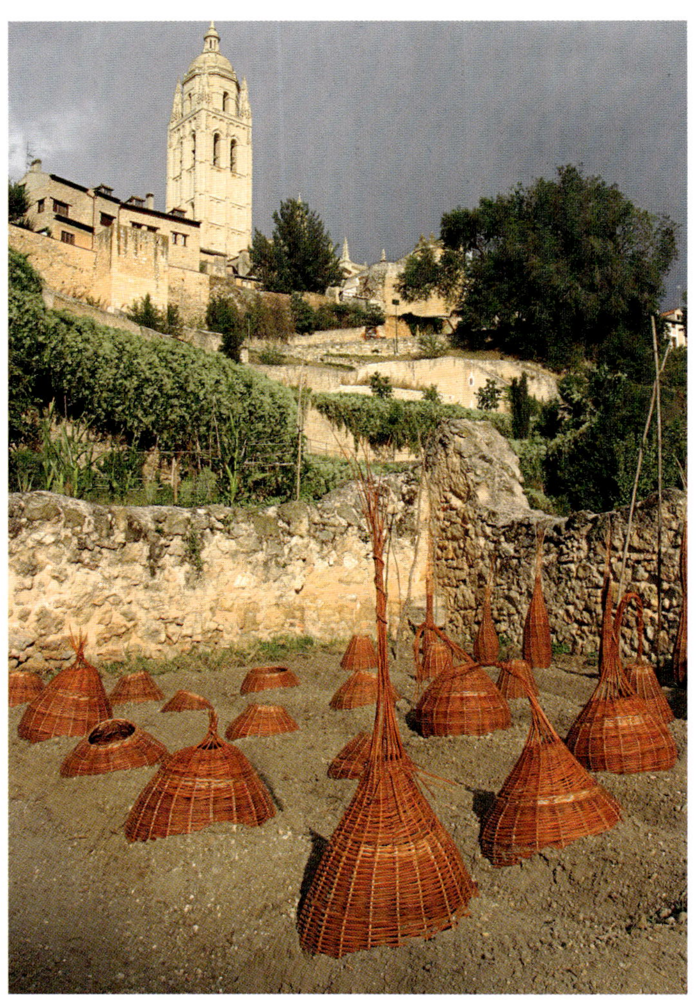

OPPOSITE: *Matriz de agua* [Navarra, Spain], 2017. Wickerwork: dimensions variable. *Photo courtesy of the artist*

Arqueología de una huerta [Segovia, Spain], 2006. Wickerwork: dimensions variable. *Photo courtesy of Juanjo Misis*

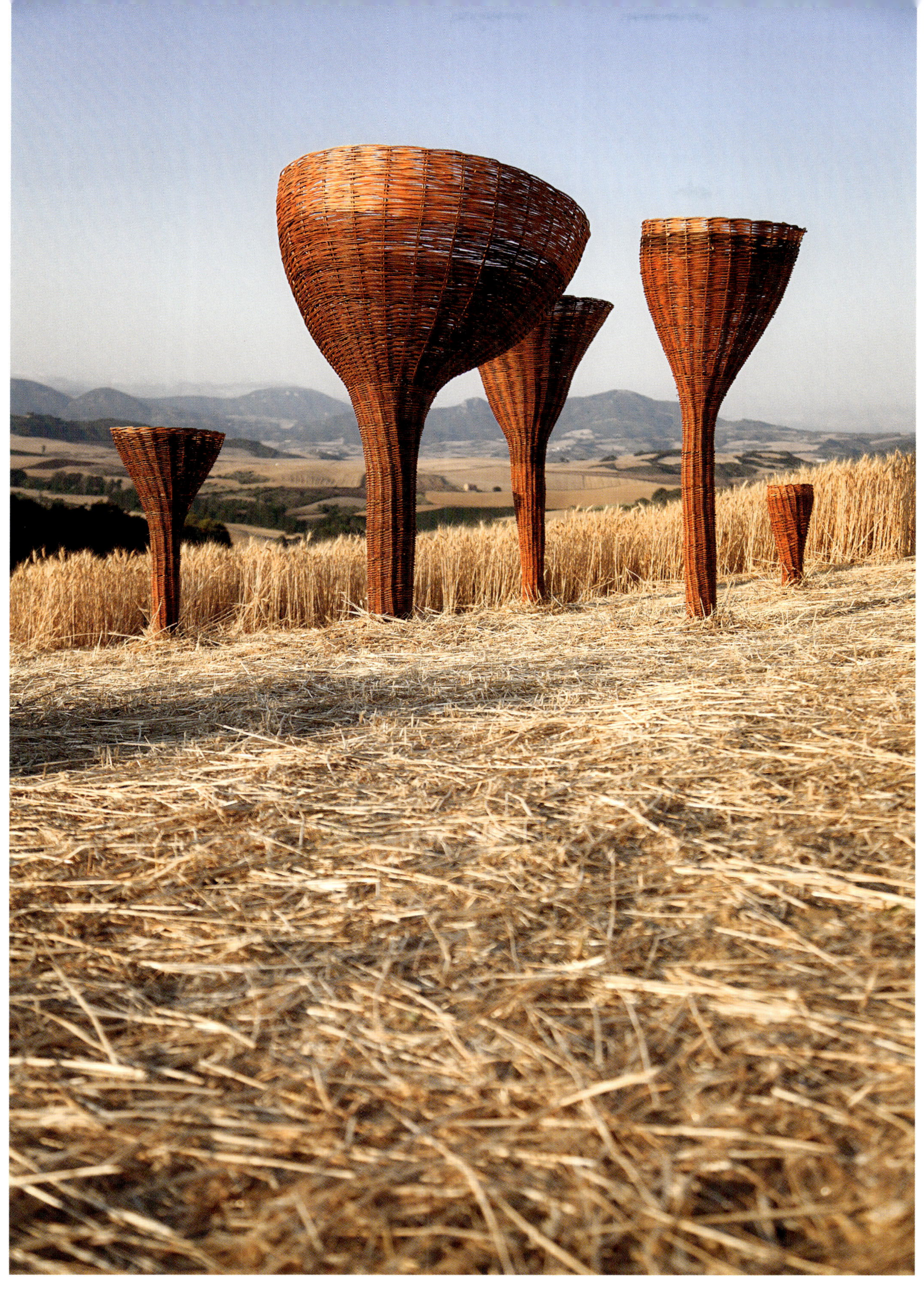

Porky HEFER

Cyclosis, 2023. Kooboo cane, steel, Chinese camphor, leather: 194 × 213 × 173 cm (76" × 83" × 68"). *Photo courtesy of the artist*

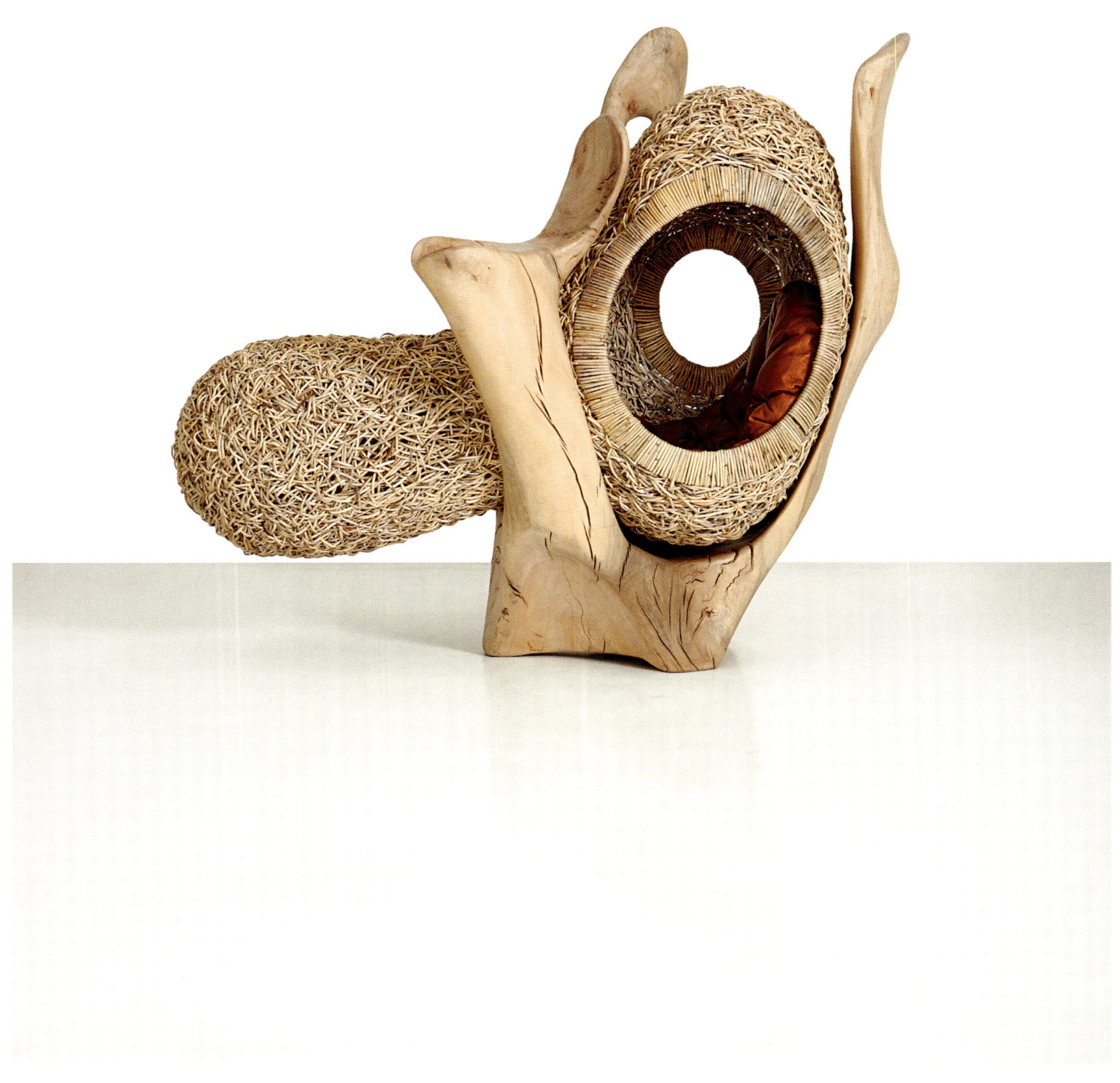

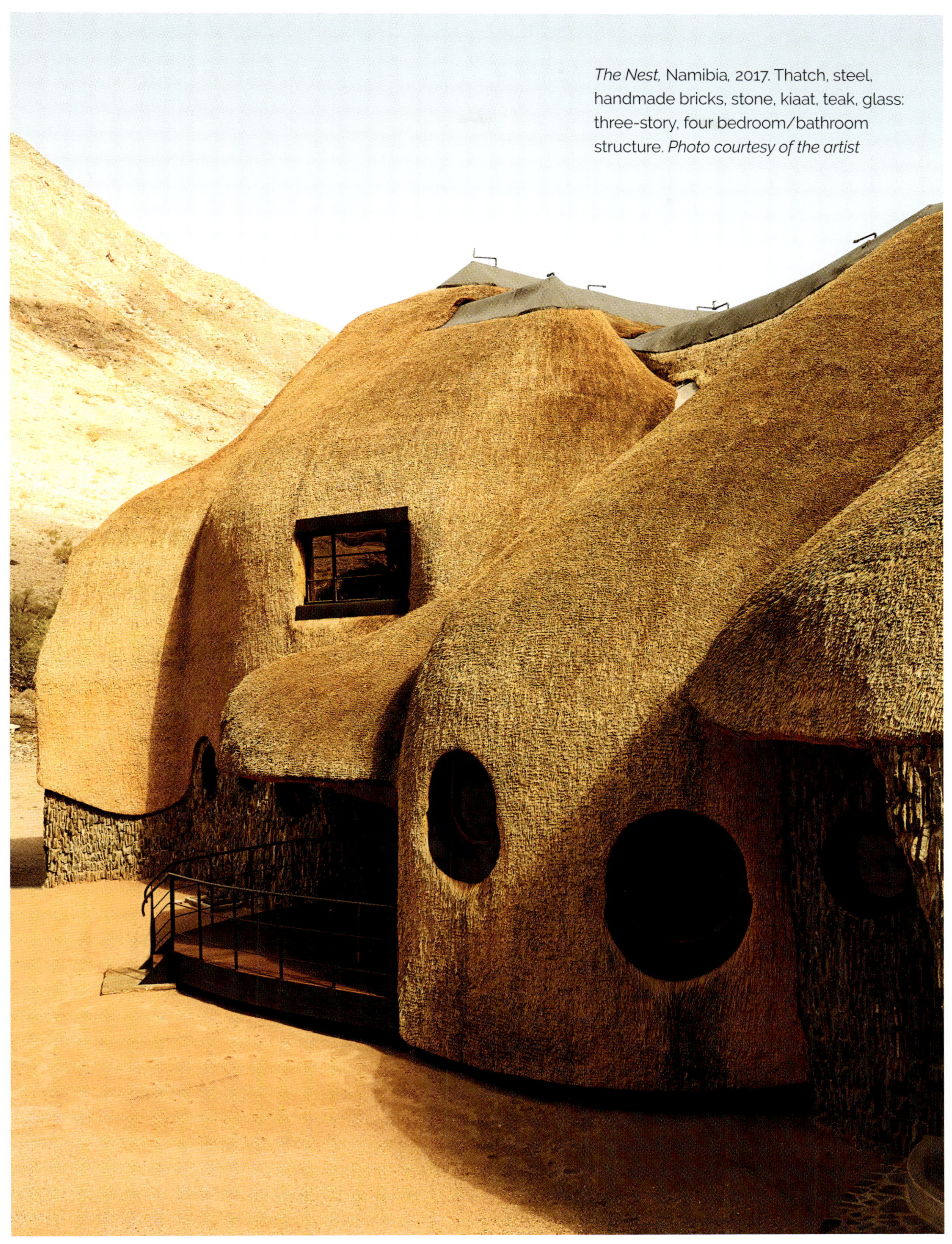

The Nest, Namibia, 2017. Thatch, steel, handmade bricks, stone, kiaat, teak, glass: three-story, four bedroom/bathroom structure. *Photo courtesy of the artist*

Ona TREPAT RUBIROLA

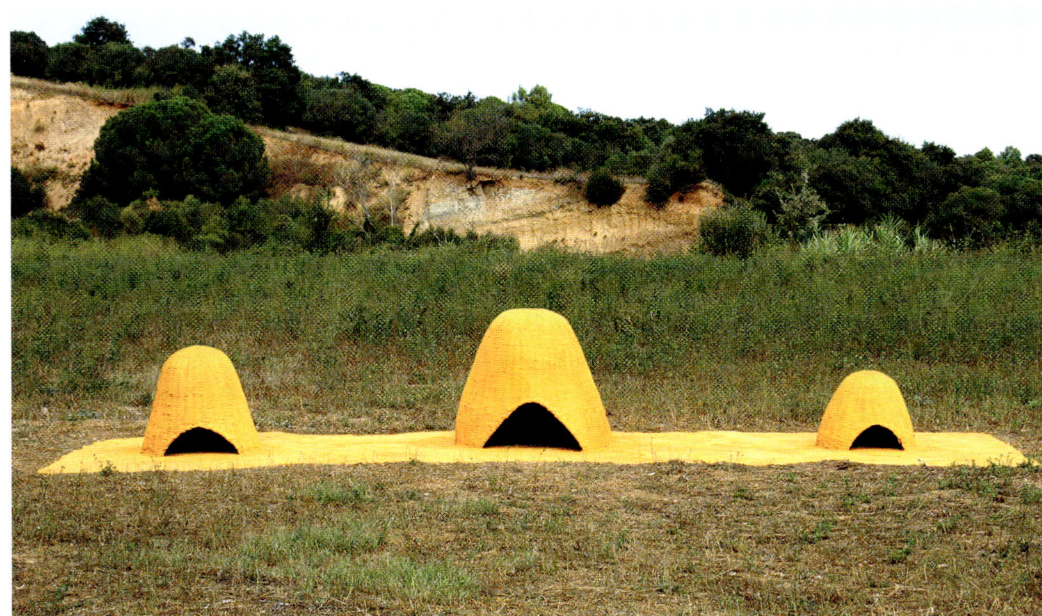

Three Mountains, 2020. Willow, clay, iron oxide: dimensions variable. *Photo courtesy of Robert Santamaria / Marc Sellarès*

Straw Braids, 2023. Rye, spelt, wheat straw: dimensions variable. *Photo courtesy of Robert Santamaria / Marc Sellarès*

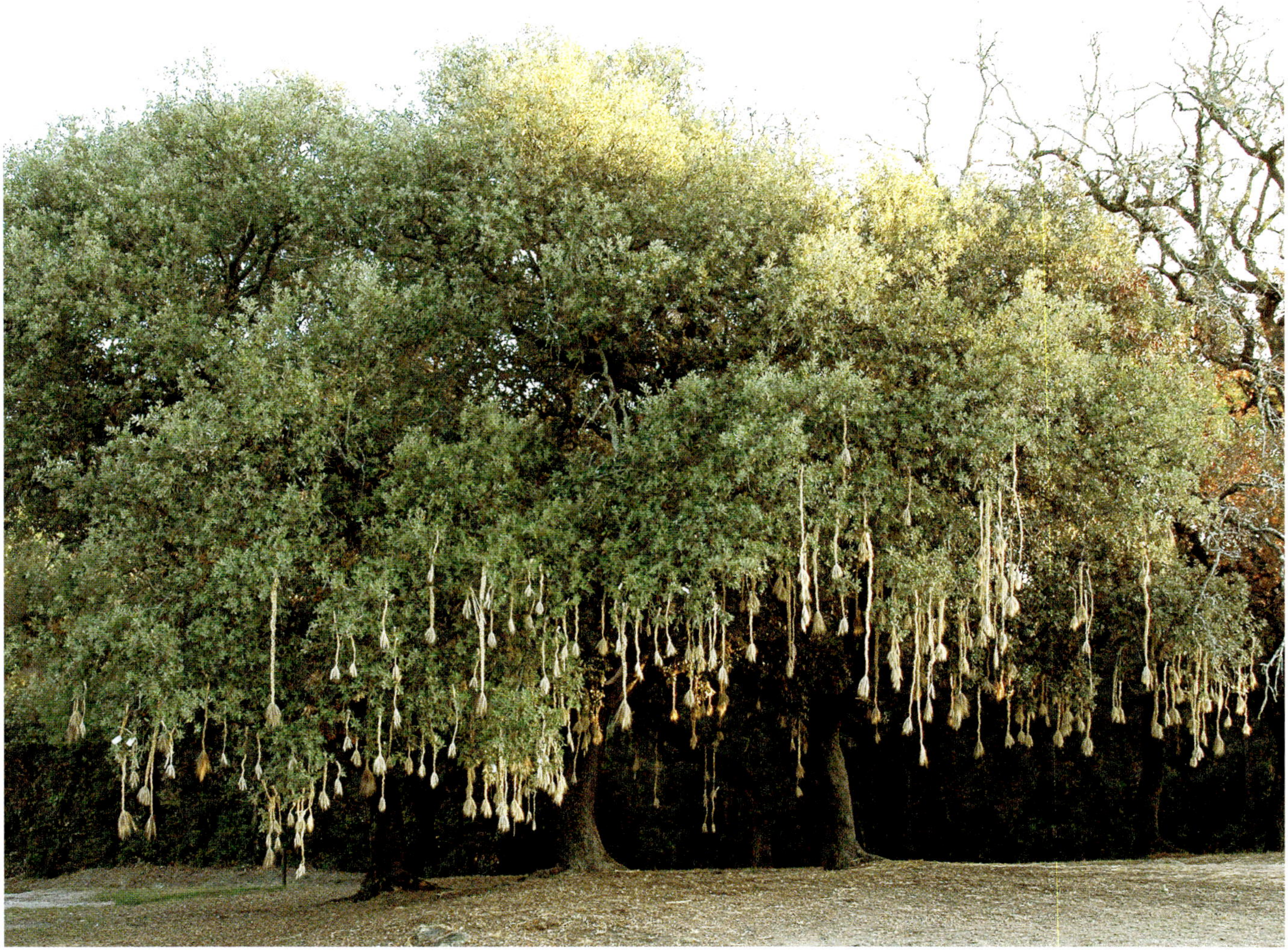

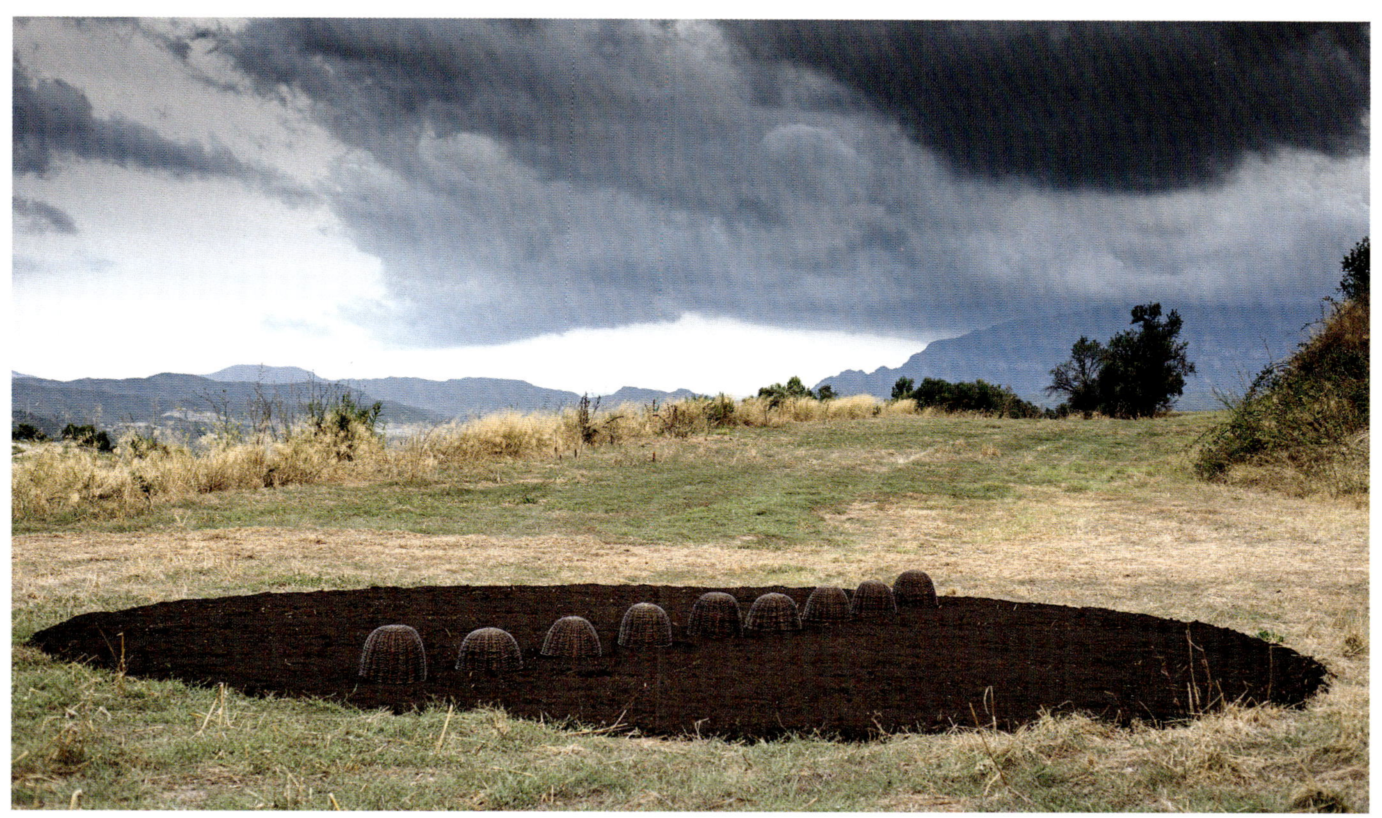

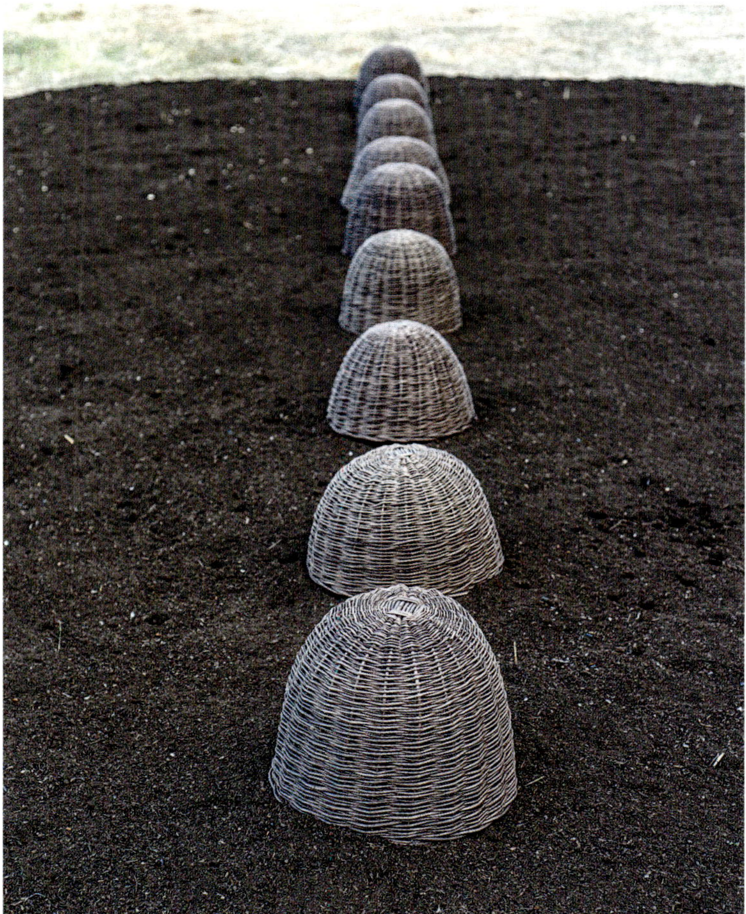

Sowing, 2020. Willow, compost land: dimensions variable. *Photos courtesy of Robert Santamaria / Marc Sellarès*

Sowing (detail).

Marie-José **GUSTAVE**

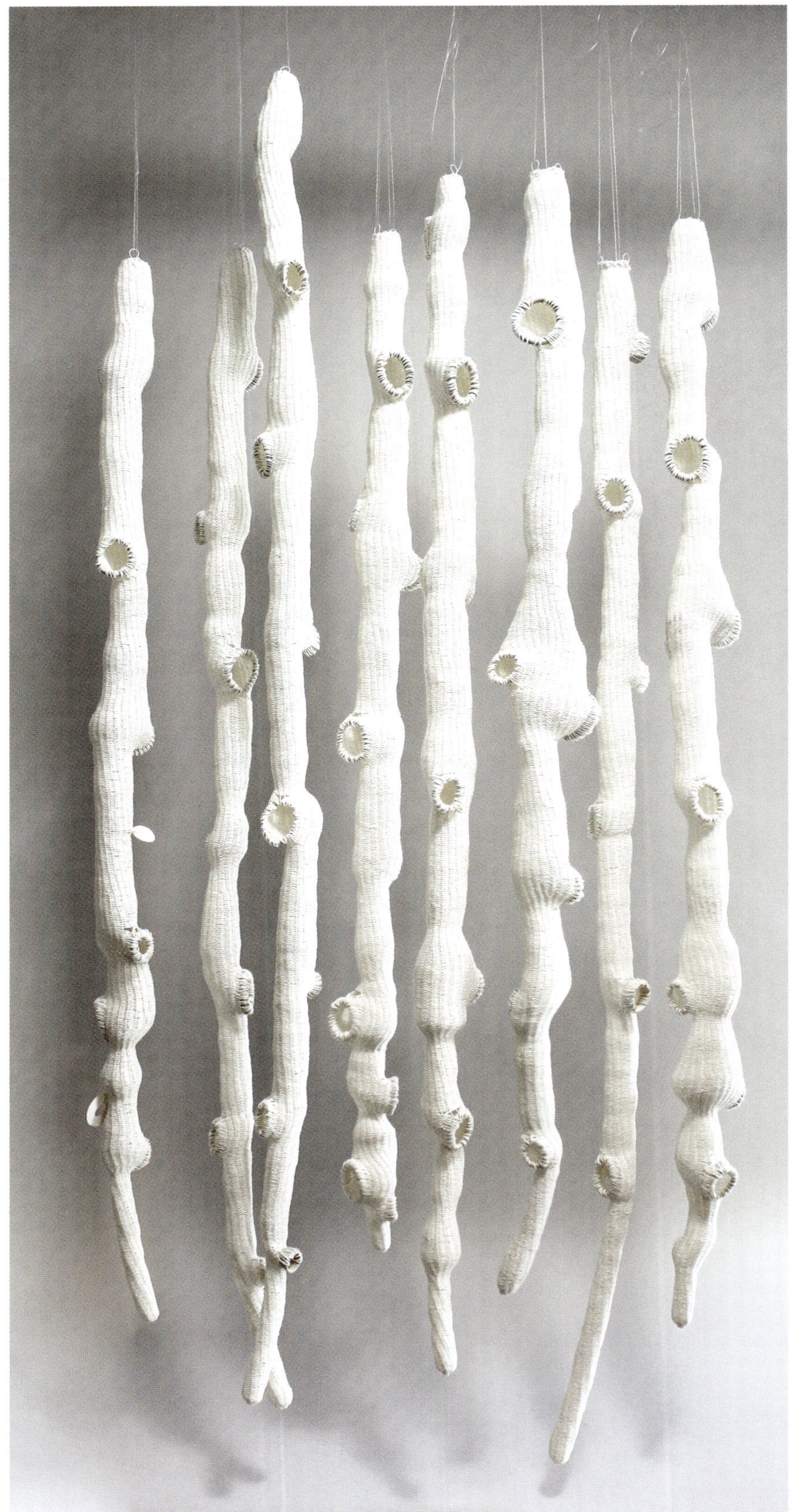

Corals, 2022. Paper wire, porcelain: dimensions variable. *Photo courtesy of La Guilde Montréal*

OPPOSITE: *Fruit,* 2018. Paper yarn: 100 × 25 cm, 104 × 31 cm (39" × 10", 41" × 12"). *Photo courtesy of the artist*

Fruit (detail), 2018. Paper yarn. *Photo courtesy of the artist*

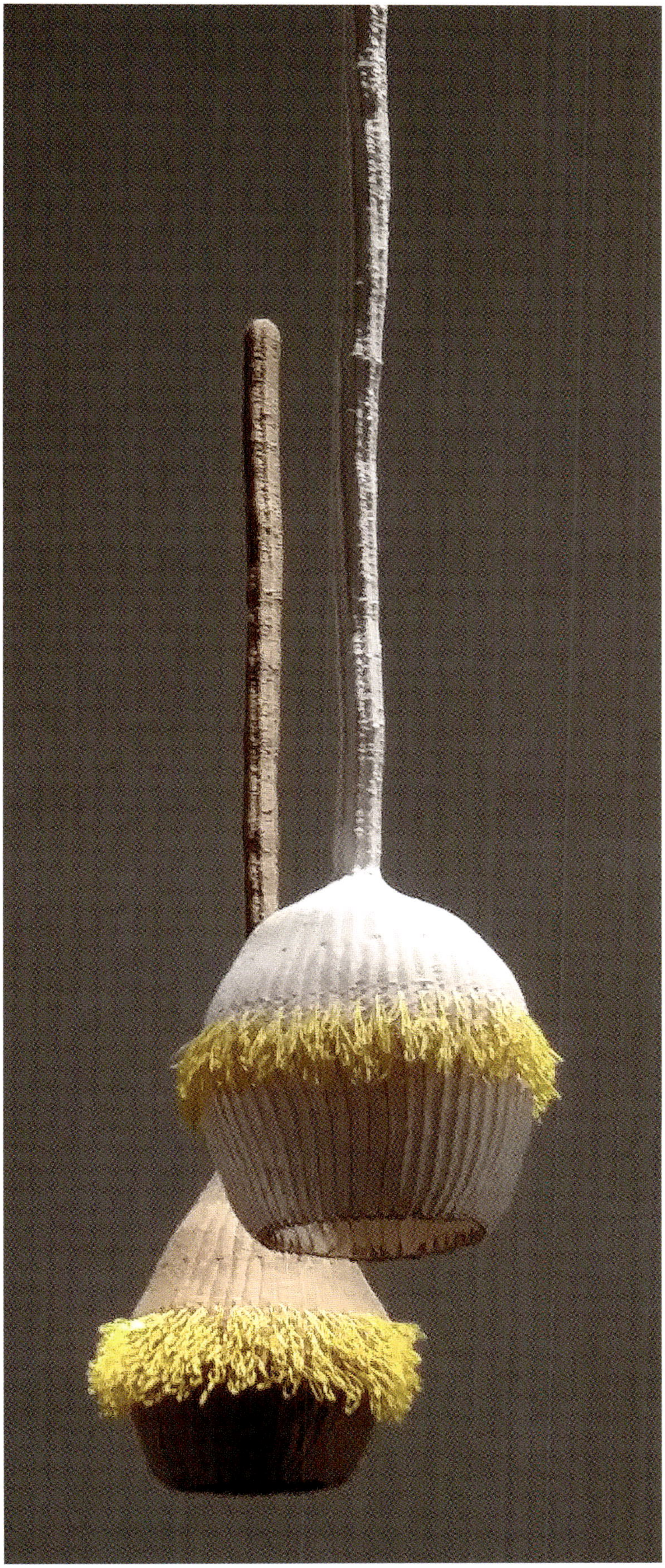

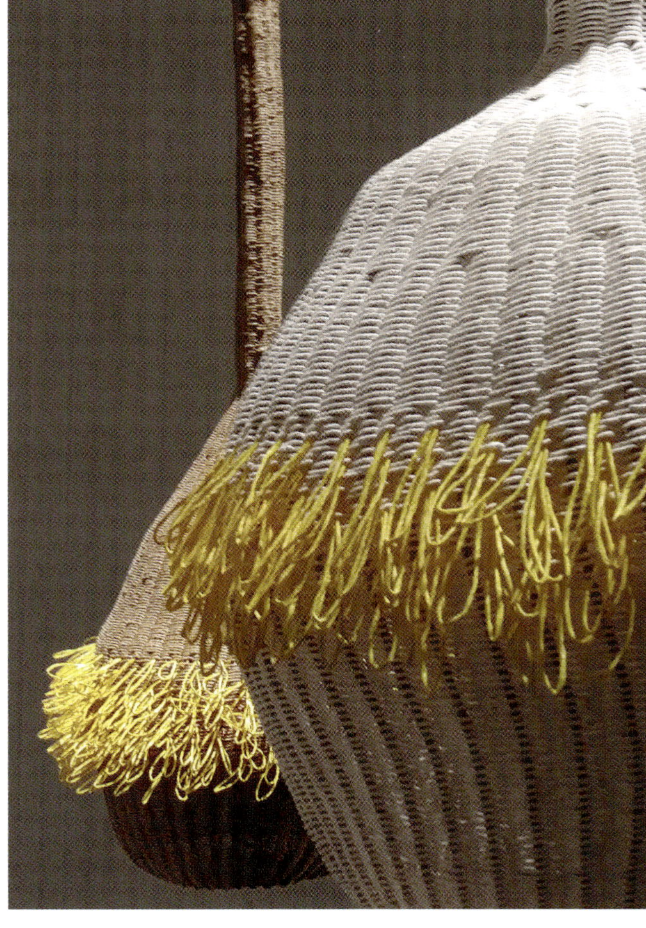

Nathalie **MIEBACH**

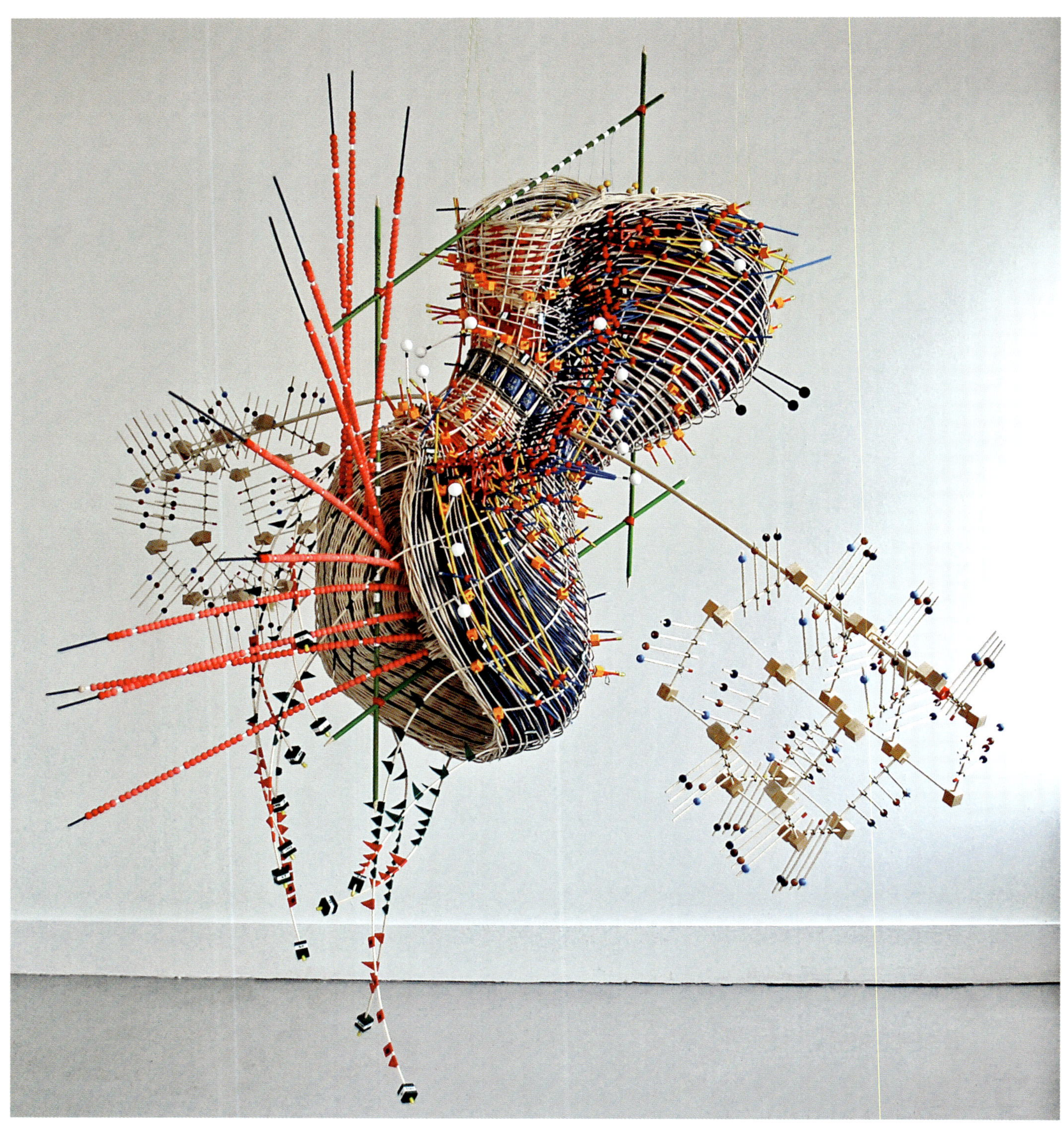

Warm Winter, 2007. Reed, wood, data: 182 × 152 × 182 cm (72" × 60" × 72"). *Photo courtesy of the artist*

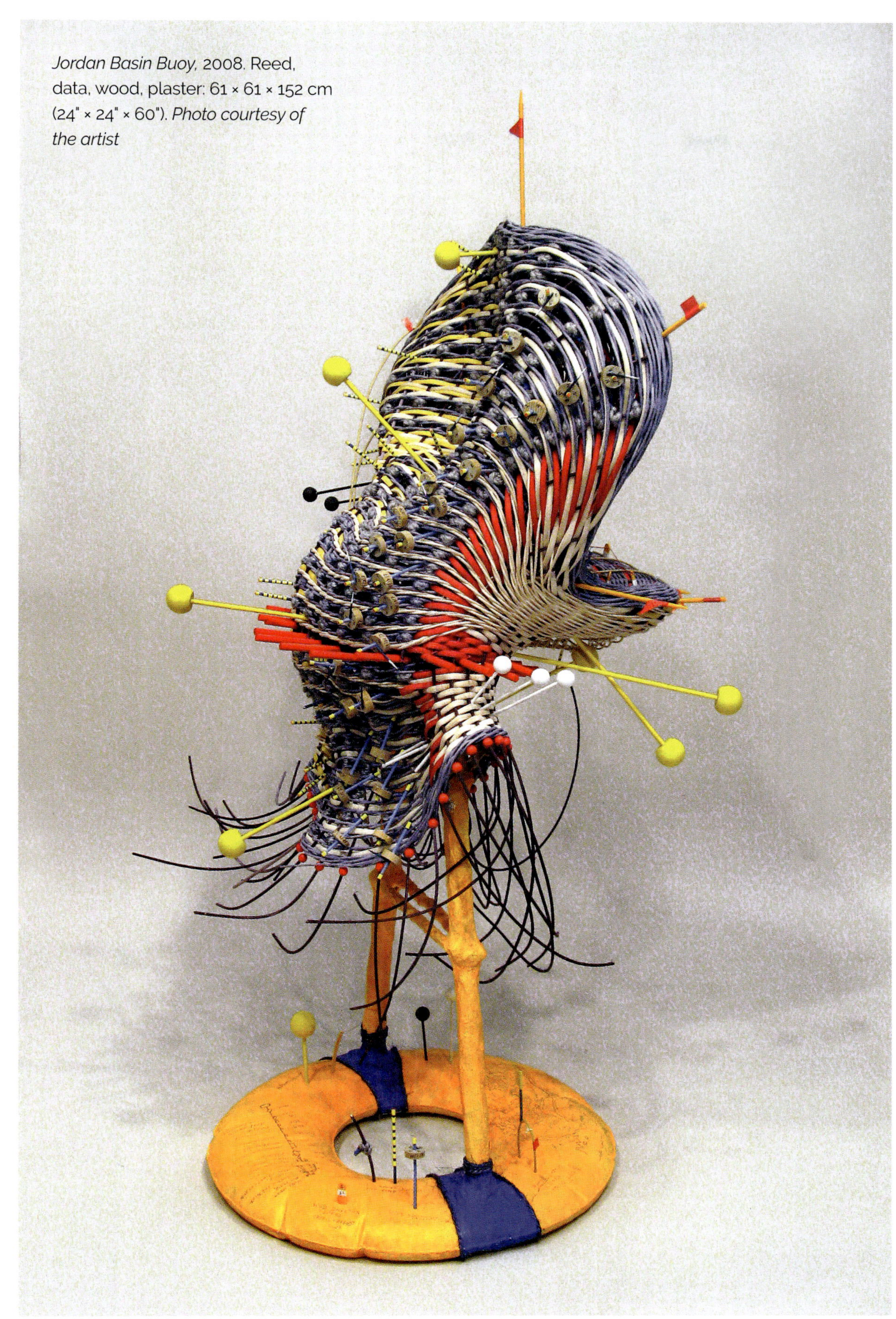

Jordan Basin Buoy, 2008. Reed, data, wood, plaster: 61 × 61 × 152 cm (24" × 24" × 60"). *Photo courtesy of the artist*

Rita SOTO VENTURA

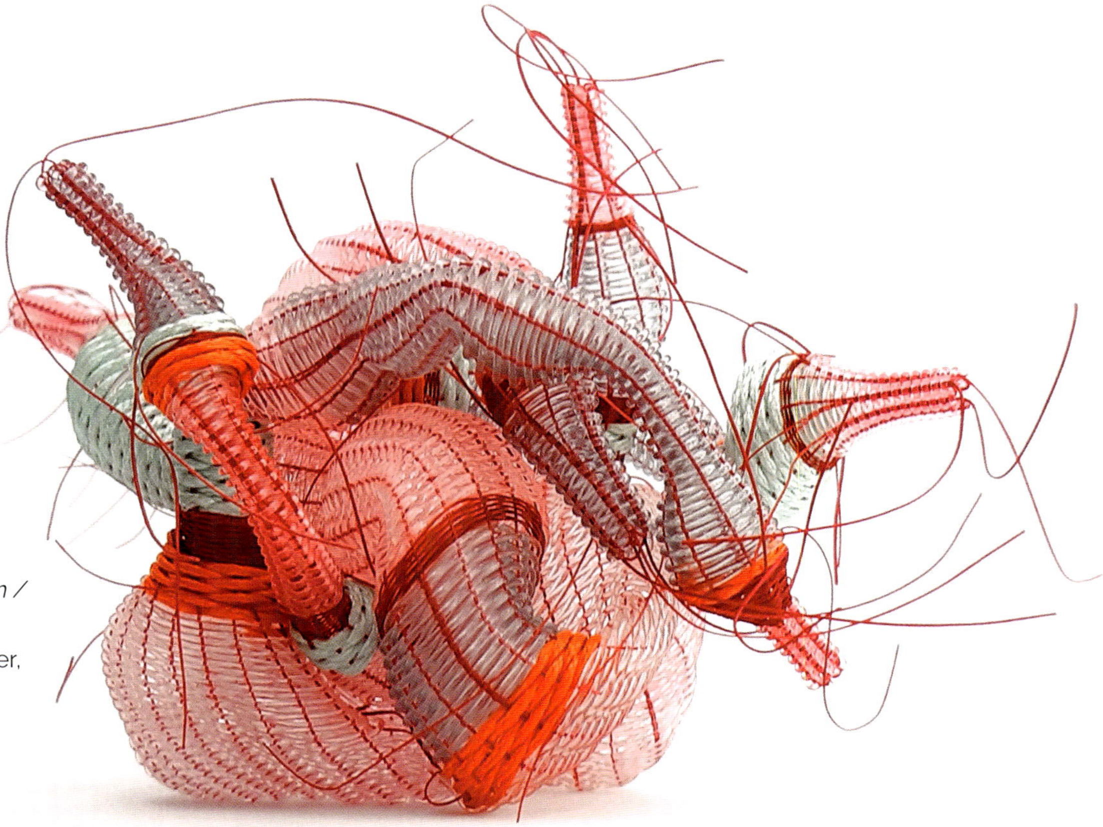

Brooch Existencial Parasitism / Parasite p.e .02B spiritualite, 2021. Horsehair, tampico fiber, silicone thread, silk thread, silver, steel: 180 × 60 × 70 mm (7" × 2" × 3"). *Photo courtesy of the artist*

Pendant Illa Manka / Amulet of the Andes, 2023. Horsehair, tampico fiber, monofilament, bamboo and cotton thread, patinated copper: 270 × 100 × 100 mm (10" × 4" × 4"). *Photo courtesy of the artist*

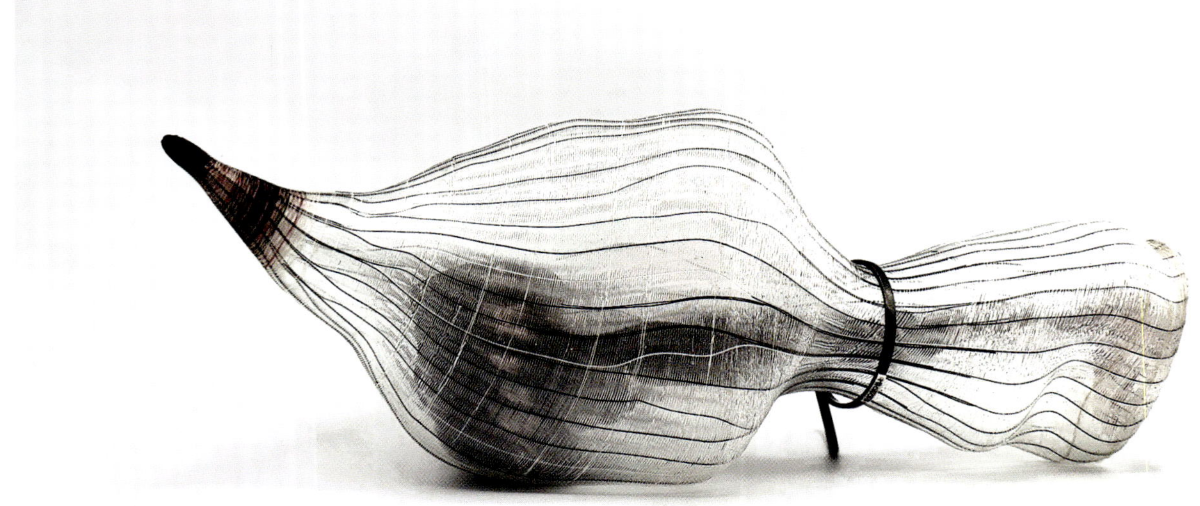

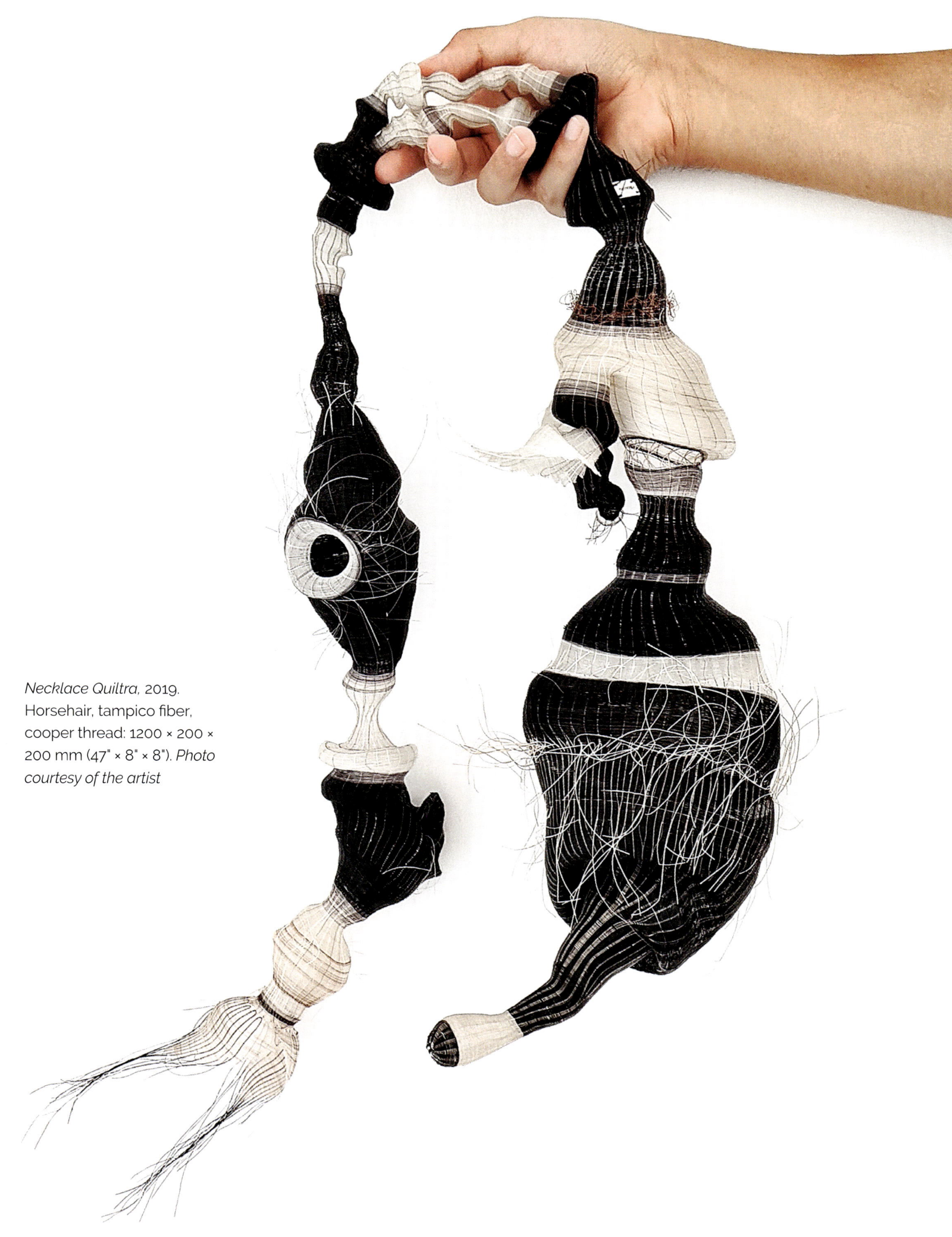

Necklace Quiltra, 2019. Horsehair, tampico fiber, cooper thread: 1200 × 200 × 200 mm (47" × 8" × 8"). *Photo courtesy of the artist*

LOOKING INTO BASKETS

by Janet Koplos

SINCE 2012 Carol Eckert's *Contemporary Basketry* blog has presented, in spectacular photographs without commentary, more than 17,000 baskets and basket sculptures from around the world. The images arrive on your computer or phone screen. You study and appreciate them. And the next day they are replaced by another inspiring set. This book alters that daily sequence by offering Eckert's honed selection representing the spectrum of contemporary work.

This book does not analyze individual works. Instead, you'll find here a consideration of the characteristics of baskets—the formal means by which they are recognized even when the definition is stretched—and notes on some allusive possibilities. You'll also find suggestions on what you might see in baskets, from the humble utilitarian to outsized abstract structures, and how you might understand what they can communicate.

An ancient form made new, baskets seem to be everywhere today, from art galleries to fashion shows to public parks. That's in addition to their traditional appearances in various contexts of practicality or decoration. The works chosen for this book, made in one form or another, of one material or another, and in a dizzying range of sizes, by makers from many nations and from any number of creative backgrounds, are nevertheless identifiable as basketry. How is that possible? It's because baskets typically have a visible, exposed structure that entails some sort of crossing of elements, orderly or not, that enclose a volume. And that's enough to define them. They are frequently made of natural materials, but that's not a requirement.

Calling out the qualities of the materials, the implications of the processes and forms, and some of the symbolism will help you see the pleasures of making and meaning in basketry. Looking at the overall characteristics of basketry encourages you to find your own explanations through a "close reading" of the works. The makers sometimes deal with personal, social, or political issues but rarely do so didactically. Some of their motivations are laid out in the artists' comments in part III. But with or without such hints, these works, like abstract art in any medium, exploit physical qualities to open a door to visual pleasure and to interpretation.

Today, basketry attracts most makers for reasons other than producing a service object. One motivation, in our increasingly virtual existence, is the self-satisfying pleasure of process, of being deeply engaged in a time- and attention-demanding creative act. Another is working with natural materials. Another is engaging with the logic of construction. In addition to these and other physical satisfactions, baskets have accrued many associations and metaphors over the millennia that can convey what the artist has in mind. On the most essential level, baskets refer to and exemplify containment, which may range from protection to transportation to incarceration. In addition, they offer options for display and for allusion. The thing "held" may be as elusive as a thought.

Basketry most often involves linear elements in some sort of reticulation. These constructive elements, no matter how fine or coarse, usually remain visible and so tell the story of their assembly. While the layering of leaves may be the prehistoric origin of bowls, the

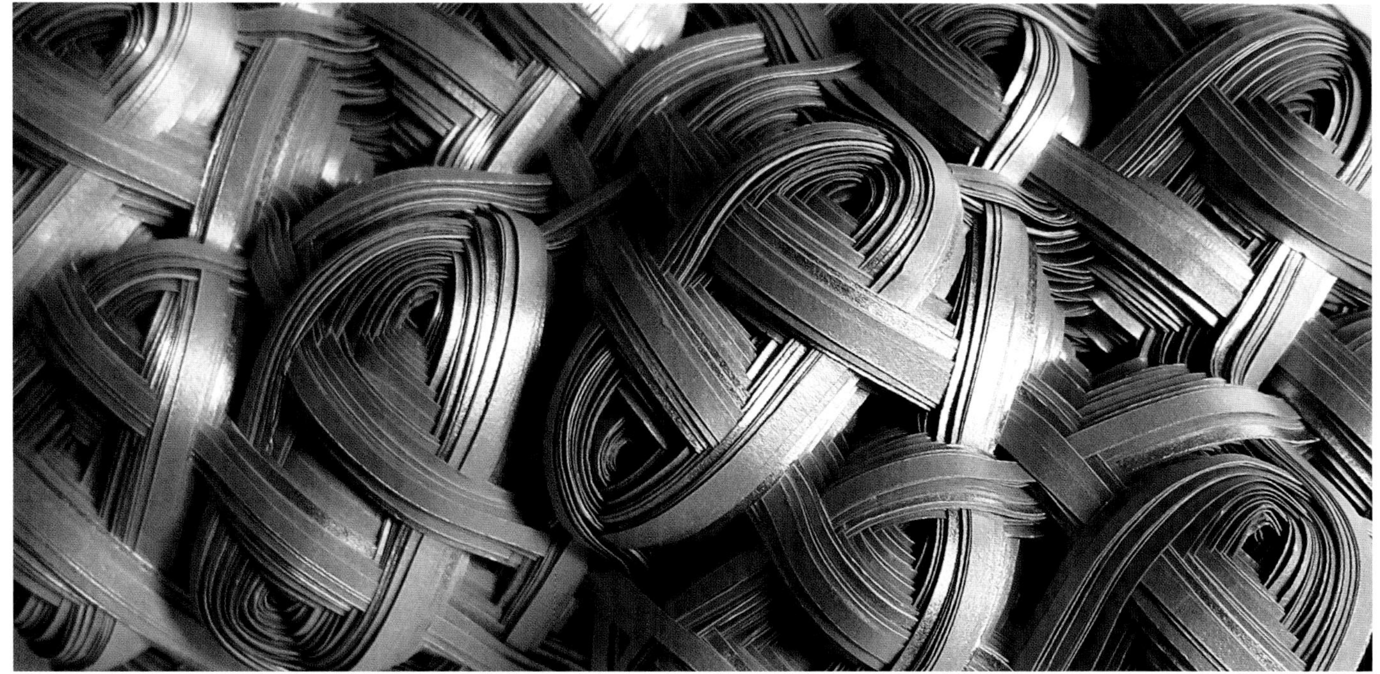

Noriko TAKAMIYA. *Cube Connection #16* (detail), 2018. Paper: 25 × 15 × 15 cm (10" × 6" × 6"). *Photo courtesy of the artist*

interlacing of fingers may be the first model for basket structure. From there, the making gets more and more complex to construct a tighter weave or achieve a certain shape. The addition or subtraction of elements, or the bending of pliable elements, yields a three-dimensional form.

Containing allows accumulation, retention, or sharing. A simple, open basket implies giving because the inner space is so easily accessed. It can also imply care, as in the case of a nest. As the form becomes deeper and more enclosing, the association shifts to a more restrictive type of containing. Baskets have served as traps and cages.

On the other hand, the visible structure can both symbolize and entail reaching outward. It's easy to understand that the structure can be added to. Because additional elements are spliced in, the basket can seemingly continue without limit. How, and how much, is added gives it intensity. Baskets show the labor that goes into making them, in the type of the constructive elements and in their intersections. (How large? How tight? How many?) In the art world, various instances of labor are often highlighted in sculptures and installations that have become more elaborate in recent years. Visible labor celebrates the effort itself, unlike mastery, which tends to conceal effort.

Finding pleasure in labor may be a response to today's digital fabrication and virtuality: Labor is real, it encourages engagement, it allows a bodily experience, it emphasizes touch. Some might regard it as drudgery, but makers seem to find comfort, even joy, in effort. Visible disclosure of labor may be part of what makes basketry satisfying today.

Because baskets contain, they are necessarily creations of volume rather than mass. Although they can be closed, they cannot be solid (unless they are depictions of baskets rather than actual ones). They must have some pocket of space within. That means that in general they are lightweight in relation to their size. Baskets may offer varying degrees of transparency, depending on the constructive particulars, on the chosen material, and on the purpose. In all basketry, density is an expressive option that establishes mood or feeling.

Let's look a little closer at some of these considerations.

Tradition

Traditional basketry continues not just in the developing world but also in the leading world economies, sometimes as an intentional effort to hold on to heritage. Today's baskets demonstrate, for example, community continuity, as in American Indigenous groups, or aesthetic schools, as in Japan. Tradition is expressed by the choice of heritage materials and techniques. The term "traditional" does not specify a single form but just points toward the existence of a valued precedent.

Traditional baskets are sometimes still used today, but they may also be made as collectibles for display, in the same way that large ceramic crocks are less often used for pickling today and more often displayed for their beauty, appearance of strength, and reference to the past.

Skills may be passed on through kinship ties or may be recuperated through individual initiative. Often a maker begins a career with traditional training but evolves into creating larger objects or nontraditional shapes, outcomes encouraged both by market forces and by a maker's own desire for challenges. Thus, for example, Mary Jackson's sweetgrass baskets have grown to the scale of 3 or 4 feet in diameter and with dramatic use of free grasses as accents, but they continue the materials and techniques of her Gullah ancestors.

Another example of how tradition can also be contemporary is baskets for ikebana flower arrangement in Japan. These might be extremely eccentric in form, like the artistic inventions of Western contemporary artists. The tradition is only that an ikebana basket accommodate a water container, which might be as unobtrusive as a small cylinder. Any basketry form is acceptable to encase it, ranging from subtle and conservative to wildly irregular.

The public needs some knowledge of precedent in order to appreciate holding to tradition or diverging from it. As in any field, knowledge brings understanding and greater appreciation.

Service Type: Offering

Considering basket forms in the broadest and least culturally determined sense, there are several archetypal categories. One of them is offering. It might also be called serving or presenting. This is a mostly open form, ranging from a flat tray to a shallow bowl that is suitable, for example, for serving food. A deeper bowl might still be used for food, with the proper implements to retrieve the contents, but in general a deeper basket suggests storage, which because of its more closed form performs the act of offering only in a more limited way. For example, perhaps only one person at a time can access it. Storage baskets can be rectangular or rounded, lidded or not, and they can even be raised on legs to keep a cache away from animals.

Another offering form is a nest. The stereotypical bird's nest is a shallow bowl form (though there are also other forms). The construction often consists of interwoven tangles of twigs, moss, strings, and other found materials, and it comprises a thick rim and a central indentation. Artists working with basketry materials play with the nest form because of its emotional resonance of protection and nurturing. Artists have devised nests large enough to accommodate sleeping humans.

Service Type: Constraining

Another archetypal basketry category is the trap. Basketry materials would not be strong enough to capture all types of animals but have been notably adaptable. Fish traps and lobster traps are probably the most familiar. What denotes a trap? Usually it is a form that can be completely closed—no welcome opening at the top—although this, like all suppositions, can be challenged with a rim that encourages sliding in but not climbing out. There is generally a door or a lid. The association of a trap with force and control makes the harshness of a rectilinear form seem appropriate, but it is not necessarily required for the performance of the function. The trap form, like the nest, is often chosen by makers for its emotional tenor—in this case threatening rather than comforting.

Service Type: Wearing

"Baskets to wear" might sound outlandish but is at least familiar—in fine-gauge materials—in the case of headgear or footwear. In traditional instances, another example of wearable baskets would be backpacks or various other means of carrying that are supported by the body. Beyond that, contemporary makers have engaged with fashion and theater to produce various eccentric garments or disguises. These give less consideration to the comfort of the wearer and more attention to the viewer's visual or emotional disturbance—or amusement. Strong and rigid materials may be used for spectacular extensions of skirts, bodices, or headgear; softer basketry materials, such as grasses, may be used for skirts, but they are easily abraded and demolished.

Service Type: Supporting

The support aspect of basketry is common. There is even a furniture form called a basket chair, which can be suspended from a pergola, a floor-based frame, or from overhead beams, indoors or out. Basketry techniques also figure in empress/lotus/peacock chairs made of rattan, in cozy versions of an egg chair in which the user is largely enclosed, and in string or wire-mesh seating. All have linear interlocking elements that are basic to basketry. Rattan and bamboo are rigid enough to be the framework of furniture and, when cut into thin strips, make comfortable seats. Basketry materials and techniques are also seen in various realizations of bench seating, such as settees, although they may not resemble basket forms. Contemporary makers have carried the basket-seating idea into unusual forms and materials, including forms that comment on social motives by requiring or prohibiting congenial gathering.

Structure

Baskets are defined by structure, but that does not mean they are defined by form, since they may be spherical, boxy, cylindrical, or irregular, and those are only the

Esmé HOFMAN. *Serious Business* (detail), 2008. Willow skeins, plastic: 18 × 34 cm (7" × 13"). *Photo by te, courtesy of the artist*

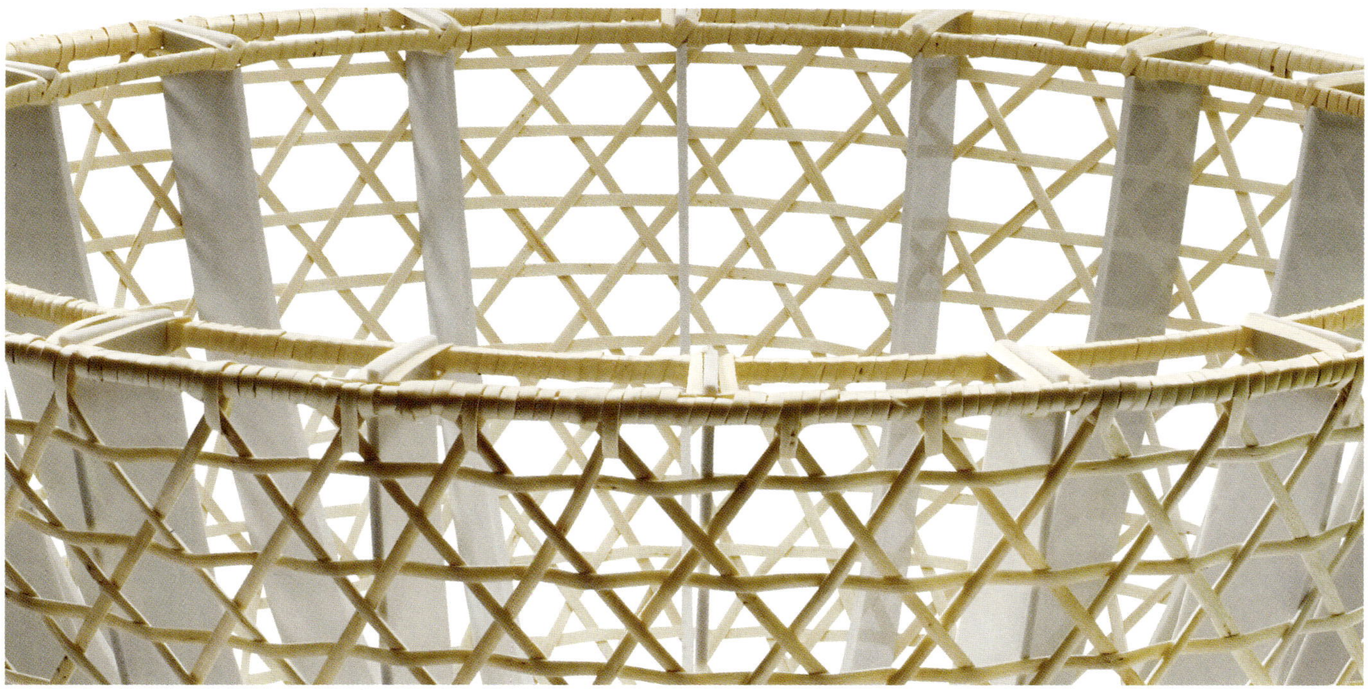

starting points. The interlocking basketry structure may be orderly, with regular intervals between elements, or the spacing may be irregular, or the elements may be bunched or entangled. The size of the elements, large or small, is virtually unlimited. Natural materials are often used, and because of their irregularity, perfect grids do not come easily in basketry (exact grids suggest machining). But a suggestion of the grid may carry allusions.

Usually the structure is visible, and often the structure is itself the primary aesthetic appeal of the basket. It is emphasized when the elements differ (in size, color, material, etc.) because that makes the intersections more obvious. Structure is also a major determinant of basket texture (material is the second major determinant) and will enable an almost infinite variety. Where the structural elements are small, any light coating material may have the surprising effect of not concealing but emphasizing the texture generated by structure. That's because it eliminates distraction and leaves only the structural pattern.

Spiraling structures test the limits of basketry if there is no vertical element holding the spirals together; a spring, for example, is not in itself a basket. But baskets can be made by coiling, so even an unfixed coil can be reminiscent of a basket. Like a spiral, a flat circle recalls basketry construction even when it is not a conventional container shape. Contemporary makers play with these resemblances and distinctions.

An aspect of structure that may be both functional and aesthetic is the handle or handles. A handle may be rigid (for example, bamboo or wood), or it may be flexible (for example, string). String may be braided for greater strength, or a different and stronger flexible material, such as leather, may be used. A single handle may be shaped as a semicircle that echoes the basket's profile, or it may rise in any shape from the points of the basket's greatest width. It may be functional in the simplest way possible, or it may be embellished at its points of attachment or at its peak, competing with the visual interest of the basket itself. Rather than a single handle, there may be smaller paired handles at opposite points, or vestigial handles as ornament. Sculptural baskets are often accompanied by eccentric handles, sometimes functioning as a drawing in the air, a counterpoint to the basket's form, a framing device, or a suggestion of outward extension.

Materials

The visual character of a basket, and thus its implied meaning, is affected by the choice of material. Willow, bamboo, wood, bark, grasses, pine needles, and other organic materials are the most common. A delicate basket can even be constructed of leaves or maple seeds sewn together in a circular form. Sometimes natural materials such as grasses or palm fronds are made into basket forms, with stems or seedheads left intact to emphasize their sources. Paper and metal create quite opposite effects. And sometimes the material is a complete surprise, such as clay, which may be carved in a leather-hard stage to resemble a basket (garlic box, strawberry basket) or may be laboriously constructed of ropes of clay. There are also organic basketry materials that are surprising today because they are rarely used expressively in the developed world; for example, gut.

Within the organic realm, the choice of material is usually due to aesthetics, availability, ease of handling, or tradition and only sometimes is symbolic of an extravisual meaning. Wood allows construction in large scale and may be a convenience rather than a symbol. On the other hand, nontraditional materials are often explicit in reference. Plastics, found objects, and the like refer to pollution, sustainability, and other environmental complaints, for example.

Bamboo is so widely found and used in Asia that it has accumulated symbolism—in Japan, it most famously means to bend but not break. And because of its ubiquity, it is the most frequent basketry material. But that does not mean one sort of look. Basket-making families who emphasize traditions tend to use fine materials to foreground craftsmanship. But today the fine materials may be used in large scale for a sculptural approach that may create a sense of movement or may attach to and mutate the architectural features of a building. This shows the flexibility of the material both literally and symbolically.

Sensory Responses

Structure and materials are the primary affective agents of basketry and are the first to come to mind when you think of baskets. Both are experienced visually but also palpably. When any kind of basket is touched, its structure can be sightlessly followed and creates various sensations of rhythm and order. Whether the elements are large or small, long floats or short segments, regularly placed or disorderly, knotted or twisted or interlaced—all will affect the sensation of touch just as much as—or more than—the roughness or smoothness of each element itself. The varied character of materials, whether natural or synthetic, also can be understood and appreciated through touch. Weight and rigidity are also understood by this physical means.

It seems that baskets operate outside the realm of taste or flavor, although it's possible that some traditions that serve food in baskets might play with this. Sound is a rarely offered option in basketry, although you may experience the sound of wind passing through large sculptural baskets in the landscape, and some baskets are inspired by a musical sense of order, and the artists may provide for music to accompany them in public showings. Smell is a pleasant side effect with some natural materials—both expected grassy odors and the fragrance associated with some kinds of bark. Native American baskets and some African examples may feature sweetgrass precisely for its odor. A basket that is handled may exude a pleasant smell, and odor is also experienced in some architectural-scale baskets when you enter them. Artificial materials may also offer odors, not always pleasant. But while these other sensory appreciations are uncommon, response by sight and touch is universal.

One other sensory response is viewers' sense of their own bodies in space in relation to the artist-constructed environment. This proprioception is an experience similarly provoked by large-scale sculpture and architecture. It may likewise be stimulated by the perception of a basket's movement, whether of a large work outdoors or of any sort of suspended basket.

Connecting/Outreach

The structure of baskets can imply extension: Because a viewer can see how the parts relate to each other, and because they are spliced or tied, or otherwise fastened to each other, it's clear that more can be added, maybe infinitely. Makers can exaggerate the length of some elements (usually verticals) to indicate how very modest the standard length usually is (and also how practical). For example, the neck might be grossly extended. This ability to be added to carries the symbolism of other kinds of outreach, such as connections to other objects or among people or between thoughts.

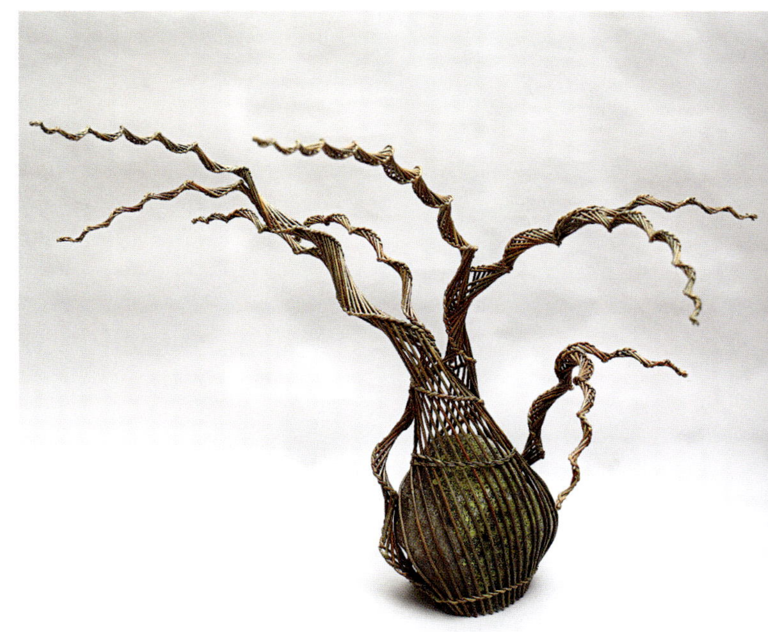

Karen GOSSART and Corentin LAVAL. *Bonsaï,* 2019. Brown willow: 65 × 105 × 100 cm (25" × 41" × 39"). *Photo courtesy of Oseraie de l'Ile*

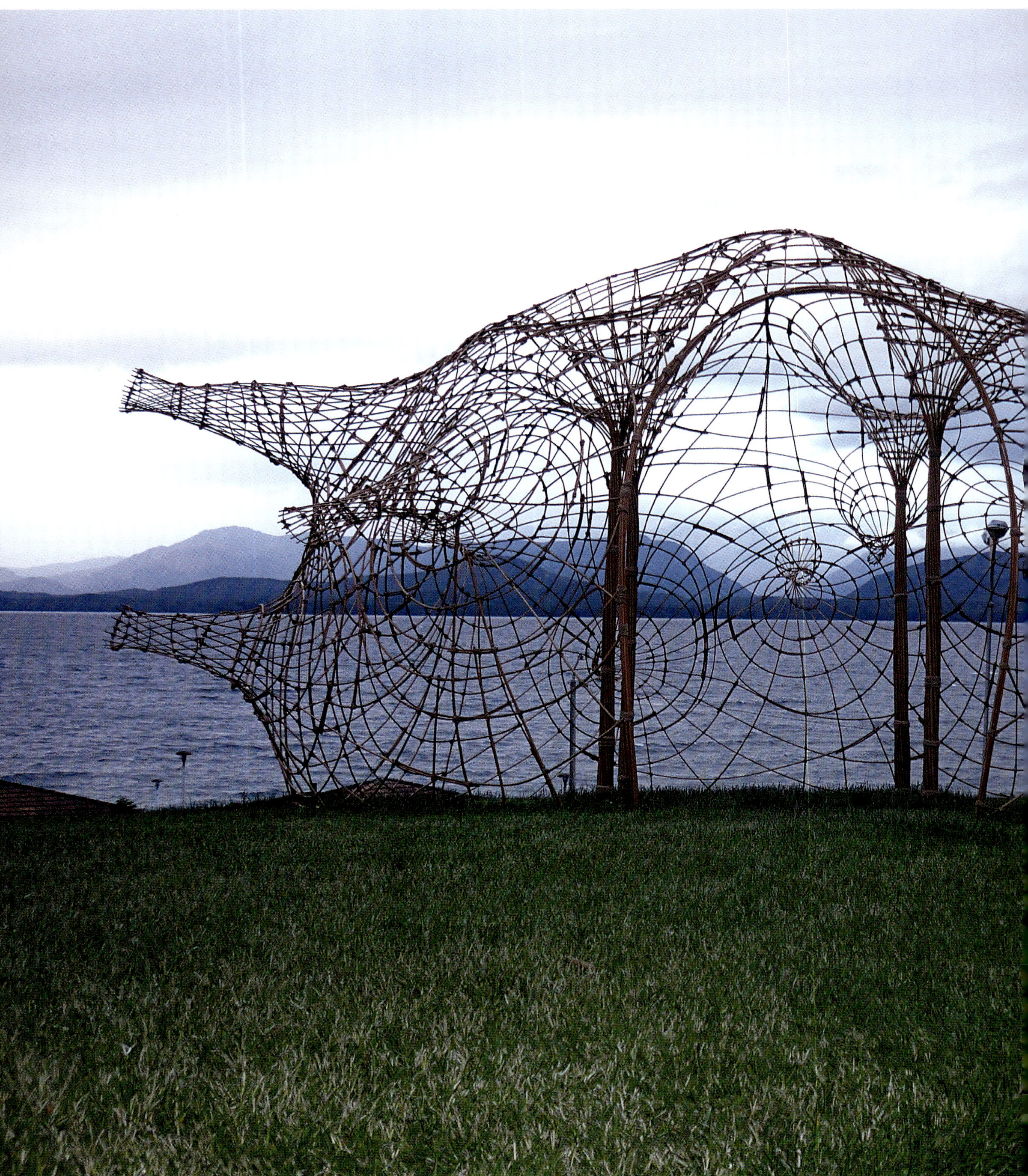

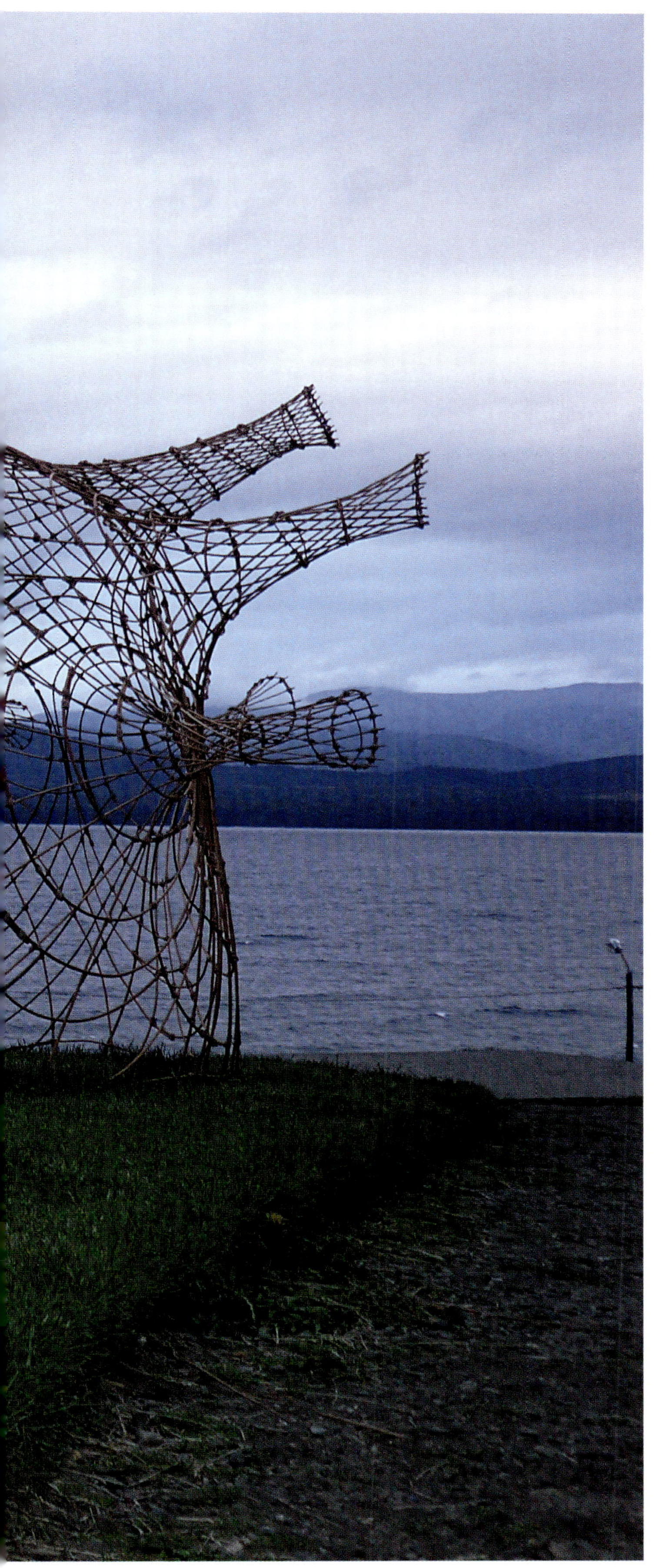

Transparency

In some baskets, the structure is visible but so decisively open or so fine that one can see through it. Such transparency allows another kind of connection or outreach, a penetrating one. The basket shows what it contains (if anything) and what's behind it, and it integrates with its surroundings by engaging with the light that passes through it and by casting shadows.

Among functional baskets, a loose, transparent structure indicates that lightweight, volumetric objects will be held, or that the material from which the basket is made is exceptionally tough. Gaps in structure may also serve purposes of ventilation. Among baskets made for artistic reasons, openwork is often exploited because transparency is a desirable feature; it can frame or outline, it can visually encompass, or it can veil. In any case, it adds another layer to the visual experience.

Additive: Repeating

As noted, the visibility of structure allows one to see how the basket is constructed. Most often, the process is additive: A basket is not carved or modeled but assembled through repetitive activity. It can start at the base with crossing elements around which a spiral is wound, or it could be constructed by interlacing elements in an over/under pattern. The specifics of technique are not the focus of this book; the essential point is that most often the process is not free movement but, rather, is a reiteration of a gesture. Therefore, there is a rhythm in the process engaged by the makers, which can be perceived in the finished basket by observing thickness, closeness, direction, pattern, and forcefulness of the elements and their interaction. Evidence of repetition is controllable by the maker and can be manipulated for impact. Different additive processes convey different

Edgardo MADANES. *Mirador*, 2014. Willow wicker: 3 × 6 m (10' × 19'). *Photo courtesy of the artist* feelings: Interlacing has a percussive precision, while coiling has a swaying, pulsing rhythm that inclines vertically. Repetition is a means of emphasis.

Additive repetition can imply outreach in a metaphoric sense—seeking connection. This idea of linkage may be demonstrated literally or suggested, and it evokes the way one person can be connected to another physically or psychically. Another image that repetition might evoke is cellular reproduction in all its aspects—constructive growth of distinct, measurable increments.

Additive: Collaging

Some artists stretch the definition of basketry by making the vessel wall of irregular pieces of material collaged together or applied over a framework. Collaged surfaces are opaque and tend to conceal structure. The most common applications are bark or heavy paper. Bark baskets may seem disorderly in surface character, since the bark pieces may be irregular in shape and because bark carries its own texture and its own markings of nature's hazards (weather, bug trails, knots), which remain apparent. But bark may also be cut into strips, making it thickly linear, so that it emphasizes extension rather than piecing.

Likewise, paper can be collaged in pieces large or small and regular or irregular. Clearly, bark or paper surfaces can vastly differ in visual weight, one looking massive and the other lightweight. These are the maker's expressive options. A basket's structure may also be covered with a thin layer of paper or fabric or coated with a thick layer of paint; these are different in that they lightly veil the structure but do not conceal it.

Additive: Relationships

Baskets, like pots and other functional objects, can be handmade in sets. Such multiples—considered for their positive volumes or for the charged negative spaces between them—activate a larger field of action. Such works put the emphasis on relationships. At its simplest, this may consist of a pair or a trio of related forms—identical, or mirroring, or telescoping in size, or relating in some other aspect. A pair of forms may seem to cling together or may seem to be in the process of splitting apart.

In functional works, repeated related baskets are simply sets, a commercial concept. But contemporary makers have found many more interesting considerations of multiplication. Stacking baskets creates a relationship that may be external (several objects touching) or may be interpreted as internal (one multipart object). Nesting baskets of graduated sizes are also an expression of relationship—usually conveying an inward feeling of snuggling comfort.

In the art world, an arrangement of many separate objects in a meaningful spatial relationship is called an installation. Many contemporary basket makers are exploring this option. An installation may consist of identical or unlike forms, but the relationship of the forms, and their placement in a context, is not arbitrary. They seem to have something to say about each other. Whether gathered on a wall or the floor, the elements can seem to cluster together in a family or community, evoking people or creatures. This is amplified when they take an anthropomorphic posture of leaning or bowing toward each other. Basketry installations can make puzzle-like compositions that encourage the viewer to ponder.

Shape or Volume

Baskets continue to be constructed in the spectrum of traditional shapes. They may also be suggested by enlargements of linear materials, such as ropes, tubes, or ribbons configured in such a way that they imply containment even if not precisely shaped as a container. They can also be constructed in nontraditional shapes, such as the human form, which has little relationship to a traditional basket except that both have interior space. (See "The Body," below.) As previously noted, it is that space—the basket's volume—that makes it functional, since it provides the space for something to be served or stored. The interior space can also be expressive. Textile constructions such as mats, nets, lacework, or cloth may bear some similarity to baskets in method or material, but they lack interior space.

Scale

Baskets can be any size, from minuscule to monumental. Functional baskets are scaled to the human hand or arm, for carrying or for reaching into. But if there's a drift in basketry in the last several decades, it's the same as in painting of the period: larger and larger dimensions. In all art, a larger-than-expected size demands that the object be individually considered, and gives it greater presence. A large basket insists on being shown on a pedestal, plinth, or wall rather than tucked into a shelf. Large scale also magnifies structure and makes it more apparent. It can make a basket intimidating.

Large scale, when it is not for reasons of enclosing a body for protection or control, can be any degree of enlargement, from just a slight but unexpected change to the production of something gargantuan: from body scale to architectural scale. An ordinary vessel form with obscuring walls in large scale may give a sense of mystery, generating concern about the unknown contents and the difficulty of releasing some sympathetic object or creature inside. An enormous nest, on the other hand, may evoke either the science-fiction notion of a gigantic bird or the thought of it being a communal shelter for animals or people. Exaggerated size alters interpretation and distorts the familiar, making it unfamiliar.

On the other hand, small scale gives a sense of preciousness. It pulls the viewer up close. Possibly it allows only one person at a time to interact with the basket, making the experience intimate. It does not preclude function, but it narrows the options.

Landscape

Large scale particularly suits two frequent themes (and sites) of contemporary basketry: landscape and architecture. In earlier times, a basket in the landscape was probably a trap, or it might be sited below a tree to catch ripe fruit or nuts. In contemporary times, a basket in the landscape is typically a sculptural form, often an organic echo of the setting in which it is placed. The form may evoke a growth pattern, shrublike or flowerlike. It may suggest the upward trajectory of a tree. Or it may poetically evoke something else in nature, from wind to clouds to moving water.

In our era of alarm about climate change, baskets embedded in the landscape are often a maker's effort to bond with nature and to demonstrate harmony with it. Basket forms attached to trees might allude to containment or to protection of the tree. They may recall

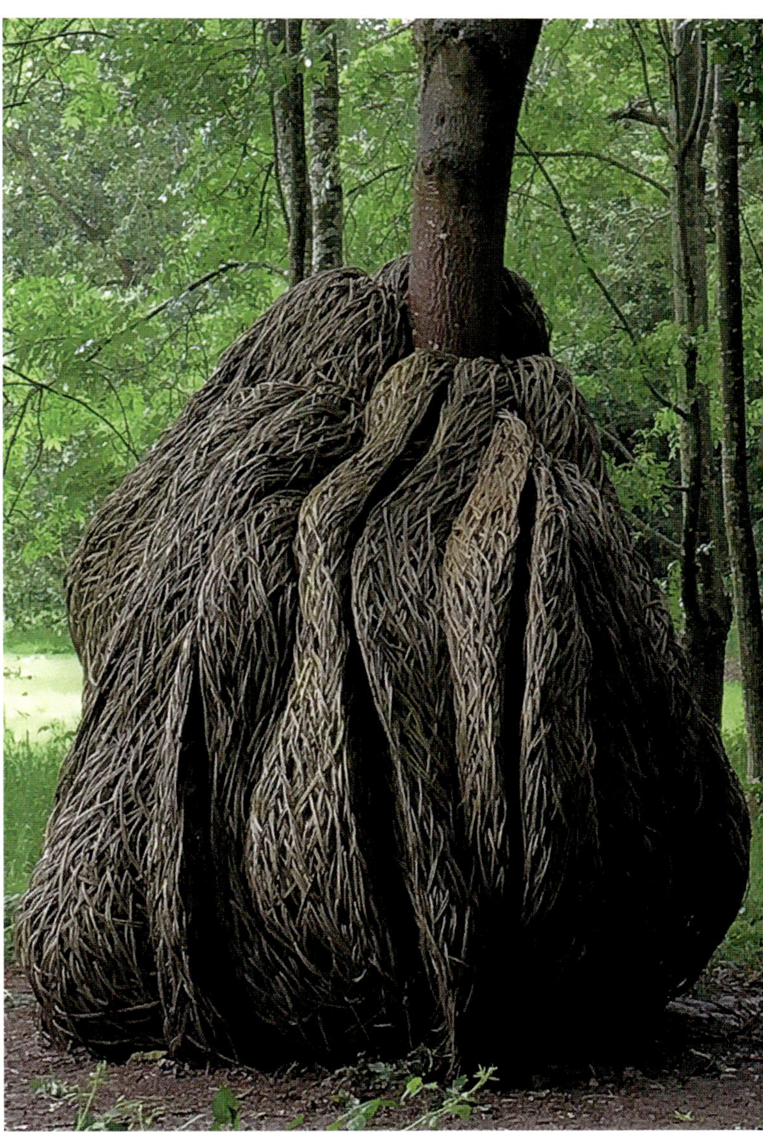

Laura Ellen BACON. *Don't Let Go*, 2019. Installation at University of Warwick, UK. Willow. *Photo courtesy of the artist*

nests or seem to be growths on a tree. More open and outward-reaching basketry constructions link trees together.

Or a basket may take advantage of the tree as a stable vertical element and sinuously wrap around the trunk. At other times, the tree is simply a convenient hangar for a sculpture that represents something else entirely. Circles—and cycles—are common in nature, yet emblematic circular forms have been used to refer to natural occurrences that we cannot see and grasp only intellectually, such as the diffusion of sound waves, or centrifugal force. They can be metaphors for the extent of impact, in a good or bad sense. Yet rigidly circular structures may seem nonnatural and therefore provocative intrusions in the landscape.

Landscape comprises not just hills and vegetation, but water as well. A favored practice in contemporary basketry is to install or float baskets in water. Sometimes this is simply an expression of natural materials in a natural setting, recalling rice and rushes and other plants the grow in water. Sometimes it suggests transport of cargo on the water. Sometimes it symbolizes movement and change and vulnerability. Often the setting is chosen for reflection, which doubles the form and elaborates the apparent structure. More playful installations at the shore or on a riverbank mock the ability of baskets to contain, since their perforated structure would not hold water. It's curious, then, that another favored familiar form used by makers is the boat shape, which may be presented anywhere—on land, suspended in trees, near or in a body of water—but could not really function. Boat forms can refer to both real and imagined travel, even supernatural transport.

Architecture

Large-scale basketry sculptures—typically of natural materials—often refer to architecture. Basket forms can be evocative additions to or reflections of buildings, where they interface between nature and architecture or pit one against the other. The combination may suggest that architecture is not immune to the strength and persistence of seemingly more-fragile natural growths—think of roots cracking concrete or rocks, or the strangler fig and banyan trees swallowing Angkor Wat.

As makers have worked in larger scale, they have devised a great variety of person-accommodating enclosures. Some resemble natural forms rather than buildings. Some interact with architecture in a plantlike way, such as winding over the roof of a building or "growing" from inside and passing through a window or door. Some are like patches on a building's wound. Others resemble snakes or snails crawling upon it. The architecture/basketry combination evokes the continuity and exchange of inside and outside and plays nature-made against human-made.

Basketry structure might function as the frame for a yurt or another sort of personal enclosure. Many sculptural basket forms set in the landscape recall tipis or wigwams, huts, coops, conservatories, domes. Domes can be powerfully suggestive, since they are an inversion of that basketry standard, the bowl. All these forms can be constructed for transparency, allowing a view of something within them or beyond them, or acting as a mark against the landscape. Or, contrarily, the basket structures may be closed and private. Basketry elements may cover a pergola much as a mat of vines would.

Basketry in relation to architecture may actually be buildings, may interact with buildings, or may comment on buildings. When basketry forms are set before a building like any public sculpture, they tend to differ in significant ways. Transparency allows the building or sky or landscape to be seen through the object; a handworked and lightweight structure contrasts with the more massive construction of the building; a circular or linear form stands out against the angularity and solidity of the building. A building is usually understood as a collection of planes, while a basket is a collection of lines.

Basketry of natural materials sited outdoors will decay. While baskets have been reproduced in bronze or other more lasting materials, the choice to use organic elements makes a statement about life cycles, ephemerality, and the natural world, and it speaks against the seemingly permanent intrusion of architecture.

Shadows/Reflections

Structure, transparency, and scale all can be exploited to visually expand and complicate a basket form through shadows or reflections. Shadows can be cast by daylight, but many makers orchestrate the additional dimension that shadows create when strategically lighted indoors, where they don't have to compete with a complex landscape background. Shadows are usually more impressive indoors against neutral backgrounds. Yet, in a gallery, emphasis on shadows can be a crutch to puff up a display by giving it unearned drama.

In the case of basketry, shadows seem justified as an extension of the linear character of the object. Shadows can express the idea of connecting because they stretch the basket into its environment. They create a ghost image, translate the three-dimensional object into two dimensions, and change a colored basket into a black-and-white version. The position of the light source determines whether the shadow replicates or distorts the basket structure.

Reflection has many of the same effects but is usually realized with baskets only in water settings. Mirrors or glass might do the same trick but are seldom presented with baskets.

Light

Baskets can be light fixtures themselves, with the structure of the basket designed to throw complex patterns of shadow. Baskets are familiar as shades for commercially manufactured lights, with the pattern of shadows adding to the decorative appeal. Probably the clearest dividing lines between a commercial product and an artist's investigation of light effects are scale and time investment . Makers take advantage of the freedom of handwork to devise lights in irregular shapes (such as soft baskets rather than rigid ones) or in showy, complex patterns (rather than small and tight designs). The basket structure for a light fixture may be as tight as lacework or so open that it seems to be a drawing in the air—in both cases, echoed by the shadow.

Colors and Patterns

The classic natural materials for baskets have their own colors but may also be receptive to dyes. In other cases, color may be applied to the surface rather than infused into the material. Baskets can also be formed of metal wire, which usually presents its own color, or from extruded or hand-rolled ropes of clay, which offer color

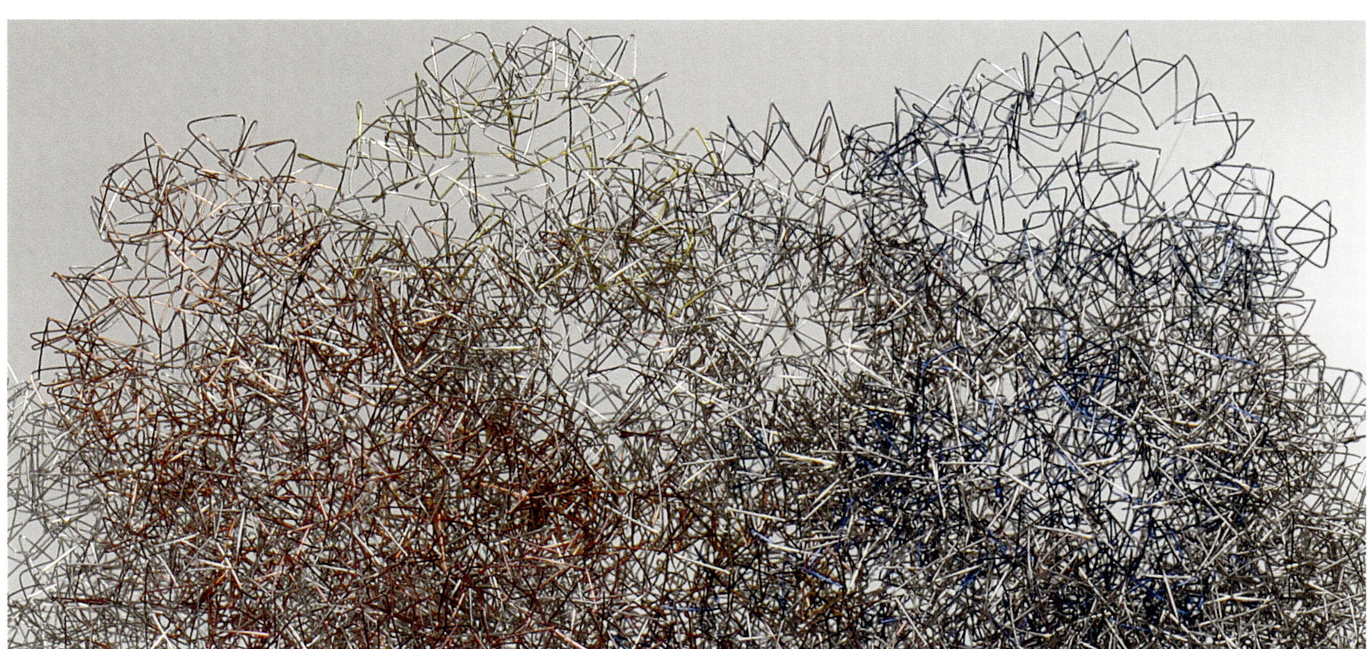

Haruko SUGAWARA. *Sunset Cloud I* (detail), 2016. Stainless steel: 20 × 30 × 17 cm (8" × 12" × 7"). *Photo courtesy of Studio Sky*

choices according to the type of clay and may also be glazed or painted. Baskets fashioned of paper, in the form of sheets, knotted ropes, twisted cords, or cut strips, can be given color when the paper is made, and can also receive paint or other coloring agents after it is used in construction.

Consequently, color is a common design element both in traditional and nontraditional baskets. The choices of the maker determine the color range, and it's largely decorative. A blue basket would not seem to carry a different meaning than a yellow one (other than the emotional temperature of colors). Yet, monochrome coloring can have a powerful impact and colors do have some established associations, although these vary from one culture to the next and are not a uniform language of expression. Any monochrome leaves the structure very clear because there is no pattern to compete with the understanding of it. This may be less true of black and some other dark colors because their darkness makes it hard to perceive minute internal shadows that reveal fine structure.

Not many materials are naturally an intense red—or if they are, the color is fugitive. Red seems to appear in contemporary baskets as an eye-catching hue, rather than having a specific meaning such as "stop" or "blood." White acts as a color in basketry because it does not occur naturally in the usual basketry materials; the closest instances are pale-beige natural materials. It is the opposite of black not just in the conventional dyad but also in the sense that its extreme paleness allows every shadow, no matter how minor or minuscule, to help define the structure or ornament. Perhaps that's why it is used in inventive baskets, both those in which tiny flecks of color stand out or those in which openwork leads to layered visual complexity rather than to transparency (because the structure remains so prominent). When white baskets appear among trees, they look alien. Thus white coloring tends to pull baskets out the context of nature to make a more conceptual point.

Color is another way to emphasize structure when it is used to distinguish segments of a form, no matter how irregular. Combining elements that are different

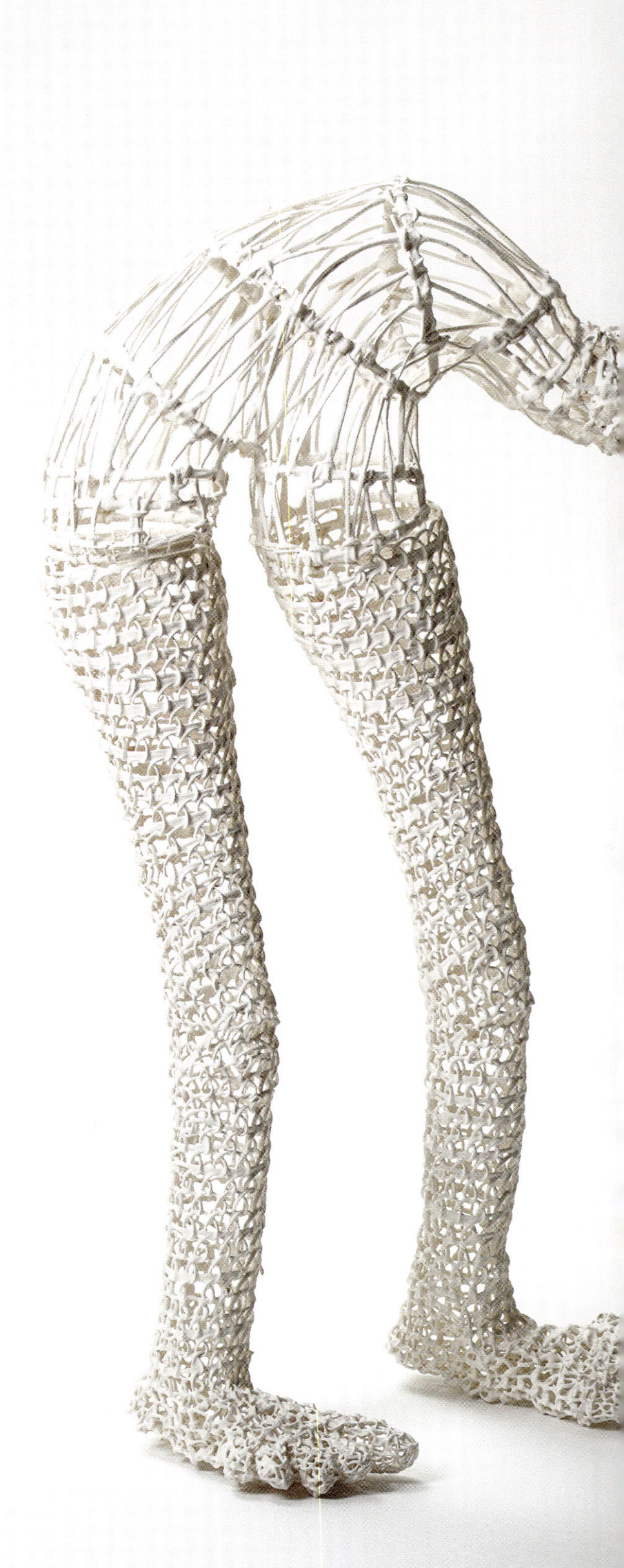

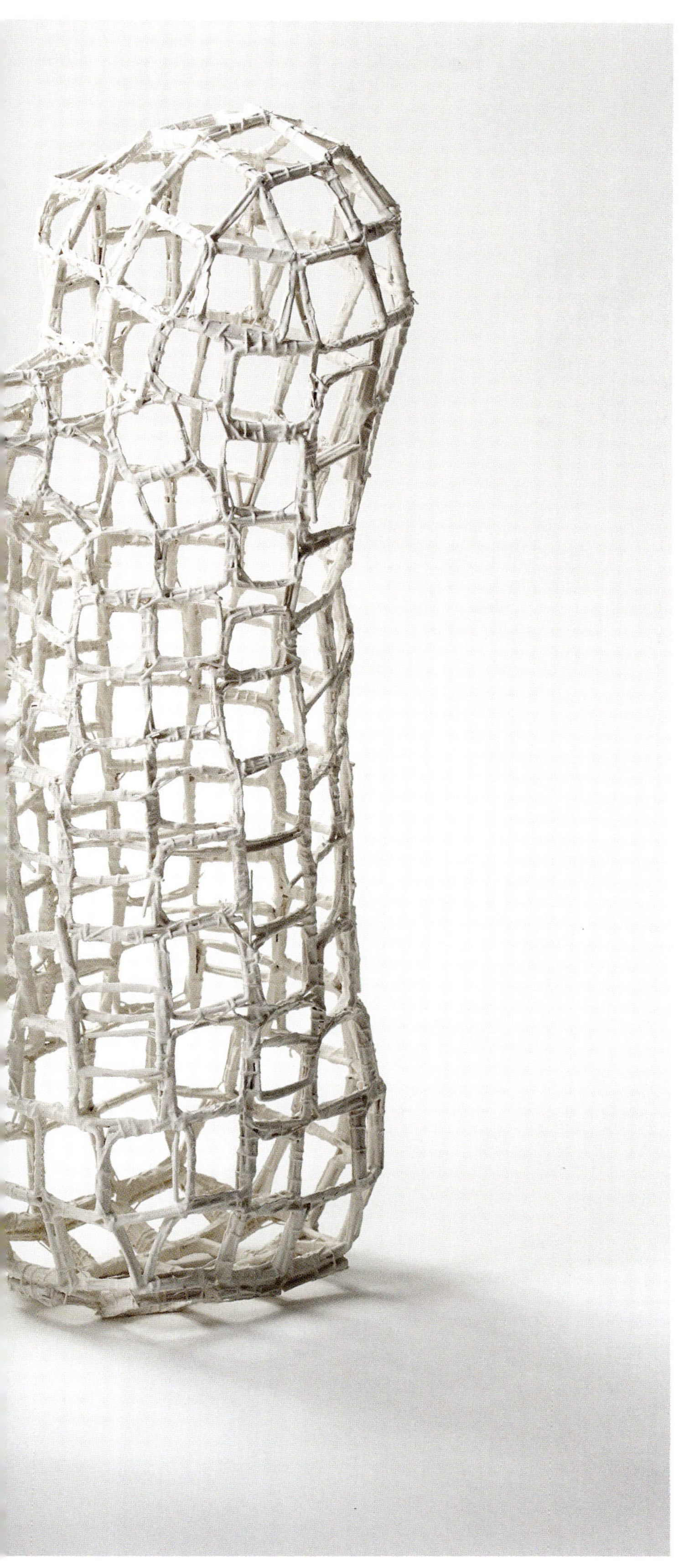

colors can make structural lines clear even in the most tangled construction. Color also enables the development of patterns. Patterns may be linear and orderly, as in some Native American basketry, but today pattern is also intentionally used to produce a chaotic—if festive—effect, a reflection upon the complicated times we live in. Adding to the complication, straight-line nonbasket elements or found objects may be added to the surface.

Stripes—revealed by color or by differences in materials type or size—can go in any direction on a basket, horizontal, vertical, diagonal, or spiraling. The conventional response to horizontal emphasis is stability and calm, while vertical implies aspiration or stretching, and diagonal or spiraling both give a sense of force and/or motion. Stripes can be employed to emphasize irregularities of contour, as, for example, a vertical stripe may seem to sway because of the dents and protrusions of a basket form. This can be an intentional optical effect. It demands careful looking.

The Body

As noted earlier, contemporary baskets have even adopted the human form as an option. It is not a natural match of material and subject, for one thing, because the tension involved in interlacing materials and the intermittency of surface have little relationship to the fleshy continuity of a body. Still, the vocabulary describing any vessel-type basket echoes that of a ceramic pot, consisting of terms that allude to bodies. Vessels have a foot, belly, shoulder, neck, lip, or mouth. Moreover, a vessel's posture may seem anthropomorphic. The resemblance is more projected or imagined than literal.

Contemporary makers, unrestricted in their considerations, have constructed figures and used them for various meanings. A figure is always immediately relatable, and we find a face or body image with only the

Stéphanie JACQUES. *Ce qu'il en reste III / What remains III*, 2015. Willow, gesso, thread; 69 × 60 × 30 cm (27" × 23" × 18"). *Photo by Patricia Mathieu, courtesy of browngrotta arts*

slightest hint. Thus the basket form can be little more than a head atop a trunk, or even less, such as a contoured form that looks like a dressmaker's dummy of a torso only. Rudimentary figures often suggest prehistoric or tribal associations. The surprise of a human form in basket materials is sometimes used as a means of abstracting or generalizing a person's pose or action. The same isolating abstraction can be seen when basketry material and structure mimic a portion of the body, such as a foot.

Deformation

To speak of deformation is to assume that there is a standard form that has been altered. In some art, the deformation of the human body suggests psychological or physical damage. In basketry, a deformed vessel might likewise appear to be aging or collapsing or to have suffered abuse. In a less distressing way, deformation can offer a sensuous tension between what is seen and what is imagined. More simply, one can follow the visual shifts and meanders of a deformed object, which encourage mental engagement with the form.

Language

Just as there is not a strong association of baskets with the human figure, there is no straight link between baskets and words. But artists have chosen to deploy language in various ways. Baskets made of used paper have introduced language when newspaper or book papers are the chosen material. Using newspaper connotes the ephemerality of language as a residue of daily life, while book pages imply an inaccessible knowledge, fragmented in the strips or patches of paper. In addition, some contemporary makers have counterintuitively constructed lettering in the process of making the basket, allowing the basket to offer text, with a specificity not native to visual art. The statements may be playful conundrums or references to serious matters.

Presentation

Another meaning implied in basketry does not derive from the character of the basket itself but from the way it is presented. Baskets tend to have a much stronger tie to their conditions of display than conventional sculpture, which requires no more than a plinth, or even just the floor or ground. In basketry, various presentations have a major impact on the meanings that can be associated with the work. For example, suspending a basket implies flexibility in the positive sense and vulnerability on the negative side, as well as light weight. Placing a basket on a pedestal increases its importance, asks that it be individually considered, and likely takes it out of the realm of function—such placement specifies a different context. A basket on a shelf is likely either functional or historic; if it is not alone, it may be part of a general statement or comparison, diminished in individual importance. It may be part of an installation. A basket mounted on the wall may conceivably be waiting for use, Shaker style, but more likely it is being called up for visual study. The more three-dimensional it is, the more difficult this placement is. But even a fully three-dimensional basket on the wall is brought to eye level, encouraging examination.

Placing a basket in nature identifies its source, declares a relationship, and accepts a shorter life than the basket would have in a more protected situation. A basket wrapped around a tree trunk or attached to a building takes advantage of the particular qualities of baskets to achieve this range. Since they are lightweight and since they are hand-constructed, they may be shaped to their "host," whether a natural or a man-made form. Baskets shown in association with machinery in a landscape setting, such as with farm equipment or emerging from the hull of a boat, are usually large scale and nontraditional in form, to resist the visual strength of the machinery. Some baskets engage with the floor or ground not by simply resting up on it, but by sprawling, covering it to evoke a mat, but not in a typical way.

Suspending allows a basket to be made without a foot to stand on. It enables every sort of complex form, including tangles—almost scribbles—that without suspension would not even have a clear up or down. Suspending allows installations that do not take up floor space and that derive meaning out of making the viewer look up. It can suggest that something was once in motion. It can make a basket seem weightless and ethereal. It can make it seem tentative and in transition. It can allude to the vulnerability or intimacy of draping, as in clothing or jewelry. It can resemble a natural form such as a wasp nest. This presentation option is especially suited to basketry, whereas the pedestal and the wall are adopted from other art forms.

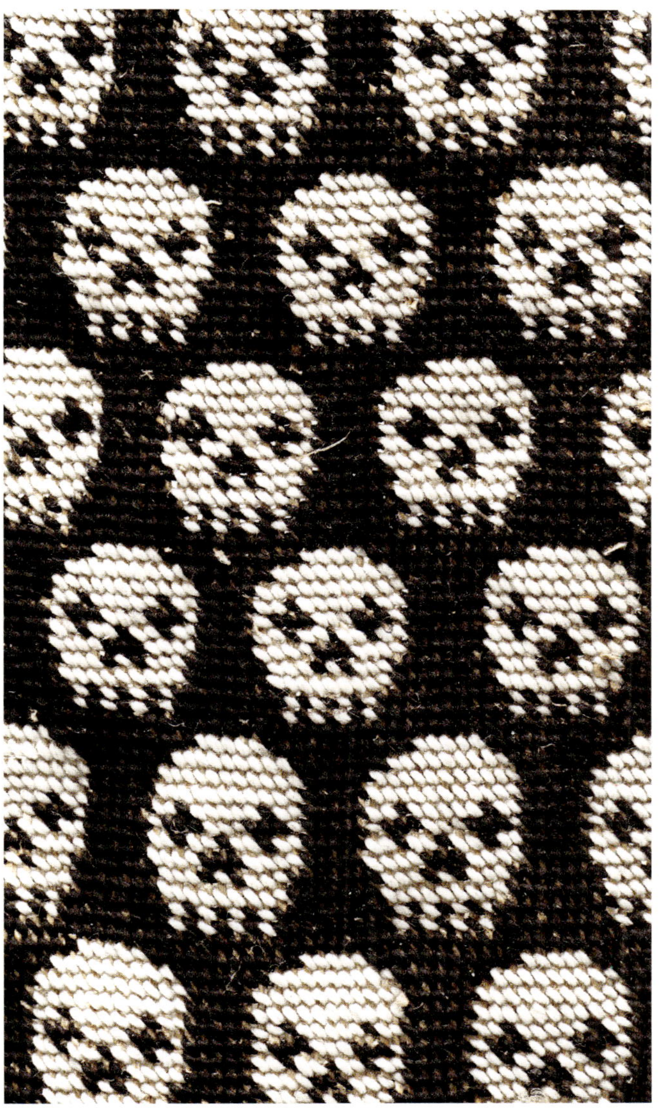

Allusion

The new attention to basketry tends to be visual more than practical. Essentially, the basket is valued as a metaphor, as something more than what it literally is. This may be most striking with the makers who come from the art world rather than the textile world. But in one sense or another, it is true of all—even those who have come to basketry through the most traditional kinds of apprenticeships, because even they tend to value their perpetuation of tradition for what tradition means philosophically and socially in a modern culture. Often the referent of the work, but not the actuality, is some form of use.

Makers identified with basketry usually construct the work themselves, or with the help of assistants, but in either case craftsmanship is a concern. But some artists who present basket forms are conceivers but not constructors, or, more often, they are artists who work in many genres and do not claim a close association to basketry. Martin Puryear is one interesting example of this because, while he has a commitment to fine workmanship regardless of his material, he has only selectively employed basket forms for various uses, including the identification with traps and cages. In a looser sense, he makes enclosures of thought. Tadashi Kawamata conceived of applying agglomerations of wooden boards to ruined buildings, with the concept that this process brought the buildings back into time going forward. The feeling his basketlike structures give is rushed, not finessed, a residue of the violence the buildings have undergone.

Other makers may have specific cultural referents or personal associations that drive the execution of work in the realm of basketry. Sometimes a title or a biographical fact will help viewers to understand the implications.

Joe FEDDERSEN. *Kamloops Residential School* (detail), 2024. Waxed linen: 24 × 22 cm (9.5" × 9"). *Photo courtesy of Dean Davis Photography.*

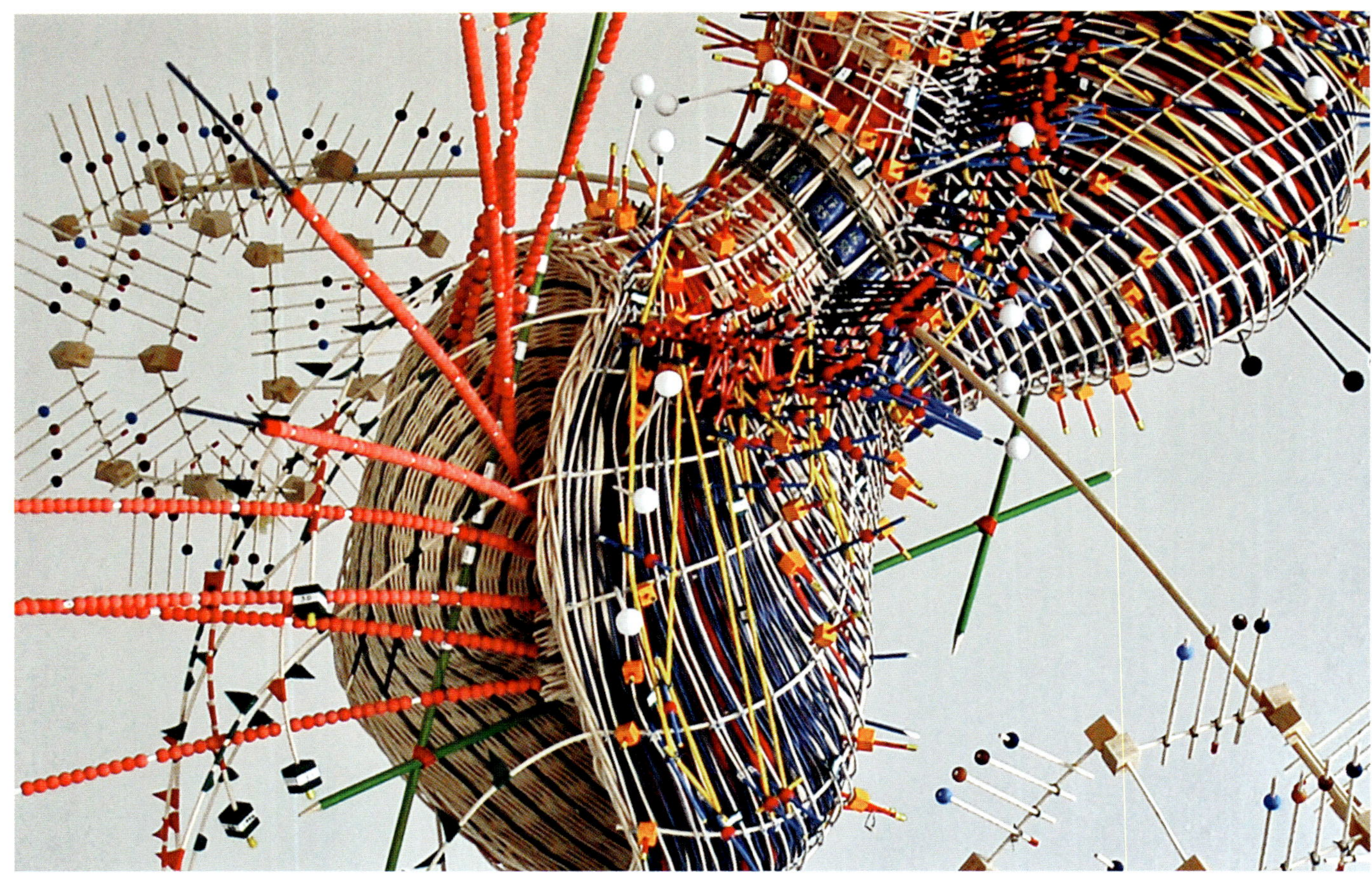

Nathalie MIEBACH. *Warm Winter* (detail), 2007. Reed, wood, data: 182 × 152 × 182 cm (72" × 60" × 72"). *Photo courtesy of the artist*

New Methods

Just as basketry as a concept easily accepts new materials, so it can embrace new methods, such as 3-D printing. While of course this would not be met with enthusiasm by traditionalists, dimensional printing can be used for structural but non-load-bearing lattice elements resembling basketry that allow the transmission of light and the movement of air in architectural settings. A basket can be accomplished by robotics.

It would seem that digital printing would yield only regular and repetitive forms. But the printer can be programmed to exceed the stability of the plastic or ceramic material being employed so that it collapses and gives the appearance of spontaneity.

Especially interesting to those working with natural materials are experimental "collaborations" with processes or creatures of the natural world, such as birds and bees as forming agents, or controlled root growth used to create a tangled-basket shape, or incisions in living trees harvested later to feature the scarred bark.

Recognizable Objects

Some baskets are made to contrast with what they contain, which may be revealed by the shape of the basket and its opening or may be visible because of the transparency of the basket. In these cases, the contents are intentional, selected, and symbolic. This is not a matter of utility but of contrast of material, weight, form, etc. The basket is given meaning by the identity of what it contains.

Artists have combined baskets with stones for a maximum contrast. Sometimes the stone is wrapped in interlaced natural materials, protected like a newborn.

Sometimes it is caged within a tiny house of shiny wire—newly, but forever, imprisoned. Rounded stones that are collected within a basket of rusty wire contrast their senses of time and resistance. In all these examples it is the disharmonious relationship of the component materials that creates a mood and provokes the viewer's mind to wander, looking for an explicit reference. The basketry is smaller, finer, more detailed, and—importantly—it is worked, manipulated, which generates an energy and tension that is at odds with the impassiveness of the stones.

Another example is eggs. Egg baskets are a traditional utilitarian form. But an egg is also a symbolic object, so it has drawn the attention of makers who present it with a soft-looking fibrous scarf or in a twig or a wire nest. Enclosing and protecting are the messages here.

But anything can be inside. Sometimes there is a basket within a basket. Frequently, when transparency allows us to see a foreign object in the interior, it is something that would not fit through the mouth of the basket—if, indeed, there is a mouth. The basket both symbolizes and exemplifies containment, and it is left to the viewer to interpret it as protecting or imprisoning.

Sometimes a maker who works consistently in basketry—rather than a sculptor who occasionally borrows the form—uses the materials or the associations of the form to convey a less-than-obvious meaning. A miscellany of familiar materials may be wired together in a basket shape as a kind of memory catchall.

In addition to containing symbolic objects, baskets may be shaped to resemble industrial objects from the real world. These works, since they re-create form but do not function, provoke questions of the original object's value; for example, when it is an appliance. A simpler object, such as a funnel, cone, or fan, when realized as a basket, may concentrate on abstract form in addition to evoking the real-life purpose. Animals made of basketry materials may be associated with their place in nature.

In Closing

The British sculptor Phyllida Barlow (1944-2023) spoke of her sculptures as "restless objects." That term seems resonant for baskets. For one thing, they are restless in the sense of being unfixed to a precise time. Although some baskets have managed to survive since ancient times, to a large degree baskets are ephemeral. They may succumb to insects or to unfavorable climatic conditions or to a poor storage environment. They may lose their shapes, but the failing forms still have a sort of melancholy beauty. And that makes another basket metaphor: the parallel to vulnerable living vessels, that is, humans or other animals. Baskets are restless in being flexible and not fixed in form, and also in the sense of being lightweight and thus portable, which means they are not fixed in place. Additionally, artists are restless and are always looking to defy expectations and to distinguish themselves and their works, so exemptions can be found to any presumed attribute, and all is open to interpretation—there is always the possibility of Something Else, as suggested by the tabs on the works illustrated here. You can find categories on your own. Baskets generate unspoken feelings, remembrances, concerns, and delights, and that's art enough.

WORDS FROM THE ARTISTS

Kim AH SAM *Australia* — PAGE 52

vivienandersongallery.com | @kimahsam

I am a Kalkadoon and Kuku Yalanji woman who grew up in Brisbane knowing little of traditional ways or my cultural connections to my father's country of Kalkadoon. The concept of my five woven sculptures is to represent my cultural identity through the stages of my life, from childhood through adolescence to adulthood. These woven sculptures represent my coming to maturity and cultural awareness. My practice is mixed traditional weaving and stitching, heavily focused on the repurposing of materials I fossick for, or which are donated to me, such as repurposed rope, raffia, bamboo, feathers, even old venetian blinds. Each woven piece is my conscious journey of growing up and finding who I am as an Indigenous woman. The forms are a corporeal manifestation of myself growing up, receiving knowledge, understanding my place in the world. I imagine my skin as a landscape, like a time journey. Making them gave me a powerful emotion, a sense of belonging, a feeling that I had already been there, and a sense of finding my cultural identity.

Laura Ellen BACON *United Kingdom* — PAGE 94

lauraellenbacon.com | @lauraellenbacon

I create my large, abstract willow forms by making a knotted willow framework and then using an informal, dense weave. Typically, I use willow in quite large quantities, but I also work with other natural materials such as reed or stone.

Much of my work is large enough for me to stand within it (either during the process or when finished), and has been driven by a desire to create an enclosure of some kind, a kind of woven space. I often build upon existing structures, allowing a building or landscape to "feed" the form, as if some part of the host site is exhaling into the work.

The thrill of making a woven space or a woven form by tying, pushing, and pulling the material into position and the accumulation and layering of materials appeals to me, as does the experience of working with my hands in a seemingly repetitive way.

My work is entirely abstract, and at first glance it can sometimes be difficult to assess if my work has been shaped by plants, natural phenomena, or the human hand. I enjoy making work that feels strangely familiar in this way, and I am motivated to draw attention to the peculiarities of the natural world.

Carolina CARUBIN *Argentina* — PAGE 58

carolinacarubin.com | @carolinacarubin

Regarding the rules proposed by different textile disciplines, I do not deny them, but I do betray them. I use traditional techniques and ready-made objects to arrive at my own production system, almost wishing to pull apart the handcrafts world.

Whether suspended in space or just lying on the floor, my soft sculptures are sinuous organisms of open existence that do not fit into traditional categories. Figures are rarely attractive. Some are hollow like skeletons; others are almost liquid membranes that leak at the interstices. They may suggest niches, nests, larvae, communities, herds, as well as deformations of the bodies that give life. Abstractions and patterns blend the animal and the vegetable.

Dee CLEMENTS *United States* — PAGE 48

studioherron.com | @studioherron | ninajohnson.com

Basketry is the oldest craft in human history. Some evidence exists of plaited and interlaced plant fibers as far back as 34,000 years ago. Basket weaving, a global craft, is a language of form and utility. It has evolved along with us since the beginning of our species.

My work examines the roles of women and their unseen labor through the lenses of ethnography and feminism. I use the language of weaving to create sculptural vessels that are metaphors for what women hold, and how early human society relegated them to crafts that have historically been done in tandem with child rearing. In the 1970s, anthropologist Elizabeth Fisher, in *Woman's Creation: Sexual Evolution and the Shaping of Society*, discussed her "carrier bag theory of human evolution"—the idea that the body was the first vessel and that the primitive basket, an interlacement of sticks and twigs for carrying foraged foods, was the next kind of carrier bag. Inspired by this theory, my baskets are corporeal sculptures. They are bulbous, pudgy, droopy, saggy, leaning or off-kilter. I use bright colors to highlight what seem like matronly curves and hyperfeminine forms. Weave patterns reference my career in textile design and the world of textiles as a historically women's field.

Ann CODDINGTON *United States* — PAGE 14

abcoddington.com | @abcoddington

I am fascinated by extending pre-Neolithic traditions of making into the present, my hands moving in similar ways as our ancient predecessors' had. Through these processes, I create a connection with ancient human beings by extending their methods for making functional objects into the present-day, fine-art basketry world.

My artwork also reflects the work of my more immediate ancestors, my mother and grandmothers, how they knit, crocheted, and did needlework for their homes and their loved ones. Tapping into this legacy of women and making is a way to reclaim and celebrate the often-invisible labor that sustains and enriches our world.

The use of familiar natural materials and techniques is an entry point into the work for viewers who can then experience themes of growth, metamorphosis, connection, birth, and aging. My work often evokes naturally occurring organic forms such as seed pods, microorganisms, and the body. I make objects that may recall something familiar, tapping into a shared universal, visual language—the way a spiral refers to a shell, a galaxy, or a human ear.

Dan COOPEY *United Kingdom / Brazil* — PAGE 36

@dancoopey

My work attempts to support basketry as an innate human expression, to reconnect on a personal level with this ancient technology—to make it feel fresh, alive, and full of purpose. To do this requires unlearning and defamiliarization, finding ways to look at and feel the fibers anew.

I am interested in histories so ancient that they are largely speculation. One theory is that at a time when baskets were lined with earth in order to carry liquids, an accidental fire caused a basket to perish, leaving the first fired ceramic vessel. One would imagine that baskets would then have been rendered outmoded. But basketry continued to be practiced across the globe by almost all cultures. This pan-cultural nature interests me.

While weaving, my body has to make great effort to tension fibers against their will. In return, the fibers create tension in my own fibers, the cord-like tendons that connect every muscle in a body. Twists and turns in the works are formed by positioning the weaving at specific angles in relation to my body. Thus the weaving is an extension of my body. I never design my works; rather, forms emerge organically out of this intimate and intuitive process. The undulations that result add strength to the forms and a fluidity that echoes wheel-thrown clay vessels, which links back to my initial interest.

Patrick DOUGHERTY *United States* — PAGE 96

stickwork.net

As a sculptor who constructs monumental site-specific works using sticks, I take great pleasure in the building process with all its problem-solving and day-to-day evolution. I love the challenge of trying to achieve the right scale for the site and to build a sculpture that seems integrated and blends well with its surroundings. Using saplings as lines with which to draw, I like to suggest in the sculpture's surface the powerful momentum of wind, water, and the hidden forces of the nature.

Part of the success of my sculptures is the way they tend to remind people of their profound connection to the natural world and seem to foster fantasies of walking away from the geometry of the city and fading back into the forest for a day. Our contemporary challenge is how to reconnect and live in harmony with the plants and animals that still share the earth. I believe that "stickworks" and other kinds of environmental initiatives can help with that awareness.

Joe FEDDERSEN *United States* — PAGE 62

joefeddersen.com | @joe_feddersen

I began weaving 30 years ago and my initial interest in the art evolved into creating contemporary Plateau root baskets that use traditional twining processes to speak to current issues. When I heard of the 215 unmarked graves of children at the Native boarding school in Kamloops, British Columbia, I struggled to comprehend the senseless taking of so many young Native lives. The tragedy became even more real to me when I learned that my grandparents had attended the school. They survived the experience but never spoke of it, leaving me to guess that they chose to suffer in silence and move on as best they could. I, however, could not forget. To express the sheer number of lost children of Kamloops, I was inspired to create an indelible memorial to lives that should never have been extinguished and that should never be forgotten. I began with

215 tiny skulls, and as I wove I thought of the children. I imagined a labyrinth starting in the center of the spiral and, working my way around and around, sought a path to an explanation for this atrocity. At the same time, I thought of my ancestors and all the horrors and injustices to which they were subjected under the policies and in the hands of church and government oppressors. I weave to honor the lost children of Kamloops and the tragedies of all Native schools.

Cheng-Tsung FENG *Taiwan* — PAGE 106

chengtsung.com | @chengtsungfeng

These two works are collaborative projects created by a community of participants who had no prior weaving skills or experience. The participants ranged widely in age, from teenagers to the elderly.

Basketry has such an approachable nature that anyone can start learning and creating. Through these two creative projects, I want to share the joy of weaving with people, allowing them to bring these basic weaving techniques into their own lives and to try various applications using different materials.

Additionally, these two pieces are quite large, achieved by magnifying two different basketry structures through exacting structural calculations and material arrangements. Due to the enlargement and extensive combinations, people can experience the structural strength and the logically meticulous aesthetics of basketry through different scales of visual and physical perception.

Most of my works are individual creations. My college training was in industrial design, but during my studies I became fascinated by the process of making traditional handcrafted items and visited those who make them. Documenting the processes, I realized that making cannot be fully taught through diagrams and texts. Especially the feel and temperature of the materials and tools in hands must be passed down from one person to another. I made my first community-oriented collaborative work in 2016.

Alexandra FERDINANDE *France* — PAGE 10

tressages-pas-sages.com | @tressagespassages

When I weave wicker, I connect with nature and my environment. I collect and use natural elements. I pick, I glean, I intertwine, I interweave, I give shape to a volume from stems, twigs, lianas.

I try to pay homage to the sensitive world: I listen to rare moments and then transcribe them in my basketry. I try to be attentive to detail, to draw inspiration from it to convey the emotions and sensations of living things.

Pearls of water glisten in the tree after the rain, a caress of sunlight crosses the foliage of a weeping willow, a gentle wind animates the wild grasses and makes the hillside dance. . . . I strive to capture the poetry of the moment. I transcribe it into my basketry to share with my fellow human beings in an attempt to reenchant the everyday.

I find a movement in the material, observe its reaction, and then capture this dynamic. I play with light and shadow, exploring the energy of contrasts and chiaroscuro. I propose variations on rhythm, power, radiance, weightlessness, and lightness.

Alice FOX *United Kingdom* — PAGE 22

alicefox.co.uk | @alicefoxartist

Hybrid Objects is a series of works exploring old tools and other things found on my allotment (garden) plot. The majority of my work is focused around using materials from the plot—found objects combined with cultivated and wild plants. Taking a playful approach to a set of old tools led me to explore ways I could bring different substances together. This resulted in forms that suggest function but are essentially sculptural. Working with only materials found on-site gives me a set of boundaries to work within and helps me achieve a sustainable approach to my artistic practice. It pushes me to be inventive and explore what is available to me, rather than relying on what might traditionally be used. I am constantly learning from the materials I work with, always finding new means of bringing them together in interesting ways.

Shoko FUKUDA *Japan* — PAGE 92

fukudashoko.com | @fukuda_shooko

Organic shapes such as curves, zigzags, undulations, and twists are the result of a combination of the flexibility of the materials and weaving phenomena.

I take inspiration from baskets, weaving linear materials by hand to create sculptural works. Since normally flexible materials are used in my work, the final form is also flexible and deforms with its own weight when it is hung. In this respect, it is kind of in between a basket and a piece of cloth and can be characterized as a soft basket or a three-dimensional cloth.

The works are constructed by the action of "winding." It is thought that the winding causes rotation, which draws out repulsion from the core material, resulting in twisting. Each piece is a combination of a core material with elasticity (springiness of the parts) and resilience (rebounding force against the applied force) added to the flexible winding material. In other words, when investigating characteristics and combinations of two materials, the way the core is stacked and the direction of winding affect and change each other. By changing the winding direction and combining multiple surfaces, anomalous twists are intentionally generated.

Naomi Wanjiku GAKUNGA *United States / Kenya* — PAGE 56

naomiwanjiku.com | @naomiwanjikustudio

My artistic journey began at the age of five in Gacharage Village, Kenya, under the guidance of my grandmother and her friends. They taught me the craft of weaving Gikuyu kiondo baskets, using yarn extracted from local migiyo shrubs. These baskets are traditionally used for gathering crops, storing harvests, and carrying gifts, but their significance extends beyond these practical uses. They are culturally charged vessels, rich with communal history and personal stories, representing the blend of everyday life and spiritual practice intrinsic to African societies.

In my contemporary work, I reimagine the traditional Gikuyu kiondo basket, merging ancestral craftsmanship with colonial-era crocheting techniques and modern materials. As an immigrant, I weave together narratives from my Kenyan heritage with my experiences in the United States, creating a dialogue between the past and present, and exploring the dynamics of continuity and change.

My baskets blend tradition and innovation, honoring cultural roots while engaging with the evolving global landscape. They uphold the values of generosity, community, and spirituality, celebrating these ideals through their innovative design and craftmanship. My baskets strive to bridge generations and geographies, and to connect individuals to a broader collective, through our shared expression of basketry.

John GARRETT *United States* — PAGE 76

johngarrettarts.com

I grew up in a house under construction. My first set of blocks was made by my dad, using scrap lumber. Once the house was built, my parents had a place for their modest collection of Native American arts and crafts, including rugs and baskets. We were all involved with Scouts. Something was always being made, or remade, at our house.

My first art class in college was weaving. I responded immediately to the possibilities presented by interlacing two sets of threads to create a web. Soon I explored forms that could be created from what came off the loom. To hold the flexible woven pieces rigid, I used wire rings as armatures. Still today I use the combination of an armature with other materials, soft and hard.

My work has been a conversation between flat, wall-hung work and three-dimensional forms; between soft, pliable materials and harder, more rigid ones. While I prefer using fiber/textile methods for connections, I have been open to using glue and rivets as possible solutions. Designs from quilts have become major elements in my current baskets, which in turn create ideas for my wall work.

Fiona GAVINO *Australia* — PAGE 88

fionagavino.com | **@fionagavino**

My practice began in the remote Northern Territory (Australia) in the late 1990s. As I pursued an interest in basket making, Yolngu elder Anne Gondjalk taught me the techniques and materials for traditional baskets and ceremonial objects. Because I do not belong to this culture, it was important for me to find my own unique artistic voice. A significant influence in this was the Ngarrindjeri woman, senior fiber artist, and master weaver Yvonne Koolmatrie, who said, "Fiona, you know you don't just have to make baskets." This led to my work in sculpture.

The American artist and Franciscan monk Jerry Bleem introduced me to the concept of bifurcated surfaces, which led to another transformative shift. In a way, I pay homage to my Filipino heritage, predominantly working in cane and rattan to make large-scale basketry. Thinking with my hands to push the boundaries of what basketry can do or say, synthesizing complexity with conceptually driven work, I take fiber to an elevated practice. The result expresses the inherent beauty and intricacy of the natural world. My work highlights the potential of design and materiality as tools for safeguarding our planet. Rather than constantly looking to invent, it is essential to recognize that the stories and resources we need are here.

Karen GOSSART and Corentin LAVAL *France* — PAGE 34

oseraiedelile.com | @oseraiedelile

Creative basket makers for nearly 20 years, we moved to L'Oseraie de l'île in southwest France in 2012, where we grow our own willow.

We weave with four hands and play with shapes and techniques, sometimes with lightness and curves, in a very spontaneous gesture, or layer after layer for a more in-depth exploration of the material and the tensions at play within it.

Sometimes it is nature that inspires us to create functional or decorative objects with unique shapes, and willow guides us. Sometimes mixing diverse techniques leads us to contemporary and graphic basketry emphasizing curves, spirals, and line, a meeting point of tradition and innovation.

The richness of this infinite potential amazes us, as a multitude of shapes can be created from just a few rods of willow. It's a real dialogue with the material, rooted in tradition and its techniques, at the service of a constantly renewed curiosity.

Marie-José GUSTAVE *Canada* — PAGE 122

mariejosegustave.com | @mariejosegustave

I use basketry in my creative work for the volumes it allows me to create. The only material I use for basketry is paper thread. I love the repetitive gesture of weaving with this very fine thread, which allows me to create organic shapes that let the light through.

This aesthetic ties in with the theme of my practice, which focuses on diversity and preconceived ideas. Through ignorance, we all have a skewed view of differences. The light on these simple forms changes our perception of the object and symbolically evokes how our view of the Other can change.

In using basketry, I also find a meeting point with other cultures, as basketry is a technique found all over the world in various forms. My work illustrates the language that enables me to communicate with others through this universal technique, for everyone, wherever they are in the world, has held a basket in their hands.

Gjertrud HALS *Norway* — PAGE 104

gjertrud-hals.no | @gjertrudhals

In earlier times the Norwegian coast was fairly bare of trees, so when I grew up in the 1950s it was still common to heat a home with peat. My grandparents carried the peat in a basket woven of twigs, which they carried on their backs. It was functionally designed; wide at the top and narrow at the bottom.

When I, many years later, started making baskets, I always had this beautiful shape in mind, though my baskets are not for practical use. They are to be considered more like sculptures. But I hope they reflect something from my background, although the techniques and materials I use are quite far from my grandparents' torvekase (peat basket).

Porky HEFER *South Africa / France* — PAGE 118

animal-farm.co.za | @heferporky

In my work in vernacular architecture and design, I try to:

- push traditional techniques and materials.
- work with traditional craftspeople and create vernacular objects that have a contemporary relevance.
- celebrate and elevate vernacular architecture and design.
- celebrate the hand and human over technology.
- work with existing systems, to strengthen and grow them rather than compete with them.
- create organic forms in an organic way.
- work with instinct rather than rules and degrees.
- create objects or environments that alter your state of body and mind.
- bring nature into the home and the home into nature.
- challenge the way we interact with the universe to find a new way of living in harmony with it.
- insist that play and discovery are parts of everyday life.

Pat HICKMAN *United States* — PAGE 30

pathickman.com

Throughout my life as a fiber artist, I am especially interested in the intimate relationship between structure and surface. When I was studying at the University of California at Berkeley, a Yupik parka of seal intestine captured my imagination as an inner skin that became an outer protective garment. Ed Rossbach, my professor, made baskets of various structures covered with skin-like materials. When I collaborated with my mentor and friend Lillian Elliott, she built structures of rigid basketry materials, which I covered with skin.

My signature material became hog casings, which I use as both skin and structure, sometimes in the same piece. Using it as a linear element, I create knotted netting, which, molded and formed, hard and dry, serves as vessel structure. That can then be covered, inside or outside, with a transparent surface of animal membrane. In my basket called *Winnow*, the netted structure is tight, the tiny knots in the netting and the direction of those knots suggesting strong movement and density—pure structure. The container—with its shadows spilling through those tiny openings—brings to mind an ordinary farm tool for separating wheat from chaff, one thing from another. *Holding* suggests openness, in the broadest definition of what a basket can be. I think of my works as visual metaphors. The material, the technique, and the form are meant to provoke the imagination, responding honestly and directly to these times.

Esmé HOFMAN *Netherlands* — PAGE 72

esmehofman.nl | @esmehofman

As a modern craftswoman I am versatile and flexible. I like to explore technical and material boundaries and stretch them. It is a challenge to create new and innovative work using age-old techniques, and collaborations with designers and artists have challenged me to reconsider the traditional ways of making.

Traditionally woven objects have a function, which often dictates the choice of technique and material. For a traditionally trained maker, the starting point is always determined by skills, and the goal is high quality and perfection. Letting go of function gives me the freedom to create objects that are independent, ones in which lines, pattern, structure, and form are decisive.

Inspiration comes from everywhere: from the shape of an old jug to the pattern of a spiderweb to colorful textiles. The beauty of antique basketry pieces also endlessly fascinates me. Every action of construction is executed with precision and skill. I am searching for a duality, a conversation, to invite people to look at my work with a different eye. My aim is to make alluring pieces that call viewers to come closer and, I hope, surprise and move them.

Joe HOGAN *Ireland* — PAGE 12

joehoganbaskets.com | @joehoganbaskets

I have worked as a basket maker since 1978, attracted by the ease with which willow could be grown and thus allowing me the chance to live rurally. I made functional baskets for many years. These needed no explanation; they were strong, durable, and, I hope, also beautiful. I came to basketmaking when the Indigenous Irish baskets were going out of use, and I became very interested in learning and passing on these techniques.

When I began to make artistic baskets, I was drawn to this activity by an urge, not fully understood, that included a desire to deepen my feeling of belonging in the world, a creature among creatures. At first I felt the need to justify or explain the existence of this new work, but this has diminished. It seems more a question of being the river by which the idea reaches the sea. This begins with honoring the urge to make that to which we are drawn. If it touches the spirit of others in some way, then all the better. The techniques and solutions I need all come from the deep well of tradition.

I have a huge sense of gratitude that I have been able to find work which has satisfied and sustained me.

Kazue HONMA *Japan* — PAGE 32

basketry-exhibition.org

I started natural dyeing and hand weaving at the first stage of my career. Then I encountered basketry. I was fascinated with its variety of material, diversity of technique, and three-dimensional form. Now my work is a compound of these three elements.

The most interesting theme is structure. A principal rule of simple technique brought unexpected pieces to me. Lines are related to geometrical law. Resiliency is connected to dynamics. At the root of basketry, there might be a mathematical or physical principle. Both man-made material and natural material have important properties to create structure. Especially the latter is quite interesting because it is "talkative" and intricate and has the great possibility of changing characteristics.

I have been collaborating with a restoration project for ancient baskets. Thousands of years ago, humanity already processed many kinds of plants for weaving useful items. My work is not functional, but it is a descendant of those ancient forms.

Ferne JACOBS *United States* — PAGE 38

craftinamerica.org/artist/ferne-jacobs

Rhythm: Repetitive movements. Four wraps around a core and connections with needle and thread hundreds of times, creating a form through the details.

Intimacy: Holding the developing form in my lap. Being involved with every stitch, slowing down time.

Devotion: Serving an inner feminine soul. Deep listening. Letting go to embrace the unknown.

Stéphanie JACQUES *Belgium* — PAGE 50

stephanie-jacques.net | @stephanie.jacques.sculpture

I see my sculptures as containers. These concave objects with two inseparable faces carry a symbolic charge. They are "holes in Being" (in the words of Donna J. Haraway). With basketry techniques, I have the possibility of constructing my sculptures from a void. The shape of this void changes with each sculpture; it defines it. My *What remains* series is an attempt to make the human body a container. The openwork surfaces of these human figures are made of scattered elements of willow skeins. The content can be perceived: an invisible interior landscape, experiences, a psychic space, etc.

I remember the emotion felt when making my first basket: the joy of building a container using my whole body, cooperating with the material. This basket opened a world to me. From then on, I was able to look for sculptural solutions based on this know-how. Often, during moments of doubt or of seeking inspiration, returning to baskets reinvigorates me. They contain ways of seeing the world.

Merritt JOHNSON *United States* — PAGE 66

flashbanggiveaway.com

I think about basket making and making woven objects as technology rooted in our relationship to land and ecosystems. Basket-making materials and methods reflect the specificities of the environments and circumstances of our lives. So the forms we make, their purposes, and their construction are continually expanding.

My baskets, most often and most consistently, are containers for ideas. Meaning is usually dependent on their failure to work as suggested by their form. My woven portable oxygen tank, infant car seat, boxing gloves, and head protection are all recognizable forms, but none are capable of functioning as the objects they represent. My woven work is often a reflection on the difference between what things appear to be and what they are. It is an attempt to envision, sustain, and create with what we have, especially when that is insufficient or impossible. By making an object that is incapable of its intended function, the shape of what is being asked of the object is shown; that could be a danger/threat, a theft or lack of protection, a dependence or need, a desire/wish or effort.

Weaving by hand requires care and persistent attention, and that's important for this work.

Tim JOHNSON *Spain / United Kingdom* — PAGE 16

@timjohnsonartist

Today, as I struggle once again to interpret and understand an unusual basketry technique, in this case from photographs of perhaps the world's oldest known basket, a 10,500-year-old storage vessel found in a cave in the Judean Desert, I repeat a familiar routine of experimentation and failure occasionally illuminated by small steps of understanding. Over the years I have researched a number of traditional baskets and uncommon techniques in this way. The process of discovery through making, practiced mostly without a teacher, is a demanding and engaging activity. Making the baskets that were essential to the daily lives of our ancestors and striving to understand their relationships with plants, tools, and techniques offers an insight into our diverse woven heritage.

With one foot rooted deeply in tradition and the other set on improvisation and innovation, my experimental approach and delight in spontaneous process-based studio practice leads me in new directions. Innovation, like research, is a long haul, a route littered with failures, but the occasional revelation makes it an exciting path to travel.

Doug JOHNSTON *United States* — PAGE 40

dougjohnston.net | @hawktrainer

The industrialization of sewing had a profound impact on global history. Yet, in many ways it was simply the culmination and continuation of hundreds of thousands of years of human evolution. As I sew with my industrial zigzag machine, coiling and stitching cordage into a wide variety of forms that may include baskets and bags, I listen to books about history, evolution, archeology, biology, and philosophy. I contemplate all the forces and events that have converged across this vast time and distance to make this moment possible in my studio. There may be awkward and humorous results, which can soften the reality that these vessels are inherently geologic and anthropologic and that they grapple with fundamental questions of our time and our nature. I came to basketry, somewhat accidentally, via work in architecture, fabrication, and 3-D printing. My interest in architecture stemmed from a fascination with how humans reshape the environment. However, basketry has taught me much more about who humans are, and our relationship to everything.

Gyöngy LAKY *United States* — PAGE 78

gyongylaky.com | @gyongy.laky

At UC Berkeley, while studying early cultures of Mexico, I became aware of Ed Rossbach, in the Design Department of the College of Environmental Design (CED). Soon I was an avid student of textiles, immersing myself in exploring basketry. The ingenuity inherent in basketry provided an insight into the handmade structures of Mexico. The Phoebe A. Hearst Museum of Anthropology, with its 8,000-plus Native Californian baskets, enthralled me. Both cultures resourcefully utilized materials harvested from nature.

My brother was also in CED, studying architecture, and many of his friends became mine, inspiring an unexpected expansion of my education. I began to understand that I was developing my art in the architectural spectrum of textiles.

Basketry taught me how to construct with my hands and connected me to civilization's introduction to the birth of creative engineering. Inventing basketry must have been the first industrial revolution. To carry more than a handful of berries would have been a major source of delight as well as benefit. That technology, over time, led humans to building houses, bridges, and other essential aspects of our constructed world. Basketry technology catapulted human beings into a future of creativity, and it catapulted me into a life-long joy of making.

Joanne LAMB *Northern Ireland / England* — PAGE 80

joannelambstudio.co.uk | @joannelambstudio

I'm driven by a desire to connect with and preserve the beauty of nature. My delicate baskets have been inspired by my impressions and memories of the landscape, combining natural materials and textile processes to create intimate yet expressive vessels. These pieces directly connect to my experiences in nature, where color and texture become tangible references to memory.

After creating a woven structure with tatami paper yarn using a mold, I then interlace textural, natural yarns including wool, mohair, and silk with tactile qualities to create an invitation to touch. I'm trying to paint with the yarns in an impressionistic way when making my vessels, so the techniques are quite loose and delicate. I love how the threads are not beaten into a fixed weave but are allowed to slide up and down, so light passes through.

I want my work to evoke a sense of being in nature; as if the vessels could be found among the flowers in a beautiful garden, before being placed on a mantelpiece to be treasured. We all need to deepen our emotional connection with the natural world. Building and creating a sense of awe and wonder is key if we are to foster respect and reverence for the living world.

Julie Bénédicte LAMBERT *Canada* — PAGE 84

papiertextile.com | @j.b_lambert

The basketry series *Les Greffes* (The Grafts) is the central part of a long-term project titled *Motifs à dire. Papiers tissés* (Text(ile) Patterns. Woven papers).

Les Greffes is a technical investigation of shapes and patterns in diagonal plaiting, and an exploration of the metaphorical links between weaving and the spoken and written language. This is why I work with paper and India ink, to stay as close as possible to the traditional medium of writing and its relationship to language.

Thus, this series is inspired by words that carry multiple meanings. Here, specifically, the many facets of the verb *articulate*.

"to clearly and distinctly pronounce (your words) so that others can understand you.

to clearly express (thoughts, ideas, etc.).

to bring out a structure.

to join, to unite functionally."*

The works in this series are articulations of two interwoven elements, intimately linked, structured, just as our words are organized and embellished with grammatical patterns. These baskets, wide open at both ends, unified by a wall, are megaphones that cannot carry the voice.

*Antidote Mobile [Software], Montreal, Druide informatique, 2008.

Jenna LEE *Australia* — PAGE 20

jennalee.art | @jenna.mlee

I have never considered myself a weaver, but instead I use the technique of combining fibers to transform materials. Transformation, transition, and translation are core to my work and are constant through lines in both my woven pieces and other ways of working.

My practice started as a way of transforming books written about First Nations Australians that should have included our voices within their pages or that presented outright incorrect information. A part of that process was considering the elements of a book—paper, ink, glue, linen thread, and cover board—and considering ways they could be pulled apart and put back together to say something new. Some people might think I weave because I am Aboriginal, but that is only partly true. I knew I had the skills to weave, which I had learned from elders and family, but that's not why I did it. I wanted a gentle act of transformation that made the original words illegible and presented a new form.

I consider my work a translated book, one that we can read through form, one where the "text" becomes texture to what the object is saying.

LEE Kuei-Chih *Taiwan* — PAGE 110

leekueichih.com | @kueichih101

Creation is a human instinct. It is an act of materializing abstract thinking, expressing poetic images of one's own experiences in life, and experiencing the relationship between man and the universe in the process of encountering the soul. Nature has its own laws of flow, as seen in water, and its rhythmic principles in time, in which people vibrate and coexist with its frequency. During the creative process, I use the connective idea of water as a catalyst for creative thinking and practice, sculpting the flow of energy in nature and responding to the laws and order of nature. When creating natural sculptures, I explore the relationships among nature, environment, and people, and thus establish a new interactive relationship with the environment. The works carry messages from all aspects of life and influence people's reactions to environmental issues. Natural sculptures are like seeds of hope sown in the world, looking forward to a new future and vision.

Laura LIO *Spain* — PAGE 24

lauralio.com | @lauralio1

TIE

BIND

JOIN

WEAVING sculptures is a praise of slowness and Artisanal Intelligence—another AI—in an age dominated by speed, machines, and industrial processes.

TIGHTEN the roots that weave us to Mother Nature with an ancestral way of doing that resists the mechanization of our industrialized societies.

NATURAL MATERIALS, whether roots, esparto grass, rattan, bamboo, or wicker, allow me to create more open or more closed weaves, including weaves with spaces between the vegetal lines. This results in sculptures in which one can see inside and also see through them. It creates qualities of lightness, openness, and strength within a clearly defined composition and structure. My sculptures, although they are abstractions, refer to communicating vessels, to seeds, to the vegetable world, to cages, pots, and nests. Meaning and material support and reinforce each other. Weaving together, they become one.

NOT ONLY human beings use these materials and techniques. Some of these woven plant materials are also used by African weaver birds and by the oropendolas of Central and South America to make their amazing nests.

Lucia LOREN *Spain* — PAGE 116

lucialoren.com | **@lucialoren_arte**

My artistic practice integrates a socio-environmental reflection on our relationship with the natural world, advocating for interventions in the landscape that are informed by awareness of the natural and cultural heritage of each location of my site-responsive work.

Traditional crafts, particularly basketry, serve as a rich source of inspiration in my creative process. They embody a material culture of recycling, rooted in local resources and promoting a sustainable approach to environmental stewardship.

Basket weaving provides me with a direct and spontaneous connection to the landscape and its inhabitants. Working with natural materials fosters a profound awareness of our material surroundings, honing both physical and conceptual skills. Moreover, it fosters a sense of community and taps into local wisdom, which is deeply intertwined with the cultural memory of the land. The intricate process of weaving allows for extended periods of creation, enabling a deeper exploration of our interconnectedness with nature and the fabric of existence.

Edgardo MADANES *Argentina* — PAGE 112

edgardomadanes.wixsite.com | **@edgardomadanes**

I work with willow wicker because I am fascinated by the geographical regions where it thrives. Furthermore, its flexibility and resilience never cease to amaze me. I delight in its aroma and the softness of its texture. The stillness that surrounds me while I work becomes a dialogue, where my breathing mixes with the subtle sounds produced when manipulating and interweaving the wicker rods.

I perceive the wicker rods as individuals within a community. Each rod has a distinct identity and bears the marks of its own journey. Each of them plays a crucial role in shaping the final form; they support and complement each other, forming a society.

Giuse MAGGI *Italy* — PAGE 42

maggiglass.com | **@fibre.e.natura**

The allure of Arab landscapes and culture deeply influences my artistic exploration and serves as a wellspring of inspiration in crafting profoundly hybridized pieces. These creations pay homage to the rich traditions of ancient civilizations, the vibrant hues of bustling souks, and the majestic and sinuous scenery of the desert.

Employing diverse and contrasting techniques ranging from glass kiln forming to basketry, I transform vases, baskets, and containers into contemporary forms.

The glass object is fused and shaped, ready for further development—this dialogue is the metaphor of my life. Fibers serve as the connecting thread between two worlds. I followed the thread that led me to the local craftsmen, who taught me how to connect things and basketry techniques. The weave acts as the permanent bond between them. The resulting artwork embodies a distinct identity, harmonizing Eastern and Western aesthetics.

The selection of fibers is deliberate and symbolic: from the ubiquitous palm utilized in traditional basketry to locally cultivated cotton, spun and woven within domestic gardens, to imported silk adorning opulent interiors.

The use of coiling technique in my basketry represents the essence of the creative process. Its gradual and slow progress fosters meditative contemplation and introspection, often sparking new ideas and innovative solutions, ultimately surprising me with the final outcome.

Anina MAJOR *United States* — PAGE 64

aninamajor.com | @aninamajor

My grandmother Saphora "Mar" Newbold was a Bahamian straw vendor. Hers were intimate pieces made with love and care from a variety of local palms. I can't help but notice the parallels between this dying craft and the deterioration of the few cherished straw items she left behind.

To engage with basketry and the weaving process reconnects me with aspects of my heritage, and working through the ceramic process provides a beautiful metaphor for feelings of loss and gain (because when the clay is fired, it loses water and the particles bond, making it a stronger, permanent form). The primary technique I use to create sculpture is a form of braiding, or as Bahamians say, "plait." It is formed by interlacing three or more strands of flexible materials such as straw in my grandmother's case or clay in mine.

This method of making baskets from natural grasses traces back to the slave trade. Many enslaved Africans used their basket-weaving skills to increase the efficiency of labor and as a means of signifying tribal identity, age, marital status, wealth, religion, and social position. The intergenerational transfer of these skills is a way to preserve our oral history and culture. My artistic language is grounded in the women-led industry of straw weaving. The work tells an autobiographical story and serves as representation of a place and a record of an experience that moves freely between cultural realms with no fixed position.

Jette MELLGREN *Denmark* — PAGE 98

jettemellgren.dk

What drives my work is the desire to experiment, to explore materials and expressions. I see woven rhythms and structures everywhere and I want to enlarge, frame, or translate these so that we see the old, respected basketry craft with new eyes. I work in many ways to build a bridge between old techniques and new design. For me, basketry is a craft that insists on constant renewal.

I am very attached to nature. Working with natural materials gives me a special feeling of connectedness and immersion, especially when I use site-specific materials in situ. With my sculptures, I would like to bring out the inherent and hidden qualities of nature, as well as to create spaces to stay and wonder. I like to play with the scale and shape of nature's own objects, such as the nest.

I often operate within a limited framework of ideas, and I feel I'm in a Zen state when I experience the synergy of creativity and technical skills.

My work ranges from small pictures and objects to larger land art installations, all with wicker as a focal point.

Josep MERCADER *Spain* — PAGE 26

tramats.cat | **@tramats**

Tramats is the basketry workshop created by Josep Mercader and Magda Martínez in Torroella de Montgrí (Catalonia), a small town near the Mediterranean Sea.

Understanding traditional basketry has been fundamental for us. We have been learning and researching for the last 30 years different basket techniques and the use of different plant materials, mainly focusing on Catalan basketry, especially the ones used for agricultural works.

However, what has influenced us the most has been the research work we carried out on traditional triangular mesh fishing traps. We looked for fishermen who still knew how to make them in order to establish a typology of fishing traps, their uses, the materials, etc. And we discovered a whole world of techniques and natural and human resources developed and transmitted in a long chain from fathers to children down the centuries, until it vanished toward the '70s of the 20th century.

One of the main goals of our workshop is to be able to apply these techniques, materials, and know-how, with rigor and craft, to contemporary projects in different fields such as architecture, marine research, and design, and also in works of purely artistic expression.

Nathalie MIEBACH *United States* — PAGE 124

nathaliemiebach.com | **@miebachsculpture**

My merging of basket weaving and science data began somewhat by serendipity in 2000. I learned basket weaving from Lois Russell. Her class fell on the same dates as my astronomy class at Harvard University Extension School. After learning weaving in the morning, I would bring my buckets, reed, and half-finished baskets with me into the lecture hall to learn about stars, black holes, and quasars. Astronomy was fascinating to me, but frustrating. As a tactile learner, I found it was nearly impossible to get a sense of the time-and-space dimension we talked about in class. At some point I realized I could use basket weaving as a three-dimensional grid through which to translate astronomical data, to get a more tactile, physical sense of what I was learning about. And that began my journey of exploring art and science.

Soon after, I began to focus on other complex scientific systems such as weather and climate change. The two pieces in this book come from an early series I did on Cape Cod, where I used my own data and ocean buoy data to better understand the interaction of weather and ocean systems. To me, basket weaving remains an important language to try to grasp complex scientific information through a tactile methodology.

Leeroy NEW *Philippines* — PAGE 108

leeroynew.com | @newleeroy

"Before we are painters and sculptors, we are weavers, potters and carvers."

This was something that my art high school mentor, Roberto Feleo, would often tell us, and this has profoundly influenced my artistic practice. The tradition of weaving using natural materials has always been present in our daily lives, especially growing up, as I did, in a small city in the Philippines. My creative influences also came from watching sci-fi and fantasy films and hearing folk tales of the supernatural shared by my grandmother.

As I pursued my interest in the arts by studying it in high school and later in university, I was consciously aspiring to build the sci-fi fantasy worlds that captivated me in my childhood. But since I had no access to high-tech materials, I decided to build my first spaceship by using structural and woven bamboo, a material we regularly used in art school. Since then, I've continued to explore the possibilities of integrating this inherently Philippine construction and crafting tradition with manipulated plastic discards, with the hopes of creating a distinct Filipino sci-fi language.

Beauty NGXONGO *South Africa* — PAGE 18

bambizulu.com | @beautyngxongo

My baskets took form and shape purely by mistake. I had no intention of making them distinctively different, but I was trying to copy Laurentia Diamini's style, which I was encouraged to do as her baskets were in demand and I was her protégé.

Just this morning, much to the agony of my body, I had to go up to the nature reserves hill, as I live in proximity to the Hluhluwe game reserve in part of Hlabisa (South Africa). I had to get the type of fine grass that I use for my baskets. It's so scarce and comes around only twice a year here. It takes forever to grow. While most weavers will use any grass, the best one is scarce. I know every coil of my basket will be symmetrical, and I am happier working with carefully selected grass and palm that is perfectly ripe, soft, vibrant, and healthy. The basket is sure to look exactly as I've imagined it before starting to weave. Working on a basket that is valuable is not all glamorous but is mostly a lot of hard work and sweat, requiring critical and careful thinking when selecting the best palm, selecting the plants to dye the palm, and monitoring the color while it cooks to bring out the best color.

Keiji NIO *Japan* — PAGE 86

https://uryu-tsushin.kyoto-art.ac.jp/detail/1041

I dye nylon and polyester materials in colorful hues under the theme of "color and form," and use the same techniques of interlacing (braiding, knitting, tying, weaving) that are traditional in Japanese crafts to create works that decorate various spaces. Kumihimo braid is a very important element of the Japanese kimono and is used as an ornament called obijime. These braided cords are made by assembling silk threads on a braid stand. But to decorate a space, I assemble the wide strings by hand, and the finished product comes from my imagination.

Annemarie O'SULLIVAN *United Kingdom* — PAGE 8

studioamos.co.uk | @studio_amos

In everything I make there's a quest for beauty, both in the movements as I work and in the final piece. It's a slow dance. I try to remember as I am manipulating a rod of willow that not long ago, it was growing in the field and wasn't planning on becoming part of a basket. I feel a great reverence for this material.

I love being part of a long, long lineage of makers and growers who've been making vessels for humankind for thousands of years. I'm extra lucky that I have the freedom to move between materials, scale, and functionality.

Somehow, I see the work as connecting cultures; I'm intrigued by the slow transference of skills across the sea roads and the land, from one country to another throughout Europe and beyond.

José Santiago PÉREZ *United States* — PAGE 46

josesantiagoperez.com | @josesantiago.p

I am an artist and educator based in Chicago. I craft sculptural works in varying scales that consider the formal and conceptual spaciousness of containers—such as baskets, ritual objects, and nets—as a category of object and field of experimentation. As a first-generation queer Latine artist, I regard my practice as a form of gathering across time, space, and difference within a polarized contemporary context that continues to reproduce colonial systems of separation and exclusion. My handmade queer containers expand such traditional forms and methods as coiled basketry and net making (things that *hold*), through intuitive and improvisational making. My works extend notions of function through the use of nontraditional materials like mylar emergency blankets and plastic lacing. These petroleum-based materials, produced through complex systems and processes of extraction and global industrialization, show the complex and asymmetrical relationships between nature and culture. Consistently choosing materials that are not traditional plant-based fibers speaks to this colonial and capitalist imbalance between human culture and the living planet. As containers, my shimmering baskets and netted structures invite viewers to imagine other ways to *hold*.

Roger RIGORTH *Germany* — PAGE 100

roger-rigorth.de | @rogerrigorth

Two essential aspects motivate my use of traditional weaving techniques in my monumental sculptures. The first is that I can create a natural-looking, three-dimensional, and light body, without limitation in size. And second, I am able to have a pattern that can be found in nature, whether it is the graphic repetition or the fur-like appearance.

A third aspect becomes important, and this is to balance the more aggressive chain-saw work as representative of male energy with a more meditative and female weaving work. It is balancing not only me but also the creation itself. To create a woven body means to have a hollow inside, which in my case is not empty. It is a home and a shelter for something that lives in the ethereal world. Or is it, at the end, just driven by my personal longing to hug a whale—an expression of my fascination with these big, wonderful creatures and urge to become one with them, which motivates my creation of big bodies.

Hisako SEKIJIMA *Japan* — PAGE 74

basketry-exhibition.org

I would like to explain my approach through two examples: one a structural analysis, the other an abstraction of the material's contribution.

I am interested in formulating primary structural mechanisms that clarify the nature of the object in relation to the technical solution. Consider two similar-looking cubic baskets from the series *Structural Discussion*. In one, an indented line is perpendicular to the edge of a diagonally plaited cube, while in the other an indented line is at a 45-degree angle to the edge of a right-angle warp/weft woven cube. Both are plaited in making indented lines, but making in the whole I experience reverse structural relationships between line and wholes. I am questioning what defines types of basket structure.

In *Grasp I,* I utilize the material's physical characteristics to realize imagery suggested by the material's natural distortion. It was made of a low-processed walnut bark strip with the coarse outside still on. That makes the bark strip distinctively curl inward as it dries. It looks as if an unseen inner space is grasped by the bark. To hold the intersections, I drilled the dried and hardened bark and inserted wooden nails to perpetuate the distortion or transformation as an image of a grasp. That is, I took what was happening as an image to be expressed. This kind of abstraction often gives me new combinations of forms and engineering ideas.

Rita SOTO VENTURA *Chile* — PAGE 126

ritasoto.cl | @ritasotoart

Fortuitously, my life has revolved around the trades, and today I operate in that creative, emotional, and sensory world that links art with crafts and design: artistic jewelry.

I learned the craft of jewelry from my father, and basket weaving through various Chilean women who cultivate ancestral techniques with natural fibers, focusing on the micro basket-weaving technique with horsehair. This technique, so typical of Chile, allowed me to develop forms that metal did not permit, and was key for my artistic exploration, which involved learning the textile language and searching for my own language of experimentation and generation of bodies, skins, and fabrics. I create biomorphic objects that are in a constant dialogue between the organic and the poetic, weaving their own imaginary.

The hours committed to this meditative and emotional work have led me to unexpected proposals, through materials and their transformation, ancestral techniques and their experimentation. Art jewelry is a means of communication that connects the body, the work, the individual, and the fabric through an ancient, primitive, earthly gesture. Today I seek to open a new dialogue, a "metamorphosis of a speculative nature," which proposes a narrative around possible futures. Through form and matter, the pieces invite us to speculate about a possible, but unknown, nature.

Haruko SUGAWARA *Japan* — PAGE 28

harukosugawara.com

I create jewelry as wearable art, and while I was searching for new techniques, I came across basketry. In metalworking for jewelry and similar crafts, you typically design first and then work according to that design. However, in basketry, the structure and the materials themselves shape the form, and this approach of pursuing form through discovery was a fresh experience for me. Basketry often uses natural materials, and I like them. Yet, I create unexpected shapes by weaving metals that I am familiar with. There are many kinds of metals, and I repeatedly experimented to understand their properties and whether their thickness would suit the technique. Additionally, originality is required—it's not just about replacing existing forms with metal—and I also needed to consider whether my designs could be adequately expressed. Basketry is the process of transforming materials from one-dimensional to two-dimensional, and from two-dimensional to three-dimensional, elevating them to art. I enjoy the process of experimenting with different methods and turning them into works of art.

Noriko TAKAMIYA *Japan* — PAGE 82

basketry-exhibition.org

My *Revolving* series started when I saw some plaited toys and containers made by Indigenous people of New Zealand and Indonesia. They make plaited containers from coconut leaflets, but their ways of plaiting are totally different, more like braiding. I had been taught that corners were necessary to make a three-dimensional object, but they seemed not to distinguish between corners and planes. I was impressed, so I tried to find different ways of plaiting, and that became my theme.

I thought that paper might be good for my experimental pieces. Paper can be cut in various widths and has a variety of colors and textures. At first, I used thick paper, but soon I found I didn't like the rough cross section. Then I used thin paper, which led to a new way to make thick plies. I plaited again and again over the first layer and found the successive plies changed the original shape, which was so interesting to me that I have continued the method to today. I am still attracted to unpredictable shapes. I preferred lustrous paper with an uneven surface, and later I began to use metallic lustrous paper.

Stephen TALASNIK *United States* — PAGE 90

stephentalasnik.com | @stephentalasnik

My work is informed by weaving. My attraction to this process evolved from a love of organic engineering; of that which is handmade and intended to function as a support, a span, a suspension, a skin; and of a reverence for grid-based linear structure.

My obsession grew out of variable repetition, which is a process associated with various types of Indigenous building, which I first saw in Southeast Asia. The unmeasured assembly of colliding or entwined lines—rigid or fluid—facilitated great feats of intuitive engineering. It was the woven grid—a near-precise union of horizontal and vertical—that provided the visual ingredients of structure. These invented space frames laminated grid upon grid until the ultimate form was defined. The rigid "woven" grid-like organization determined the unique characteristics of exterior skin, responding to an inner skeleton. There was no blueprint, only hand-drawn line upon line, utilizing flat reed and stick.

My curiosity about the grid began with two rigid structures: the Indigenous form of bamboo scaffolding and the wooden roller coaster. They appear to be woven geometrical fortresses, never intending to be seen as vessels, but they satisfy an implied function, which is exploring the linear character of that which is woven. "Gridification" is the aesthetic and structural attraction of the art of the weave.

Eneida Lombe TAVARES *Portugal* — PAGE 70

eneidatavares.pt | @eneidalombetavares

The crossing of different territories through basketry—places, materials, techniques, people—has been my main vehicle. From an emotional place, my origins, I begin exercises that connect Angolan mateba (fiber from a species of African palm tree) and pine needles (from a tree mostly native to the Northern Hemisphere and abundant in the Portuguese landscape). I integrate these contexts.

Pine needles were the answer to my questions "How to transfer this emotional place to objects via design?" and "What objects?"

These questions led me to the spiral technique, which led me to ceramics and so on, going around, evolving, and poetically returning to the same place. I would say that the objects I choose to develop come from a place of familiarity and timeless needs, including homeware objects (vases, rugs, furniture) or accessories such as hats and backpacks, among others.

The dialogue between materials and techniques also naturally appears in collaborative projects with other artists and designers, as an essential element in the creative process.

Lisa TELFORD *United States* — PAGE 54

stoningtongallery.com | @haidaweaver

I am a Git'ans Git'anee Haida weaver. I come from a long line of weavers including my grandmother, mother, aunt, and cousins. My daughter continues the lineage. I learned traditional techniques of Haida basketry from Delores Churchill and Haida cedar garments from Holly Churchill.

It has been important for me to pass on tradition and maintain a high standard of perfection. I harvest and prepare my own material, using red and yellow cedar bark and spruce root in my work. Harvesting cedar bark requires that I travel hundreds of miles from home, and it takes many hours of preparation time. The bark is traditionally stored for one year, and then further processing is required before weaving may start.

I stuck strictly to the tradition of form follows function from 1992 until 2004, when I jumped off the cliff into contemporary cedar clothing, cedar shoes, cowboy boots, and neckties.

Haida basketry was essential for survival years ago. I continue the tradition, celebrating the beauty of nature.

Ona TREPAT RUBIROLA *Spain* — PAGE 120

onatrepatrubirola.com | @onatrepatrubirola

My work combines my way of looking at the world of crafts and the strategies and mysteries of the arts themselves. I am interested in the relationship between the material and the invisible. Through the languages, shapes, and symbols of weaving and braiding plant fibers I try to open a framework for reflection between matter and spirituality.

The narratives of popular culture and traditional arts have always inspired me with an honesty, beauty, and truth that I have struggled to find in the visual arts; also with their inherent relationship with territory. The idea that one of the first artifacts that humans developed was a container woven from plant fiber for harvest, amazes me. Maybe that is why I pay special attention to the mythical or symbolic idea of basketry as an element of identity, community, ritual, and cosmogony. The act of weaving thus becomes a text, a story. Braiding represents the act of becoming, of multiplication and growth. To weave and narrate, we need a thread, a path, and a denouement.

My creative process is rooted in deep knowledge of the material and the technique. I merge craft practice and artistic research. For me, the creative process is a kind of antidote to the existential question about the fragility of existence.

Karin VAN DER MOLEN *Netherlands* — PAGE 102

karinvandermolen.nl | @karin_van_der_molen

In my career as a professional artist, I have increasingly focused on environmental/site-responsive art. I take time to research and experience the location for the artwork. I try to find the "entrance" to that place, in order to formulate an artistic answer to it. The central theme of my work is the human relationship with nature. Because I live in an urban, digital, global world, by using natural materials for my site-specific artwork, I try to entice myself and others to get closer to or even "enter" nature. Working with the materials that local nature offers deepened my relationship with nature through creating. Now I also weave waste, recycled, and other materials into the willow and reeds, since I am compelled to relate in my work to the contemporary challenges that nature and humans face. Nature often mirrors the consequences of human activities in the environment. Researching cause and reaction and my own position, I use contemporary basketry to encourage, amplify, and intensify a deep experience of the place and time in which we live.

Lois WALPOLE *United Kingdom* — PAGE 44

loiswalpole.com | @loiswalpole

Trained in sculpture, basketry, and product design, I have worked as an artist / basket maker since 1984. Sculpture gave me a desire to create in three dimensions, basketry offered me many choices of materials and techniques to create with, and product design taught me about our relationship to material resources.

Materials that are considered to be of no further use, or ignoble, many of which are plastic of some type, attract me. I try to give them a new life in another context, so that they might be viewed in a more positive light. Often these materials still have plenty of life left in them when we, unthinkingly, consign them to landfill. But they also have patinas and marks that tell us how they have been used or abused by us. I try to heal those scars and at the same time give the viewer something interesting to look at.

North Atlantic Drift is an installation of over a hundred small baskets made from plastic and rope washed ashore in Shetland, which I have combined with natural materials from the same environment and basketry techniques that were once traditionally used in Shetland.

Asim WAQIF *India* — PAGE 114

asimwaqif.com | @asimwaqif

On a research trip to Assam last year, I stepped into a newly built brick-concrete house and was struck by the heat. There were only two tiny windows, and the galvanized steel roof was radiating. A nearby older house made with ikra and bamboo with a thatch roof was airy and cool, but in disrepair. The government only provides grants to make durable houses. As a result, almost no new houses of the traditional type are being constructed in rural India.

Contrast this to boutique studios in Mumbai and Milan, where bamboo is being hailed as a wonder material in terms of sustainability. However, few economic or creative opportunities trickle down to the artisans themselves. The creative roles have been usurped by designers, while fabricators are expected to merely follow instructions.

Today some architecture is being developed using parametric design, whose biomimetic forms appear to me to have a lot in common with basket weaving. Parametric design uses algorithms to generate forms, and 3-D printers and CNC machines for fabrication. The entire creative process is in a CAD environment.

I am experimenting with improvising and scaling-up artisanal bamboo- and cane-weaving techniques to create large-scale parametric forms. My seemingly vernacular structure is embedded with an interactive electronic system that creates a game-like environment. The viewer's experience is contemporary and nostalgic at the same time.

Deloss WEBBER *United States* — PAGE 68

delosswebberartist.com | @delwebber

Discovering ikebana basketry opened doors to something earthy in my artist brain. I've never had an art class or a class on weaving; however, I grew up with the sound of my mother's shuttle in the other room. I've had the great fortune of many friends with wonderful basket collections that were shared with me. I realized early on that I am an autodidact. My process is to study an object or image in an exercise of deconstructing and reverse engineering. One of my themes is to emulate recognizable objects with an injection of irony or symbolism (stone baskets, for example).

The ikebana philosophy of marrying heaven, man, and earth has been the guiding force in my journey of discovery and invention. In art making, this practice led me to an aesthetic of natural materials approached with high craft. My work is a dance blending accident and nature; it is an embodiment of the Japanese concept of wabi-sabi, or appreciating imperfect beauty.

Masako YOSHIDA *Japan* — PAGE 60

basketry-exhibition.org | @atelier_udo

This is what I thought when the production of the work *Sing* was finished:

The emotions that welled up inside me took the form of the work.

I was working on *Sing* in the days when the end of the coronavirus infection was not in sight, and the war in Russia and Ukraine had started. The tragic news made my heart ache.

A child's parallelogram-shaped mouth looked like it was singing a song.

I thought that the act of singing is the same as the act of making things, and that it gives people joy and strength.

Acknowledgments

WE ARE GRATEFUL for the cooperation of the artists presented in these pages, or in some cases the galleries that made possible their inclusion. We also wish to acknowledge others not shown here, for as the *Contemporary Basketry* blog has demonstrated, there are thousands of other makers worthy of attention. Among the motivations of the book is the hope that this representative sampling will encourage readers to discover more of the world's basketry riches.

On a more practical level, we are grateful for the staff of Schiffer Craft Publishing, in particular the superb editing of Sandra Korinchak—thoughtful, encouraging, and sometimes eye-opening but never coercive!

Perhaps we should acknowledge that although we have known of each other and respected each other's work for decades, we had met in person only once before we began this collaboration. And our work with each other was accomplished entirely by email until we had another opportunity to meet in person when the book was in its late stages. It has been a happy experience!

Index of Artists

About the Authors

Carol Eckert is an artist and curator focused on contemporary basketry and fiber art. She has served as president of the National Basketry Organization and is the founder of the widely followed blog *Contemporary Basketry*. She is a contributor to many publications, including *Rooted, Revived, Reinvented: Basketry in America*. Eckert is active in a range of textile art organizations including the Surface Design Association. caroleckert.com | @caroleckertart | contemporarybasketry.blogspot.com

Janet Koplos is a former senior editor at *Art in America* magazine and a renowned journalist. She was awarded a National Endowment for the Arts critic's grant, and has served on the American Section of the Association Internationale de Critiques d'Art and the College Art Association's Frank Jewett Mather Award Committee. Koplos has taught at Parsons School of Design, Pratt Institute, the University of the Arts, and the Rhode Island School of Design. She is author of numerous books including *Contemporary Japanese Sculpture* and *What Makes a Potter* (Schiffer).

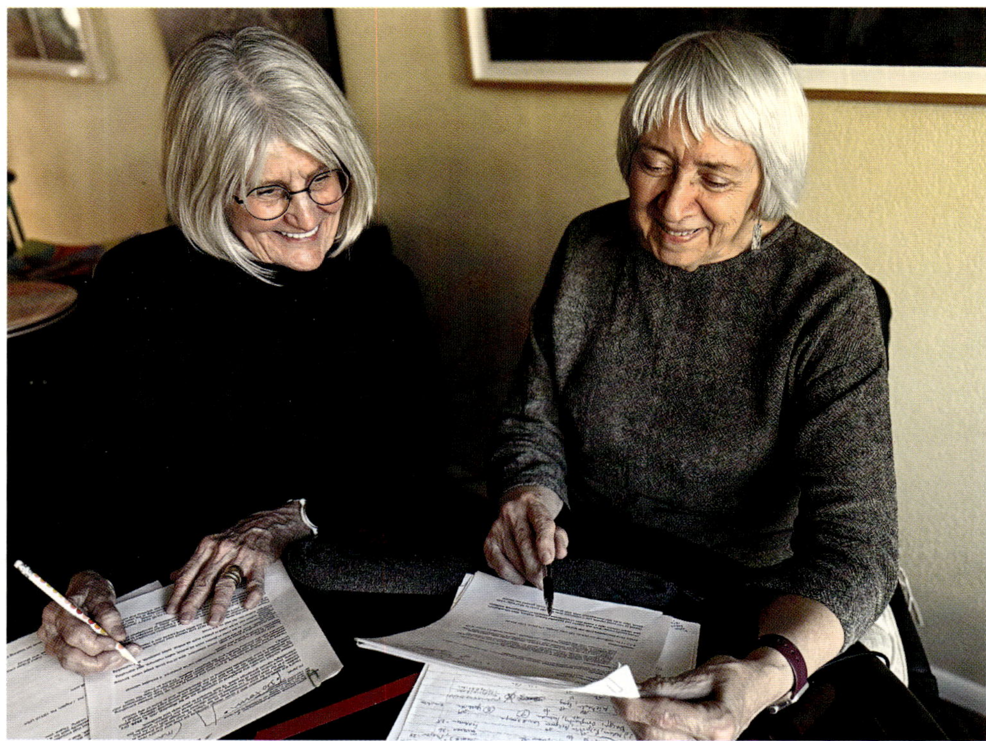

Carol Eckert *(left)* and Janet Koplos *(right)*